AF621735

Historicizing Academic Freedom

Also Available from Bloomsbury

Dominant Discourses in Higher Education, Ian M. Kinchin and Karen Gravett

Academics' International Teaching Journeys, edited by Anesa Hosein, Namrata Rao, Chloe Shu-Hua Yeh, and Ian M. Kinchin

Class, Race, Disability and Mental Health in Higher Education, Mike Seal

Utopian Universities, edited by Miles Taylor and Jill Pellew

Changing Higher Education for a Changing World, edited by Claire Callender, William Locke, and Simon Marginson

Locating Social Justice in Higher Education Research, edited by Jan McArthur and Paul Ashwin

Subjectivity and Social Change in Higher Education, Liezl Dick and Marguerite Müller

Social Theory and the Politics of Higher Education, edited by Mark Murphy, Ciaran Burke, Cristina Costa, and Rille Raaper

Historicizing Academic Freedom

On Universities, Scholarly Indeterminacy, and World Ordering

André C. Drainville

BLOOMSBURY ACADEMIC
LONDON • NEW YORK • OXFORD • NEW DELHI • SYDNEY

BLOOMSBURY ACADEMIC
Bloomsbury Publishing Plc, 50 Bedford Square, London, WC1B 3DP, UK
Bloomsbury Publishing Inc, 1359 Broadway, New York, NY 10018, USA
Bloomsbury Publishing Ireland, 29 Earlsfort Terrace, Dublin 2, D02 AY28, Ireland

BLOOMSBURY, BLOOMSBURY ACADEMIC and the Diana logo are trademarks of Bloomsbury Publishing Plc

First published in Great Britain 2026

Copyright © André C. Drainville, 2026

André C. Drainville has asserted his right under the Copyright, Designs and Patents Act, 1988, to be identified as Author of this work.

Cover image: After Us, Liberty, 1949, Constant A. Nieuwenhuys. Tate, Purchased 1983. © Constant A. Nieuwenhuys. Photo: Tate

All rights reserved. No part of this publication may be: i) reproduced or transmitted in any form, electronic or mechanical, including photocopying, recording or by means of any information storage or retrieval system without prior permission in writing from the publishers; or ii) used or reproduced in any way for the training, development or operation of artificial intelligence (AI) technologies, including generative AI technologies. The rights holders expressly reserve this publication from the text and data mining exception as per Article 4(3) of the Digital Single Market Directive (EU) 2019/790.

Bloomsbury Publishing Plc does not have any control over, or responsibility for, any third-party websites referred to or in this book. All internet addresses given in this book were correct at the time of going to press. The author and publisher regret any inconvenience caused if addresses have changed or sites have ceased to exist, but can accept no responsibility for any such changes.

A catalogue record for this book is available from the British Library.

A catalog record for this book is available from the Library of Congress.

ISBN:	HB:	978-1-350-57601-8
	PB:	978-1-350-57600-1
	ePDF:	978-1-350-57602-5
	eBook:	978-1-350-57603-2

Typeset by Integra Software Services Pvt. Ltd.
Printed and bound in Great Britain

For product safety related questions contact productsafety@bloomsbury.com.

To find out more about our authors and books visit www.bloomsbury.com and sign up for our newsletters.

To Clara, with whom I am learning to be free—
in the hope that she, too, is learning as joyfully as I am

NOTE ON THE COVER

The cover features a painting by Dutch painter and architect Constant Nieuwenhuys—a founding figure of the COBRA movement (1948–1951) and of the Internationale situationniste (1957–1972). How Nieuwenhuys titled—and later retitled—this work invites reflection on the contingent nature of freedom and stands as warning against its appropriation, nowhere more relevant than in current debates on academic freedom.

The painting's original title, *À Nous la Liberté* (*To Us, Freedom*)—borrowed from that of René Clair's 1931 film satirizing factories as carceral spaces—captured the mitigated enthusiasm with which the COBRA movement greeted liberation from Nazi occupation. Painted in Amsterdam, the work answered what Nieuwenhuys perceived as the "false freedom" celebrated by the Rijksmuseum's *Kunst in vryheid* (Art in freedom) exhibition, the first show of contemporary Dutch art held after the war. After COBRA dissolved, the painting's title was changed to *Après Nous la Liberté* (*After Us, Freedom*) to convey—so Nieuwenhuys later wrote—both "doubts about the possibility of 'free art' in an unfree society and, at the same time, ... hopes for the freedom all men are longing for."

Though certainly marked by postwar disillusionment with liberation, as well as by the gendered universalism of its time, Nieuwenhuys's doubts and hopes nevertheless resonate at the uncertain juncture we now find ourselves, trapped between the old world-system of territorial states, which—bolstered by a rising tide of authoritarianism—refuses to die, and a new world order not yet born.

Après-nous la liberté is held in the collection of the Tate, London. The quotations from Constant Nieuwenhuys are reproduced in the catalog entry for *Après nous la liberté* on the Tate website. https://www.tate.org.uk/art/artworks/constant-after-us-liberty-t03705.

CONTENTS

BY WAY OF ACKNOWLEDGMENTS: A FOREWORD

This book began as a talk presented to the *#MustFall: Understanding the Moment* conference, which took place at the University of the Free State in Bloemfontein, South Africa, in October 2016.[1] How I came to be invited to speak in Bloemfontein matters very much to explain my faithfulness to this brief event, which was attended by a handful of scholars and activists, and thus the subject matter of this book.

That the invitation to Bloemfontein had come from my friend Leonhard Praeg, then Professor of Philosophy at Pretoria University, is most relevant. I had met Leonhard a decade previously while on a semester-long teaching stay at Rhodes University in Grahamstown that had been arranged by Professor Louise Vincent of the Department of Political and International Studies. Reading an article I had published on the pedagogical relevance of avant-garde techniques, Professor Vincent had invited me, as simply and collegially as that, to work with her students. Lecturing in a historically white university in postapartheid South Africa in English from notes written in French to students who would have been brought up in any of the eleven official languages of South Africa in a politics department about Salvador Dalí's tight red shoes and André Breton's automatic writing, I, of course, learned as much as I hope to have taught—about South Africa, authors and ideas students and I shared (or not); ways of being, teaching, and learning; forms of power and counterpower, in the classroom and beyond.

Here already, entwined in the beginnings of an explanation of how this book came about, is a rough idea of what it is about. Writing was an act of freedom rooted in the circumstances of university life. It happened because colleagues in the Political Science Department at Laval University questioned the relevance of avant-garde techniques in the teaching of a graduate seminar on methodology and because I answered them by writing an article that came to be published in a peer-reviewed journal (Drainville 2003), which found its way, quite by academic happenchance, to the desk of an unknown colleague from South Africa who was sufficiently engaged in her own professorial practice to read it and had mettle enough to follow up on her curiosity by extending an invitation.[2] It also happened

---

[1]A video of my talk was made by Aryan Kaganoff. At the time of writing, it was still available for viewing on Vimeo (https://vimeo.com/196144143), as was "Metalepsis in Black" (https://vimeo.com/193233861), about the #MustFall conference as a whole.

[2]In 2002, Professor Vincent won the Vice-Chancellor's Teaching Award at Rhodes University. I understand this helped her secure funds for my stay.

because students at Rhodes University were, as are students everywhere, simultaneously engaged and indifferent, full of questions and silences, and because I answered them, as professors do everywhere, contextualizing questions and reading into silences, clarifying ideas that I had put forth. On occasion, I recontextualized, or redefined, them on the fly; it also happened that I rushed back to the office after class to scribble down fresh insights lest they evaporate. This dialectic plays out more or less in the same manner in every classroom in every university. It was activated in Rhodes in ways that students and I were both more alert to, in large part, because I was a visiting professor teaching an unfamiliar subject in a familiar manner. At Rhodes, students and I were strangers to each other, playing known parts with unknown partners, attentive to the tenuousness and possibilities of our relationship. This fostered a sense of indeterminacy and possibility that I take to be essential to what I will term *freedom in thinking*.

Meeting Leonhard, I felt the shock and thrill of recognition. This is a rare feeling in one's life. At once a gift and a burden, it is certainly an event to be faithful to; ignoring it would be pissing away life's possibilities. For a decade after Rhodes, Leonhard and I succeeded in maintaining a sense of continuity in our relationship. Distance, that great inhibitor, could have bogged us down in what Jacques Derrida called *The Politics of Friendship*—a book Leonhard gave me when he left Québec City after a lengthy sabbatical. Instead, it gave us time to learn the exigencies of friendship. In the end, whatever lesson Derrida had to teach us, he taught despite himself; it took me as long to admit to Leonhard that I could never get past the first few pages of *The Politics* as it did him to confess that he had barely read it himself but had been waiting for an occasion to gift it to someone who would neither read it nor pretend to have done so.

For many years after our Derrida moment, Leonhard and I concocted reasons to see each other in learned conferences, during research trips, or sabbatical stays abroad. We never applied for funding or published together, never gave institutional shape to our encounters, but wherever we met, whether in a bar in New York's Lower East Side or walking to that place near Granada where the last Nasrid ruler is said to have last sighed, an invisible college of sorts was in session, providing both an experience of *freedom in thinking* and a lesson on the demands of such freedom.

In March 2016, as the student movement in South Africa was all about *#RhodesMustFall*, Leonhard invited me to participate in a gathering of *Thinking Africa*, a project-of-projects aimed at decolonizing African studies that he had set up at Rhodes University a few years before and taken with him to the University of Pretoria. I accepted his invitation without hesitation, in the joyously indominable spirit of our friendship. In a rapid-fire exchange of SMS—while I was walking my dog on the Plains of Abraham in Québec City and Leonhard was in his kitchen in Grahamstown (now Makhanda)—a scheme was conceived and an obligation created.

What Leonhard asked of me was to draw a big picture, "what a real sociologist would do." "The parallel with global '68 is being bandied about," he wrote (texting in full sentences, as only parents and professors do), mentioning in passing the goings-on at the University of Missouri (Mizzou), Yale, and Oxford. "What," he asked, "could be the link between happenings in South Africa and all that is 'out there' in the great abstract space of neoliberal hegemony?"

There was certainly much out there to draw from and help give context to events in South Africa. In the year or two before *#RhodesMustFall*, students had taken action not only at Mizzou, Yale, and Oxford but also at the Universidad de los Andes in San Cristobal, Colombia; York University in Toronto; CUNY and NYU in New York; the Universität Wien in Vienna, Austria; Makarere University in Kampala; the Universitat Politècnica de Catalunya in Barcelona, Spain; the Université Félix Houphouët-Boigny in Abidjan, Côte d'Ivoire, and in many other institutions being repurposed as organizations in the making of new knowledge economy. By sociological profiling, I could have assembled a repertory of students' actions or testified to similarities in the use of the internet, the horizontality of mobilizations, their common leaderlessness, spontaneity, or fungibility. I could have cast campus politics as an instance of the politics of place against the placelessness of neoliberal globalization, written of student resistances, or hinted at the possibility of an abstract one-world movement of students.

The truth of my friendship with Leonhard revealed itself to me in how I allowed to weigh on my work the thought that I would betray it by letting myself be content with integrating South African happenings in ready-made narratives. Throughout summer 2016, my desk at home in Québec City was tangibly linked to South Africa. By the time *Thinking Africa* gathered in Bloemfontein, it had been almost eighteen months since struggles had begun on South African campuses, with University of Cape Town political science student Chumani Maxwele hurling a bucket of human excrements at the statue of Cecil John Rhodes. During that period, the movement had hopped and skipped from campus to campus, moving capriciously in appearance from its *#RhodesMustFall* beginning, to challenging the culture of violence against women on South African campuses (*#PatriarchyMustFall*) to opposing tuition fees (*#FeesMustFall*) to protest against the leadership of African National Conference President Jacob Zuma (*#ZumaMustFall*). The term *fallism* had begun to be used with the sort of shallow knowingness that recognizes events in their own terms only to leave protagonists strangers both to their own history and from happenings elsewhere, stranded in reified singularity. Historicizing fallism, I labored to give substance and intelligence to the big picture my friend Leonhard had asked me to draw in terms that students in South Africa would recognize.[3] This book is the end result of that effort. Thanking people who made it at once possible and

[3]The text of my conference was published as "Gatherings of Academic Crowds as World-Historical Events: On the Passage of a Few Students through Brief Moments in Time" in Lis Lange, Vasu Reddy, and Siseko H. Kumalo, eds., *University on the Border Crisis of Authority and Precarity*. 1 ed. Vol. 3, *On Higher Education Transformation* (African Sun Media, 2021), 41–96.

necessary, my first thoughts, of course, go to my friend Leonhard Praeg, a professor of two continental philosophies, kind scholar, fearless person, and genuine colleague. The confidence it took him to stand outside the locked-up terminal of Federico García Lorca Airport in Granada in the middle of the night on nothing but trust in our nascent friendship that I would show up to drive him into town created conditions that made it possible for me to ask myself questions I did not have answers to. Having resigned his position as Head of the Philosophy Department at Pretoria University, Leonhard now stands outside the managerial university. It is my understanding that *Thinking Africa* does not exist anymore, and it is my hope that the big picture drawn here gives such an open-ended project a clearer sense of what possibilities for freedom were lost in its disappearance.

I began writing this book as my colleague Martin Hébert and I were in the process of translating Eric Wolf's *Europe and the People Without History* into French. I wish to thank Martin for his friendship and collegiality. One professor thanking another thus may sound trite, but all of us who make our living working in neoliberal universities know how rare it is to work with someone in the true spirit of collegiality, not as cosigners of a grant application or as members of committee of some sort but out of curiosity, moved by a shared sense of the importance of intellectual work, and the pure pleasure of thinking things through. Translating Wolf was a spontaneous decision. One evening, I emailed Martin asking if he had on hand the pdf of the French translation of a chapter of *Europe* because I wanted to assign it to students. Being told that such translation did not in fact exist, I suggested, as simply and collegially as Louise Vincent had invited me to South Africa, that we translate the thing ourselves. Immediately, I wrote to the University of California Press to inquire about translation rights. Within a week, Martin and I had secured rights and begun discussing with publishers. That, after having embarked so casually on such an exacting task, we both remained faithful for so long to our sense of *Europe*'s importance forty years after its original publication, I recognize as expressions of the unique possibilities for freedom offered by academic life.

Europe and the People Without History, I had first read almost forty years before, in a PhD seminar given by Professor Robert W. Cox in the Department of Political Science at York University. Professor Cox died in 2018. I remember him as much for the books on his reading list as I do for his unboasting, gentleman farmer-like, approach to intellectual work. There was real grandeur in Professor Cox's modest ways. An article he published in *Millennium* that would become fêted as a founding document of the Neo-Gramscian International Political Economy, began thus, in the plainest fashion: "Sometimes ago, I began reading Gramsci's *Prison Notebooks*." Here, in the simplest sentence possible, is the most eloquent statement of intellectual freedom. "Sometimes ago, I began reading" the professor wrote, letting readers know he was in a situation in which he was free to read, committed to thinking, and moved by a sense of being a peer among peers enough to articulate his thoughts for others to consider. Professor Cox, I also remember for a small handwritten note he sent me many years after I had left York, when I was caught in the middle of a storm-in-an-academic-teacup triggered in part by my refusal to join an academic protection racket (freedom, when treated as a privilege, can be parlayed into power), and by a novel I had written about the murderous alienation of a professor in a neoliberal university.[4]

Leo Panitch, who passed away while I was writing this book, was my PhD director at York University. That title, he had been generous enough to waive when I told him, presumptuous as only a young man in political science can be, that I did not wish to work in the usual, pedestrian manner, handing in chapter after chapter to my director, waiting like a schoolboy for his approval before being allowed to move on. It was an *oeuvre* I was working on, a *thèse* to end all theses, and I could only imagine it being read whole and admired for all that it was. "Then," Leo proposed, "I will be your Jewish grandmother." "We will meet once in a while, in my home. I will teach you how to make chicken broth and we will discuss your work." I could never be anyone's Jewish grandmother—though I did learn how to make proper broth—but in my relationship to students I hope to have stayed true to what I learned from Leo, that it is the responsibility of professors to help create conditions in which students can be free to explore their own thoughts in their own manner.

Trained as a political economist, I come from a discipline marginalized by the colonial organization of knowledge, which was all but erased by the neoliberal restructuring of intellectual work. I was lucky to find a good home in Université Laval's Department of Sociology. Here, I teach, read, and write about what enthuses me, with few obligations besides those I define myself. I am, in other words, as free as any scholar can be in a university. Twenty years after having arrived here, I remain thankful to three colleagues whom I knew very little at the time, who worked hard to put me in this situation of considerable privilege: Olivier Clain, Denys Delâge, and Gilles Gagné. Working alongside them, I hope to have learned a depth of engagement in scholarly life without which any talk of freedom would amount to little more than empty boasting. In the same breath, I also want to thank Pamela Colombo, Gérard Duhaime, and Dominique Morin, colleagues who became friends as I was writing this book. Their comradery has given substance and meaning to collegiality; it has been invaluable.

[4]*The Yellow Notebooks of Valérien Francoeur, heuristic murderer* was never published in the English original. It was, however, translated into French by Michel St-Germain, winner of a Governor General's award for his translation of Naomi Klein's *No Logo*, and published as *Les carnets jaunes de Valérien Francoeur, qui a crevé quelques enflés* (L'Effet Pourpre, 2002). The book was subsequently translated into Romanian by Fiona Dobrescu as *Eu, Valérien Francoeur, care mi-am împuşcat colegii* (Editura Cartea Românească, 2002).

It is my experience that students are rarely aware of the influence they have in shaping social relations of knowledge production. Yet, anyone who has ever attended university classes knows the wonder of those moments when the Idea itself seems present in the classroom—an enchanted space between professors and students, beyond that which either could have willed into existence. In such moments, we are reminded that freedom does not exist as an exclusive privilege of professors, or as an abstract mission of universities, but as a living relation between scholars. At Laval, I wish to acknowledge students who took part in the seminar on *Histoire globale des révoltes étudiantes* (The global history of student resistances) that took place as I was beginning to work more seriously on this book and those from the seminar on *La liberté en situation universitaire* (Freedom in university situations), which took place as I was nearing the end of my labors. From the former, I particularly remember François Bourassa for his generosity to younger students; Nicolas Chartier-Edward for his modest eloquence; Arian Omeranovic and Pablo Roy-Rojas for their subversively unassuming intelligence; Sebastian Vielnas for his sincerity; and Charles Olivier P-Carrier for his understated mercuriality. From the latter, I especially want to thank Leonard Marcoux for his exacting persnicketiness and Maggie Hébert, who was working on her master's thesis on academic censorship on the question of Palestine, for her doggedness. Their engagement helped preserve weekly gatherings from falling into the humdrum, keeping alive a relation without which there can be no scholarly freedom.

Historicizing Academic Freedom is not a prudent and thorough discussion of events and authors but a broad attempt to historicize what contemporary debates about academic freedom have come to reify, by thinking through the relationship between the *longue durée* history of world ordering and the always-circumstantial *praxis* of actually existing scholars. It is at times as thin on the bone as it is ambitious, and as dependent on specialized works. In writing it, I have not stood on the shoulders of giants, a position from which one can get only a God's-eye view of things, but among peers whence one can be free to "stand apart from the prevailing order of the world and ask how that order came about and how to transform it."[5] In that as well, this book is the product of the very freedom it wishes to problematize.

Historicizing Academic Freedom is a *sui generis* proposal. It is about academic freedom but in ways that problematize the hegemonic discourse on academic freedom. It shares widespread concerns for the erosion of

[5]"To stand apart from the prevailing order of the world and ask how that order came about and how to transform it" is how Robert W. Cox defined the purpose of critical theory, which he contrasted with problem-solving theory "that takes the world as it finds it, with the prevailing social and political relationships and the institutions into which they are organized as the given framework for action." Robert W. Cox, "Social Forces, States and World Orders: Beyond International Relations Theory," *Millennium—Journal of International Studies*, 10, 2 (1981): 126–55.

academic possibilities while also recognizing those possibilities as privileges born of the late-colonial ordering of the world. In doing so, it challenges the very categories through which scholarly collections are organized, which made it difficult to have the manuscript considered for publication. For intervening so generously at a key moment in this process, I want to thank Emily Andrew, senior editor at McGill-Queen's University Press, who suggested I write to her colleague Mark Richardson at Bloomsbury Publishing, who in turn, forwarded my manuscript to his colleague Alexander Bell. To Alexander, I owe special thanks for his engagement, rigor, and exacting fidelity. Working with him, I very much felt that the unalienated sense of freedom with which I had been working for so long would remain intact through publication. I could not have asked more from an editor. In the same breath, I want to thank reviewers, who were open enough to engage the book on its own terms, and who offered thoughtful, uncomplacent suggestions. It is an ingrate task to review a manuscript; their collegiality sustained a sense of relation that is at the very core of *freedom in thinking*.

Finally, I want to acknowledge the generosity of friends and colleagues who took the time to read parts of my manuscript before it was published. Their engagement has allowed me to finish this work as I began it, with a deep sense that my freedom as a scholar was intimately linked to an active relationship with others who are as committed as I am to think matters through rigorously in my own terms. Without that connection, I could not have written with any intelligence about *freedom in thinking*. With this debt in mind, I am happy to thank Nahla Abdo; Greg Albo; Nora Almeida; Pepijn Brandon; William Carroll; Lara Montesinos Coleman; Fiona Dove; Barry Eidlin; Maria Epele; Abdullah Farooq; Samir Gandesha; Dalie Giroux; Talbot Imlay; James Mittelman; Henk Overbeek; and Maya Wind.

I began working on this book a decade ago, not realizing it was a book I was working on. In the ever-busy world of the new knowledge economy, it is a great privilege to have spent so much time on a single, indeterminate, path, thinking as I went along. This privilege, I owe to my position as a tenured professor and to Laval University's station at the margins of the academic continent. There is a Thoreau-like freedom to be found working in Québec ("a breathing chimney at the corner of the continent" wrote Leonhard Cohen in *Beautiful Losers*), out of many loops, sheltered from what E. P. Thompson termed the "exigencies and alarums… of academic work" (1971: 78). This has allowed me to work at my own pace and in my own manner. I hope my book does justice to this great privilege.

Parts of this book build from previously published works. The beginning of the Introduction and the discussion of the dispersal of Paris's *studium generale* in Chapter 1 build on my "A struggle of civilization against barbarism: about universities as autonomous zones" (2016). In Chapter 3, the discussions of the Rodney riots in Jamaica and of the computer center incident at Sir George Williams in Montreal build on shorter accounts published in my "Gatherings of Academic Crowds as World-Historical Events" (2021). In Chapter 4, the discussion of the Maple Spring in Québec is abridged from my "Present in the World Economy: Québec's Students in the Springtime" (2013b).

André C. Drainville
Québec City,
November 2025

OUTLINE

Academic freedom is a phrase that originated in the late moments of the world-system of territorial states, which has acquired an almost totemic importance in the last twenty years, as the making of the global knowledge economy redefines the condition of knowledge production. Dusted off like academic gowns at convocation, it lords over present circumstances, binding scholars to mythologies that blind them to the substantial freedom embedded in situated *praxis*; to their own history as scholars; and to broader happenings in the world. To historicize that which it has come to reify, we need to rise from the abstract to the concrete and look into what scholars have made of the circumstances in which they have found themselves.[1]

For the pain it takes to include all, a work of such unbound ambitions can only be remarkable for what it inevitably leaves out of its consideration. If Southern Song academies during Mongol control over Eurasian trade routes, why not the Academy of Gondishapur at the time of the Sassanian Empire; the Patriarch School in Constantinople before the Fourth Crusade; the *Sungkyunkwan* in Seoul during the Joseon dynasty; or the Buddhist school of Takshasila? If the great dispersal in Paris, why not the hanging of the clerks at Oxford? If the fight over women's degrees at Cambridge, why not the long and acrimonious campaign for the admission of women at the University of Toronto? If the censuring of W. E. B. Du Bois at the University of Atlanta, that of Paul Sweezy at the University of New Hampshire, or of Bertrand Russell from Trinity College or from City College in New York, why not the ousting of Christian Wolff at the University of Halle or the forced resigning of Edward A. Ross from Stanford University? If the Université Autonome et Populaire in Paris, why not the University of Woodford square in Port of Spain, the Pavement University in Trafalgar square, or Black Mountain College, which was established by Rollins College professors dismissed for having refused to sign a pledge of allegiance, an act that led to their censure by the American Association of University Professors?

There is no good answer to such questions, except to acknowledge that a single author could never undertake the limitless task of accounting for

[1]In the *Grundrisse*, Karl Marx presented political economy as a way of "rising from the abstract to the concrete," "the only way in which thought appropriates the concrete, reproduces it as the concrete in the mind" (Penguin 2005 [1857]), 141.

every moment by which the little tradition of scholarly actions is defined.[2] Why not then mandate an empire of scholars to craft a one-to-one scale map of events or command a school of painters to create a collection of life-sized tableaux depicting scholars in lifelike action, as if caught in the very acts of defining their freedom? Because working thus would betray the irreducible uniqueness of situations. Abstract ensembles would be created in which scholars would remain strangers to themselves. We may as well let algorithms do our thinking.

Each scholarly action is an event unto itself; each in its own way contributes to defining a freedom that can only be deciphered by a kin working dialectically, animated by a subjective sense of indeterminacy and possibilities, faithful to ideas as they take form.

To get a sense of *freedom in thinking*, I intently fell down the rabbit holes of many situated struggles. Only by extracting myself as many times as I fell down, and by continuously triangulating findings, could I hope to remain faithful both to the circumstantiality of freedom and to the relative coherence over time of the moral community of scholar giving it shape. Time and again I fell down and surfaced, until the to-and-fro between the specifics of situations and the structure of world order seemed seamless enough for me to have a sense that I was looking at instances of the same. My moment of discovery over, I stopped to take stock of what I had found. This book is the result of this reckoning. It is, to borrow from the language of scholastic disputations, my *propositio*—an invitation to *responsio*.

Acquainting myself with the little tradition of scholarly actions, I did not shy away from moments that get overlooked in the literature on *academic freedom*, from those that cast a crude light on scholarly *praxis* or from those that have mostly been examined in other contexts. The Wartburg book burning (1817) has received scholarly attention mostly as an anecdotal moment in international relations (the Wartburg festival coincided with the fourth anniversary of the Battle of Leipzig); as a postscript to the Protestant reformation; or a preface to Nazi *auto-da-fé*. Though the Reformation itself began as an academic disputation, and the Wartburg festival was a critical moment both in the history of German student unions and in the construction of Germany's imperialist vision, it is almost never discussed as a scholarly event. The "No Women at Cambridge" protests (1897); the travails of W. E. B. Du Bois in Atlanta (1897–1910, 1933–1944); Rodney

[2]"Little tradition" is a loaded phrase. In "Protest and Profanation," James C. Scott, building from Christopher Hill (1970), contrasted *little* and *great* traditions in agrarian societies. Defined by the creeds of ruling elite, the latter readily appears as a relatively coherent and continuous pattern of thought, beliefs, and behaviors. The *little tradition*, by contrasts, is a looser ensemble existing in "what amounts to a 'shadow society,' only visible to itself and others in moments of 'normative opposition to the politico-religious tradition of ruling elite'" (Scott 1977: 4).

riots in Jamaica (1968); the occupation of the Sorbonne in Paris (1968) or that of the computer center at Sir George Williams University (1969); *#RhodesMustFall* protests in South Africa (2015); events surrounding safe space protests at the University of Missouri (2015); controversies stemming from the teaching of critical race theory in Florida (2015); or the censuring of Angela Davis at Butler University (2021) are rarely considered part of scholarly history, and they are certainly never considered part of the story of *academic freedom*. My intention is to consider these episodes and a handful of others as scholarly events in their own right—not to add a superficial measure of gender, racial, or political diversity to the discourse on *academic freedom* but to see through what the reification of *academic freedom* obfuscates.

The book is divided into four chapters. In each, a lengthy introduction examines how social relations of knowledge production got aligned with world ordering at specific junctures, defining the circumstances in which scholars took actions that gave shape to *freedom in thinking*.

Chapter 1 looks into the brief moment during which Mongol control of Eurasian trade routes made the *world-economies* of China, the *Dar al-Islam*, and Europe part of an integrated system for the first time since the Roman Empire, creating conditions conducive to the autonomy of reflexive instances. Academies, madrasas, and universities are expressions of what scholars made of these circumstances. Three events are considered: the restauration of the White Deer Grotto Academy (1179–1181), the building of the al-Mustansiriya *madrasa* in Baghdad (1227–1233), and the strike at the University of Paris (1229–1231).

The world-system of territorial states that took shape between the long sixteenth century and the latter part of the nineteenth century resolved rather than multiplied linkages and relationships between peoples of the world. The world-system of universities was an expression of this resolving; it is discussed in Chapter 2. In the first part of the chapter, I look into the making of national systems of knowledge production in Germany between the Prussian defeat at the battle of Jena-Auerstedt and the beginning of the First World War (1806–1914); in England between the repeal of the Corn Laws and the First World War (1846–1914); in France during the years of the Third Republic (1871–1914); and in the United States during Reconstruction (1865–1877). With these as context, five episodes are considered: the Wartburg book burning (1817); "No Women at Cambridge" protests (1897); the reform movement at Cordoba University (1918); the *de facto* banishment of W. E. B. Du Bois from the University of Atlanta (1897–1934); and the case of Paul Sweezy versus the University of New Hampshire (1954–1957).

The twentieth-century crisis of world ordering is the object of Chapter 3. In the Introduction, I examine how the worldwide wave of "anti-systemic movements" (Arrighi, Hopkins, and Wallerstein 1989) created a sense of global propinquity that incited scholars everywhere to take actions.

Six events are then briefly considered: the free speech movement at the University of Berkeley (1964); student occupations at the Sorbonne in Paris (1968); ANPO protests in Japan (1968); the Tlatelolco massacre in Mexico (1968); the Rodney riots in Kingston, Jamaica (1968); and the "computer center incident" at Sir George Williams University in Montreal (1969). These are well-known and oft-mythologized episodes often buried under the immense condescension that the literature on academic freedom reserves for student protests. They are worth revisiting as scholarly events.

Chapter 4 looks into the making of the new knowledge economy. In the Introduction, I situate universities in the new global system of knowledge production. Nine episodes are considered: student riots in London (2010); the long winter of student protests in Chile (2011–2012); the *Printemps érable* in Québec (2012); the setting up of a safe space at the University of Missouri (2015); *#RhodesMustFall* protests in South Africa (2015); the canceling of Angela Davis at Butler University (2021); the protracted strike movement at the University of California (1983–2022); the censuring of critical race theory in Florida (2020–2023); the setting up of Gaza solidarity encampments on US campuses (2024).

Periodizing is a reductive expedient that must be justified. Here it serves to highlight how distinct structures of world order overdetermined possibilities for scholars to institute self-regulated relations of knowledge production and how, above and beyond circumstantial considerations, scholars have time and again struggled for indeterminacy. This is the freedom to which scholars' actions always return. Having restored scholars to their own history, we are better equipped to think about freedom not just in thinking but also in acting in the world. This is discussed in the Conclusion of the book.

Introduction

The world of humankind constitutes a manifold, a totality of interconnected processes, and inquiries that disassemble this totality into bits and then fail to reassemble it falsify reality.

—ERIC WOLF,
EUROPE AND THE PEOPLE WITHOUT HISTORY

In the time it would have taken a child born in the year the Organisation for Economic Co-operation and Development (OECD) published *The Knowledge-Based Economy* (1996) to finish their doctorate, the University—by some accounts the second-oldest institution with a continuous history in the Western world (Rothblatt and Wittrock 1993)—had been in appearance all but molecularized to bits by neoliberal managerialism and those bits folded into global "knowledge supply chains" (Mak and Ramaprasad 2003), flattening scholars' unique sense of totality.

This recomposing has been so broadly swayed by global concepts of control and so specifically shaped by situated struggles over the reinvention of every fact and facet of the university way of life that it has been difficult to gain both insight into and perspective on it. Between attempts by global governing agencies to make universities "driver[s] of productivity and economic growth" (OECD 1996: 3) and arcane tussles over safe spaces, speech codes, and tuition fees, we can hardly think for the vertigo. Yet, this is the gap we must look across if we are to understand that struggles now taking place in universities, no matter how singular, overwrought, or mundane they may seem—at times even to those who are most concerned by them—are signposts of a profound transformation in social relations of knowledge production. What is at stake in this transformation is nothing less than the possibility for scholars to engage in relatively autonomous and self-inventing relations of knowledge production.

Such relations exist in situation; they are always in the process of defining themselves, and, therefore, always at stake. They are the *sine qua non* conditions of what, borrowing from Arendt, we will term *freedom in thinking* (Arendt 2009). How scholars' actions always return to it is the subject of this book.

Academic freedom is a catch-all phrase invoked by everyone and their foes to mean everything and its opposite. A malleable, at times shifty, signifier, it looms over debates about the reinvention of universities, especially at the core of the old world-system of states and universities.[1] Here, I understand it not as a finality inherent to the mission of universities, as an expression of the professional privileges of titular professors, or as a political value linked to democratic governance but, as a regime of freedom instituted in a particular moment in *world ordering* to regulate and reproduce social relations of knowledge production.

I will call *world ordering* the shifting ensemble of disputed processes by which "contacts and connections, linkages and interrelationships" between peoples of the world are organized and the world itself is given form as a social and economic formation.[2] Between the long sixteenth century and the latter half of the nineteenth century, as the world morphed from an arrangement of relatively porous *world-economies* linked by war, cosmopolitan thinking, and long-distance trade toward a more integrated international division of trade, labor and states, a world-system of universities took shape that was increasing dedicated to the mass production of knowledge—a move Immanuel Kant decried in "The Conflict of the Faculties" (1798). The term

[1]The terms *core* and *periphery* are more problematic concepts than they were half a century ago, when world-system theorists used them, after Fernand Braudel, to distinguish positions within what Christopher Chase-Dunn and Barry Gills (2003) called "the old inter-state system." Now, "the centre of gravity has moved from inside nations to elsewhere" (Sridhar 2004: 9). At the "core" of world ordering is not a country or group of countries anymore but a *nebula* of meeting places beyond the reach of all nationally organized societies where transnational capital makes itself into a class in the process of defining global concepts of control. What it is now de rigueur to call the Global North and the Global South both stand, each in their own way, at the periphery of the world ordering. Still, I will continue to refer to countries of the core and periphery throughout this book, simply because it remains relevant do so. It was in the core—not in the periphery—that academic freedom was instituted as a regime to regulate and reproduce social relations of knowledge production. And it is there—as argued in Chapter 4—that the new, neoliberal iteration of academic freedom meets the old, giving impetus to an infinity of minute struggles that current debates bind together through reification. World ordering does not make itself outside of its own history: By distinguishing between core and periphery, we can historicize scholarly *praxis*, give substance to freedom in thinking, and see what is at stake in current debates.

[2]"Contact and connections, linkages and interrelationships" is a phrase Eric Wolf used in his introduction of *Europe and the People Without History* (1982) to contrast a relational, processual, view of the history of humankind with one based on the acceptance of the world as a mere assemblage of "static and disconnected" things: "nations," "societies," and "cultures."

academic came to be used in this context as a marker of desuetude. Engaged in theoretical speculations of little real-world importance—in Jonathan Swift's *Gulliver's Travels*, members of the Academy of Projectors, their hands sooty and their beards long, extracted sunbeams out of cucumbers and calcined ice into gun powder—*academics* became defined by association to outmoded ways of thinking and *ancient régime* institutions: the Accademia Platonica, the Académie des Beaux-Arts, and others. Whereas the "ingenious pursuers" who defined intellectual work during the first scientific revolution (Jardine 2000) shared a grounding in experimental methods from which they garnered a unique sense of freedom—contingent *dixit* Descartes on relative indifference to the orders of truth and utility (Schulthess 1980)—*academics* remained enfettered in predefined routines and obligations (Burke 2013; Hall 1959). Theirs was the domain of unquestioned notions, not freedom.

In the latter half of the nineteenth century, as the world-system of states was reaching its achieved form and modern research universities were being installed as coordinating instances of national "scientific-technical" production systems (Hacking 1982; Karady 1998; Nowotny 1991), the waning of *academics* was complete, and *academic freedom* became the legitimizing notion of a utilitarian market of ideas instituted to enable "professors and students to carry on their roles."[3] Tied to a particular "idea of the university" and bound to an "implicit contract between university and society" (Collini 2017), it was a two-faced phrase that misnamed its subject—it was professors, not *academics* who were the privileged subjects of *academic freedom*—and leaned on a superannuated referent to assign new obligations.[4] Before *arbeit macht frei* was *bildung macht frei*.[5]

In the twentieth century, universities in core countries of the world-system of states grew into hubs of technoscience and as "ideological state apparatuses" (Althusser 2014). The idea of *academic freedom*, increasingly detached from social relations of knowledge production actually taking place in real-world universities, endured as a justifying notion and as an object of struggle, particularly in core countries. At the periphery, it was made part of the "accoutrements of every newly independent states" (Hayhoe 1994: 361). Appeals to it were made to "cover up contemporary faults, corruptions, tyrannies" and to lay claim within "the embattled imperial contexts out of which [universities] came" (Saïd 1994: 16).

---

[3]Wilhelm von Humboldt (1982) is quoted from "On the Spirit and the Organizational Framework of Intellectual Institutions in Berlin."

[4]The "idea of the university" alludes to John Henry Newman's text of 1852, the origin point of the American Association of University Professors' *1915 Declaration of Principles on Academic Freedom and Academic Tenure*.

[5]*Arbeit macht frei* ("Work sets you free") is, of course, the infamous phrase written atop the archway at the main entrance gate to the Auschwitz-Birkenau death camp. *Bildung macht frei* ("Education sets you free") was a slogan of nineteenth-century reformers who championed the cause of the Humboldtian University. On this, see Reitter and Wellmon (2016: 12).

The "crisis of universities," which began in the mid-1960s, was a modality of the crisis of state-bound knowledge regimes and of the world-system of states writ large. It was met by fastening an increasingly fragmented and diverse lot of organizations to a globally integrated system of knowledge production geared toward finding new avenues for capital "to reconquer the entire social space from which the previous [world] system had tended to separate it" (Gaudemar 1980) as well as "to bring more orderly and reliable responses to social and political issues that go beyond the capacities of states to address individually" (Weiss and Gordenker 1996: 17). Its aura gone (for what could be left of it after McDonald's University, a perfect parody of scholarly sublime, began awarding degrees in "hamburgerology"?), the university endures as an organization in a world of organizations—a switchable part of a globally integrated enterprise.

Academic freedom has become in this context the name of a more intensive regulation of social relations of knowledge production. Appropriated by university administrators, it has become the ever-pervasive legitimizing notion for the preemptive foreclosing of scholarly relations (Butler 2006: 11–12). To think what its making puts at stake, we have to look into the situated doing of scholars.

Like *academic*, *scholars* is a term that by etymology points toward that which took place two millennia ago in a grove of olive trees in the northern suburbs of a large city at the center of a regional empire that was in many respects very much a world unto itself. By usage, however, it invites historicization: Scholars are intellectuals in relation, meeting in preexisting circumstances that their actions shape. Looking into their doings, we will see active bodies of people engaged in the real world of instituted relations laboring to put themselves in situations where they can enter into relatively indeterminate, self-governed, relations of knowledge production: *freedom in thinking*.

Scholars in World-Ordering Situations

With Antonio Gramsci's *Quaderni del carcere* as a focal point, the concept of hegemony became a household notion in social sciences early in the 1980s. Used with reference to transnational capital's "revolution from above" (van der Pijl 1984), it helped scholarship come to terms with the depth of the crisis of the Bretton Woods world order and the radicalness of capital's way out of it. Used retrospectively, it helped situate the new neoliberal world order in the continuity of *Pax Americana*, *Pax Britannica*, *Pax Mongolia*, *Pax Romana*, etc.

"Hegemony" also gave an oppositional sort of coherence to studies of protests "kicking off everywhere" (Mason 2013) against the ways and consequences of global neoliberalism. Understood with reference to counterhegemony, distinct episodes of struggle (factory and land occupations in Argentina and Brazil; antisummit protests in Washington, Seattle, and Genoa; International Monetary Fund [IMF] riots in Abidjan and Cairo; antiausterity *indignados* gatherings in Madrid and Barcelona; gas and water wars in Bolivia; global street parties in London and Adelaide, etc.) could be thought of as relatively coherent parts of a historic bloc. In a context where end-of-history scholarship was promoting ideas that there was no alternative to global neoliberalism, this was of immense intellectual and political importance.

But for all that it contributed to giving scholars a means to stand apart from the neoliberal order of the world, the literature that constituted itself around the concept of hegemony tended to presume rather than question capital's ability to articulate a global "common purpose and vision ... embedded in distinct, reproducible, social relations" (Hajnal 1989: 21–22). Positing hegemony, it separated the order of the world from the domain of social relation and made it seem an abstract totality made in capital's image, which could, in time, be remade in its own by another, more progressive but still as abstract, subject (Drainville 1994). In such a scenario, freedom could only be imagined as an abstract thing, not the way of being and struggling of happening bodies of people.

This is how discourse has made academic freedom seem.[6] To lift that veil, we need to conceptualize the world not as an abstract totality all dressed

[6]I have used the phrase *academic discourse* argumentatively, in a totalizing and quite dismissive manner, to sharpen the contrast with my own thinking. Though a utilitarian understanding of freedom is widely shared in the literature, as is a Euro-centered sense of history which neither reaches beyond the nineteenth century nor concerns itself with the contingencies of world ordering, there is, in truth, no single academic understanding of academic freedom. It is a literature, not a discourse. A proper review of it is well beyond the scope of this Introduction and would, in the end, add little to the argument put forth in the book. Still, as we enter into it, a few works can be briefly mentioned. Bill Reading's *The University in Ruins* (1996); C. Nelson's *No University Is an Island: Saving Academic Freedom* (2010); Ellen Schrecker's *The Lost Soul of Higher Education* (2010); R. C. Post's *Democracy, Expertise, and Academic Freedom* (2012); Stanley Fish's *Versions of Academic Freedom* (2014); J. L. Turk's *Academic Freedom in Conflict* (2014); Joanna Williams' *Academic Freedom in an Age of Conformity* (2016); Jennifer Lackey's *Academic Freedom* (2018); Henry Reichman's *Understanding Academic Freedom* (2021); and Maria Slowey and Richard Taylor's *Academic Freedom in Higher Education* (2024) are well-known works that would find a place in any reading list on academic freedom. For all their singularities, they share a common, implicit sense of history. With the possible exception of Joan Wallach Scott's *Knowledge, Power, and Academic Freedom* (2004), they tend to evoke rather than problematize the making of the new knowledge economy; far from praxis, they remain more concerned with the conditions under which scholars act than what they make of them. Evan Gerstmann and Matthew J. Streb's *Academic Freedom at the Dawn of a New Century* (2006); Carlos Alberto Torres's *Education and Neoliberal Globalization* (2008); M. Seckelmann, P. Collin, and T. Biebricher's *Academic Freedom Under Pressure?* (2021); Michael Ignatieff and Stephen Roch's *Academic Freedom: The Global Challenge* (2018); Timo Aarrevaara et al.'s *Universities in the Knowledge Society* (2021); R. Watermeyer, Rille Raaper, and Mark Olsen's *Handbook on Academic Freedom* (2022); Asli Vatansever and Aysuda

up in Latin locutions but as a field of practice. To do so, we must look into how scholars have acted in the circumstances they have found themselves in. Those, we will understand as *situations*.

Situation is a term that brings thinking back to a phenomenological understanding of subjectivity. It draws attention to the circumstances under which people act that Jean-Paul Sartre objectified as *data*. How these circumstances are recognized and what course of action people commit to are taken to reveal them to themselves as subjects, and to define "that freedom to which what we do always comes back" (Sartre 1988: 55).

For Sartre, *situations* were moments in proximate places: an evening out at the theatre (Contat and Rybalka 1976) or, say, Paris at the time of the German occupation (Sartre 1949). Always, what mattered was what the subject could see with its own eyes and make intelligible to itself (Bains 1997). The "surrounding world" was an abstraction peopled by abstractions: *le juif*, a ghostly object of suffering part of an "abstract historic" community (Sartre 1985: 68); *le colon* (a caricature of Fanon's own *colon*); *la négresse* (Remley and Albert 2013); and *Blacks*, likened to untouchables (Sartre 1996: 84).

In many ways, it was a wholly provincial, flat-earth view of the world that Sartre put forth.[7] World order was taken for granted, never conceived

---

Kölemen's *Academic Freedom and Precarity in the Global North* (2023); and Frédéric Mégret and Nandini Ramanujam's *Academic Freedom in a Plural World* (2024) all share a global/comparative perspective, but none are concerned with problematizing the relationship between situated actions and world ordering. They take the order of the world as a given. C. A. Torres's *Theoretical and Empirical Foundations of Critical Global Citizenship Education* (2017); Elspeth Tilley's *Creative Activism: Research, Pedagogy and Practice* (2022); Derek R. Ford's *Teaching the Actuality of Revolution* (2023); and Kim A. Case and Leah R. Warner's *Creating a Faculty Activism Commons for Social Justice* (2025) lie at the intersection of pedagogical practices, academic activism, and social movements. They are part of a tradition that is often understood with reference to Paulo Freire's *Pedagogy of the Oppressed* (1970); Henry Giroux's *Theory and Resistance in Education* (1983); or bell hooks' *Teaching to Transgress* (1994). *Historicizing Academic Freedom* aligns with this tradition but broadens and historicizes its referents. To understand what freedom can be found in pedagogical relations, it also draws from Chu Hsi's *Articles of Instruction* (1180); Pierre Abelard *Sic et Non* (1120); Immanuel Kant's *The Conflict of Faculties* (1798); John Henry Newman's *The Idea of a University* (1852); Emily Davies's *The Higher Education of Women* (1866); W. E. B. Du Bois's "In Defence of the Sociological Laboratory at Atlanta" (1898); George Sabine's report on the dismissal of Professor Herbert A. Miller from Ohio State University (1934); Guy Debord's *Rapport sur la construction de situations* (1968); the Universidad Nomáda's *Manifesto* (2001), among other works.

[7]On flat ontologies and the "*a priori* expurgation of scale," as a defining trait of European modernity, see Leitner and Miller (2007: 121) and Marston et al. (2005).

of as data except on occasions when "slaves and monsters" involved in anticolonial struggles brought the gift of second sight to the colonizer's feet.[8]

Of greater interest to our attempt at understanding the relationship between social relations of knowledge production and the structure of world order will be multiscalar notions of situations, drawn principally from critical anthropology and Black existentialism, that consider the disputed, deeply situated, process of world-ordering part of the circumstances in which subjects act, defining their freedom.[9]

---

[8]"Slaves and monsters" references a phrase used by Sartre's in his "Preface" to *The Wretched of the Earth*: "the European has only been able to become a man through creating slaves and monsters [I]in the notion of the human race we found an abstract assumption of universality which served as cover for the most realistic practices. On the other side of the ocean there was a race of less-than-humans who, thanks to us, might reach our status a thousand years hence." The "gift of second sight" recalls W. E. B. Du Bois on double consciousness: a form of world-historical consciousness. Sartre's own take on second sight ("the shock of being seen") is detailed in "Orphée noir," an essay which originally appeared as Preface to *Anthologie de la nouvelle poésie nègre et malgache de langue française* edited by Léopold Sédar Senghor and later republished as a postscript to Albert Memmi's *Portrait du colonisé*.

[9]Assembling anything resembling even a sketch of a genealogy of the relevant literature is well beyond the scope of this Introduction, but a few works can be listed to give a sense of my position. Some are contemporary to Sartre. In his "Analysis of a Modern Situation in Zululand" (Gluckman 1958) Max Gluckman, for instance, used the term *situation* to drag anthropology out of its defining preoccupation with timeless ethnic groups and other fixed-and-bound entities, to recenter it on what Bronisław Malinowski (1939) had termed "points of contact" between colonizers and colonized. Doing so, he apprehended world ordering in a more situated, contingent, and constitutive fashion, restoring Bantu people to a manner of agency (Gluckman 1940). In *Psychologie de la colonization* (1950) and in articles published in *Esprit* (1950, 1951, 1965), Octave Mannoni situated the broad process of colonialization in the same manner, recognizing colonized people as subjects of history made in scale-straddling, event-bound circumstances. In *La situation coloniale*, Georges Balandier (1951) likewise understood colonialism as a situated process of worldwide subjection-from-beyond-and-within which engaged colonized people as accomplices in their own subjugation. Other works of interests in the study of situations circumscribed by word ordering are works of what has come to be termed *Black existentialism*, as discussed in Lewis Gordon's *Existence in Black* (1996) and "Black Existentialism"(2014) and in Vereen et al. (2017). Franz Fanon and James Baldwin are early figures of reference. In *Peau Noire, Masque Blanc* (1952) and in *Les Damnés de la Terre* (1961), Fanon scaled colonialization down to specific, uncertain, situations: A single colonial administrator speaking *petit-nègre* to the *colonisé*, in effect saying "You, stay where you are," and the whole subjugating order of the word could be brought to bear on the tiniest, most specific, circumstances. Immediately, the *colonisé* was at risk of becoming pathologically dislocated; in a movement just as abrupt, it could make itself a world-historical subject by reaching for his machete or letting it be known to the *colonisateur* and to himself that it was close at hand. James Baldwin also understood world ordering from situations. A lone cop standing at the corner of Fifth Avenue and Forty-Second Street in New York, grumbling "Why don't you n—… stay uptown where you belong" to a thirteen-year-old adolescent on his way to the public library; the whole racial order of the world was brought to bear on a specific situation and thus made clearer, more contingent (Baldwin 1962: 21). The cop grumbled because he was fearful and ignorant, and the adolescent took conscience of his fragility. What he did with this knowledge defined him not as an abstract figuration of consciousness, nor as the person he would have been had he been born elsewhere—say in the

Universities and university-like institutions became privileged sites through which knowledge in and of the world came to be organized as the world-system of states took shape between the long sixteenth century and the latter half of the nineteenth century, and they have remained indispensable to the making of the new knowledge economy in the twenty-first century. This makes it inevitable that, as we look into *situations* in which scholars have acted in the century-and-a-half that social relations of knowledge production have been governed by *academic freedom*, it is professors and students that we see. They were professors and students, not scholars, who in 1848 formed Academic Legions in Vienna and occupied barricades in Paris—unreliably according to Karl Marx and Friedrich Engels, and most often on the bourgeois side (Draper 1977: 534–38)—and professors and students who acted out on Market Square when the Senate of Cambridge University voted against awarding degrees to women; burned books at Wartburg; occupied the computer center at Sir George Williams University; organized teach-ins during protests against wars in Vietnam and Gaza; set up free universities in Berkeley, Paris, and Barcelona; defended the safe space at the University of Missouri; and took part in *#RhodesMustFall* protests in South Africa.

But unavoidability does not a concept make. Laboring to historicize what the term *academic freedom* has come to reify, we will need to take a step back from instituted positions and think not of professors and students performing as professors and students would—but of scholarly *praxis*. Looking into critical moments in the *longue durée* history of world ordering, we will unearth a living community of scholars struggling to defend the possibilities to engage in relatively autonomous and indeterminate relations of knowledge production. Therein, we will see, lies *freedom in thinking*, the cause and consequence of scholars' self-realization.

Possibilities for the relative autonomy of reflexive instances are conditioned by the structured, multiscalar ensemble of relations of which they are part. Always, autonomy is a matter of what we might term a *politics of usefulness*—not a neutral or transparent calculation of utility but the shifting process by which scholars and instituting powers legitimize their doings by referencing an always deferred, never realized, horizon of social necessity.

"old country" of the South (Baldwin 1959: 72)—but who he was at that particular juncture in "'the common history—ours': singed by freedom, a force," as Baldwin put it, "that burns away illusions" (Lapenson 2013: 204). More contemporary works of Black existentialism have also influenced our understanding of situations: Robert Birt's *The Quest for Community and Identity* (2002); Bernard Boxill's *Blacks and Social Justice* (1992); Robert Gooding-Williams's *Look a Negro* (2011) and *In the Shadow of Du Bois* (2011); Tommy Lott's *The Idea of Race* (2000); Lucius T. Outlaw's *Critical Social Theory in the Interest of Black Folks* (2005); Naomi Zack's *Philosophy of Science and Race* (2014) and *White Privilege and Black Rights* (2015); and Lewis Gordon's *Freedom Justice and Decolonization* (2020).

The politics of usefulness allows scholars to negotiate a measure of relative autonomy, but it does not determine what they make of it. The central proposition of this book is that, beyond whether the structuring of social relation favors or hinders the autonomy of reflexive instances, scholars everywhere lean as much as they can toward indeterminacy. At the very core of this movement lies *freedom in thinking*.

Indeterminacy is not a provisional, preambular, state of affairs—a mere suspension of relations, a "giddy moment," to evoke Terry Eagleton on the ineffable flicker of difference (Bhabha 1992: 50)—before the gears of thinking get engaged and intellectuals take up their mission, what Julien Benda in *La trahison des clercs* (2003) called their vocation. It is neither a vocational calling nor a ready-made creed but the essential quality of a living relation—changing, multidimensional, multiscalar, plurisituated, multitemporal—connecting scholars with one another; with authors both dead and alive; with concepts culled from their own practice and that of others, past and present. It takes subjective form in seminar rooms, conference venues, and amphitheaters where classes are held, and in fleeting encounters in hallway and street corners when scholarly engagement is at its most fragile and the to-and-fro of *propositio* and *disputatio* is looser and, at times, most fecund. It is even at stake in scholars' relation to artificial intelligence. It is not the expression of free will but a set of values, a moral order of sorts, that remains hidden to scholars themselves and to others until actions are taken, and seen to be taken, in defense of the possibility for scholars to create situations where perfectly useless notions can be thought through with self-determined rigor.[10]

Freedom in thinking only gets articulated episodically, yet it can be seen more clearly in the *longue durée* of the little tradition, at once within, above, and beyond discourses and instituted relations, in concordance with, in opposition to, or in perfect indifference to *academic freedom*. To recognize it in its own terms, even if only as a plausible hypothesis, we have to look into moments of practice.

I will begin inquiring into the history of the relationship between the structure of world order and scholarly *praxis* by examining the "long thirteenth century" when the expansion that followed Genghis Khan's reunification of Mongolian tribes (1206) brought the broad complex of

---

[10]The term *moral* is used not with reference to any normative morality to which scholars would have been obliged (a way to understand "moral," *dixit* Thompson, which "brings on a rush of polemical blood to the academic head") but more materially, as an expression of a mutual engagement, the terms of which are both embedded in existing customs and conventions, duties and mutual obligations, and constitutive of the subjectivity needed to articulate them in concrete circumstances (Thompson 1991: 260, 271). "Perfectly useless" alludes to Abraham Flexner's 1939 defense of academic indifference to the "angry current of daily life." Flexner was a founder of Princeton University's Institute for Advanced Study. "The Usefulness of Useless Knowledge" is the title of an essay he published in *Harpers* (179, June/November 1939, 544–52).

Eurasian trading routes under relatively coherent administrative control, making China, the *Dar al-Islam*, and Europe "interactive components of a unified system" for the first time since the Roman empire (O'Rourke 2007: 108).[11]

China, the *Dar al-Islam*, and Europe, I will understand as *world-economies*. In the first chapter of *The Perspective of the World*, Fernand Braudel used the term (with hyphen, approximating the German *Weltwirtschaft*) to designate "fragments of the world ... economically autonomous section[s] of the planet able to provide for most of [their] own needs ... to which ... internal links and exchanges give a certain organic unity" (Braudel 1984: 22). What is important for our purpose is less the separation intimated by the nouns—which encourages us to see the term *world-economies* as separate, self-contained, entities—than the bond acknowledged by the preposition on which the phrase pivots: unto themselves as fragments, *world-economies* were for Braudel nevertheless *of* the world, defined as much by their enmeshment in worldly ties (mostly of long-distance commerce for Braudel) as by their internal dynamics.

Beginning with the Mongol moment, I want to think from a critical juncture when the *world-economies* of China, the *Dar al-Islam*, and Europe were brought into a relatively plural, transactional, articulations that created in each condition conducive to the relative autonomy of reflexive instances.

In China, scholars acted within the limits and possibilities of a strong articulating state historically constituted at the intersection of attempts to control (i) external relations of commerce, diplomacy, and war with nearby polities and with the Afro-Eurasian *world-economy* and (ii) the digging of

[11]*Genghis Khan* (*Ghengis Khan* in French; *Gengis Khan* or *Jenghiz Khan* in Spanish; *Dschinghis Khan* in German; *Cambuskan* in *The Canterbury Tales*) is a common transliteration from the original Mongol that I will use in deference to prevailing usage. This is a simple and, for the most part, forthright way of working to which I will remain faithful throughout the book. It owes to the experience of working with my colleague Martin Hebert to translate Wolf's *Europe and the People Without History* into French. Wolf, in many regards, already wrote in translation: between English and German; between European and American anthropological traditions; between disciplines divided by the colonial organization of knowledge; between the desire for a synthetic narrative and concerns for situated histories; and between academic freedom and the constraints of the cold war, and so on. Translating *Europe and the People Without History*, Martin and I strove to resolve issues in what we came to call *la manière la plus Wolf possible* (the wolfest manner possible): avoiding jargon, striving for unencumbered, readily recognizable, language, simple phrases, and unfettered syntax. In the wolfest manner possible, I have avoided translating foreign-language terms altogether when the original appeared to be in customary use. I have also eschewed tonic accents, except when they have entered common usage. When several transliterations seemed to vie for usage, I committed to the simplest and most agile, much in the way that Wolf committed to the term *polity* to designate all manners of distinct political formations. In the spirit or readability and to facilitate linkages with the scholarly literature, I have also kept terminological digressions to a minimum. When they seemed necessary, I tried to relegate them to footnotes, as I am doing now. For the most part, I have done the same with discussions of conceptual and theoretical propositions.

canals, irrigation ditches, and dams to defend areas of settlement against floods and secure water supplies in periods of drought (Kuhn 2011: 72). How these enterprises combined to curtail the autonomy of reflexive instances found perhaps its clearest expressions in the consecration of Confucianism as State ideology and in the development of the imperial system of examinations. These were mutually reinforcing events: The former gave the Chinese State legitimizing notions that emphasized social harmony and the unity of knowledge and practice; the latter produced a class of scholar-official for whom there was "no clear dividing line between political power and scholarly knowledge" (Hayhoe 2001: 329). When Mongol control over trade routes increased opportunities for long-distance commerce, a middle class of merchants took advantage of an "unprecedented economic expansion of the Chinese market economy" to develop independent relationships to the outside (Liu 2015: 57). This increased domestic possibilities for autonomy. The neo-Confucian "academy movement" of the Southern Song period (960–1279) is an expression of this autonomy. At the heart of its "revolution in education" (Bary 1989: 186) was the putting of scholars in deliberately constructed relations of learning, at distance from the State examination process. In relatively autonomous and self-invented situations, a "true way" could be discovered from which the ruler's mind could be rectified (Schirokauer 1993: 127–30, 219).

In the *Dar al-Islam*, Mongolian control over Eurasian trade routes boosted opportunities for merchants to develop broader and more varied relations with the outsides. The resulting rise in profit (which also owed to the revival of maritime trade routes with East Africa, the Persian Gulf, India, and China) fostered conditions conducive to relative autonomy of reflexive instances (Fındıklı 2022: 130). The "*madrasa* movement" which took place during the waning years of the Abbasid caliphate is a product of these circumstances. Hundreds of *madrasas* ("the place to give lessons") were built in the Islamic world in this period. Always, they combined places where scholars lived and learned in a separate, purposely built, architectural ensemble. As prosperity increased, better-funded *madrasas* formed a scholarly system increasingly coherent unto itself in terms of *praxis*, more detached from ways of learning inherited from the prophetic tradition and autonomous from the political world of caliph, sultans, and princes (Gilbert 1980: 108–13). Gathering in communities where they "enjoy[ed] relative freedom with respect to the content and mechanisms of knowledge transmission" (Günther 2022: 480), the *ulama* ("those who know") made itself into something resembling a self-regulated class of professional scholars (Ephrat 1993: 174–90).

In the European *world-economy*, Mongol control of Eurasian trading routes coincided with the short renaissance of the first half of the thirteenth century: By 1210, "it was well advanced, by 1250 its work [was] largely done" (Haskins 1955 [1927]: 10). In the midst of a "new Europe" (Le Goff 2009) shaped by the contending claims of the *sacerdotium*, *imperium*, and merchants, scholars drew from privileges harking back to Roman civil law, as well as a more recent culture of disputation (Novikoff 2013) to secure a measure of impunity they shared with lepers, mendicants, and other outcasts living in self-governed communities (Ryke 2002). Unbound by military levies and civic obligations, scholars could travel and ply their trade. Like all manners of self-governing corporations, they constituted themselves into *universitas*. By the fourteenth century, that term was used exclusively to designate members of scholarly orders and the buildings where their activities took place.

Distinct from one another as institutions, academies, *madrasas*, and universities were remarkably alike in the social relations of knowledge production they instituted. Everywhere scholars exploited the possibilities for autonomy opened up by relatively plural linkages between relatively porous *world-economies* to put themselves in relatively self-constitutive and indeterminate social relations of knowledge production.

The Mongols "trod lightly on the world they conquered": They invented no aesthetic, did not enforce a common language (though the Uyghur script did become broadly recognizable along Eurasian trading routes), and built no significant engineering works except for bridges (Weatherford 2005: 14, 169). However commonplace references to *Pax Mongolica* might have become when "hegemony literature" was laboring to trace the deep roots of neoliberal world ordering; it was not a political or ethical order that Mongol expansion gave form to and exploited but a relatively plural and open-ended transactional arrangement between relatively porous *world-economies*. As the risks of long-distance trading diminished, so did possibilities to collect protective rent (Abu-Lughod 1991: 155). Requiring "booty to continue to exist" (Buell and Fiaschetti 2018: 17), Mongol organization dissolved into competing polities ruled by Genghis Khan's progenies.

The short moment of Mongol control over Eurasian trade routes ended synchronously, as global history goes, with Mongol incursions into Eastern Europe and parts of the Balkans in the 1230s–1240s; the siege and destruction of Bagdad in 1258; and the capture of the Southern Song capital of Hangzhou by Kublai Khan in 1276. In Yuan China (1271–1368), academies were first banned as sites of spurious learning and then made bearers of state orthodoxy. In the *Dar al-Islam*, the *madrasa* form continued to spread, but the autonomy of actually existing *madrasas* diminished in the absence of enabling tensions between the unifying ambitions of the Abbasids and regional drives for self-rule. In Europe, universities proliferated as instances of state-building, not expressions of scholarly autonomy. Everywhere, scholarly relations lost indeterminacy.

Between the long sixteenth century and the mid-twentieth-century crisis of world ordering, an increasingly integrated and hierarchical system of territorial states gave political form to the international division of trade and labor. "[V]irtually all interrelations among peoples [became] dimensions of their respective states' relations with one another" (Arrighi, Hopkins, and Wallerstein 1989: 4). In place of porous *world-economies* linked in relatively plural fashions, territorial polities sought command of linkages between fixed populations, creating conditions unfavorable to the autonomy of reflexive instances.

In the Westphalian core of the world-system, knowledge in and about the world was organized by bureaucratic states acting as "sponsoring authorities" for a national systems of social relations (Fuchs 1963: 434). These systems were the product of a double movement. In the first, states separated a new genus of research universities from the lot of institutions (academies, *écoles*, salons, learned societies, private laboratories, etc.) that had carried the burden of intellectual activities between the first scientific revolution (*c.* Newton, Locke, and Descartes) and the second (so-called by Samuel Taylor Coleridge in his 1819 *Philosophical Lecture*). This was a moment of disembedding. Everywhere, it was shaped by particular configurations of inherited institutions, by specific dynamics of state and empire-building, and, perhaps most importantly, by places occupied by states in the international division of trade and labor. The closer national systems of knowledge production were to the core of world ordering, the more scholars were cut off from the possibility of "culling inductively from the fullness of experienced human life in one or another part of the world" (Wallerstein 1996: 367).

In the second moment, research universities were pulled in the direction of fulfilling the myriad tasks necessary for the proper functioning of society and empire: to insure "high levels of control necessary to prevent irregularity, unpredictability and inefficiency from interfering with the orderly flow of commerce" (Foucault 1997: 214); to produce "more exact knowledge on which to base decisions" (Wallerstein 1996: 6); "to develop experts for various branches of the public service" (American Association of University Professors [AAUP] 1915); and "to participate in commissions, compile and publish data on finance, trade, wealth, demography, crime, education, transportation, agriculture, and industry" (Cohen 1996: 4).

Academic freedom was part of the interlocking ensemble of market-based freedoms that, as a whole, made up the late-imperial world of market regulation. By it, scholars were separated into two functional categories: (i) professors, established as privileged bearers of freedom to research and teach, (ii) and students, who bore the ancillary freedom to learn. Between them, a relatively autonomous and self-regulated "free market" of ideas was set up that extended the prevalent mode of regulation of social relations to the domain of knowledge production.[12]

[12]"Free market of ideas" references a phrase customarily used by the US Supreme Court in matters relating to academic freedom. The first reference is attributed to Justice Louis Brandeis's concurring opinion in *Whitney v. California* (1927). The first Supreme Court decision that explicitly referred to universities as marketplaces of ideas was *Sweezy v. New Hampshire* (1957), discussed in Chapter 3.

As universities grew into "axial institutions" of modern bureaucratic states (Barker 2008: 51), *academic freedom* clarified the terms and purposes of scholarly autonomy. So settled did scholars become in the folds of instituted privileges, so perfectly contained in their doings, that they almost never challenged the limits imposed by the division of their labors. Actions that did, we might say, were as rare and fleeting as wildcat strikes during the period when Fordism was a hegemonic mode of regulation of social relations in countries at the core of the world-system of states or direct action during the hegemony of parliamentary socialism (Panitch and Leys 2001). Looking into these rare moments, we will see scholars negotiate the terms of their indeterminacy, the condition of their self-realization.

At the periphery, by contrast, the instituting of *academic freedom* was part and parcel of a more dislocating movement, by which existing institutions of knowledge production (*yachahuasis* in the Inca empire; *calmecas* in the Aztec world-economy; *daigakkōs* in Japan, etc.) were severed from contexts and scholars "re-educated [as] negative mirror image of their metropolitan masters," tasked with "propagat[ing] a world-view favorable to imperialist hegemonic culture" (Swai 1980: 33). As postcolonial states instituted bloodier iterations of Fordist regulation (Lipietz 1987: 69–103), scholars were brought more tightly into the folds of developmentalist schemes. Their struggle became wrapped in the general movement of society, making *freedom in thinking* indissociable from broader notions of freedom.

The mid-twentieth-century crisis of the world-system of states was a crisis of a world-ordering process predicated on resolving social relations by settling social forces in place—what David Harvey termed "the spatial fix" (1985). The worldwide wave of "anti-systemic movements" (Arrighi, Hopkins, and Wallerstein 1989) that crested in 1968 was cause and consequence of this crisis. Just as it put into question every dimension of the world-system of states, it upended the regime of *academic freedom* instituted to regulate social relations of knowledge production.

In core countries, the convergence of the "current of anti-imperialism and [the] ocean of student discontent" gave antisystemic mobilizations the allure of a student rebellion (Ehrenreich and Ehrenreich 1969: 63): "agents of world change" is what C. Wright Mills called students in his "Letter to the New Left" (Mills 1960). Used everywhere (*Neue Linke* in Germany, *Nieuw Links* in the Netherlands, *Nouvelle Gauche* in France, *Nuova Sinistra* in Italy, etc.), this reference underscored both the relative inventiveness of student tactics and their new sense of global propinquity. Everywhere, students occupied buildings and public places, held sit-ins and teach-ins, and they established "free," "open," and "critical" universities that instituted self-constitutive, relatively autonomous, and indeterminate social relations of knowledge production. Professors sometimes took part in students' actions, but for the most part, they waged rearguard struggles in defense of a vanishing regime of freedom of which they had been the center.[13] At the periphery of the world-system of states, what Rosie Douglas in his letter of Invitation to the Congress of Black Writers in Montreal called the "fantastic outburst of the peoples of the world" (West 2005: 4) did not appear as a sudden wave coming in from the open sea but as a moment in the *longue durée* organizing of social relations. The struggle of scholars in this context did not find expression in the founding of new universities, nor in any explicit articulation of *freedom in thinking*. Rather, it was folded into the general movement of society.

From the middle of the 1970s, a global strategy out of the crisis of world ordering began to be articulated in a loose network of private and semiprivate enclaves: the Mont Pelerin Society, the Trilateral Commission, the Bank for International Settlements, the Brunner Conferences in Interlaken, the World Bank, etc.[14] What Phillip McMichael called the "globalization project" (2000) initially took form as a most intransigent program applied with Ceasarist impunity, as if there really was no such thing as society. In countries at the core of the old world-system of states—what Samir Amin called the "global north" (Sridhar 2004: 5)—neoliberal concepts of control begot wholesale deregulation, monetarism, debt and deficit targeting, as well as all manners of attacks on every modality of the Keynesian social compact. In peripheries—what everyone now calls the Global South—it brought harsh conditionality, structural adjustment programs, the stripping of public assets, and state authoritarianism.

Strikes and the fungibility of money at the core, "IMF riots" in peripheries, and the plain resilience of inherited sociability everywhere

---

[13]The first teach-ins in the United States were organized on March 24–25, 1965, by the University of Michigan Anthropology Professor Marshall Sahlins and the Faculty-Student Committee to Stop the War in Vietnam (Jorgensen and Wolf 1970: 28). On May 15 of that year, a "National Teach-In" took place in more than one hundred universities which was in part financed by a "pay-in" of professors, according to the November 15 issue of *Michigan in the World*, "Resistance and Revolution: The Anti-Vietnam War Movement at the University of Michigan, 1965–1972." That summer, the teach-in movement grew throughout the United States (Nader 1997).

[14]How transnational capital gathering in exclusive locales made itself into a class through the invention of "neoliberal concepts of control" was the principal preoccupation of "Neo-Gramscian international political economy (IPE)." This school of analysis is sometimes referred to as the Italian school, Transnational Historical Materialism (TNHM), or the Amsterdam school. It was there that the concept of hegemony first gained traction in the analysis of neoliberal world ordering. For a general introduction, see Jessop and Overbek (2019). I published an article that simultaneously recognized the contribution of TNHM to the understanding of the structural power of transnational capital and took it to task for presuming rather than problematizing its hegemony. At the basis of this error, I argued, was an un-relational understanding of class formation at the global level. See Drainville (1994).

brought a rapid end to what Kees van der Pijl termed "the short interregnum of the transnational counter-revolution" (van der Pijl 2006). To contain resistances, global regulatory agencies began concerning themselves with constructing a vast architecture of collaboration dedicated to defining the terms of a "global framework for actions and policies" (Commission on Global Governance 1995).

Totalizing cold-war *exterminism*, which had rested on the crude and singularly compelling threat of mutually assured destruction (Thompson 1982a, b), the World Bank and others began finding in all manners of very real dangers, problems, needs and challenges—such as climate action failure, fiscal crises, natural disasters, pandemics, world hunger—reasons to install problem-solving practices as the nexus of all social relations. To securize social relations, solutions must be sought if not found. This has fostered a state of permanent urgency in which active compliance becomes the only possibility: "in hair-trigger situations" *dixit* E. P. Thompson *à propos* of cold-war *exterminism*, "the very notion of 'political options' becomes increasingly incredible" (Thompson 1983: 10).[15]

Global governance is the name of this depoliticizing scheme, and "global knowledge" its specific form of intelligence (Drainville 2021). It is the product of a global system of knowledge production of which universities are a part—not as mission-bound institutions but as organizations in a world of organizations. There, two iterations of *academic freedom* come into conflict—nowhere more spectacularly, or to greater effect, than at the core of *world ordering*. Each in its own ways endeavors to regulate social relations of knowledge production. The first, instituted a century ago, is a free market of ideas bound by the privileges and responsibilities of titular professors. The second, centered on the ability of university administrators to foreclose scholarly relations (Butler 2006: 12), is contemporaneous to the global knowledge economy. As they clash, abstract ideas of academic freedom get summoned by both professors and university administrators, obscuring the substantial freedom being born of myriad prosaic struggles over "the [new] rules of academic engagement" (Gindberg 2017: ix). These, we understand as part of the little tradition of scholarly actions.

Never has *world ordering* reached so deeply and intently into the folds of social relations of knowledge production. Never, by the same token, has the idea of *academic freedom* been so frequently invoked in such abstract

[15]Forty-five years after the Trilateral Commission's initial manifesto set the tone for neoliberal managerialism, by declaring that "we seem to be… in a cultural crisis which may be the greatest challenge that confronts Western societies, inasmuch as our incapacity to develop appropriate decision-making mechanisms—the ungovernability of our societies—is a cultural failure"; see Crozier et al. (1975). More recently, Schwab and Malleret (2020) seized the occasion of the coronavirus pandemic to assemble an exacting compendium of global risks and challenges (organized into categories: economic, geopolitical, technological, environmental, and societal) and to put forth an argument for more tightly coordinated terms of global governance.

ways. To see through what such invocations obfuscates, we must look into scholarly *praxis* as it takes form in situations of world ordering. Only then can we begin to see a moral community of scholars taking shape, struggling under circumstances beyond its control to define the terms of its self-realization.

750–1258	Abbasid caliphate
1050–1230	Twelfth-century renaissance in Europe
***c.* 1206–1250**	Mongol control of Eurasian trading route
1127–1276	Southern Song dynasty, China
1179–1181	**Restoration of the White Deer Grotto Academy**
1227–1233	**Building of the al-Mustansiriya *madrasa* in Baghdad**
1229	The phrase ***libertas scolastica*** first used by English grammarian Jean de Garlande
1229–1231	**The great dispersal, University of Paris**
1236–1242	Mongol incursions into Eastern Europe and the Balkans
1258	Siege and destruction of Bagdad
1276	Capture of Hangzhou by Kublai Khan

Timeline originated on behalf of the author by Alexandre Gravel.

1

The Mongol Moment

In the twenty-five years after *Temüjin* becoming *Genghis Khan* unified nomadic tribes of the Mongolian steppe, mounted warriors vowing allegiance to him subjugated more people and conquered more land than Roman legions did in four hundred years (Weatherford 2005).

To understand this history as having been made by "monsters drinking the blood of their victims and devouring the flesh of dogs, rats, and men alike" (Kuhn 2011: 90) is to hearten a tale aligned with Eurocentric ideas of the pre-Westphalian world as a lawless realm that could only have been brought to some sort of order by being organized around territorial polities.

How Mongols organized transactions across Eurasian plains is a more prosaic but no less wondrous story. In the century that followed the unification of Mongolian tribes, thousands of miles of traveling routes were marked off and hundreds of postal stations erected, repaired, or improved where, at the end of the day, fodder for horses could be had and travelers could rest knowing that the commodities they carried were under safe keeping. Offenses against people and property were everywhere penalized; tithes imposed; weights, measures, and taxes standardized and articulated to local practices (May 2013). Paper currency (still a wonder to Marco Polo a century later) entered common practice, and a broad network of communication was brought under jurisdiction of the *Yeke Yasaq*—a relatively coherent collection of edicts and pronouncements customarily attributed to *Genghis Khan* himself (Morgan 1986; Buell and Fiaschetti 2018: 177).

As merchants, clerics, scholars, artisans, and officials, being offered safety and rewards (Burbank and Cooper 2010: 93), took to what German geographer Ferdinand von Richthofen later termed the "Silk Road," long-distance commerce among China, the *Dar al-Islam*, and Europe, that had "dried to a narrow trickle of uncertain caravans grew more reticulated" (Abu-Lughod 1991: 137, 144).

In the thick of multiplying relationships between *world-economies* lie the deep roots of a scholastic movement that instituted more autonomous and self-defined social relations of knowledge production. To understand its making, we must consider how the Mongol organization of relations between *world-economies* transformed in each the conditions of scholars' actions.

*

The history of higher education in China is customarily traced back to the school of Confucius in Xiangtan, founded during the period of the warring states (475–221 BCE).[1] There, teaching was articulated around values of self-cultivation, family harmony, and the unity of knowledge and practice (Wu and Zha 2018: 602), and made to lean in the direction of a life lived "in accordance with the highest code of conduct that can be expected of a true gentleman and his love for others, his human-heartedness" (Hamburger 1959: 236). Each day, time was spent on exercises ritualizing good conduct, respect for others, reciprocity, mastery of gestures, and feelings.

In the context of the "Hundred Schools of Thoughts" movement with which began the classical period of Chinese philosophy (sixth–third centuries BCE), the term *school* should be understood broadly, with reference not just to a built form, a particular pedagogy, curriculum, or formally institutionalized set of practices but also to social bodies of pupils and followers defined by their relationship to movements of thought and ideas and to the philosophers who personified them: "[G]overnment officials or scholars, traveling from one feudal state to another … offering ideas for social reform … [e]xpressing their ideas in conversations, official documents, or short treatises" (Editors 2017). The privileged setting of their public allocutions were private schools, which had become "the normal way of education" after the collapse of the Western Zhou dynasty (1046–771 BCE), when government schools folded (Gu et al. 2018: 2). Confucius was the most eminent of many philosophers; his school was a defining instance.

During the Han dynasty (206 BCE–220 CE), schooling in China was given a more formal structure and turned toward state service. This passage was underlined in 124 BCE with the founding of Tai Xue, the "Institute of Supreme Learning." Retroactively consecrated in the nineteenth century as the "first imperial university institutionally created for political reasons" (Li 2018), it installed Confucius as " the authority spirit guide of all government-run schools" (Huang 2020: 2) and Confucianism as "ruling thought" (Hayhoe 1994: 368) or "state cult" (Tu 1998: 4)—an appropriation that was very much built-in Confucius's concerns for practical matters of governance (Liu 1973: 483).

---

[1]In accordance with contemporary usages, before the common, or current, era (BCE) and current/common era (CE) are used in place of BC and AD, whenever context makes the distinction necessary.

Located in the capital city of Chang, an important outpost at the eastern end of Asian trade routes, Tai Xue was the central node of a state-integrated system of provincial-, prefectural-, and county-level institutions that "made possible a ladder of success" for sons of local merchants and administrative elites (Hayhoe 1994: 368). Recruited by recommendation of important families for their incorrupt character (de Crespigny 1991: 27), "filial sons and honest subjects" (Martin 1880: 57) learned how to organize and participate in ritual ceremonies; to play music; and to write poems and government documents. They trained in archery and chariot riding and prepared themselves to take the imperial bureaucracy exam (Hu 2011: 26–27). After graduation, they were integrated into state service as scholar–official (Marginson 2011: 600).

Complementing state-run schools, private academies of classical learning (*shûyuàn*) were also established during Han period, usually in bucolic settings by retired officials and traveling scholars, who, by virtuosity of scholarship, attracted disciples—sometimes by the thousands (Lee 1985: 14). Away from the capital, academies developed with relative unconcern for state service (Walton 1999a). "[O]riented toward the past, historically minded and conservative" (Liu 1973: 484), they focused on rhetoric, phraseology, calligraphy, and painting, in programs of learning based on "the connection between research and teaching, freedom of teaching, freedom of learning, the predominance of self-study in [the] learning process" (Gu et al. 2018: 4).

Through the Period of the Three Kingdoms (220–280 CE) and the Jin dynasty (265–420 CE) as well as the Sui dynasty (581–618 CE), territorial fragmentation encouraged the militarization of Chinese polities and the vocationalization of state-based education. As *Tai Xue* was reduced to merely qualifying students for admission into state service, private academies withered, fostering among scholars an idealized sense of remoteness—perhaps best exemplified by the "Seven Worthies of the Bamboo Grove," quasi-mythological figures associated with the short-lived "Pure Conversation Movement."[2]

During the Tang dynasty's renaissance (618–907 CE), Chinese state-building was predicated on the development of the equal-field system, in which land was distributed to the peasantry in proportion to the number of people in each household, contingent on productivity. This required the establishment and maintenance of registries of households and land occupation, the measurement of yields, the collection of taxes, and the development of administrative procedures. Additionally, penalties had to be

[2]Soon after it began to take form (*c.* 235 CE), the "Pure Conversation Movement" "turned toward an elitist, aesthetic hedonism, specializing in witty repartee, paradoxical sayings, wine drinking, sexual affairs, and other behavior scandalous to Confucian mores" (Collins 2009: 170–71). One style-setter would practice *ch'ing t'an* (pure conversation) "while [holding] in his pale hands a feather-duster with a jade handle, with which to sweep away, symbolically, the dust of this vile world" (Balazs and Wright 1964: 248–49).

defined, grievances heard and adjudicated, and infrastructure built, among other bureaucratic functions (Gernet 1999: 215–40). These tasks were carried out by a growing body of scholar–officials who acted as "an integral part of the machinery of the state" (Martin 1880: 21). To guarantee competence and conformity with Tang state ideology—based on a proscription of foreign influences and a return to national values—a broader network of higher education was established (Gernet 1999: 255), which was dedicated to the recruitment, training, and selections of scholar–officials. At its center was Tai Xue. There, senior scholars–officials ruled over authoritative interpretation of Chinese classics and set the terms of the Imperial examinations. In addition, the Tang state established two new institutions of higher education in the capital: the "Directorate of Education," open to young men from aristocratic background and high-ranking families, and the "School of Four Gates," into which could be admitted students from humbler backgrounds. The Tang state also set up several professional and technical schools in the capital: the "School of Law," the "School of Calligraphy," the "School of Mathematics," the "School of Painting," and so on (Hu 2011: 39–40).

The Tang state also gave private academies situated at the margins of the education system "relatively free space for development" (Wu and Zha 2018: 603). This allowed scholars funded by local families to establish relatively autonomous institutions of learning, where students, sheltered by a "unique … relationship between students and teachers" (Li 2018: 2), could engage in studies without fear of government intervention.

The brief period of the Five Dynasties and Ten Kingdoms (907–979 CE) was characterized by rapid fragmentation of territory and increased emphasis on technical and military training. "[A]mid the confusion of perpetual war" (Martin 1880: 11), the state-centered network of higher education again withered. For their part, private academies deteriorated, folded unto themselves, or disappeared altogether.

The period of Northern Song dynasty (960–1127 CE) marked a second renaissance of the Chinese state (Gernet 1999: 290–310). Within the confines of a territory made smaller by the expansion of the Liao kingdom of the Khitans; the Xia kingdom of the Tanguts; and the Jin kingdom of the Jurchens, Chinese state-building was premised on: (i) the appeasement of proximate threats by payment of what amounted to annual ransoms in the form of silk cloth, silver, tea, and gold (Deng 2013: 19) and (ii) the development of long-distance ties of diplomacy and commerce with the Srivijaya empire in South Asia, the Tamil Chola dynasty in South India, the Kara-Khanid khanate in Transoxiana, and the Fatimid caliphate in the Eastern Mediterranean and North Africa. Obligated to outside polities and markets, the Northern Song state took form in the twin pursuit of economic growth and social control (Elman 1989: 380) through a series of broad reforms—the so-called "new policies" that "stress[ed] statecraft and institutional innovations" (Liu

1973, 488). The "equal field system" was broadened and systematized; supervision of outputs tightened; credit schemes expanded for farmers and merchants; local irrigation works were promoted; labor and foodstuff markets regulated; shipbuilding, coal, and iron-mining capacities were improved. As a consequence, population grew steadily and household size increased in the countryside and in the cities (Deng 2013).

In education, Northern Song reforms expanded the network of state-run schools and created China's first truly integrated, empire-wide, school system (Chaffee 1985a: 78). Four intentions shaped this organization: (i) to widen the social basis of the state by encouraging the inclusion of the sons of merchant and local gentries (De Weerdt 2020); (ii) to diminish the influence of traditional aristocrats and military families (Lee 1985: 20–21); (iii) to assure broad ideological uniformity (Hu 2011: 86); and (iv) to increase the juridical and administrative capabilities of the state (Ming-kin 2020: 49). Key to fulfilling these objectives was the "Three Hall System" (Ming-kin 2020: 196). It divided students, whom it financed, into categories arranged in concentric circles. The "outer hall" was made up of prefectural and sub-prefectural schools (Zheng 1994: 194). Based on performance, a proportion of students could be brought into the "inner hall" of *Tai Xue* and then into its "upper hall." Regulating movements was a tiered system of imperial examination leading from prefectural contests to the imperial examinations organized by the office of the Imperial Secretary held in presence of the emperor (Gernet 1999: 268).[3] Upper hall students "with outstanding academic results and proven moral conduct would be nominated for office without passing the civil service examination" and personally introduced to the emperor (Ming-kin 2020: 7).

On the outskirt of the outer hall but, nonetheless recognized formally by the Northern Song state through the allotment of land and salaries, the granting of calligraphic signboards, the bequest of books libraries (more common with the expansion of printing in the tenth century), were private academies. There, the sons of merchants and local gentries who had not qualified for admission into government schools could study classical texts and maintain their family's hope that they would in time succeed in imperial examinations—a key moment in the formation of "the Confucian gentry as a non-aristocratic elite class … with political status and social prerogatives" (Elman 1989: 379).

Established in the tradition of Tang-era private schools, often on former sites of Buddhist temples, academies were located in remote areas as *de facto* autonomous centers of scholarship (Hayhoe 1994: 368). There the *curriculum* tended to be broader than what was considered in preparation for imperial examinations, and the work of learning could be carried out in a lively and informal atmosphere that in itself was an implicit challenge

[3]Success rate of examinations can be found in Kuhn (2011: 122–23).

to imperial intellectual authority (Hayhoe 1994: 370). All academies were arranged in a similar same manner, which echoed the "three hall system":

> the academy included a central ceremonial hall, usually called the "Hall of Great Completion"; in front of it was a lecture hall, called the "Hall of Clarifying Human Relations", and wings of dormitories were places symmetrically along corridors to the left and right. There was often a library and a sacrificial hall for the worship of Confucius and his disciples, as well as a kitchen, granary and bathhouse
>
> (Walton 1999b: 27)

Four Northern Song academies were granted calligraphic signboards by the emperor, a mark of singular recognition: the Taishi Academy (997 CE), the Yingtianfu Academy (1009 CE), the Yuelu Academy (1015 CE), and the Shigu Academy (1035 CE). Once removed from the four great *shûyuàn*—granted not a calligraphic signboard but a copy of the Nine Confucian Classics—was the White Deer Grotto Academy (977 CE) on Mount Lu-shan, which frequently appeared in Southern Song iconography, evoking contemplative escapism (Nelson 2000).[4]

In 1127 CE, the Jurchen Jin dynasty captured the Northern Song capital of Bianqing, exiling the Songs south of the Yangtze River, into the "most economically advanced, populous and prosperous" region (Walton 1999b: 87). In the half century of its existence, the Southern Song dynasty followed the path of Northern Song state-building strategies, accelerating the transformation of Chinese political economy from the "hierarchically defined and capital-based aristocracy of the Tang Empire" toward a modern administrative state (De Weerdt 2020: 10). It was, in the succinct formula of Linda Walton, "an era marked by profound change in the economy, technology, thought, and the social and political order" (Walton 1999b: 5). Social welfare programs, including retirement homes and pauper's graveyards, were put in place or expanded; a nationwide postal service was organized; shipbuilding capacities increased; seaports significantly improved (that of Quanzhou, located at the end of the "maritime silk road" doubled in capacity); the construction of roads and bridges accelerated, driving growth in quarrying, masonry, and overland transport industries (Deng 2013: 25). This brought about a rapid development of commercial activities and long-distance trade, growth in population, and higher urban concentrations, mainly in the lower Yangtze basin and in Sichuan.

Also in continuity with the "new policies" of the Northern Song period, Southern Song reforms in education worked to increase accessibility and conformity. The network of state schools was broadened and increasingly

[4]The academy was named for the pet white deer kept by Li Bai and his brother Li She, who lived as recluse on Mount Lu-shan.

politicized; the canon of knowledge used in the imperial examination system was standardized; the number of exam takers increased at all levels; and promotion became increasingly contingent upon compliance (Hayhoe 2001; Ming-kin 2020).

Most remarkable was the growth of private academies—in numbers, autonomy as well as coherence of purpose (Hongbo 2009: 134). As many as five hundred were created in this period (Walton 1999b: 228). Often founded by scholar–officials "either frustrated or disgusted" with the increasing authoritarianism of the state-run education system (Liu 1973: 485), they complemented rather than disputed the education offered in government schools (Chaffee 1985b). Most professors were state officials, though few made government their full-time career, and students would often conjugate a stay in academies with examination studies (Barreira 1999: 333). This was facilitated by the organization of Song state schooling, arranged triennially. During the first year or two, young men would sometimes step away from studies in state schools and spend time in academies to develop a broader posture toward knowledge and cultivate better habits of learning. Only in the last year would they study in earnest for examinations (Chaffee 1982: 328).

Bucolic seclusion was central to the relative autonomy of academies (Walton 1999b: 80–81). Underwritten by charitable estates—a form of endowment that spread during the Southern Song economic expansion (Chaffee 1982: 317–18)—it allowed academies a measure of autonomy vis-à-vis the centralizing state (Lee 2013). Sheltered in "Confucian rusticity" (Chaffee 1985b: 49, 188), masters and students worked in their own manner toward the "correct interpretation of the classics … for statecraft application" (Liu 1973: 488).

In contrast both to government schools, dedicated to examinations, and to Taoist and Buddhist temple schools, which served essentially contemplative purposes, academies' teaching strove for the unity of self-cultivation and "of service to the ruler and to society" (Chaffee 1982: 326). This intent is best captured by the injunctions of scholar Chu Hsi, complied in *Reflections on Things at Hand*:

> In learning … do not reach for the clouds or overextend yourself. Simply examine words and deeds, and there is your reality. Nowadays when people discuss Tao [AD: the first principle], they mention only principle and do not discuss actual events … Their words are lofty, but aimless and indefensible. They drift onto the road of emptiness and heresy.
>
> (Hsi 1991: 74)

The unity of detachment and involvement in statecraft defined academies as intellectual centers of the Neo-Confucian "True Way movement" (Walton 1999b: 6). It also informed how social relations of knowledge production were organized. Immersed in an ambiance of "consciousness, awareness, and sensitivity" (Liu 1973: 92–93) and arranged in ascending orders of knowing and relevance—from "companion-in-learning" to "fellow-in-learning," to "fellow-in-explication" (Liu 1973: 494)—students and professors worked together from a more coherent and comprehensive *curriculum* than in government schools (Lee 1985: 27), animated by a greater sense of community and common purpose (Walton 1999b: 6), reinforced by comportment practices and ritualized behavior.

> In reading books you must draw up your body and sit erect, pay careful attention to what you read and repeat silently to yourself. Free your mind and immerse yourself, and undertake a personal investigation.
>
> (Hsi 1991: 91)

On occasions, the relational dimension of knowledge production was performed in public: "(L)egends recount how over a thousand people came to hear Zhang Shi and Zhu Xi (Chu Hsi) teach and debate at the *Yuelu* academy in 1167" (Tillman 2020: 27).

As the "True-Way movement" grew into "a powerful intellectual movement touching on virtually every aspect of social, economic and political theory" (Lee 1985: 24), academies became more deliberate in their ways—sometimes affectedly so—more attentive to the relationships underwriting *freedom in thinking* and more critical of the instrumentalization of Confucius's thought by the Song state, as well as of Song authoritarianism in general.[5]

*

In the *Dar al-Islam,* the Abbasid drive for unity found its clearest expression in what is customarily termed the *House of Wisdom*. Though sometimes used broadly to refer to all manners of libraries, hospitals, observatories, private homes, literary salons, bookstores, and gardens where took place the work of translation by which the Abbasid Golden Age is often defined (Gutas 2012: 1), the term is more properly used to refer specifically to the *Bayt al-Hikma* in Baghdad. Founded as the personal library of Caliph Harun al-Rachid (763–809), it is reputed to have grown into the largest book depository in the world (Al-Khalili 2011: 57). There, "a small army of

---

[5]Ways of being in academies were also performed in deliberately antiquated manner of dress and behavior: "Though times had changed, [academy students] searched among Northern Song portraits and earlier records to recover bygone styles and dress accordingly. Among other features, they chose to wear a tall hat with a pointed top, a beret like gear for casual wear, a roomy gown with broad sleeves, and a fine white-gauze shirt underneath. Their mannerism was strict: they sat squarely with their back erect, walked in measured steps looking straight ahead, bowed slowly and deeply to express sincere propriety, spoke in dignified ways with few gestures ... [M]any people looked upon their lofty air as strange, stupid, snobbish, arrogant, or more like that of a Taoist than a Confucianist" (Liu 1973: 497).

scholars" (Lyons 2010: 63) worked along strict lines of authority under the order of a superintendent of translation (İhsanoğlu 2023: 29), tasked with ensuring a proper articulation between the work of translation itself and political efforts to legitimize the transition from the cultural order of the Damascus-based Umayyad dynasty to that of the Baghdad-based Abbasids, and thus from Persian to Arabic as a language of rule (Von Grunebaum 1970: 138; Algeriani and Mohadi 2017: 179).[6]

In *madrasas* by contrast, scholars labored with some autonomy and a measure of self-regulation. Underwriting both were *waqfs*, which were inalienable endowments set up by wealthy individuals to insure "the perpetual immobilization of property for pious purpose" (Van Leeuwen 1999: 40). Long acknowledged in Islam (Gaudiosi 1987: 1233), w*aqfs* took on more formal attributes at the end of Abbasid hegemony, when prosperity born of long-distance commerce floated development in trade, agricultural, and manufacturing (Daun and Arjmand 2018: 100).[7] Under *waqf*, a piece of land, an orchard, a building, or group of buildings could be sheltered from tax and passed on in perpetuity through a single line of descent without threat of being seized: "[O]nce made *waqf*, the property became inalienable. It could no longer be the subject of any sale, disposition, mortgage, gift, inheritance, attachment, or any alienation whatsoever" (Makdisi 1981: 38). Income derived from *waqf*-endowed properties could be directed to predetermined beneficiaries or managed in the equivalent of a blind trust by a caretaker acting within limits prescribed by *waqf* deeds (Koehler 2014; Kuran 2001).

Under *waqf*, better and more securely financed *madrasas* grew into broad architectural complexes made up of mosque, boarding houses, professorial residences, and libraries, often with copyists and booksellers occupying outlining buildings nearby (Ephrat 2000: 7). Professors, who prior to the *waqf*-underwritten *madrasa* movement sometimes had to hire themselves out as copyist (Makdisi 1961: 52), came to stay in their positions longer and exercised greater authority as *waqf* administrators, caretakers,

---

[6]In the context of Abbasid rule, the term *translation* should be understood broadly to encompass not only the rendering into Arabic of works written in Greek, Persian, Indian, and Syriac but also the broad process by which those works were gathered, read, appropriated, preserved, and commented upon and use was made of them to "treat the sick, design ... temples, palaces, bridges and canals, [and] develop more sophisticated weapons" (Al-Khalili 2011: 55).

[7]The Abbasids shared claims of direct filiation to prophet Muhammad with other Caliphates. In 833, Abbasid Caliph al-Mamun, describing himself as "the heir of the prophethood," ordered an inquisition (*miḥna*), with the intent to subject all scholars to a rationalist reading of the Quran, and thus assert political control over "all matters, worldly and religious" (Nawas 1994: 620). Sunni leaders, whose authority was rooted in tradition rather than filiation, were persecuted, sometimes flogged to death (Makdisi 1981: 138). A pivotal moment in the relative separation of faith and State in the Islamic world (Lapidus 1975), the *miḥna* ended fifteen years after it had begun, with Caliph al-Mutawakkil ending the controversy over the createdness of the Quran (and thus the possibility that it be incarnated in a particular filiation), opening room for distinct interpretative traditions.

and beneficiaries (Van Leeuwen 1999: 67). Traveling more, they gained coherence as members of a relatively self-regulated and autonomous class of professional scholars (Pedersen et al. 2009: 1123). Bestowed scholarships and provided with board and lodging, larger cohorts of students, who had come from farther away on better-traveled routes, engaged in longer, more formal courses of study and developed a stronger, more cohesive and consequent *esprit de corps* (Brentjes 2018: 136; Hussain 2013: 107). On occasion, this brought them into conflict with caliphal authorities in defense of the inviolability of *madrasas* (Levy 1928: 269), led them to protest the hiring or dismissal of particular professors (Bougamra 1983: 104), or caused them to clash with students from other schools or with local residents (Ephrat 2000: 4).

The case for the autonomy of *waqf*-endowed *madrasas* should not be overstated. Even when better financed, and more tightly connected to one another across the whole of the Islamic *world-economy*, *madrasas* "remained an inherently open and permeable body [which] included not only professional teachers, but a host of educated and semi-educated individuals active on the margins of intellectual life" (Berkey 1995: 54). Professors and students did not meet there in a vacuum, isolated from social obligations and ties of loyalty and service developed outside of them (Daun and Arjmand 2018: 24; Chamberlain 2002).

But we would be remiss not to recognize endowed *madrasas* as purposely created sites of relatively distinct relations of knowledge production, simultaneously entwined in context and autonomous from it.

This can perhaps best be appreciated by considering disputations. "Polyvocal events," as Brinkley Messick called them, were very much a medieval pastime throughout the *Dar al-Islam* (Messick 1992: 34). They brought all manners of people in contingent, living relations where they could assert themselves as subjects in the modern sense of the term. In the specific context of madrasas, they permeated all relations. At their most spectacular, they involved prominent scholars on a visit or newly hired professors asked to give their inaugural lecture—a practice that "came into prominence somewhere around the middle of the eleventh century" (Makdisi 1981: 154). After an initial statement, they would engage in discussions with their audience. In such moment, they both stood the risk of being exposed and were given a significant occasion to establish credibility as bearer of knowledge (Ephrat 1993: 5, 142) by displaying the connection between personal qualities and knowledge.

Madrasas were colleges of law. There, jurisprudence (*fiqh*: "the queen of Islamic sciences") occupied a hegemonic position vis-à-vis grammar, literary arts, poetry, and so on (Makdisi 1981: 9, 90). It was *fiqh* that was the privileged object of disputations and *fiqh* that gave them contexts. Beneath the spectacle of public disputations were ordinary events folded in the quotidian course of studies. Classes in *madrasas* began with blessings on the Prophet and other religious formulae. Afterward, formal lectures took place, from notes "enacted fortuitously in time" (Chamberlain 2002: 143) and submitted for the consideration of students who were at liberty to ask questions verbally or present them in the form of written notes (Pedersen et al. 2009: 219–20). This provided students with occasions to engage in a lesser disputation and professors with opportunities to offer tiny spectacles of professorial competence.

> Like a shower of rain, questions were sprinkled upon him from all sides, and these he did not fall short to answer, and was prompt to do so, delaying not. A number of notes were passed to him and, gathering them together in his hand, he began to answer each one, throwing away each note as he dealt with it, until he had come to the end.[8]

Classical Arabic requires orality: "the word had to be *heard* from an authoritative speaker, not merely *seen* already written. For the written word is lifeless; only the consonants are written. The speaker breathes life into the inert consonants, resurrecting them by vocalizing as he speaks" (Makdisi 1989: 179). In mosque schools, spoken words were learned by dictation and inscribed by repetition in the mind of students (Makdisi 1961: 10). "I understand" in this context meant "I have assimilated and can recite" (Mohamed and Korani 2015: 36). In *madrasas* by contrast, the spoken words of a professor would be written down "as heard" by students (Makdisi 1961). Sometimes, they would be copied and published under a professor's own name, alongside a record of disputation, commentaries, abridgments, and so on (Al-Faruque 1987: 256, 12). This obliged *madrasa* professors to their own words and built a record that acquired the character of a *curriculum*.[9]

At the end of a lengthy period of study—usually four years of basic studies, followed by an indeterminate period of fellowship during which he served as an apprentices and repetiteur for younger students (Pedersen et al. 2009)—a student of jurisprudence could aspire to claim *id̲j̲āza*, which was the license to teach jurisprudence and issue legal opinions (Ābdel-Latif 2020: 640–41). This too was an event validated by disputation: Facing his professor in front of assembled peers, the disputant had to show that he knew by heart an extensive set of disputed questions and have ready answers for them (Makdisi 1981: 132; Weijers 1999).[10]

---

[8]Sebastian Günther (2022: 484) quotes from Ibn Jubayr's account of a lecture given "on Friday May 18, 1184" by Shafi'i leader Radi al- Qazwini, at the Nizamiyya *madrasa*.

[9]There was no word for *curriculum* in high medieval Arabic (Chamberlain 2002: 87). Progress in studies was not validated by formal diplomas until colonial reforms of the nineteenth century. Vincent Monteil, "Préface," in Ibn Khaldoun, *Discours sur l'histoire universelle* (al-Muqaddima) (Beyrouth, 1968), II: 897.

[10]The *id̲j̲āza*, the right to teach *fiqh* and issue legal opinion, in many ways prefigured the European *licentia docentis* (Makdisi 1989: 175). It did not, however, express the professional autonomy of a body of scholars organized into a corporation (Fındıklı 2022: 135). Instead it remained "essentially informal, flexible, and linked to persons rather than to institutions" (Ephrat 2000: 8).

*

During what Charles Haskins termed "the European renaissance of the 12th century" (Haskins 1955 [1927]), feudalism reached its apogee as a mode of production (agricultural techniques improved, outputs swelled, surplus and population increased, etc.) and began to disintegrate from pressures brought on feudal rents by the growth of long-distance trade; from its inability to appropriate surpluses; and from the transformation of property relations and class structures in rural society.[11] It was in this critical juncture that the European *world-economy* took form, both as a relatively coherent set of social relations and as an object of representation (Bloch and Bloch 1995: 126).

In the transition from the social order of the feudal world to capitalist modernity, a broad movement of autonomy manifested itself in the emergence of new forms of money and credit (Le Goff 1986); in cathedrals that set in stone a more aspirational relationship to the sacred (Panofsky 1951: 102); in contrapuntal polyphonies celebrating a more complex and dialectical relation to the world (Novikoff 2013: 147–48); in vernacular *chansons de geste* celebrating emancipatory self-consciousness (Gally 1987); in uprisings of peasants and town dwellers (Cohn 2012); and in the push to incorporation (Cavanagh 2016).

In the context of late medieval Europe, the term *corporation* (from the Latin *corporare*, meaning "to form into a body") should not be understood as referring primarily to legally constituted business enterprises imbued with perpetual rights, as it would come to be after the emergence of joint-stock companies in the sixteenth century (Mougeot 2002: 26). Rather, corporations—including guilds in England, *arte* in Italy, *innung* in German-speaking regions, *neering* in Dutch, and *jurandes* in France—were part of an ongoing and often contentious processes of social differentiation and recognition. They were forms of association as much as expressions of collective self-consciousness. Everywhere, they "built [from] the same structures and answered to the same exigencies" in roughly the same manner, welding members together in organizations that could lay claim to rights and privileges on the basis of the capacity to regulate themselves (Mougeot 2002: 5).

To distinguish their work from that of unskilled laborers, artisans organized into corporations that structured training and validated hierarchies of skills; to limit individual liabilities, apportion profits, organize traveling, secure rights to hold fairs and privileges of extraterritoriality, merchants too

[11]This rudimentary enumeration limits itself to juxtaposing opposed sides in the so-called "Brenner debates" on the European transition from feudalism to capitalism. Prompted by Brenner (1976), the debate contrasted analyses that emphasized external trade dynamics (which, for the most part, aligned with the world-systems theory) and those stressing the role of internal class relations. A succinct account of the debate is provided in Blackburn (2017).

organized into corporations, as did "thousands of towns in northern Italy, France, England, and Germany" to facilitate raising tax and levy (Kuran 2005: 792). Even the Catholic church (through Gregorian reforms) made itself into an ecclesiastical corporation, freeing itself from an encroaching laity and from "the pretentions of the Germanic emperor" (Le Goff 2009: 60). To counter the consequences of the great schism of 1204, it created subsidiary corporations endowed with a measure of operational autonomy (Howe 1988).

"Like any other trade ... scholars also ... made themselves into corporations" (Le Goff 2009: 121–22). To distinguish those from mendicant orders, perceived as rivals (Le Goff 2009: 123), and to underline a subjective sense of themselves as a coherent and relatively autonomous social ensemble (Weijers 1987: 25), they appropriated the term *universitas* in broad usage to designate any aggregate body of persons with common interests and independent legal status, "whether of barbers, carpenters, or students did not matter" (Haskins 1965 [1923]: 9).[12]

Leaning on their capacity to meet the demand for educated priests, administrators, mediators, lawyers, physicians, and clerks, scholars organized into corporations gained autonomy from feudal, ecclesiastic, and urban authorities, securing exemptions that would come to be recognized as *libertas scholastica*—a phrase first used by English grammarian Jean de Garlande in 1229.[13] By it, scholars were simultaneously sacralized as "honest and learned men through whom the truth can be ascertained" (Bernstein 1978) and set apart as subjects of the "right to impunity," which feudal society reserved for outcasts in *exsilium* living in self-regulated communities (Friese and Wagner 1998).

Libertas scholastica took form not by grand design but through the situated interventions of economic, political, and ecclesiastic authorities vying for hegemony over the general organization of the "New [capitalist] Europe of Christian Mandarins" (Le Goff 2009: 126). Always, it was the result of situated compromises.

At the University of Bologna, students came from privileged, often noble, backgrounds. "[Y]oung men of substance with experience of worldly affairs and accustomed to positions of responsibility," arrived more qualified into formal studies (Cobban 1971, 39). Studying in a city that played a central role in the revival of Roman law in Italy, at a time when it answered

---

[12]The term *universitas* was first used specifically to designate a community of masters and students in reference to Paris's *universitas magistrorum et scolarium*.

[13]As a regime of privilege, *libertas scholastics* can be thought of as a corporate variation on the antique *status civitas*. Where Roman law had made the rights and privileges of individuals citizens contingent on their acceptance of the place they occupied in the overall political hierarchy, the transition from feudalism to capitalism gave occasions for all manners of groups and association organized into corporations to claim collective rights (*ius*), prerogatives (*consuetudo*), exemptions (*immunitas*), and privileges (*privilegium*) based on their capacity to regulate themselves. On this, see Taylor (2016) and Weijers (1987: 6).

demands born of long-distance trade better than the archaic and essentially rural customs of the Lombards (Haskins 1955 [1927]: 388), they made themselves privileged subjects of scholarly privileges. They were exempted from all levies, taxes, tolls, and customs duties (Blasi et al. 2002), and in times of food shortage, they were granted the right to "purchase grain whenever and wherever they wished, and in quantity necessary for themselves and their retainers" (Kibre 1962: 29). Professors, by contrast, occupied lesser positions as hired hands (Riché and Verger 2006: 194).[14] After 1189, they were required to sign an oath promising not to teach elsewhere (Cobban 1971: 36), or even "to absent themselves from class, even for a single day, without good excuse and then only after approval by the class, the councilor, and the (student) rector" (Cardozier 1968: 946). Moreover, they were "required to abide to student-approved regulations, swear obedience to the (student) rector, and follow procedures prescribed by students in the conduct of class" (Cardozier 1968: 944).[15]

> He must begin with the bell and quit within one minute after the next bell. He was not allowed to skip a chapter in his commentary or postpone a difficulty to the end of the hour, and he was obliged to cover ground systematically, so much in each specific term of the year.
>
> (Haskins 1965 [1923]: 10)

In Paris, masters and students were younger than in Bologna; indeed, many masters were younger than students in Bologna, and they were less wealthy and came for the most part from outside the city (Cardozier 1968: 945). Gathered in autonomous nations—each with distinct "statutes, archives ... books ... schools, chapels ... places of assembly ... sources of revenue [and] special feast days and patron saints" (Kibre 1948: 20)—they benefitted from an implied privilege of ecclesiastical immunity as members of the church (Kibre 1954: 551), and from the protection of the French king as denizens of his capital (Weijers 2015: 15). When *libertas scholastica* were formalized, they incorporated protections against civic authorities (Weijers 2015: 20). After a bloody brawl between students

[14]In 1158, Frederick Barbarossa, wishing to guarantee immunity to visiting representatives of the Diet of Roncaglia, issued an edict that guaranteed safety for those "who travelled or resided in imperial lands for purposes of study ... who exile themselves for love of learning" (Kibre 1954: 549). Barbarossa's *Authentica Habilita* is "the first important medieval grant of privileges intended primarily for lay students and professors of canon and civil law" (Kibre 1954: 549, 551). The model of student-controlled universities came to prevail throughout southern Europe (Cobban 1971: 34).

[15]Privileged subjects of *libertas scholastica*, Bologna students were also sometimes preferred objects of disciplining. Reacting to a housing crisis brought about by the same commercial expansion that had given wealthy students leverage, Pope Clement III, "prohibited rich students from taking away lodgings from poor students [and] threatened with excommunication anyone who took another's lodgings before the expiration of his term of residence" (Kibre 1954: 558).

and city officials in 1200, King Philip Augustus assured the former of special protection by obliging "all the burghers of Paris" to testify on behalf of ill-treated students whenever they saw abuses of power, and by forbidding *prévôts*, *baillis*, and judges from seizing property belonging to students or from sending them to prison for any wrongdoing (Riché and Verger 2006: 188). All matters involving scholars, including criminal cases, were to be presented first to the Bishop of Paris for arbitration. In 1215, Cardinal Legate Robert de Courçon, acting on behalf of Pope Innocent III, provided in writing the first extant status and privileges of the University of Paris. As if to make explicit the conditions under which a measure of freedom was awarded the city's *universitas magistrorum et scolarium*, de Courçon outlined the first *curriculum* for the teaching of arts. Some texts that were being taught (most notably Aelius Donatus's *Ars grammar* and Aristotle's *Topiques*) were relegated to a list of complementary courses to be taught only on holidays (Verger 1999: 158–159) or forbidden altogether (Piché and Lafleur 1999: 153).[16]

At Oxford, scholarly privileges were shaped by rivalries among the Crown, the Church, and the local judiciary in a manner often precipitated by town and gown riots, recurrent in the years between the "hanging of the clerks" (1209) and the St. Scholastica's Day riots (1335). Both events began as *faits divers* seemingly unrelated to scholarly matters: The first stemmed from the accidental killing of a woman by a student, and the second arose from a tavern brawl over the quality of wine. In both cases, townspeople clashed with students, and both ended with increased privileges for scholars gathered in collegiate corporations at the expense of the city. After the hanging of the clerks, student rents were fixed for ten years, the town was made to pay reparations, and citizens were obliged to provide food and other necessities at reasonable prices to students. Following the St. Scholastica Day riots, the town of Oxford was fined, the mayor and town bailiff were imprisoned in London, and penance was imposed: Each year on the anniversary of the first day of the riots, the mayor, the bailiff, and sixty townspeople would be made to attend a mass at the University Church in memory of scholar killed, a practice that endured until 1825 (Cobban 2017). As scholarly privileges became more clearly defined, the power of Oxford's endowed colleges (Balliol, Merton, University College) grew at the expense of merchant influence (Munby 2007: 59). From an essentially commercial town, Oxford transformed into a preserve of scholars, "firmly under the control of the university" (Munby 2007: 57). To guarantee the

---

[16]After the great strike in 1229–1231, Pope Gregory IX broadened the right to teach (*licentia docenti*)—previously granted by the Archbishop of Paris—to include the whole of Christendom (*licentia ubique docendi*), and he put forbidden texts under review of a commission of masters, charged with expunging them from "any hint of error." This commission never actually met and censorship quickly fell into desuetude. By the end of the 1230s, Aristotle's natural philosophy, frequently "read" publicly in Paris, was reinstated in the *curriculum* of the University of Paris.

comfort of the *studium generale* and remove any obstacle to study, in 1305 King Edward I prohibited "tournaments, jousts, tiltings or other games with spears" near the city (Kibre 1954: 561).[17] That same year, in reply to a scholar's complaint "that the pavements were so torn up and broken that the student and masters were seriously impeded from walking about through the city, also that they were repelled by the reeking substances which were placed and collected in the streets and byways," the King issued a writ mandating that "the paving of the streets in the city of Oxford should be repaired ... that each holder of property repair the street in front of his holding ... that the lanes be cleared of all ill-smelling wastes and that the snow be removed from the streets" (Kibre 1954: 562).

Before the end of the thirteenth century, fifteen universities in Europe had attained a degree of institutional permanence. Besides Bologna (1088), Paris (1150), and Oxford (1167), some form of *libertas scholastica* had been instituted in Modena (1175), Palencia (1208), Cambridge (1209), Salamanca (1218), Montpellier (1220), Padua (1222), Naples (1224), Toulouse (1229), Orleans (1235), Siena (1240), Valladolid (1241), Northampton (1261), and Cumbria (1288). Each university, to be sure, is the product of its own history. The University of Cambridge was born of the exile of Oxford's clerks, and the University of Toulouse was granted privileges as a political maneuver by the King of France, who sought to assert his authority over Count Raymond VII. In Orléans, the *studium generale* was given papal recognition in 1230, when Boniface VIII mandated students in exile from Paris to comment his *Liber Sextus Decretalium*. Five years later, Pope Gregory IX granted the Orléans cathedral school its *licentia docenti*; half a century after that, Pope Clement VI issued the bulb by which the university was granted full privileges. In Montpellier, Guilhem VIII, in a bid for power, answered demands from merchants—who had just obtained privilege of commerce with the Muslim world—and from Jewish doctors in exile from the Almohad caliphate by granting teaching privileges that were not his to grant in 1181. In 1220, these privileges were confirmed by Bishop Conrad, Pope Honorius III's legate (Riché and Verger 2006: 194–95). This is the date traditionally cited as the founding of the University of Montpellier, though it could as well be 1137, when a school of medicine was first established, or 1289, when Pope Nicholas IV issued the *Quia Sapientia*, the bull by which he officially recognized the *studium generale*, more than a hundred years after it had established itself.

Occupying relatively autonomous positions at the margins of the overfull social order of late feudal Europe, members of the academic corporation—carrying with them tools of their trade (small, easy-to-manipulate books

[17]The phrase *studium generale* is used here not in the political–judicial sense of a chartered corporation defined by privileges and statutes but, rather, in the sociological sense of a self-regulating community of scholars held together by shared practices of learning, disputation, commentary, and rituals (ceremonies of inception, vestments, etc.).

written in fast script), free as *colporteurs* and as dangerous to local-bound powers as *brigands, béguards*, and *beguines*—placed themselves in situations where they could enter in self-inventing and radically indeterminate relations of knowledge production.[18] For the first time in Europe—in a manner that helped define what it meant to be in Europe—teaching was organized "into the form of permanent institution of learning" (Haskins 1965 [1923]: 1). Where monasteries, favoring meditative perseverance, had barely troubled themselves with codifying teaching at all (Waddell 1966)—preferring instead a study regimen that favored individual exercises (*littera*, *sensus*, *sententia*)—scholars gathered in self-governed communities and performed a relatively coherent corpus of texts through instituted disputations (Novikoff 2013; Le Goff 2009: 130). Time and again, the same authors—Priscianus Caesariensis, Pierre Lombard, Claudius Galenus, Aristotle—were introduced by masters and questioned by students (Weijers 2015: 173). In the back and forth between professorial propositions and student disputations, *libertas scholastica* defined itself.

*

Situations are the conditions of situations. Mongol control over East Asian trading routes defined the terms of a relatively transactional relationship between relatively porous *world-economies*, creating in each conditions conducive to the relative autonomy of reflexive instances. To see what scholars in Southern Song China, the *Dar al-Islam*, and Europe made of their common possibilities, we have to see into specific circumstances.

The Restoration of the White Deer Grotto Academy (1179–1181)

For the breadth and influence of his scholarly work, "often compared [to that] of Thomas Aquinas" (Liu 1973: 489) and for his political visibility as state official and figurehead of the "True-Way" movement, Chu Hsi (1130–1200) was the most prominent neo-Confucian scholar of the Southern Song

[18]"Tools of intellectual technicians" is what Jacques Le Goff called small books produced in numbers by scribes and paper makers organized in the *pecia* system (Le Goff 1991: 181–223). "Fast script" refers to a handwriting style characterized by swift execution, where characters were spaced to facilitate reading and phrases were punctuates for ease of reading that came equipped with schematic diagrams, table of contents, annexes, and lists of abbreviations. Lacking in elaborate flourishes or decorations, it was the preferred style of books written in what is referred to as "scholastic Latin," closer in syntax to vernacular languages than classical Latin. On this, see also Weijers (2015: 160, 176).

era (Bol 1992: 298).[19] The ways of teaching and learning he defined in the process of gathering support for the restoration of the White Deer Grotto Academy outlined a model which "served ... for many future academies throughout China" (Tillman 1991: 4).[20]

The impetus for renovation came in 1179 when Chu Hsi, acting as Prefect of the Nan-K'ang Military District, responded to reports of drought-related distress in high-lying fields with a visit to Mount *Lu-shan*, about seven kilometers away from the capital (Tillman 1991: 6). There, he came upon what he took to be the ruins of the White Deer Grotto Academy.

Though certainly well aware of the political sensitivity of his request—the Northern Song White Deer Grotto Academy had been closed in part because it was accused of harboring dissidents—Chu actively sought political and material support for the revival of the academy. He labored in the capital to secure state recognition, but it was only by leaning on a local sense of autonomy that he was able to secure the resources needed for restoration (Walton 1999b: 80–81). In the same manner that he had established community granaries as permanent institutions of relief—sheltered from seasonal market fluctuations and from political contingencies (Glahn 1993)—Chu secured for the White Deer Grotto Academy "rice fields for perpetual financial support" (Walton 1993: 275), as well as provisions from endowed estates, integrated into Southern Song state-building as means "to stabilize and harmonize social relations" (Tillman 1991: 7).

Despite Chu's prior assertion that "the notion of self-cultivation as the basis for a larger human renewal would lead to political and economic reforms" (Kim and Kim 2013: 19), the restoration of the White Deer Grotto Academy did not begin with an explicit challenge to Southern Song state education but, rather, with strategic arguments on behalf of the probity, rigor, and relevance of academy teachings. Those were rooted in a distinctly utilitarian reading of Confucius's work (Ho 1976: 15) that stressed the

---

[19]Though widely used when discussing academy movement in Southern Sung China, the term *neo-Confucian* is an anachronism; the term was actually coined by Jesuits in the sixteenth century (Kim and Kim 2013: 18). Introducing Chu Hsi as the most prominent neo-Confucian scholar, is to situate him in an ensemble that neither he nor his contemporaries would in fact have recognized. But it is correct in evocation of his centrality: "In the opinion of many historians [he] outshined Confucius himself" Kuhn (2011: 103). So consequent was Chu Hsi's reading of Confucius on Chinese, Korean, and Japanese thought that his position came to be defined as Chu Hsism. See Wittenborn (1991: 11).

[20]The restoration of the White Deer Grotto Academy is widely recognized as a defining moment of the South Song academy movement, but it was no means an isolated event. Indeed, the restoration of Northern Song academies can be considered key part of the Southern Song repertory of scholarly actions. Often symbolic—restored academies were often significantly smaller than the originals—restorations served both to affirm the prominence of individual scholars and to assert the autonomy of scholars in general. Of the four great Northern Song *shûyuàn*, only the *Yingtianfu* academy was not restored. Chu Hsi himself is "credited with the founding of seven academies in addition to the White Deer Grotto Academy and with teaching or lecturing at another dozen." See Chaffee (1985b: 49).

centrality of the "Four Books" (the *Great Learning*, the *Doctrine of the Mean*, the *Analects*, and the *Mencius*), briefer and more readily intelligible than the "Five Classics" around which authoritative interpretations of the Confucian canon had hitherto been organized (Gardner 1984: 64).[21] Summoning neo-Confucian watchwords, "terms such as 'principle' … 'material force' … 'sincerity' … 'quietude' … 'investigation of things'" (Lee 1985: 24), Chu drew the contours of a scholarly practice that emphasized the dialectical unity of knowledge and action ("[they] always need each other").[22] Whereas consciousness could be arrived at intuitively (Wittenborn 1991: 40), knowledge—born in the inexhaustible intermingling of the examinations of self and things—remained an elusive end unto itself (Chan 1963: 605–11).

For the revival of the White Deer Grotto Academy, Chu Hsi wrote "a short and easily memorized guide to study" (Chaffee 1985b: 54), the "Articles of Instruction." During the Southern Song expansion of academies, it defined for True-Way scholars what it was to learn the right way (Bol 1992: 338). Contrasting the ways of learning in academies with happenings in government schools—where the authority of professors relied on examination-related instrumentalities and "people devote themselves to recording and memorizing ornamental phrases so as to fish for fame and obtain profit and office"—Chu Hsi enjoined students to learn from a curriculum made up of the "Four Books" tightly arranged in order of reading from the most accessible to the least accessible, in an atmosphere of "lively debates" nurtured by his own teaching—Chu's teachings are the "greatest of all the S[o]ng 'record of speech'" (Bol 1992: 339).

> Study it extensively, investigate it accurately, think it over carefully, sift it clearly, and practice it earnestly.[23]

This atmosphere of lively debates was cause and consequence of the social compact at the heart of neo-Confucian academies (Bol 1992: 339). Whereas in Confucius's own school, the self-transformation at the basis of knowledge has been nurtured by an "intimate dialogue … among friends and disciple" (Kim and Kim 2013: 18), in the White Deer Grotto Academy, the seeking "of what we do not know" and the attendant improvement of "the ability of what we are not yet capable of"—practice for Chu Hsi—was predicated upon a more deliberately constructed and rigorous ambiance (Hsi 1991: 74).[24] Only by constituting themselves into an active and disciplined community of practice (Bol 1992: 338) could academy scholars

[21]It was around the "Five classics" that were organized the Northern Song state compilations of Confucius's work that served as centerpieces of civil service examinations Kuhn (2011: 42).
[22]Chu Hsi *On Learning* in his work (1991: 75).
[23]The "Articles of Instructions" are widely translated, cited, and paraphrased. They are cited here from Tillman (2020: 33).
[24]"Seeking the knowledge of what we do not know, and seeking the ability of what we are not yet capable of is called 'learning.' Ceaselessly carrying out what we know and are capable of is what I mean by 'practice'" (Hsi 1991: 74).

become capable of defining a place to stand apart from the imperial order (Hayhoe 2001: 329).[25]

> When things are investigated, knowledge is extended; when knowledge is extended, the will becomes sincere; when the will is sincere, the mind is rectified; when the mind is rectified, the personal life is cultivated; when the personal life is cultivated, the family will be regulated; when the family is regulated, the state will be in order; and when the state is in order, there will be peace throughout the world.[26]

In the months that followed Chu Hsi' initial visit to Mount *Lu-shan*, "the White Deer Grotto was the scene of much activity" (Chaffee 1985b: 41). Executed by corvee labor working from a model based on the layout of the Temple of Confucius at Qufu (Tillman 1991: 4), restoration was completed in less than a year. To mark the event, Chu Hsi declaimed a poem to assembled guests:

> The rebuilding of the ancient hall happily is now complete.
> The whole company of worthies will hear the barking of the deer.
> (Chaffee 1985b: 44)

The next spring, Chu invited Lu Jiuyuan—a prominent idealist philosopher with whom he disagreed publicly—to lecture at the White Deer Grotto Academy on a topic of common concern: "The superior man is conversant with righteousness, the inferior man is conversant with profit" (Schirokauer 2019: 123). Thus did teaching begin at the White Deer Grotto Academy with a scholarly disputation.

In 1234, Mongols conquered the Jurchen Jin territory, initiating the "last, greatest, longest, and most difficult of all the Mongol conquests" (Wright 2022: 118), which ended in 1276 with the capture of the Southern Song capital of Hangzhou. The "Great Yuan" state then established by Kublai Khan subsumed all external relations under tight control, shrinking possibilities for the autonomy of reflexive instances. Higher education was placed under political control and tasked with preparing students for examinations. "Though neither a faction nor politically very active" (Liu 1973: 485), the "True-Way movement" was soon banned as spurious learning (Liu 1973: 485–500). In short order, however, "the Mongol empire [took

[25]For Chu Hsi, collective self-restraint was a reflection of personal rigor. In the years that followed the restoration of the White Dear Grotto Academy, his followers found in the "Articles of Instruction" reason to develop disciplinary practices defined by strict precepts which instructed students to "to stand erect … and not to stand on one foot or lean to one side," "to … speak respectfully, to … keep clothing neat … to look and listen properly without staring or cocking the ear" (Schirokauer 2019: 123, 128).

[26]Schirokauer (2019: 128).

on] the trappings of a Confucian state" (Kuhn 2011: 106). Rebranded the "School of Principle," the "True-Way movement" moved "from proscribed heterodoxy to state orthodoxy" (Walton 1999b: 6) and was integrated into the state-building process as a form of cultural propaganda (Liu 1973: 502). Chu Hsi was made into a "paragon of orthodoxy" (Chaffee 1985b: 60) and his teachings—henceforward referred to as "correct learning"—became required reading for civil service examinations (Gardner 1984: 58).[27]

In the late Ming period (1368–1644), neo-Confucian academies again became centers of dissidence (Elman 1989: 389), and their interventions into the quotidian affairs of the state were once more made them object of critique (Gernet 1999: 382). The Donglin academy, the "last great *shûyuàn*"—restored with support from the local gentry—was deemed a site of "ethically intense and militant Confucianism" (Dardess 2002: 1) and considered a threat to political order (Elman 1989: 388). It fell into disrepair, only to be restored again in 1603. In 1625, Donglin principals were once more branded threats to public order (Dardess 2002: 124). Teachers and students were publicly chastised, arrested, and sometimes tortured (Elman 1989: 395). Land that had been bestowed upon the academy was sold off, and soon after, the halls of the academy were "completely torn down by imperial order," as were those of most other academies (Elman 1989: 395). No new academy was permitted to established itself in China until the mid-eighteenth century (Elman 1989: 403).

The Great Dispersal (1229–1231)

In Paris, as elsewhere in the European *world-economy*, riots, strikes, and exile (*tumultus*, *cessatio*, and *migratio*) were part of the rough repertory of actions through which the *studium generale* asserted its autonomy—defining *libertas scholastics* as a distinct modality of *libertas civica* (Rashdall 1824: 16). The two of course were kin in externality: "[U]niversities stood outside the jurisdiction of the cities that gave them a home, just as cities themselves existed outside the jurisdiction of the feudal districts in which they were located" (Backman 2009: 248).

Perhaps the clearest expression of *libertas scholastica* that took form at the time can be found in Pierre Abelard's *Sic et Non*—a loose collection of quotations and glosses complied between 1121 and 1122 (Marenbon 1997: 61). In *Logica ingredientibus* (1115–1118) and in *Theologia scholarium* (*c.*1120–1135), Abelard applied the "art of the dialectics"—which he had become acquainted with during scholarly peregrinations (Verger 1991: 67)—to the study of sacred texts. Rather than being content to celebrate the

---

[27]Chu Hsi's works retained a central place in the formation of civil servants in China until the Xinhai Revolution of 1911 (Chan 1963: 589).

divine unity of sacred words (Asztalos 1992: 411), he began by delineating contradictions between biblical and patristic sources, trusting that the study of their interrelation would reveal deeper truths—a manner of inquiry that, of course, left him open to accusations of attempting to understand God by way of reason (Jolivet 1977: 307, 318). In *Sic et Non*, Abelard applied "the arts of the dialectics" to relations between masters and students. He urged the former not to lecture authoritatively from reified truths (Jolivet 1977: 313–16) or by presenting ready-made answers to antinomies. Instead, he encouraged them to present ideas for student's consideration, initiating a relatively indeterminate learning relationship (Taillandier 1861: 627; Gimpel 1975: 163–65).

The corporate privileges of Paris's *studium generale*—a loose gathering of masters and students organized into nations, each with distinct "statutes, archives ... books ... schools, chapels ... places of assembly ... sources of revenue ... special feast days and patron saints"—were first recognized by Pope Celestine III in 1194 (Kibre 1948: 20; Le Goff 2013). The earliest recorded "town and gown" riot in the city happened six years later (McNair 1898: 37). It began with a tavern brawl involving German students, "in which some German students assaulted and severely beat the tavern keeper following an attack on one of the retainers of a German nobleman" (Kibre 1962: 86). In retaliation, "friends of the tavern keeper and other bourgeoisie, including the provost of Paris" raided the hostel where German students were staying, seriously injuring many (Kibre 1962: 86). Petitioned by masters, King Philippe II, drawing from Frederick Barbarossa (Verger 1991: 68), responded by giving assurances of royal protection, immunizing students from arrest by the city's provost or his justices, except in the commission of the most heinous crimes (Kibre 1954: 552). Vying with him to fix the terms of the relationship between clerks and the papacy, Pope Innocent III—who had studied theology in Paris and jurisprudence in Bologna—also acknowledged the autonomy and integrity of Paris's *studium generale*. In *Ex litteris vestris*, a series of notes written between 1208 and 1209, he threatened excommunication for anyone caught striking a clerk and granted other privileges and exemptions to the *studium generale* organized into a *universitas* (Coutin 1969: 21). In 1215, papal legate Robert de Courçon formalized this recognition by transmuting them into status that organized the *Universitas Parisiensis* into relatively independent and self-governed faculties. Thus, through competing sleights of hand of King and Pope, an "institutional mutation" happened; the *studium generale* of Paris had become an institution (Gorochov 2009: 53–54).

Benefitting from privileges of residency but struggling for affordable housing, Paris's *studium generale* began migrating to the left bank of the Seine (Wei 2012: 111). There took place a strike that initiated Europe's longest and most consequent exile of masters and students. As had the riot of 1200, it began with a barroom brawl between students and townsfolks (Le Goff 2013: 77). On February 26, 1229—Shrove Tuesday, a day of feasting before Lent—some theology students, having gone drinking in the nearby village of Saint-Marcel (Gorochov 2012: 405), found themselves in a dispute over the price of wine (Gorochov 2012: 399). The dispute degenerated into a fight during which students received a trashing from patrons. The next day, students returned to Saint-Marcel armed with swords and sticks. They broke into the *cabaretier*'s house and smashed wine barrels before setting out on a town-wide riot. In the tumult, town people rained blows on students, killing perhaps as many as 320 students according to Cistercian chronicler Raoul of Coggeshall—who wrote of bodies being thrown into the river Seine (Gorochov 2012: 405). One scholar was summarily executed by "the provost and the royal justices" (Kibre 1954: 533).

The next day, masters interrupted classes, signaling the beginning of a strike. Together with students and elected provisors (Gorochov 2012: 412), they petitioned Pope Gregoire IX and Blanche of Castile—Queen of France during the regency of Louis IX—detailing twenty-one conditions that had to be met before classes would resume (Kibre 1962: 92). Unacknowledged and unsafe, Paris's *studium generale* left the city *en masse*—borrowing a strategy previously used by students from the University of Bologna, who exiled themselves in Vicenza (1204–1209), Padua (1222), and Vercelli (1228), as well as by Oxford students, who went into exile in Cambridge and elsewhere in England (1209–1214; Gorochov 2012: 414).

Whole in leaving, Paris's *studium generale* dispersed in exile—often with students following in formation behind masters (Gorochov 2012: 416)—to join other *studia generalia*. Some went to Angers, Reims, Montpellier, Orléans, or Bologna. Others accepted an invitation extended by the Count of Toulouse, who promised "that they could read the books of Aristotle's natural philosophy which had been banned at Paris; that they could enjoy all the scholastic liberty they desired; … that they need not yield the reins of government to anyone; [and that] they need … fear [neither] the malice of the people nor the tyranny of the prince" (Kibre 1962: 92). As in 1200, English students—the largest nation in Paris (Gorochov 2009: 55)—went to Oxford on the invitation of Henry III: "In every way … we will make it possible for you to enjoy the liberty and tranquility which pleases God and which ought to be yours to enjoy fully." (Kibre 1954: 554).

On April 13, 1231, Pope Gregory IX made his own bid to persuade members of the *studium generale* to return to Paris. His bull *Parens scientiarum universitas*—the *Magna Carta* of Paris's scholars for Jacques Le Goff (2013: 78)—gave scholars a series of assurances:

1. *Licencia docendi*, the license to teach, valid throughout Christendom (Verger 1991: 71), would only be granted by the university's *chancellier* following an inquiry led by no fewer than six masters from the University of Paris (the term "inquiry"—*inquisitio*—was particularly resonant in the midst of the first papal inquisition, initiated in 1231 by the Papal bull *Excommunicamus*, authored by Gregory IX himself).

2. The *chancellier* would retain authority over matters of admissions, programs, and discipline but only the archbishop, the pope's direct representative, would have the power to jail students (Davy 1931: 301).
3. Harm previously done to members of the *studium generale* would be investigated and reparation made.
4. A commission of three masters would look into Aristotle's *Libri naturales*, with an eye to integrate the most useful passages into the *curriculum* (Gorochov 2012: 450).
5. The question of the devolution of assets belonging to students who had died without descendants would be examined—a matter of considerable importance for the perpetuation of the corporate rights of the *studium generale.*

Parens scientiarum universitas was the product of protracted negotiations (Gorochov 2012: 400–1) and, as such, only the most salient moment in a broad campaign to settle relations among scholars, the papacy, and the city. In the week that followed its publication, no fewer than fourteen papal bulls were issued that explicitly detailed *libertas scholastics* as a particular regime of freedom (Gorochov 2012, 2009).[28] In the months and years afterward, the *studium generale* gained privileges over the controlling of rents; students were entirely exempt from being called to appear in front of ecclesiastical tribunals; and their right to barricade a block of student houses on *rue Coupe-Gueule*—and thus the power to impose levies—was acknowledged (Le Goff 2013: 75; Wei 2012: 294, 24).

The Mongol moment ended for the European *world-economy* not with conquest but with the prolonged occupation of the Caucasian borderland by *Batu* and *Kadhan Khan*, grandsons of *Genghis Khan*. In the political consolidation that followed—a run-up to the rise of modern territorial states—universities in Europe developed not as expressions of scholarly self-rule but as extensions of political and religious power. As they did, the limits of scholarly autonomy were fixed more strictly, and scholarly relations of knowledge production brought under tighter political reins. At the University of Paris, Averroism was censured (Piché and Lafleur 1999: 195) and the wearing of academic vestments made mandatory (Riché and Verger 2006: 207). At the University of Orléans, student nations were forbidden from holding assemblies (Cobban 1971: 58). At the University of Toulouse, professors were summoned to Rome to sit in judgment of King Philippe II, who answered Gregory IX by forbidding the whole of the *studium generale* from leaving the kingdom (Kibre 1954: 82). During the Hundred Year's war, universities were created by political fiat in Poitiers (1431), Caen (1432),

[28]A comprehensive list of Gregory IX's bulbs, dated between April 13, 1231, and May 10, 1231, can be found in Gorochov (2012: 457).

and Bordeaux (1441). In *reconquista* Spain, universities were created by royal decree in Castile (1212), Salamanca, Castille and Leon (1241), Girona (1446), and Barcelona (1450). In Italian city-states, universities flourished in the loss of their autonomy. At the University of Bologna, that had defined the model of student-run universities, all matters *universitari*, including the hiring of professors and the granting of student privileges, were put under control of communal officials (Cardozier 1968: 948). Though the position of Rector continued to be filled by a student representative until Napoleon's invasion (Cobban 1971: 43, 53), a Board of Governors made up of notable citizens became the university's *de facto* deciding instance (Cardozier 1968: 948). Deprived of instituted power, students answered with infrapolitical irony: Conjuring feudal subjection, they took to calling professors *dominus meus* (my lord) rather than *magister* (teacher), effectively recusing any and all possibility of social relations of knowledge production (Le Goff 2013: 144). When the University of Padua was brought under control of the Republic of Venice, citizens were forbidden from attending any other university (Bayen 1973: 46). At the University of Naples, established by Emperor Frederick II as a "war machine against papacy" (Le Goff 2013: 159), the *studium generale* was forbidden from leaving the kingdom of Sicily to teach or to study (Kibre 1962, 1954: 81). In the Holy Roman Empire, universities proliferated as entirely "artificial creations" wholly under political control (Rashdall 1824: 213): In Prague, the university was founded (1348) by Charles IV as a means to assert royal prerogatives, and in Marburg (1527), Philipp I made academic privileges dependent on the acceptance of Lutheran reforms (Bayen 1973: 52). Everywhere, student movements lost power and relevance (Cobban 1971: 29), impoverishing social relations of knowledge relations.

By the beginning of the long sixteenth century, there were as many as sixty universities in Europe. At a juncture when the accoutrements of feudality "continued to impress the mind long after they had ceased to structure social relations" (Huizinga 1956: 57), professors continued to capitalize on their status as near-aristocratic nobility (Le Goff 2013) and students behaved unrulily, but *libertas scholastica* had dissolved into mere institutional formality.

The Building of the al-Mustansyria Madrasa (1227–1233)

Baghdad was an intentional city "[s]o perfect in its planning and creation that ... it was as though it had been poured into a model and cast."[29] It was built following the Abbasid victory over the Damascus-based Umayyads, on

[29]The quotation is from Baghdad-born geographer al-Ya'qūbi (d. 898) cited in Ephrat (2000: 21).

the west bank of the Tigris River—simultaneously connected to the world and protected from it by a network of canals. In 945 CE, the Shi'i Buyids conquered the city. For a century, they ruled over it as an "independent and autonomous government" (Ephrat 1993), keeping the Abbasid caliphs as titular figureheads. In 1055 CE, the Sunni Seljuks ousted Buyid rulers. They too kept the Abbasid caliph in place, while governing the city not as the political and cultural center of a pan-Islamic caliphate but as a provincial capital, equivalent in importance to Cairo, Cordoba, Ghazni, and Shiraz (Ephrat 1993: 42–43).

Having lost political centrality, Baghdad remained "a veritable cultural cosmopolis in the classical Islamicate World" (Günther 2022: 474), as well as "a major link in the world-wide chains of transmission of Muslim learning" (Ephrat 1993: 80). It was "'the place to go' for anyone pursuing knowledge and education" (Günther 2022: 474). Scholars from the whole of Islam "came to the city to study with the greatest masters of the time" (Ephrat 1993: 45).

It was in these circumstances that the *madrasa* movement reached Baghdad. The city's first *madrasa* was the Nizamiyya founded in 1065 and endowed by Seljuk *vizier* Nizam al-Mulk.[30] By *waqf* deed, it was reserved for the *Shafi'i* school of jurisprudence (Makdisi 1961: 38).[31] Only *Shafi'i* professors could serve as administrators, and they alone could wear professorial robes (Bougamra 1983: 86–87)—which they did immodestly by some accounts (Levy 1928: 268). Already, we see in this preclusion a sign of the relative autonomy of *waqf*-endowed *madrasas*. If Nizam al-Mulk had founded the Nizamiyya *madrasa* solely in his quality as agent of the Sultan, "then one would expect the madrasa to have been a *hanafi* one, since the Sultan was *hanafi*; only *hanafi* students would have been allowed to study there" (Makdisi 1970: 263). But Nizam al-Mulk founded the Nizamiyya *madrasa*—by *waqf* deed—in his own name, as a pious patron of learning (Makdisi 1970: 263). In doing so, he answered practical considerations: to counteract Shi'ite propaganda, to position Seljuks favorably within the Sunni revival, and "to generate loyal functionaries for administration"—

[30]Nizam al-Mulk is the honorific name given Persian scholar Abu Ali Hasan ibn Ali Tusi when he was appointed vizier in 1064. The Nizamiyya was one of two *madrasas* he founded in Baghdad.

[31]Before the *miḥna*, Islamic schools of jurisprudence (*madhhabs*) were designated by the name of the city or region whence they originated, in a manner that was coherent with the political the organization of the *Dar al-Islam*. Hence, there were the *madhhad* school of the Medinians, that of the Iraqis, and so on. After the *miḥna*, schools of jurisprudence came to be identified by the name of influential scholars (Makdisi 1989: 176). In Sunni Islam, there were four main schools of jurisprudence: the *Shafi'is*, named after theologian Muhammad ibn Idris al-Shafi'i; the *Hanbali*, named after Ahmad ibn Hanbal; the *Hanafite*, established by Abu Hanifa; and the *Maliki*, founded by Malik ibn Anas. This last school produced few *madrasas* due to an interpretation of the law of *waqf* prohibiting founders from retaining control over the trusteeship of endowed institutions. See Pedersen et al. (2009).

all in the most *realpolitik* fashion possible, by centering social relations of knowledge production on a school of jurisprudence which (i) recused "provincial dependence on traditional community practice as the source of precedent" (Editors 2018); (ii) underwrote the ascendency of Sunni Seljuks over Baghdad's Shi'ite population; and (iii) leaned on the idea of the duality of revelation (Musa 2007: 164) to allow for circumstantial interplays between interpretations of Islamic traditions and practices that were "generally valid" and those that were applicable to particular situations (Hasan 1966: 241).

Installing the Nizamiyya *madrasa* as an agency "of social control and legitimation" (Fındıklı 2022: 133–34), Nizam al-Mulk underwrote the place of "the legal scholar as the person responsible for ascertaining the significance and use of religious knowledge" (Lindholm 1999: 378), allowing for a prudent measure of scholarly autonomy (Bougamra 1983: 47–73).

Two hundred years after the founding of the Nizamiyya *madrasa*, the al-Mustansiriya *madrasa* was founded by al-Mustansir Bi'illah, the penultimate Abbasid caliph. Caliphs before had funded the building of mosques, lodges, and mausoleums, but this was the first time that a Caliph arranged directly for the funding of a *madrasa* (El-Hibri 2021: 251). To do so, al-Mustansir Bi'illah combined many *waqfs*: Where all *madrasas* before, including the Nizamiyya *madrasa*, had been the product of an individual endowment, the al-Mustansiriya *madrasa* was the result of a political combination. As a built ensemble, it represents the achieved form of Abbasid architecture, and as a political creation, it is the expression of the post-*miḥna* ambitions of the late Abbasid caliphate. It was also the first "multisystem" *madrasa* (Ephrat 2000: 93) and, as such, the highpoint of the *madrasa* movement.

When it opened for study on April 6, 1233 CE, the al-Mustansiriya *madrasa* was the largest of the city's endowed *madrasas*, half of which belonged to the *Hanbali* school of jurisprudence (Günther 2022: 478). Occupying an "unprecedently large" area on the eastern bank of the Tigris river (Hillenbrand 2022: 323–24), it housed the biggest library in the city, perhaps in the whole of the Islamic world (Polastron 2009: 106), as well as a remarkably coherent architectural ensemble of housing baths, dormitories (around three hundred students are believed to have resided at the al-Mustansiriya *madrasa*), a public hospital, kitchens, two mills, storerooms for food, drinks, and medicines, houses (more than one hundred), as well as a water-power clock so magnificent with its "metallic doors mirroring the movements of celestial objects and the dropping of metal balls into vessels to tell the passing hours" that poets composed verses in its honor (El-Hibri 2021: 255).[32] Beside it was a private garden with an observatory.

[32]The al-Mustansiriya *madrasa* was "105.50 m long and 49.80 wide" (Strika and Khalil 1987: 65). Its library is said to have housed more than 80,000 rare books and to have included a system for borrowing books, with paper and pens provided by the college for copying material (Tayeb El-Hibri 2021: 252).

There, al-Mustansir Bi'illah "used to sit near a window and watch what was going on and even listen to the lectures and discussions with the students" (Hillenbrand 2022: 328).

Remarkable as an architectural ensemble and as a statement of Abbasid ambitions, the al-Mustansiriya *madrasa* also testified to the circumstantial untying of scholarly *praxis* from doctrinal debates. Outside its walled perimeter, conflict between students of different Sunni traditions, and between them and the majority Shafi'i population, were integral part of the life of the city (Ephrat 1993: 47). Sometimes, they even lead to open conflicts (Neggaz 2020: 302–8). Inside the al-Mustansiriya *madrasa*, however, all four Sunni schools of jurisprudence were given equal treatment as modalities of scholarly relations—as they had indeed at the official inauguration, a "solemn occasion which sealed its place as the city's preeminent *madrasa*" (Hillenbrand 2022: 323), attended by sixty-two representatives from each school (Günther 2022: 483). Equal contingents of students had like access to their own *hammam* and mosque in a distinct corner of the *madrasa* built in the traditional four-*iwan* plan (Strika and Khalil 1987: 66); the quarter to the right of the *qibla* [the way to Mecca] was given to the *Shafiʿis*, the quarter to the left to the *Hanafi*'s, and so on (Ibn-Baṭṭūṭa 2016: 332). Each was given equal stipend and food allowance and had equal access to subsidiary buildings (Strika and Khalil 1987: 68).

The al-Mustansiriya *madrasa* sanctioned an equality between jurisprudential traditions in which the maturity of scholarly *praxis* found full expression. In all four corners of the *madrasa*, a professor, presenting a "solemn figure in his black clothes and turban," sat under a small wooden canopy, "on a chair covered with rags, with assistants repeating lessons and taking notes" (El-Hibri 2021: 252).[33] Everywhere, Quran and *hadith* were taught, as well as calligraphy, mathematics, engineering, astronomy, medicine, and the natural sciences. Routine disputations took place in each *iwan*. In the open courtyard, disputations took place between scholars of different schools under the eye of Caliph al-Mustansir Bi'illah. Those transformed Islamic disputations (*ʿilmal-naẓar*) into a science unto itself, a way to draw meaning from discourse, and let it rest to be picked up again (Pehlivan and Ceylan 2022: 1).

In the first moment of Abbasid Caliphate—before the *miḥna* and Mongol control over trading routes in Asia—the *house of wisdom* organized translation, and Islamic schools of jurisprudence were known for the places whence they originated, mimicking the political organization of the *Dar al-Islam*. In the second moment, schools of jurisprudence gained a

[33]Ibn Battuta, who visited the al-Mustansiriya *madrasa* roughly a century after the Mongol conquest of the city, is cited by Sebastian Günther (2022: 483).

measure of autonomy from both political authority and *hadith*. In the last moment, doctrinal differences were brought under the empire of common scholarly practice.

In 1258 CE, the armies of Hülegü Khan laid siege to Baghdad, bringing an end to Abbasid fame and grandeur (Hillenbrand 2022: 334). The library of the al-Mustansiriya *madrasa* was looted and its books thrown in the Tigris River, blackening the waters (Polastron 2009: 108). The structure itself only survived as a hollow shell. Visiting a century later, Persian scholar Hamdallah Mustawfi still referred to it "as the most beautiful building ... in Baghdad" (Le Strange 2018 [1900]: 269). As the *Dar al-Islam world-economy* fragmented into distinct polities, *madrasas* ceased to be relatively autonomous sites of distinct social relations: In the Seljuk empire and the Hafsid, Mamluk, Marinid, and Delhi sultanates, they were instrumentalized to confer legitimacy on political rule over lay populations (Abdel-Latif 2020: 651). Despoiled of their professional autonomy, *ulama* scholars were either integrated into the ordinary working of regional polities or else they returned to more traditional roles as bearer of an abstract, somewhat removed, idea of pan-Islamic unity (Daun and Arjmand 2018: 25). In the Sultanate of Egypt, Ayyubid rulers went as far as claiming power over the hirings and dismissals of *madrasa* professors (Gilbert 1980: 127).

Conclusion

"[W]hat made Mongols count in world history was the connections they made" (Burbank and Cooper 2010: 93). For a brief moment at the beginning of the thirteenth century, the Eurasian plains "were crisscrossed by trade routes and cultural corridors along which much information about the world, as well as various religions, percolated east and west" (Forsyth 2013: 123). "[G]oods were transferred, prices set, exchange rates agreed upon, contracts entered into, credit—on funds or on goods located elsewhere—extended, partnerships formed, and ... records kept and agreements honored" (Abu-Lughod 1991: 8). This induced a boom in long-distance trade among the *world-economies* of Southern Song China, Europe, and the *Dar al-Islam*, which defined the conditions of their transformation. In Southern Song China, it lessened state control over external relations and underwrote a commercial revolution that buoyed local drives for autonomy. In the *Dar al-Islam*, it reinforced the movement away from Abbasid unity, bankrolled *waqfs*, and increased both the collective coherence of the *ulama* and its autonomy vis-à-vis tradition and politics. In Europe, it contributed to the crisis of feudality, kick-started the development of capitalism (Anievas and Nişancıoğlu 2015: 77), bracing merchant's claims against political and papal power.

Everywhere, the development of relatively open, transactional linkages between relatively porous *world-economies* created conditions favorable to the relative autonomy of reflexive instances, giving scholars room to maneuver and increasing the impact of their actions.

Situations, of course, belong to themselves. The tensions between Abbasid centralization and regional aspirations for autonomy were not the same as those that existed between state-building initiatives and a rising sense of "localness" in Southern Song China (Walton 1999b: 80–81). Disputations in the *Dar al-Islam* and in Europe were as distinct from one another, and from the "pure conversation movement" taking place in China as the *licencia docentis* was from the *idjāza*, or Confucian rusticity from the walled-off isolation of the al-Mustansiriya *madrasa*. Hsu Chi's *Articles of Instruction* and Pierre Abelard's *Sic et Non* are not the same book; scholars did not gather in a *studium generale* as they did as fellows-in-explication; and the autonomy granted managers of *waqf* deed was not simply an iteration of *libertas scholastica*.

Academies, *madrasas*, and universities were not the undifferentiated outcomes of a homogenizing process of globalization. They are the circumstantial inventions of actually existing scholars acting in the context of particular configurations of social relations.

Looking into what neo-Confucians, *studia generalia*, and the *ulama* made of the propitious circumstances they found themselves in, we are offered a first opportunity to think though the relation between the little tradition of scholarly actions and the structure of world order: Before *academic freedom*, in a critical juncture when relatively porous *world-economies* were put into relatively open relations, scholars took advantage of possibilities for relative autonomy of reflexive instances to construct situations where they could meet relatively apart from existing social and political arrangements and engage with one another in self-inventing, relatively indeterminate relations of knowledge production.[34]

[34]The phrase "Construction of situation" references Guy Debord's *Rapport sur la construction de situations et sur les conditions de l'organisation et de l'action de la tendance situationniste internationale*. Debord was a principal of the Internationale Situationniste, his *Rapport* was written for the *Internationale Lettriste* (IL) and discussed by the Mouvement pour un Bauhaus Imaginiste (MBI). When the IL and the MBI merged with the COBRA group to create the Internationale Situationniste, the *Rapport* served as a common basis for discussion. It was never published in the *International Situationniste* (IS) review but in the appendix to the reprint of IS reviews published by A. Fayard in 1997 in Paris. It is widely available in translation as "Report on the Construction of Situations and on the International Situationist Tendency's Conditions of Organization and Action." It is cited here from the Anarchist Archives: https://theanarchistlibrary.org/library/guy-debord-report-on-the-construction-of-situations. On the construction of situations, see also "Problèmes préliminaires à a construction d'une situation," *Internationale Situationniste* 1 (June 1958): 11–13, and Uwe Lausen, "Répétition et nouveauté dans la Situation Construite," *Internationale Situationniste* 8 (January 1963): 57–59.

c. **1492–1973**	World-system of territorial states
1806–1917	State-building Germany
1817	**Wartburg book burning**
1871	**Civil service examinations mandatory, England**
1875	**Loi sur la liberté de l'enseignement supérierur, France**
1870–1940	**Third Republic, France**
1865–1877	Reconstruction, United States
1897	**No Women at Cambridge protests**
1914–1918	First World War
1915	Declaration of Principles on Academic Freedom and Academic Tenure, United States
1897–1910 **1933–1944**	**W. E. B. Du Bois, Atlanta**
1918	**Reform movement, Córdoba University**
1954–1957	**Paul Sweezy vs. the University of New Hampshire**

Timeline originated on behalf of the author by Alexandre Gravel.

2

A World-System of Universities

As the world-system of states was reaching its achieved form in the latter half of the nineteenth century, a world-system of universities took shape that structured the production of knowledge in and of the world. At its core was a new genus of research universities operating as coordinating instances of national systems of knowledge production. There, in the bosom of *world ordering*, a regime of *academic freedom* was instituted to organize and reproduce social relations of knowledge production. It bounded scholars to disciplines and split them into two groups bearing distinct, functionally related freedoms. Professors, the privileged subjects of *academic freedom*, bore the freedom to research and teach: *lehrfreiheit* in Humboldtian parlance. Students, for their part, had the freedom to choose what and how they wanted to learn: *lernfreiheit*.

This is the context in which scholarly *praxis* defined itself at the turn of the twentieth century. To gain knowledge of it, it is useful to begin by outlining the history of national systems of knowledge production. To that end, we can look into happenings in Germany, England, France, and the United States.

*

In Germany, the instituting of academic freedom was indissociable from the process of state-building.

Prior to the Restoration period, the establishment of universities in the German-speaking world—apart from the University of Würzburg, founded in 1402 in recognition of an established *studium generale*, and the University of Leipzig, established in 1409 by German-speaking professors and students in exile from Prague—was more influenced by volitions of political authorities than by the recognition of an established academic tradition. The University of Vienna was founded (1365) by the Habsburg Duke of Austria as a gesture of defiance toward both Charles VI and Pope

Innocent VI; the University of Heidelberg (1386), the University of Erfurt (1392), and the University of Cologne (1388) were founded by decree of Pope Urban VI during the Western Schism (1378–1415); and the University in Ingolstadt was founded (1472) by Louis IX, Duke of Bavaria, to assert his independence. The University of Halle (1694), arguably the first modern university in the German-speaking world, was founded by Frederick III to train Protestant clergy and missionaries, as well as to "advance the worldly practical purposes of men and the benefit of society" (Ringer 1990: 17). During much of the eighteenth century, it served as the principal *alma mater* of Prussian officials.

Through the first (1792–1797) and second coalitions (1798–1802), debates over university reform—involving most notably Immanuel Kant, Johann Fichte, and Friedrich Schleiermacher—answered broadly to Enlightenment ideas of the manners in which scholars could be engaged in disciplined intellectual activities, and, as such, worthy of being considered the "most valuable element of the moral culture of the nation" (Fichte 1847 [1794]). In the "Conflict of Faculties" (1798) Kant operationalized ideas on individual autonomy and self-governance into an argument in favor of a model university unencumbered by political or religious interference, where disciplined scholars could be free to pursue knowledge and truth under the ethical and moral guidance of philosophers.[1]

After the Congress of Vienna, debates were given focus by state-building priorities and centered on the possible creation of a new university in Berlin—Prussia's capital and the center of intellectual life in the German-speaking world—to replace the provincial University of Halle, which had been occupied by French troops during the Napoleonic Wars (Piché 2007: 133).[2] Animating discussions was the "flurry of memoranda, letters, and bureaucratic maneuvering" written by philosopher Wilhelm von Humboldt following his 1809 appointment as head of the newly created Section for Culture and Education of the Prussian Ministry of the Interior (Menand et al. 2017: 105).

"On the internal and external organization of higher academic institutions in Berlin" is Humboldt's best-known text on university reform.[3]

---

[1]Though Kant's differentiation between "higher faculties"—theology, law, and medicine—and the lower faculty—philosophy—prefigures the colonial partitioning of knowledge into disciplines, he uses the term *discipline* to refer to the self-control and rigor of scholars rather than to the methodologically distinct academic fields on which would rest later arguments for the self-governance of modern universities.

[2]A four-person commission was appointed in June 1810 to draft provisional statutes for the new university; Friedrich Schleiermacher served as secretary. Frederick William III approved the final report on October 1810, but final approval for work on the University of Berlin to begin was not given until April 1817, after the Congress of Vienna.

[3]Key documents in the debate over the creation of a university in Berlin can be found in translation in Menand et al. (2017). These include Friedreich Gedike's "Report to the King Friedrich Wilhelm II of Germany"; Friedreich Schleiermacher's "Occasional Thoughts on German Universities in the German Sense"; Wilhelm von Humboldt's "On the Internal and External Organization of Higher Academic Institutions in Berlin," "Request for the Establishment of the University of Berlin"; and "On Germany's Educational System."

It was written in 1810 but remained unknown until 1893, when it was rediscovered in the archive of the Berlin State Library by historian Bruno Gebhardt. First published in 1903, the text began its career as "perhaps the most discussed document in the modern history of universities" (Wittrock 1993: 317n33), only during the Weimar Republic (1918–1933).[4]

What came to be consecrated as the Humboldtian university (*die Humboldtsche Universität*) was conceived both as a model research institution (Östling 2018: 12) and as a coordinating instance for Berlin's many established centers of intellectual activity—serving, in this sense, as a "showpiece" of state reform (Anderson 2004: 53). Ensuring the articulation between those two roles was a utilitarian reconciliation of institutional autonomy and political purpose. For Humboldt—whose work *On the Limit of State Action* later served as the epigraph for Mill's *On Liberty* (Crouter 2005: 146)—universities could best realize their own purpose and more effectively serve the state "realize the state's ends ... on a far higher plane"—if the state refrained from interfering in their affairs (von Humboldt 1976: 244–46).

The seminar was the paradigmatic expression of Humboldtian compromises between *bildung*—wisdom and virtue—and *wissenschaft*—disciplined knowledge and, thus, between the freedoms to teach, research, and learn on the one hand and "the needs of the state" on the other (von Humboldt 1970: 248). There, professors and students—their freedom protected by a State that "understands that intellectual work will go on infinitely better if it does not intrude" (von Humboldt 1970: 244)—could engaged in debates secured in the knowledge that they were not there for themselves or one for the other but, rather, for science (von Humboldt 1990: 274).

> Research could be unified with teaching only as long as scholars provided instruction that prepared students for state exams. *Bildung* could remain the core of higher learning only as long as that learning produced an educated workforce for the modern civil service and army. The unity of natural sciences and humanities prevailed only as long as the broader notion of *Wissenschaft* under which they were contained served those professional goals
>
> (Levine 2021: 20)

[4]On "Mythos Humboldt," a neologism that underlines both the consecration of the University of Berlin as a model research university and that of Humboldt himself as the embodiment of the modern academic reformism, see Ash (1997).

After Berlin, the University of Bonn (1818), the University of Munich (1826), and the University of Giessen (1826) were founded in quick order, all on the model of the University of Berlin (Ringer 1990: 75).[5] These are the defining Humboldtian universities, exemplary instances of the Humboldtian "academic social contract" (Levine 2021: 20).

*

The broad reorganization of education that took place in Tudor England—marked by Henry VIII's closing of monasteries (a grab of chantry lands) and the subsequent founding of grammar schools—concerned itself only with primary and secondary education. Oxford and Cambridge, the only universities in England at the time, remained wholly private concerns.[6] Mired in scholasticism, yet relatively autonomous and enjoying a monopoly on higher education, they occupied ambiguous positions within the *nebulae* of private societies, zoos, laboratories, aquariums, and gardens, giving shape to the first scientific revolution.[7]

It was only in the nineteenth century that the bureaucratic state taking form at the intersection of domestic and late-colonial reform movements began concerning itself with organizing a system of higher education suited to the task of training "the youth of our middling rich people [for] state service and … the eventual governance of the outside world" (Soffer 1987: 173).[8]

To develop the scientific and technical knowledge required to prepare students for civil service examinations—mandatory across most of the British civil service after 1871—seven new "civic universities" were granted charter, where ideas of *lernfreiheit* and *lehrfreiheit*, "imported and vernacularized," (Finn 2022: 23) served to organize scholarly work: the University of Durham (1832), the University of Birmingham (1900), the University of Manchester (1903), the University of Liverpool (1903), the University

[5]The University of Frankfurt was founded in 1914, just before the First World War. In the immediate aftermath, the University of Hamburg (1919), the University of Cologne (1919), and the University of Münster (1919) were established.

[6]The Act of Union (1707) added the University of St. Andrews (1410), the University of Glasgow (1451), the University of Aberdeen (1495), and the University of Edinburgh (1583) to the UK's list of historic universities.

[7]Their autonomy, Oxford and Cambridge owed both to Henry VIII's interventions on behalf of the Anglican church and to the support of a growing merchant and gentry class eager "to raise or confirm their status as gentlemen by education" and to secure positions as "excellent servants to the clergy," *dixit* Thomas Hobbes in the *Leviathan*, as cited by Hill (1972: 244). Citations are from Perkin (1984: 20, 28).

[8]"[T]he youth of our middling rich people" is from Thomas Campbell's "Plan for a Greater London University," cited here from Whyte (2015: 36).

of Leeds (1904), the University of Sheffield (1905), and the University of Bristol (1909). Apart from the short-lived *New College*, founded by Oliver Cromwell, it did not outlive the Commonwealth of England, and *London University*, which existed solely as an administrative and examination body until the 1930s, these were the first university-like institutions founded in England since the middle-ages.[9] All grew from existing colleges, were located in provincial cities at the heart of the industrial revolution, and were funded directly by the Chancellor of the Exchequer (Asztalos 1982; Shinn 1980) with backing from private endowments (Jones 2018). While the authority of "representatives of local and national wealth, power, and status" was established by statutes—which never referred explicitly to notions of academic freedom—it was "in practice severely circumscribed by conventions which dictated that they should have little say in academic matters: none in matters of *Lern und Lehr freiheit*, [and] little in matters of appointment" (Jones 1985: 281). In civic universities, scholars were *de facto* free to govern themselves.

Oxford and Cambridge, for their part, offered "no practical training that would assist members of the rising middle class" (Lawrie 2014: 56) or bolster utilitarian arguments in favor of academic freedom. There, the shift toward usefulness rather involved a broad transition away from preparing clergy for church and community service (Levine 2021: 22) toward training civil servants in "schools of statesmanship" (Soffer 1987:176).[10] This

[9]London University was established in 1826, incorporating the Imperial College of Science and Technology (1731) and the London Hospital Medical College (1785). Given standing not as a corporation but as a joint-stock company (Jeremy Bentham was an initial shareholder), it did not initially have degree-granting power. In 1830, London University founded the London University College School. In 1836, it transformed into University College, London, affiliating with King's College, London to create the University of London, an "examining machine" (Ashby 1966: 6) that also existed as an administrative collage of already existing and newly created colleges, institutes, and school: the Imperial College of Science and Technology (1731), the London Hospital Medical College (1785), the School of Pharmacy (1842), St. George College (1842), and others. By 1851, there were "no less than twenty-nine general colleges and nearly sixty medical colleges" affiliated to the University College, London (Perkin 1984: 32), which complemented work done by the Royal College of Chemistry (1845), the Government School of Mines (1851), and the Royal Engineering College (1872). The Slade School of Fine Art (1871) was established as part of the University College, London, as were the London School of Economics (1895) and the School of Oriental Studies (1916). In 1907, the University College, London merged with the University of London, becoming the University of London, University College. Only in the 1930s did the University of London itself become a teaching university, acquiring for that purpose a freehold in Camden. In 1976, University of London, University College regained a measure independence, becoming the University College London (without the comma).

[10]The University Act of 1882 can be considered a pivoting point in the transition. Before, "around 90 percent of Fellows of Oxford colleges were required, after a period of time, to take Holy orders" (Finn 2022: 22).

transition was not marked as it was in civic universities by the conspicuous establishment of new administrative units or formal programs of study but, rather, by a subtler move away from seeing the university as a permanent retreat from the plebeian exigencies of the world toward understanding it as a transitory place where young men could learn to govern themselves and lead others (Soffer, 1987: 168). It expressed itself in the creation of affiliated schools; engagement in the "university extension movement"; and financial support for "civic universities"—University College of Bristol, for example, was partly funded by an endowments from Balliol College, Oxford.[11]

In British colonies, the creation of universities—and, with it, the role of academic freedom in the regulation of scholarly relations—varied depending on each colony's position within the imperial hierarchy of things, thoughts, and peoples. In white-settler colonies, scholars' self-rule functioned as an extension of indirect rule. In North America, as British colonies moved toward integration as a self-governing Dominion (which Canada became in 1867), colleges established during the colonial period—where scholarly autonomy was rooted in ecclesiastic privilege—became modern research universities: King's College, founded by the Church of England in 1827, became the University of Toronto in 1853; that year, Bishop's College, founded by Anglicans in 1836, became Bishop's University; McGill College, founded in 1821, became McGill University in 1885; Queen's College, founded by Presbyterians in 1841, became Queen's University in 1912. There, a timorous iteration of *academic freedom*—a term "very little heard in Canada before the First World War (Horn 1998: 13)"—was given shape by "a deep aversion among academic men to entering into an organization whose purposes smacked of trade unionism ... a fear of administrative reprisal [and] a certain timidity which the academic mind had acquired through years of ivied isolation" (Horn 1998: 10). No institution of higher learning was created by or for people of French descent—deemed "without

[11]Affiliated schools of moral science, history, law, natural sciences and modern history, mathematics, and physics were created by both Oxford and Cambridge beginning in the 1850s, but students enrolled there could not matriculate until after they had completed the classical program of *Literae Humaniores*. The Cambridge extension movement began in 1873. At its origin was a series of lectures on the subject of gravitation given by James Stuart, a tutor, to schoolmistresses in Liverpool, Manchester, Sheffield, Leeds, and Nottingham. It was Stuart's "dream to create ... a sort of peripatetic university of professors which should circulate in the big towns" Perkin (1984: 47). As it developed, lectures were ordered and paid for by town, cities, civic committees, and benevolent associations on subjects of interest to their clienteles: "The northern miners are keen for instruction in science: suburban ladies prefer the literature and art of mediaeval Italy or Germany" (Browning 1887: 61). These lectures were not given by professors but by lecturers, who often had to contend with the boisterousness of their audience. For a broad overview of classes given in the context of the Cambridge extension movement, see Welch (1973).

history of literature," and thus excluded from the magical circle of instituted freedoms.[12] Natives for their part were relegated to residential boarding schools, where took place what the Truth and Reconciliation Commission recognized as "cultural genocide."[13] This we understand as a modality of the worldwide "epistemicide" that took place during the colonial organization of knowledge production (Grosfoguel 2011). In Australia, "sandstone universities" were established for white settlers of English descent in Sydney (1848), Melbourne (1853), Adelaide (1874), and Tasmania (1890). There as well natives were confined to residential boarding schools.

In resource-extraction colonies, by contrast, the creation of universities—modulated by a utilitarian idea of the distinction to be made between those deemed useful to the governing of state and empire and those whose need for improvement justified a more interventionist mode of government—was an extension of direct rule. In South Africa, the South African College, established in the Cape Colony at the end of company rule (1795), continued to educate the sons of white colonists in both Dutch and English through the first period of British occupation (1795–1803), the Dutch Colonial period (1803–1806), and the years of the Cape Colony (1827–1899). After British victory in the Second Boer war (1899–1902) and the creation of the Union of South Africa (1910), it was integrated into the University of Cape Town (1918), as "an essential component in the ... building [of] a racialized and patriarchal modern state" (Hendricks 2018: 26). Stellenbosch College, established in 1881 by Dutch Reformists, acquired university status at the same time. Founded after the discovery of gold in the Transvaal (1886), the South African School of Mines (1896) was renamed the Transvaal Technical Institute in 1904 and the Transvaal University College in 1906.

---

[12]The citation is from Lord Durham's *Report on the Affairs of the British North America* (1839), a defining document of British colonial rule. After rebellions in 1837, John Lambton, First Earl of Durham, was mandated by Prime Minister William Lamb to inquire into the origins of events and find ways "to repair the mischiefs which has already been done ... and lay the foundations of order, tranquility and improvement." In English Upper Canada, Lambton saw legitimate political demands stemming from a reasonable and industrious people. In French Lower Canada, he rather saw in rebellions the expression of the ontological debility of "an old and stationary society in a new and progressive world ... a people with no history, and no literature." A copy of Durham's Report can be found on the site of the Canadian Research Knowledge Network: https://www.canadiana.ca/view/oocihm.32374/3?r=0&s=1. In New France, the highest institution learning at the time of British conquest (1760) was the Séminaire de Québec (1663), founded by François de Montmorency de Laval, the first archbishop of New France. After the British conquest, the Séminaire endured as a center for the formation of priests and the catholicization of natives. In 1852, the Université Laval was born of it. Until the 1960s, the Catholic Church remained strongly opposed to the notion of academic freedom. On this, see Curran (1990).

[13]The commission was appointed in 2008 following the Indian Residential Schools Settlement Agreement, the largest class action suit in Canadian history. Its final report (December 2015) is available on the website of the National Center for Truth and Reconciliation, University of Manitoba: https://nctr.ca/records/reports/.

Two years later, a part of it moved to Pretoria, becoming the University of Pretoria in 1930. Another part became the University College of Johannesburg (1920), which grew into the University of Witwatersrand (1922). Rhodes University College (1904) was federated into the University of South Africa in 1918; in 1951, it became a separate university. Apart from the Fort Hare Native College, administered by Rhodes University, there were no Black colleges in South Africa—indeed in the whole of British Africa—until university colleges for nonwhite communities were created by the apartheid Republic of South Africa in 1959.[14]

In the Caribbean, the white population was too small to warrant the institution of colleges or universities. Slavery, of course, did not allow Black colleges to be established (Braithwaite 1958) even if only, as Bishop Berkeley had argued in *A Proposal for the Better Supplying of Churches in our Foreign Plantations*" (1725), to teach slaves "[t]o obey in all things their masters according to the flesh, not with eye-service as men-pleasers, but, in singleness of heart as fearing God" (Berkeley 1725).[15]

In British India, company rule supported a multitude of scientific societies—some reserved for scholarly exchanges between "curious and learned" British men, others dedicated to "the translation [and discussion] of scientific material into the local idiom and thereby initiating the process of naturalization and domestication of modern science" (Raina 2011: 952).[16] After the 1857 war of independence, the British government assumed direct

---

[14]Fourah Bay College in Sierra Leone, established by the Anglican Church Missionary Society in 1827 and affiliated with Durham University in 1876, stayed the lone postsecondary institution in British Africa until the interwar period, when colonial policy moved to replace missionary schools with technical and industrial colleges—a shift driven by the belief that "the educational methods which had been hammered out for the freed slaves in the postbellum period [in the United States] were particularly relevant for black Africans in the 20th century"; that such methods were more suitable for administering colonies economically (Motani 1979); and that they were better equipped to contain "radical" influences coming from America (Nwauwa 1993). In the wake of the Phelps-Stokes Foundation Reports on *Education in Africa* (1922, 1924), the Uganda Technical College was founded in Kampala (1922), the Achimota College in Accra (1924), and the Yaba Higher College in Lagos (1932).

[15]After the Second World War, the creation of universities in British colonies, accelerated by "colonial developmentalism" was accelerated by British desires to mitigate the influence of American universities on African elites and placate anticolonial sentiments. On this, see Hargreaves (1973: 26–36); Nwauwa (1993); and Steinmetz (2017).

[16]Among scholarly institutions founded in the years of company rule were: In 1781, the Calcutta *madrasa* established by the East India Company—appropriating the name of Muslim institutions of higher learning established in India since the eleventh century—to instruct "sons of Muslim gentlemen" (Suman 2020) in the ways of *nawabi* administration. In 1784, the Asiatick Society was founded on the model of the Royal Society in London to house the transactional exchanges of "all curious and learned" British men (Steadman 1977: 466). Benaras Sanskrit College was founded in 1792. In 1825, the "Asiatic Society of Bengal" was created to accompany the transition away from emphasis on Sanskrit, Persian, and Arabic languages training toward "vocational, integrated, Western, curricular-based teaching, more useful both politically and administratively" (Zaman 1999: 308). Two documents are usually

control over the British Raj and set up a colonial iteration of the system of knowledge production taking shape in the UK. In this system, the possibilities for scholarly autonomy were curtailed by colonial anxieties over universities becoming sites for the development of national consciousness (Guha 2007); the combined—though sometimes divergent, and always contested—efforts of colonial officers, scientists, educationists, missionaries, and others to "re-engineer" education to produce not knowledge but "manpower for the efficient management of empire" (Raina 2011: 945); an all-embracing concern for the development of an "intellectual Compradors" class (Alatas 2000: 29–32); a tutelary conception of colonial education (Alatas 2000: 25); the subordination of teaching to examination (Seth 2007: 24); and imperial control over curriculum (Seth 2007) and language (Evans 2002).

At the center of this system were three universities, all established in 1857—Calcutta, Bombay, and Madras—which Dhruv Raina described as "concretizations of ideas of utilitarianism" (Raina 2011: 954).[17] Contemptful of any conception of scholarly freedom, they emphasized rote repetition over knowledge, memory over meaning, the thoughts of others over one's own thought, and learning by heart over understanding and explaining.[18]

*

In France, the absolutist state—endeavoring to regulate social relations of knowledge production—labored to curb "the rush to faculties" (Chartier 1982: 389) and instead encourage the plowing of land and service to the King "in arts and army."[19] What mattered to the Académie Française—created in 1635 to give the French language "firm rules ... and to make it pure, eloquent and capable of handling the arts and sciences"—the Jardin des plantes (1626), the Académie des Beaux-Arts (1648), the Académie Royale

referenced to contextualize the turn from orientalism toward utilitarian, English-language education in India: Lord Macauley's "Minutes on Indian Education" (1835), which emphasized the need for instruction in English "the language spoken by the ruling class," and Charles Wood's "Dispatch on General Education in India (1854), which argued for education "not only to produce a higher degree of intellectual fitness, but also to raise the moral character of those who partake of its advantages, and so to supply [the East India Company] with servants to whose probity you may with increased confidence commit offices of trust." Both documents are cited from the Internet Archives: https://archive.org/details/Minutes201311; https://archive.org/stream/dli.csl.5554/5554djvu.txt.

[17]Punjab University, the first in a majority Muslim area, was established in 1911.

[18]This list builds on a series of dichotomies outlined by Lord Curzon in a speech given at the University of Calcutta's convocation ceremony in 1902, as cited in Seth (2007: 30).

[19]The first citation is from Jean-Baptiste Colbert, Louis XIV's minister of everything. The second is from Archbishop Richelieu, the King's *éminence grise*. Both are freely translated from Chartier (1982: 395).

de Danse (1661), the Académie Royale des sciences (1666), or the Académie des inscriptions et belles-lettres (1663) was not the manner in which knowledge was produced in any modern sense of the term but the conformity of outcomes.[20] In this context, private academies, museums, companies, and universities—that had shrunk into dogmatism and conformity (Minot 1991: 29)—were for the most part left to their own practice, censured only when the need arose: *laissez-penser et censurer* we can think of as a prolongment of *ancient régime* power of *laissez-vivre et faire mourir*.[21]

In colonies, as well, the French absolutist state stayed at arm's length from organizing social relations of production. Even the *Code noir* (1619), arguably the deepest incursion of the absolutist state into relations of production in slave-holding colonies at the time of France's first overseas empire (Roberts 2019b: 3–4), did little more than impose minimal constraints on the *laissez-vivre* of masters and the *faire mourir* of slaves, remaining entirely unconcerned with social relations of knowledge production.[22] In white-settler colonies, the state was content with mandating religious orders

[20]The citation is from the *Lettres patentes pour l'établissement de l'Académie française*, signed by Louis XIII, in January 1635. The *Lettres* are available from the website of the Bibliothèque Nationale de France: https://gallica.bnf.fr/ark:/12148/bpt6k76291j.image.

[21]In *Il Faut Défendre la Société*, a lesson given at the Collège de France in 1976, Michel Foucault discussed the transition from premodern sovereign power—that remained content to let social relations be and only punished excesses in the most spectacular fashion (*laissez-vivre et faire mourir*: let live and make die)—to modern biopower, bent on *faire-vivre et laissez mourir*: to make live and let die (Foucault 1997). Of special interest here is the lesson of March 17, 1976 (Foucault 1997: 213–35), that offers a resumé of the course. An electronic version of the book was published in 2012 by *L'association pour le Centre Michel Foucault*: https://monoskop.org/images/9/99/Foucault_Michel_Il_faut_defendre_la_societe.pdf.

[22]The development of the Spanish colonial system offers a variation on the theme of the relation between absolutist state and colonies in the organization of social relations of knowledge production. Spanish universities, though never wholly integrated into the workings of the absolutist state, were central to defining its purpose and limits. It was at the University of Salamanca's Council of Geographers that Columbus pleaded his case for sponsorship to Isabelle of Castille and Ferdinand of Aragon; there as well that Francisco de Vitoria, drawing from Spanish Dominicans, made a colonialist's case for freedom to travel, which legitimized Spanish incursions into Indian society, endorsed the forced travels of Africans slaves; and underpinned, a century before Grotius's *De jure belli ac pacis* (1625), a state-based idea of freedom in the world. In colonies, the Spanish state delegated to colleges and universities created by Catholic orders the tasks of catholicizing and Hispanicizing the native population; of developing amiable relations with the sons of former "ruling class," to control the native masses; with filling local needs for educated specialists who could educate officials to be in charge of the administration and the Catholic clergy and thus help to administer colonies. Spanish colleges and universities also exported the inquisition to colonies, hearing confessions and keeping records of them. In all, fifteen colleges and universities were established in the Americas during the Spain's colonial period. All were mandated by the state and administered by Catholic orders, privileged subjects of *libertas scolastica*. Between the Spanish conquest and Bolivarian wars, "Spanish universities in the new world conferred 150,000 academic degrees" (Ashby 1966: 10). See Crum (2016); Charria Salamanca (2016); and Silverblatt (2007).

to instruct *colons* to be better believers and more productive farmers or to occupy modest role as minor clerks in *colonies*' administration.

It was only in the eighteenth century that the French state began to concern itself with organizing social relations of knowledge production—and then only with consideration for the training of architects and engineers, the *corps de métier* responsible for designing with drawing up plans for colonial fortifications and "regular cities ... with parade grounds and caserns."[23] The founding of the École Royale du Génie de Mézières (1748) and the École Royale des Ponts et Chaussée (1747), despite their narrow focus, marked in this respect an important change in the relations between the state and higher education in France. Though instructions at these institutions drew minimally from a set *curriculum* and prioritized practical over scholarly learning, both detached learning away from trades and corporations, instead aligning it with state- and empire-building. In many ways, this prefigured what would happen to knowledge production in the latter part of the nineteenth century. Similarly, the École Militaire de Paris (1750), though initially lacking a formal teaching program or dedicated faculty, did conceive of the training of soldiers in utilitarian terms as worthwhile both in itself and for the making of national society. To broaden the social basis of the state, the École adhered to strict yet inclusive admission criteria (what would now be called "positive discrimination"), favoring specific categories of students, ranging from the sons of impoverished nobility to soldiers' orphans (Laulan 1957; Chapron 2014).[24]

After the revolution, the French State suppressed the corporatist privileges of guilds and religious orders (Nourrisson 1928), and it began to invest itself in *éducation publique*—a term first used by Mirabeau in 1790.[25] Religious colleges and *écoles centrales* were replaced by *lycées* (Brambilla 2009) and universities—dismissed by d'Alembert as absurd institutions useful only to a small number of citizens (Didier 1995: 84) and by Diderot as "centers of scholastic futility" (Chouillet 1985: 52)—were abolished altogether during in 1793, during the *terreur.* In their stead, more purposeful *grandes écoles* were established to create the class of experts that was deemed indispensable

[23]« Tracer les rues d'une ville régulière avec sa place d'arme, ses casernes, etc. » is taken from Guillaume Leblond, « Éléments de fortification à l'usage des jeunes officiers (1742) » cited in Guillerme (1989: 72).

[24]Volume V of the *Encyclopédie ou Dictionnaire raisonné des sciences, des arts et des métiers*, devoted a long, praising article to the École militaire de Paris that emphasized its public utility function. A searchable, "digital, collaborative and critical" version of the *Encyclopédie* is available on the website of the *Bibliothèque Nationale de France*: http://enccre.academie-sciences.fr/encyclopedie/.

[25]Mirabeau's « Travail sur l'éducation publique » is reprinted in Bronislaw Baczko *Textes et projets de l'époque révolutionnaire. Présentation, notices d'introduction et notes* (Droz 1982: 71–104), alongside Condorcet (1792: 177–257). Condorcet's argument in favor of school reform is most thoroughly laid out in *Cinq mémoires sur l'instruction publique* (1791), reprinted in Yastrebtseva (2015: 10).

to the proper functioning of society and empire (d'Irsay, 1933, 171; Marga 2006: 429): the École centrale des travaux publics (1794), the École spéciale de médecine (1794), the École Normale (1795), the École des Mines (1793), the École spéciale des langues orientales (1795), the Écoles supérieure de pharmacie (1803), the École Centrale des Arts et Manufactures (1829), the Institut d'agronomie (1876), the École Supérieure de Télégraphie (1878), the École des Hautes études Commerciales (1881), the École Supérieure d'Électricité (1894), and others. The expansion of this system followed the logic of functional specialization: "Whenever the need for a new kind of specialist was felt, it was met with the establishment of another teaching institution" (Weisz 1983: 20–21). The Académie Française, abolished in 1793, was reinstated in 1803 and integrated into the Institut national des sciences et des arts (1795). The École normale supérieure was created in 1808 to prepare students for scientific research, admission into *grandes écoles*, and for high positions in state service.

To give direction to the "public mind" and provide the French State with means not only to construct bridges, train linguists and instruct soldiers in the arts of war, but also to "direct political and moral opinions," Napoléon reinstated universities—initially as an abstract body of people "exclusively responsible for public teaching and education throughout the Empir[e]," and then as a loose collection of individual faculties (of theology, medicine, law, sciences, and letters) under administrative supervision. As part of a broad revamping of higher education, two *ancient régime* academies (the Académie des Sciences and the Académie des Beaux-Arts) were also reinstated, as was the statewide system of tenure (*habilitation*), which had remained untouched since the thirteenth century.

By the end of Napoléon's second reign (1815), the principal institutions of France's knowledge production system—*lycées*, *collèges*, *grande écoles*, *instituts*, *musées*, *bureau*, and so on—had been put in place, with a rough division of labor between them. Coordinating it was the Université Impériale (1808), which took as its model the "well-oiled organizational and pedagogical coherence" of Jesuit colleges.[26] Academic freedom had no place in that system apart from the freedom of expression and thought instituted by the Declaration of the Rights of Man and of the Citizen.

During the short Bourbon restoration (1815–1830), *grandes écoles* and universities most closely associated with *bonapartisme* were closed altogether. Professors were suspended, and student movements put under tight surveillance: "only complete political submission was acceptable" (Anderson 2004: 740).

In 1850, the loi Falloux instituted a modest form of autonomy for lycée-level teachers, but it was only during the first years of the Third Republic

[26]Translated from the *Loi relative à la formation d'une université impériale, et aux obligations particulières des membres du corps enseignant* (May 10, 1806) available from https://www.persee.fr/doc/inrp0000-00002000ant2318831.

(1870–1940) that French universities were transformed—"in their body and in their soul" wrote Louis Liard—and established as defining institutions of a new system of knowledge production linked to state-building and the development of France's second overseas empire in Indochina, Africa, and the Caribbean.[27] At the *lycée* level, a new genus of specialized school was created to answer demands for practical learning from a new middle class of merchants and colonial administrators (Chapoulie and Briand 2019). Henceforth considered a mundane activity—on par with dancing or associated with the vulgar skills of commerce—the study of language was integrated into the *curriculum* and began to be thought as a form of knowledge in itself (Pouly 2007).

In higher education, the key legislation was the 1875 *Loi sur la liberté de l'enseignement supérieur*, the centerpiece of a broad reform of national education. It allowed for the creation of private universities, restored the autonomy of universities, and established free and equal faculties—with no special role reserved for the faculty of theology—urging them to "live and act: *vivez et agissez*" (Weisz 1983: 83). In 1896, the *Loi relative à la constitution des Universités* replaced the Université Impériale—which had never been more than an administrative instance—with a coordinated system of research universities modeled after the German system (Weisz 1983:3).[28] In all, fifteen universities were created (or re-established in the case of the Université de Paris). Each was a singular product of particular circumstances: In Lyon, it was the municipal council that called for the regrouping of faculties into a university; in Clermont-Ferrand and Bordeaux, professors pushed for same; in Montpellier, the university came as a by-product of celebrations held on the occasion of the 600th anniversary of the foundation of the scholastic university (established in 1289, abolished in 1793); and in Dijon, it was the municipal council which took the lead in the founding of the university. Everywhere, the master word was usefulness (*utilité*) and a utilitarian idea of *academic freedom* subsumed the instituting of higher learning to the development of society (Charle 2018).

In colonies, usefulness was a function of valorization. The disciplining of teaching by "colonial science"—"a most useful and practical science," which began installing itself in the *curricula* of metropolitan universities in the 1830s (Singaravélou 2009: 89)—and the modest development of universities—the Université d'Alger (1906) and the Université Indochinoise

[27]Louis Liard was a philosopher and educational reformer. He served as Director of Higher Education (1884–1902) during the Third Republic and later as Vice-Rector of the Sorbonne. He is cited here from *L'enseignement supérieur en France*, his major work, in Liard (1890: vi).

[28]In the context of the *Loi relative à la constitution des Universités*, the term *coordination* should be understood in the broadest sense, as referring not to an integrated set of practices or mandated ways of doing, but to an idea of the university "[which] presented itself spontaneously and imposed itself on publicists and orators as the single adequate symbol of the task to be achieved" (Weisz 1983: 81).

(1909)—were means to tie the works of scholars-in-training to France's *mission civilisatrice* (Goscha and Larcher 2016; Legrandjacques 2019).[29] *Academic freedom* in this context can only be understood as either a mirage or a tool of coloniality.

*

In the United States, the hodgepodge of "little sects and colleges" inherited from the early postcolonial period stayed enchanted worlds unto themselves, "full of poetry and the happy intellectual life of the young," until they were organized into a national system of technical-scientific production during Reconstruction (1865–1877).[30]

---

[29]The phrase "valorization of colonies" is taken from the "Politique Générale de mise en valeur des colonies" (1917) that signaled the French State's turn toward developmentalism. It is often associated with Jules Ferry who, after having starved the Commune (*dixit* Marx), headed the French Ministère de l'instruction publique, while serving as the chief propagandist of French colonial expansion. Everywhere, disciplines organized and hierarchized the works of scholars. In France, useful disciplines (sociology, finance, maritime law, child diseases, mental illness, comparative grammar, education science, applied mathematics, ethnology, mineralogy, etc.) installed themselves as defining instances of universities, first by means of the mass creation of professorial chairs (hundreds were instituted in the years immediately following the *Loi relative à la constitution des Universités*) and then as departments (Liard 1890: 52). Complementing the work of disciplines were all manners of study programs brought under the broad heading of colonial science, "a most useful and practical science" which in the 1880s began installing itself in the *curricula* of metropolitan universities and institutes. At the Faculté des lettres of the University of Paris, there was a section specialized in colonial history and a research chair in colonial geography, financed by the Undersecretariat of State for the Colonies. In 1899, the École coloniale was established as the first *grande école* specifically dedicated to teaching colonial administrators. At the École Libre des sciences politiques one-fifth of all courses were about colonies. Between 1899 and 1920, all nine French business schools opened colonial sections where practical teaching was provided. At the École de commerce in Lyon, there were courses on rice growing; at the College de France there were courses on colonial geography, colonial economy, and tropical studies. At the University of Bordeaux, a chair of colonial geography was created the city's chamber of commerce in 1899. The École vétérinaire (1917), the École Supérieure de pédagogie (1917), the École Pratique d'agriculture (1917), the École de sylviculture (1917–1918), and the Institut d'Ethnologie (created in 1925 by the Ministry of colonies) all offered courses dedicated to the administration or valorization of colonies. On this, see Singaravélou (2009: 90).

[30]"[A]nyone with a charter could start a college in their own religious community and many did just that … by the time John Brown made his raid [1859] there were in the United States 182 colleges and universities" (Levine 2021: 24). Among them were the New College, established (1636) by Congregational puritans in the Commonwealth of Massachusetts, renamed three years later for pastor John Harvard, who bequeathed it his library; the College of William & Mary, founded by Episcopalian Anglicans (1693) in the colony of Virginia; the Collegiate School, founded (1701) by Congregational puritans in New Heavens, Connecticut, and renamed for benefactor Elihu Yale in 1718, fallen administrator of the British East India Company; King's College, founded by the Church of England (1754) and renamed Columbia after the American Revolution; and Queen's College, founded by Calvinists (1771), and renamed after benefactor Henry Rutgers (1825).

Congressman Justin Smith Morrill of Vermont is a figure of reference of that transition. In December 1857, Congressman Morrill—acting as Chairman of the Standing Committee on Agriculture—introduced legislation to create a national program by which Congress would "endow a system of industrial universities" aimed at increasing the worldwide competitiveness of the United States. To that effect Congressman Morrill also sponsored an increase in import duties—the so-called Morill Tariff. In the impossible days of the Kansas outrage—"the beginning of the end of slavery" (Gilman 1867: 502)—Morrill's bill could not muster the two-thirds majority required to override President Buchanan's veto and become law.

Within months of Abraham Lincoln's election in November 1860, all eleven slave-holding states of the South had seceded, giving impetus to state-building in the North. The Act Donating Public Lands to the Several States and Territories which may provide Colleges for the Benefit of Agriculture and the Mechanic Arts was passed by Congress and signed into law on July 2, 1862. To "arrest the deterioration and spoliation of the soil in America," the Morrill Act encouraged "economic development through research" and expanded opportunities for everyone—"but especially to the sons of toil"—to receive training in "such branches of learning as are related to agriculture and the mechanic arts, in such manner as the legislatures of the States may respectively prescribe, in order to promote the liberal and practical education of the industrial classes in the several pursuits and professions in life." Land was awarded in proportion to each state's representation in the Congress (30,000 acres for every senator and representative), with "at least one college [established] in every state."[31] "Now all the states would have universities ... in exchange for producing educated farmers, scientists, and engineers who would ensure the competitiveness of their states and [of] the United States" (Levine 2021: 35).

Land-grant colleges are "the most famous products of the industrial movement in education" in the United States (Hofstadter and Metzger 1955: 380). What are now customarily referred to as "1862 institutions" comprise a mixed group: preexisting colleges that were granted land to expand or reestablish themselves (e.g., New Haven's School of Forestry and Natural Resources, which was later incorporated into Yale University; Newark's College of Agricultural Science, later incorporated into the University of Delaware; Burlington's College of Agriculture and Life Sciences, later part of the University of Vermont); colleges founded between the passage of the Morrill Act and the end of the Civil War (e.g., Kansas's College of Agriculture; New York's College of Agriculture and Life Sciences; Maine's College of Natural Resources, Forestry and Agriculture); colleges

[31]The text of the Morill Act (1862) can be found online on the site of the National Archives: https://www.archives.gov/milestone-documents/morrill-act. In the same spirit as Morill, President Lincoln established the National Academy of Science (1862), "to enlist the expertise of elite natural scientists in the service of the state" (Lewontin 1997: 10).

established during Reconstruction—largely on land expropriated from Indigenous people (e.g., the East Florida Seminary, later incorporated into the University of Florida; the Franklin College of Arts and Sciences, later incorporated into the University of Georgia; the University of Mississippi; the Virginia Agricultural and Mechanical College, later incorporated as the Virginia Polytechnic Institute and State University).[32]

Acting "in fact if not in name" as national schools of science (Gilman 1867: 497), the 1862 institutions served as "the scientific arm of the state" (James 1905: 623–27). Complementing their labor was a varied lot of privately endowed schools and colleges, technical colleges, and institutes (e.g., West Point, the Rensselaer Polytechnic Institute, the Worcester Polytechnic, the Massachusetts Institute of Technology, the Stevens Institute of Technology); institutions reserved for Afro-Americans, referred to in insight as historically Black colleges and universities (e.g., Howard Normal and Theological School for the Education of Teachers and Preachers, later as Howard University, Tuskegee Normal School for Colored Teachers, later Tuskegee University; the Atlanta Baptist Female Seminary, that became Spelman College; the Fisk School, later Fisk University; the State Normal College for Colored Students, later incorporated as Florida A&M University); and women's colleges, also eligible for capacity grants (e.g., Vassar, Wellesley, Radcliffe, Mount Holyoke, Bryn Mawr, Smith, Spelman, and Barnard).[33]

Giving coherence of purpose to this "[i]ncreasingly scientific, utilitarian, and professional" system of higher education was an implicit notion of institutional autonomy, operationalized through the elective system "duly installed [in] all universities and colleges worthy of the name" (Mills 1969: 40). First introduced at Harvard in 1869, it gave young men who were "eager to find gratuitous help toward a specific career" (Veblen 2015 [1918]: 171), the freedom to choose among courses organized into disciplines (Mills 1969: 53) and freedom from "administrative coercions in the learning situation" (Hofstadter and Metzger 1955: 387)—*lernfreiheit* in the American context. *Lehrfreiheit*—the freedom to teach and conduct research—remained unarticulated, even at John Hopkins University (1876), which is largely acknowledged as the first modern research university in the United States (Levine 2021: 26).

Only at the beginning of the twentieth century—during the "age of reform" brought about by the rise of financial capital and the concomitant end of isolationism (Hofstadter and Metzger 1955)—did the idea of academic freedom take a more explicit form in the United States. Meeting

---

[32]For a detailed chronology, see Table 1-1 "Locations and Names of 1862 and 1890 Land Grant Colleges of Agriculture and Related Colleges and Schools of Forestry and Veterinary Medicine" in National Research Council (1995). About land-grant universities as "land-grab universities," see McCoy et al. (2021) and Stewart-Ambo (2021).

[33]Upward of 120 women's colleges are estimated to have been created in the United States between the end of the Civil War and the First World War (Harwarth et al. 1997).

in December 1915, just a few months after the sinking of the *Lusitania*, the nascent American Association of University Professors (AAUP) endorsed a "Declaration of Principles on Academic Freedom and Academic Tenure" that put forth a wholly utilitarian idea of academic freedom. It emphasized privileges accruing to titular professors from their specific responsibilities

> [t]o investigate truth, critically to verify facts; to reach conclusions by means of the best methods at command, untrammeled by external fears or favor, to communicate this truth to the student, to interpret to him its bearing on questions he will have to face in life.
>
> (Dewey et al. 2003)[34]

From those responsibilities followed: freedom of inquiry and research; freedom of teaching within the university or college; and freedom of extramural utterance and action.[35]

The AAUP's 1940 "Statement of Principles on Academic Freedom and Tenure" further details and qualifies this professional understanding of academic freedom, removing it further from social relations of knowledge production, and instead inscribing it in a contract-like relationship between professors and the state:

> Teachers are entitled to full freedom in research and in the publication of the results, subject to the adequate performance of their other academic duties; but research for pecuniary return should be based upon an understanding with the authorities of the institution. ... Teachers are entitled to freedom in the classroom in discussing their subject, but they should be careful not to introduce into their teaching controversial matter which has no relation to their subject. Limitations of academic freedom because of religious or other aims of the institution should be clearly stated in writing at the time of the appointment. ... College and university teachers are citizens, members of a learned profession, and officers of an educational institution. When they speak or write as citizens, they

[34]Three firings in particular have direct bearing on the founding of the AAUP: that of historian Edward Bemis, dismissed in 1895 from the University of Chicago for his views on foreign policy, which ran afoul of those of William Rainey Harper, the university's funder; that of Edward A. Ross, a professor of economics at Stanford University, fired in 1900 following pressure from Dorothy Jane Sanford, widow of railroad baron Leland Stanford, the university's founder, for his opposition to the use of immigrant labor in constructing California's railroads; and that of Scott Nearing, dismissed in 1915 by University of Pennsylvania's Board of Trustees for his outspoken opposition to American militarism and imperialism.

[35]Remarkably in a context defined by the rise of anti-German sentiment following the sinking of the *Lusitania*, the AAUP's 1915 Declaration was never denounced for its relationship to Humboldt or to German state-building, except obliquely by the American Defense Society, which encouraged vigilance against professors or intellectuals suspected of espousing German ideas or sympathizing with the enemy. On this, see Wilcox (1993).

> should be free from institutional censorship or discipline, but their special position in the community imposes special obligations. As scholars and educational officers, they should remember that the public may judge their profession and their institution by their utterances. Hence they should at all times be accurate, should exercise appropriate restraint, should show respect for the opinions of others, and should make every effort to indicate that they are not speaking for the institution.

*

As the world-system of territorial states reached its achieved form in the latter half of the nineteenth century, categories through which social relations could be rendered visible and actionable—thus giving concrete form to what James Scott described as the state's drive to make society legible (Scott 1998)—were defined in national systems of knowledge production. In adequation with the dynamics of world ordering, these systems were organized hierarchically, allowing for relations of knowledge production to be fixed and reproduced, everywhere according to the limits and possibilities set by local configurations of authority, and by positions occupied in the international division of labor, trade, and power. At the apex of this hierarchy were research universities in core countries. There, *academic freedom* defined the broadly inclusive conditions under which *scholars* deemed useful to the proper functioning of state and empire could enter into relatively autonomous, disciplined, and purposeful relations with one another. To see what values they upheld beyond those linked to the subsuming of relations between the people of the world under the dynamics of inter-state relations—what freedom scholars, in effect, gave form to beyond *academic freedom*—we have to look into moments of action.

*

The Wartburg Book Burning (1817)

Anathema as book burning may seem to the work of scholars, it is nevertheless intrinsically linked to the manner in which modern knowledge in and of the world was constituted. From the burning of a million books and manuscripts on the Plaza de Bib-Rambla at the end of the Spanish *Reconquista* (Lowenthal and Hamilton 1987: 7) to that of Indigenous codices in the Americas (Grosfoguel 2013: 80), the act of consigning books to fire was part of the making of the modern world-system of states and universities and, thus, of the initial ordering of scholarly relations within the world-system. These events signaled a foundational expunging of memory and revealed a feral, undomesticated sort of freedom that was later circumscribed by the instituting of *academic freedom*.

The 1817 Wartburg festival was two-days' long commemoration of the tricentenary of Martin Luther's pining of ninety-five theses to the door of the Castle Church (*Schlosskirche*) in Wittenberg. Luther was a professor of moral theology at the University of Wittenberg, and his pinning was, explicitly, an invitation to a *disputatio* (*Disputatio pro declaratione virtutis indulgentiarum*), prefaced in a most scholarly manner:

> Out of love for the truth and from desire to elucidate it, the Reverend Father Martin Luther, Master of Arts and Sacred Theology, and ordinary lecturer therein at Wittenberg, intends to defend the following statements and to dispute on them in that place.

Disputations were defining moments of scholarly life in medieval universities (Le Goff 2013: 101). At Wittenberg, the doors of the Castle Church were frequently used for such purpose, by Luther himself as well as others. How strong the answer of the academic community to a particular invitation was a measure of a professor's reputation and of the ability of his peers to constitute themselves into a happening assembly of scholars. The disputation that was to have followed Luther's posting of the Ninety-Five Theses never took place—not for lack of academic interest but for the opening by Archbishop von Hohenzollern of an inhibitory process against the "presumptuous monk" (Mullett 2014: 104). This led Gabriele della Volta, head of the Augustinian Order, to censor Luther. In 1520, Pope Leo X issued a bull (*Exsurge Domine*) that officially condemned forty-one of Luther's theses and threatened him with excommunication.[36]

Three centuries later, the Wartburgfest commemorated Luther's pinning of his theses, alongside the fourth anniversary of the Battle of Leipzig—harbinger of Napoleon's eventual defeat at Waterloo. It took place at a critical juncture, at the beginning of the transformation of the German-speaking world from a loose ensemble of distinct polities into modern bureaucratic state (Levine 2021: 12). This broad political shift coincided with efforts to organize medieval universities—plagued by "professorial absenteeism … student brawling … intellectual conservatism" and facing competition from protestant academies—into a national system of knowledge production centered on modern research universities (Grendler 2004: 23, 26).

[36]The first *disputatio* to follow the pinning of Luther's theses happened in Heidelberg in 1518, on the occasion of the triennial of the German branch of the Augustinian order. In 1519 the Liepzig *disputatio* involved Luther; Johan Eck, Professor of theology at the University of Ingolstadt; Nicolaus von Amsdorf, Wittenberg Professor of theology; and Andreas Karlstadt, Dean of Theology at the University of Wittenberg. Luther was excommunicated by papal bulb (*Decet Romanum Pontificem*) in 1520.

This was the context in which German students, traditionally organized into *Korporationen* and *Landsmannschaftens*—both descendants of medieval corporations and "wholeheartedly devoted to the particularistic concepts of the individual German principality of which their members were nationals"—began organizing themselves into a political movement of liberal-minded, reform-oriented, fraternities: the *Burschenschaften*. The first was founded in Jena in 1814 by veterans of the campaign against Napoléon. In 1815 and 1816, the movement spread to all major universities in German-speaking states (Eyck 1955: 27). By 1817, *burschenschaft* had become the principal organization of German students. In 1818 the Allied German Federation of Burschenschaft (*Allgemeine Deutsche Burschenschaft*) was founded to agitate for national liberal state; "love of Fatherland was its 'guiding principle'" (Anderson 2004: 74).

On October 18, 1817, the Jena *Burschenschaft* organized a festival at Wartburg castle near Eisenach (Luther's hideout in 1521). Roughly 500 students participated—mostly *burschenschafters* but also a minority of *landsmannschaftens* and some *korps* sporting "old German" dress and long flowing hair parted in the middle, in the manner of Albrecht Dürer (Leerssen 2011: 261). Styling themselves participants in a "holy war" for the German nation (Clark 1996: 552), they marched in processions, and sang hymns and patriotic songs celebrating Luther, the Reformation, and victory in the Battle of Leipzig.

The first day of the Wartburgfest was largely spent on "the drafting of utopian resolutions and constitutions, the writing of fiery and gory poetry, and the signing of ineffective petitions" (Eyck 1955: 28). Two manifestos were adopted. The first bore a long-winded title that in translation would read: "Principles and resolutions of October 18, generally debated, thoroughly considered, unanimously approved, and presented to the fellow-students for approval and to the whole fatherland for appraisal." The second manifesto was titled "Basic features of a future German constitution." In the evening, Friedrich Ludwig Jahn (emblematic figure of the allied gymnastic and student movement) led a small group of students to a peripheral bonfire commemorating Luther's burning of *Exsurge Domine* (Fishburn 2008: 6).[37] Into the fire went books considered un-German—for the most part works opposed to Jahn's gymnastics movement (Press 2009: 633)—as well as "various symbols of absolutism and French influence" (Anderson 2004: 73): an Austrian corporal's cane, a *Code Napoléon*, a uniform from the Uhlans cavalry, and a pigtail from a Hessian officer's wig (Lutz 1976: 5; Ritchie 1988: 628).

A modest event that "took place miles away from the Wartburg castle on an unremarkable hill, at the behest of a middle-aged man and with the

[37]Luther himself, of course, was subject of notable book burnings in Louvain, Cologne, and London. The latter, organized by Henry VIII in the churchyard of St. Paul's Cathedral, was the first public book burning in England. On this, see Fishburn (2008: 6) and Cressy (2005: 362).

hands of fewer than six students" (Press 2009: 623), the Wartburg book burning was nonetheless telling as a moment during which revolutionary romanticism fused with youthful excesses to define the term of a rough sort of scholarly freedom closer in spirit to the hard-drinking and dueling of *landsmannschafters* than the modern understanding of academic freedom (Ray Lutz 1971: 216; Mazón 2003: 32–35).

After Karl Ludwig Sand—a Waterloo veteran and founding member of the *Burschenschaft Teutonia*—assassinated August von Kotzebue, whose books had been burned at Wartburg, the diet of the German Confederation leaned on the pretext of a far-reaching conspiracy to overthrow the government to adopt the Carlsbad Decrees (1819), that delayed constitutional reforms and curtailed freedom of speech. Made subject to niggardly disciplining—in 1820 the Jena *Burschenschaft* was forbidden from singing in the town square—and confined to little gestures of protests, in 1821, Jena students did just what was forbidden, gathering *en masse* to give "three cheers for the German fatherland and three cheers for academic freedom" (Ray Lutz 1971: 229–30)—their organization outlawed and their leadership imprisoned (Mazón 2003: 43), *Burschenschafters* retreated into an ethos of "honorable students" (Jarausch 2012: 83, 87), metamorphosing from "schoolboy to citizen of the academic community" (Jarausch 2012: 85).

When the fascist state in Germany foreclosed all possibilities for scholarly autonomy, the wild, spontaneous freedom of Wartburg repeated itself as a meticulously orchestrated, photographed and filmed, spectacle.[38] Again, events were consciously organized to emulate Luther's burning of *Exsurge Domine* (Fishburn 2008: 32), and again they unfolded as explicitly academic affairs initiated by students and professors, "the putative guardians of cultivated *bildung*, of civilized values and of the scholarly culture of the books" (Aschheim 2012: 118).

The *auto-da-fé* of May 10, 1933, in Berlin began with "great ranks of students [b]olstered by uniformed brown shirts of the SA and marching bands" proceeding in a torchlight parade toward Opera square (Opernplatz), across from Humboldt University (Fishburn 2008: 32).[39] A crowd of perhaps 40,000, politely tucked away behind "two ranks of photographers and film-makers" (Fishburn 2008: xv), "stood in a drizzle to watch the show"

[38]The fascist State rejected self-administration as an organizing principle of university governance and cast academic freedom as a form of antisocial behavior. As much as one-fifth of professors and lecturers were fired or dismissed in the first four years of the Nazi regime—perhaps as much as a third in social sciences and economics (Ash 1997: 6; Paletscheck 2001). To fill vacancies, the Nazi state actively created dedicated new chairs of study, in such domains as racial science, racial hygiene, military history, folklore, and prehistory—the latter a hobby of Heinrich Himmler (Grüttner 2005: 90).

[39]After the war, Opernplatz was officially renamed Bebelplatz in honor of Arthur Bebel, a founding figure of Germany social democratic party. It is the site of "The Sunken Library," a memorial by Micha Ullman. Every year, Humboldt University students organize a book sale there.

(Birchall 1933: 1), as students performed the burning of approximately 20,000 books by authors deemed degenerate opponents of the regime. Mounted on "a tiny swastika-draped rostrum" (Birchall 1933: 12), Reich Propaganda Minister Joseph Goebbels addressed the crowd. Recalling Wartburg, he vilified "un-German" enemies of freedom (Eyck 1955: 28–29) and proclaimed "the death of Jewish intellectualism" (Birchall 1933: 1).

> Thus you do well, at this nocturnal hour, to commit the evil spirit of the past to the flames. That is a great, powerful, and symbolic act ... that will show the world: here the spiritual basis of the November Republic sinks to earth, but from these ruins, the phoenix of spirit will rise victorious
>
> (Lowenthal and Hamilton 1987: 10)

That night and in the days that followed, *Burschenschaft* students staged book burnings at thirty universities across the Reich—"on the *Römerberg* in Frankfurt; the *Schlossplatz* in Stuttgart; the *Königsplatz* in Munich; and in Bonn, Dresden, Göttingen, Hamburg, Heidelberg" (Aschheim 2012: 117). Everywhere they followed the Berlin script (Norwood 2009: 7) "including marching parades, torches and speeches" (Fishburn 2008: 32). And everywhere, "particular attention was paid ... to the careful selection of suitable speakers to give academic tone to the proceedings" (Ritchie 1988: 638). They were professors and students who kindled the flames, "not the *Volk* of the people without a book, but precisely [the people] which lived by the book" (Ritchie 1988: 638). "Not a single university protested publicly" (Lowenthal and Hamilton 1987: 17).

The only university that was not theatre to an *auto-da-fé* was that Freiburg, where Rector Martin Heidegger gave his now (in)famous address on "The self-assertion of the German University" in which he called upon the faculty to remain true to the intersecting essences of academia and the German nation, urging them reject academic freedom as "ungenuine and only negative" (Heidegger et al. 1985: 471). True freedom, Heidegger argued, was forward-looking: it bound professors and students to "Knowledge Service," the intellectual counterpart to Labor and Armed services (Heidegger, Harries, and Heidegger 1985: 477).

After the Second World War, the Allied Military Government in Germany signed Order No. 4 on the "Confiscation of Literature and Material of a Nazi and Militarist Nature," which prohibited "works that promoted Nazism, fascism, militarism, racism, *völkisch* ideas, anti-democratic views, and civil disorder" (Peiss 2019: 146–47). In a directive that must have "sounded most familiar to the Germans" (Anon 1946), it "required schools, universities, and public libraries, as well as booksellers and publishers, to remove ... works from their shelves and deliver them to Allied authorities" to be "placed at the disposal of the Military Zone commanders for destruction" (Peiss 2019: 147). This prompted fears of what the *Wall Street Journal* termed a "bigger and better book burning" (Chamberlin 1946).[40]

No Women at Cambridge (1897)

In her conclusion to *Knowledge Across Cultures*, Ruth Hayhoe noted the "remarkable historical coincidence" of the simultaneous exclusion of women from formal participation in scholarship in Southern Song academies and early European universities (2001: 330–31). Had she looked into doings in the *Dar al-Islam* that she would have seen another iteration of gendered segregation: during the Ayyubid dynasty, growth in *waqfs* reinforced a "complex and uneven" (Berkey 1992: 162) separation of men and women as patrons, managers, caretakers, and beneficiaries of endowed *madrasas* (Islahi 2018).

Following the analyses of Sylvia Federici (2004) and Maria Mies (1986), the simultaneous parting of genders in the *world-economies* of China, Europe, and the *Dar al-Islam* appears less a coincidence than an early modality of the gendered separation of production from reproduction. Everywhere specific—rooted in the Ming's state reliance on patrilineal kinship in China; in the efforts of lords, patrician merchants, bishops, and popes in Europe to contain antifeudal struggles; and in territorial politics in the *Dar al-Islam*—this separation everywhere testified to the beginnings of the fixing of social relations to place.

In the emerging world-system of states, gendered segregation in knowledge production was shaped by the doings of a myriad of relatively independent academies, institutes, and laboratories. Men and women were differentiated as both bearers and object of science: "as gynecological knowledge became 'scientific', women ceased to be mid-wives, while men became obstetricians" (Applebaum 2000: 465).

Liberal-colonial world ordering was the political expression of the international division of labor. As the bureaucratic state took charge of reproducing social relations, it also defined the ways through which gendering structured social relations of knowledge production. In Germany, women were widely admitted in public universities (Mazón 2000), yet the intertwining of academic and national citizenships set higher education apart as a man's domain (Mazón 2003). In France, gender segregation was governed by discipline. Medicine, for instance, was the privileged domain

[40]The Allied aim to make German citizens active participants in their own denazification was eroded by petty infighting between the agencies charged with implementing Order No. 4, as well as by mounting protests in the United States. In the end, Order No. 4 fizzled in the aimless "amassing of books" (Peiss 2019: 164).

of women, as was the case in Belgium and Switzerland (Tikhonov Sigrist 2009: 62). In the United States, gender segregation took form during Reconstruction, through the establishment of women's colleges.

In England, the place of women within the national system of knowledge production—broadly delimited by Victorian idea of gendered spheres—varied according to institutional proximity to the state. Civic universities admitted women sooner in greater numbers (Gibert 1994: 407). There, gender segregation was governed by disciplinary boundaries as well as by unwritten, sometimes capricious rules "which university authorities simply took for granted" (Gibert 1994: 409). At the University College of London, for instance, women were permitted to study in the Faculties of Arts, Law, and Science but were barred from Engineering and Medicine—with the exception of courses in public health and hygiene.

Functioning as autonomous worlds unto themselves, scholastic universities maintained an inherent kind of gender separation through practices going-on in academic clubs, literary and debating societies, and through performative codes of dress and conduct.

> We were asked always to wear gloves in town. ... We must not ... take a boat out on the river in the daytime unless accompanied by a chaperon who must be either a married woman or one of the college dons.
>
> (Gibert 1994: 405)

At Cambridge, access to lectures was sometimes left to the discretion of individual professors. Physiologist Michael Foster and anatomist G. M. Murphy allowed women to attend their courses, but only in galleries overlooking the lecture hall, where "they sat modestly ... in a little row by themselves" (Marsha 1997: 447). In Frank Balfour's lectures on embryology and animal morphology, "men and women were squeezed together" (Marsha 1997: 425). At Trinity College women could attend Henry Sidgwick's lectures "provided it were fixed at an hour when there would be no crowding on the staircase" (Tullberg 1975: 71).

At both Oxford and Cambridge, more formal segregation took shape as Britain's system of knowledge production was being consolidated and academic freedom instituted to regulate social relations of knowledge production, through the creation of separate colleges that formed "alternative communities" of women scholars (Vicinus 1985). At Oxford, there were Lady Margaret Hall (1878); Sommerville College (1879); St. Hugh's College (1886); and St. Hilda's College (1893); at Cambridge, Girton College (1869) and Newnham College (1871). All were founded in the wake of the failed "Ladies' Petition for Women's Suffrage," during a critical period of "deadlock and discouragement," when the women's emancipation movement was "quietly withdrawing" from the ineffective politics of representation and redirecting its energies toward the defense of more consensual, middle-class values of education (Strachey 1928: 283).[41]

Becoming the fulcrum of women's struggle, the question of access to higher education was made into an issue of national concern by "the domination of public life by Oxford and Cambridge men" (Tullberg 1975: 14). At its core was the struggle for degrees at Cambridge, "a man's university" and, as such, the custodian of a "world-famed tradition" (Man 1897).

The pivotal figure here is Emily Davies, a leading member of the London National Society for Women's Suffrage. Following the defeat of the 1866 suffrage petition in Parliament, she cofounded Girton College—the first residential college in England to offer women a university-level education in 1869 and served as its Mistress from 1873 to 1875.

---

[41] After a very public campaign, notable in part for its strategic use of printed media, the issue of women's suffrage became in the 1860s "the subject of a major national debate " (Bostick 1980: 131). John Stuart Mill presented the "Ladies' Petition for Women's Suffrage" to the House of Commons in June 1866. A year later, Parliament voted to reject it, prompting the women's movement strategic move away from the politics of representation toward education. This move built on as association that Emily Davies had already made. In *The Higher Education of Women*, written and published after the "Ladies' Petition for Women's Suffrage" has been presented in the House of Commons, but before Parliament had voted on it, she had made an argument for the full inclusion of women in higher education, which was at once strategic in its emphasis that only by leaning on the full contribution of educated women could the British state fulfill its mission, and far-reaching in arguing that only by developing "the habit of impartiality and deliberation—of surveying a wide field of thought—and of penetrating, so far as human eye can see, into the heart of things" could women ever develop the "attitude of mind favourable for the consideration of complicated questions of any sort" and thus carry out the missions which were in keeping with the limits and possibilities of their gendered selves (Davies 1866: 44–45). Wrapped in Victorian utilitarianism were arguments for scholarly autonomy and rigor that Chu Hsi would not have repudiated.

"Women who think at all can scarcely help thinking about the condition of the poor, and to arrive at sound conclusions on so vast a subject involves an acquaintance more or less complete with almost every consideration which comes within the range of the politician. Unpaid work, such as the management of hospitals, workhouses, prisons and reformatories, and charitable societies, naturally devolves upon the leisurely classes, and offers a field in which cultivated women may fitly labour. And the moment they enter upon such work or attempt in any way to alleviate the sufferings of the poor, they find that a strong, clear head is as necessary as a warm heart.

"Sanitary laws and regulations have been enacted, and no doubt with good effect, but boards of health and inspectors can do but little without the intelligent co-operation of the women, on whom it depends to enforce personal and household hygiene in every family. Many other social questions might be mentioned on which women are required to know and to act," (Davies 1866: 44–45).

In 1880, a "Memorial for Grace"—in effect, a petition to amend the university's governing statutes—was circulated in the Newcastle area by William Steadman Aldis, Professor of Mathematics at Durham College, and his wife, Mary Aldis, an astronomer and prominent advocate for women's admission to Durham. The petition called on Cambridge's Senate to grant properly qualified women the rights: (i) to attend courses (hitherto a privilege left to the discretion of individual professors); (ii) to sit for Tripos examinations (for which women were only allowed to register by special permission); (iii) to participate fully in the governance of the university (and thus become part of the Senate); and (iv) to earn degrees.[42] The petition gathered more than 8,000 signatures (Tullberg 1975: 73). A vote was passed in the Senate that granted women the right to attend classes and take examinations but not to participate in university governance or earn full degrees. This left Cambridge women who had fulfill degree requirements "with curious pieces of paper known as certificates of degrees ... and no letters after their names" (McWilliams-Tullberg 2014: 117).

Over the following decade, Cambridge received fifteen memorials concerning the question of granting degrees to qualified women (McWilliams-Tullberg 2014: 131). In 1896, "a veritable campaign was mounted" (Marsha 1997: 449). Among the memorial submitted, three called for granting women formal recognition of degrees but not participation in the self-governance of the university (Marsha 1997: 428–49). A syndicate was appointed to consider proposals, composed in majority of members viewed as being "in favor of full concessions to women" (Anon 1896). Of the fifteen memorials considered (McWilliams-Tullberg 2014: 131): three asked for formal admission to both examinations and degrees, two for admission to examinations, and the rest asked for admission to degrees (Tullberg 1975: 78–79).

Published in February 1897, the "Report of the Degrees for Women Syndicate" recommended that

> women who have done all that men are required to do, in the way of residence and examinations ... be admissible to the title of B.A. They are to pay the same fees for the titular degree that men pay for the full degree; but they are not thereby to acquire a Bachelor's rights. After three years they may pay the full M.A. fees, and receive the title of M.A., but they will acquire no vote in the Senate, no power to sit on committees, no right to use the library, the museums, or the laboratories of the University.

[42]"Previous Examinations" were first held in 1824. At inception, they consisted of examination in Greek and Latin. From the 1850s, disciplinary topics were added: Mathematics (1854). Both examinations were abolished in 1960 as part of a broad revision of matriculation requirements. "Tripos Examination," corresponded to honors. They too came to be defined by disciplines (McWilliams-Tullberg 2014: 13).

> If they have made valuable and original contributions to science or letters they may five years later aspire to the title of D.Sc. or D.Lit.
>
> (Anon 1897a: 609)

Against the majority proposal, a minority report argued for the continuation of segregation by means of granting women symbolic degrees bearing feminized titles—*Magistra in Litteris* and *Magistra in Scientia*—"which [could not] be mistaken for [degrees] conferred on men, and which, being of new invention, [had] no traditional associations, and no suggestion of privileges withheld" (Anon 1897a: 609).

"[T]wo thousand Cambridge men gave … their support" to the majority proposal and the issue came to a Senate vote on May 21, 1897 (McWilliams-Tullberg 2014: 137). On the day of the vote, "M.A.s streamed to Cambridge from all parts of the land to cast their votes" (McWilliams-Tullberg 2014: 141). Chartered trains carried alumni from King's Cross Station in London (Anon 1897b). A crowd gathered on Market Square. Undergraduates in boater hats attempted to break into Newnham College on nearby Regent Street, cheered on by men in mortar boards and gowns. A banner was hung from a balcony overlooking the square, quoting adapted from Shakespeare's *Much Ado About Nothing*: "Get you to Girton Beatrice, get you to Newnham. Here's no place for you maids."[43] Seemingly impervious to the Bard's ironic intent, another placard cited both *The Taming of the Shrew*'s Hortensio—a wingman to Petruchio, whose attempt at controlling his wife ended risibly with him confounding the sun and the moon—and from the comically bookish King of Navarre, who at the beginning of *Love's Labour's Lost* stated his thoughtless intent to separate scholarly pursuits from life itself:

> I see she's like to have neither cape nor gown
> No woman shall come within a mile of my court[44]

Another banner drolly aligned alliterative slogans with increasing emphasis:

> No gowns for the Girtonites!
> Non Plus the Newnhamites!!
> Frustrate the Feminine Fanatics!!!
> Prudent Proctors Prance on Physical Impossibilities!!!!
> Satisfied Angels Want to Supersede Beaten Apollos!!!!![45]

---

[43]The text of the banner is a play on a line delivered by Beatrice in Act 2 Scene 1: "Get you to heaven, Beatrice, get you to heaven; here's no place for you maids."

[44]An image of the flyer can be found in Griffin (2020). Griffin's article borrows its title from a 2019 exhibition at Cambridge's University Library, part of a line-up of exhibitions, events, and displays exploring the past, present, and future of women at Cambridge. On this, see https://www.cam.ac.uk/RiseEvents.

[45]An image of the flyer can be found at https://cudl.lib.cam.ac.uk/view/PR-UA-01897-POSTER/1.

Drawing on a recognizable figuration of the "new woman"—bearer of greater social freedom if not of the right to vote (Rubinstein 1977: 47)—the effigy of a red-hair, blue bloomer-wearing, woman cyclist was suspended from the window above Macmillan's bookshop on Market Square (Tullberg 1975: 138).[46]

When voting members of the Senate began to leave chambers, and it was announced that the motion to award women degrees had been defeated—by 1,713 votes to 662—"the huge roar of male voices could be heard for miles around[d]" (Smith 2022). On Market Square, shop windows were broken and a bonfire lit. "Pandemonium broke loose," an eyewitness recalled, as "a hail of fireworks and rotten eggs were thrown at the dons in celebration" (Smith 2022). "The noise of the explosions and the cheers and the counter-cheers were deafening" (Tullberg 1975: 139).[47] Caught up in events of its own making, the crowd overrode ruling class reserve, erupting in what could only be understood as the patriarchal lynching of a free woman's effigy. So violently was the cyclist taken down that "a piece of the balcony [was] carried with it" (Anon 1897b). Once fallen, it was immediately trampled.

> The figure lost his (sic) head and hands and showed what it was made of. It was rushed away and on the Market-hill appeared on top of a cab, an excited mob of undergraduates surging below. The cabby struggles frantically, for about a dozen men were soon in the cab, on the top, and on the horse. After some persuasion, the cab with the remains of the figure, the bicycle, and the cabby on the top proceeded on a journey round the town, accompanied by horns blowing, wooden rattles, and discordant noises from human throats
>
> (Anon 1897b)

"[M]aimed and decapitated" the figure was pushed through the gates of Newnham College (Finan 2013) as women students inside looked on "disgusted and possibly terrified" (Ross 2020: 11).

---

[46]The Cambridge campaign happened in the brief moment when cycling was fashionable among upper-class women in England. In the late 1880s, the diamond frame, chain-driven safety bicycle on pneumatic tires had broadened the practice of cycling beyond the masculinist realm of the high-wheeled petty-farthing (Horton et al. 2016: 156). By the spring of 1895, cycling had begun to attract society ladies. For the following two years, "cycling was in vogue with fashionable people, including both British an Continental royalty. After 1897, the mass manufacturing of bicycles and lowering prices ended the short cycling craze for the upper class" (Rubinstein 1977: 49–55). "Bloomers"—the emblematic vestment of upper-class women cyclists—are named for American women's rights' activist Amelia Bloomer. In England, its wearing was defended by the Rational Dress Society (1881) renamed the Rational Dress League. In 1897, women were still prohibited from riding bicycles on the streets of Cambridge (Gibert 1994: 405).

[47]Tullberg cites an extra-special edition" of *Cambridge Weekly News* dedicated to the event, titled "The Triumph of Man."

A few months after events on Market Square, the self-consciously "law-abiding" National Union of Women's Suffrage Societies (NUWSS) was formed to lobby for political representation.[48] As principals of the Cambridge movement "turn[ed] from supporting higher education as the primary means of improving the position of women in British Society to advocating women's suffrage" (Marsha 1997: 451). The issue of degrees for women rescinded. Between 1897 and the First World War, "almost nothing was done by Cambridge University that might be interpreted as furthering the women's claim to membership" (Tullberg 1975: 143). Only after the Second World War did Cambridge began offering a full degree to women. It was the last institution of higher education in the UK to do so.[49]

The Reform Movement, Córdoba University (1918)

The Universidad Nacional de Córdoba (National University of Córdoba) has its roots in the Collegium Maximum, established in 1613 by Father Hernando Trejo y Sanabria, Bishop of Córdoba. Having begun in 1621 to offer course in higher education, the Collegium was granted authority to deliver diplomas in 1622 by Philip IV, King of Spain (Aroca 2017: 48). Its ability to define for itself the manner of its functioning, exceptional in the context of Spanish colonization administration (Haring 1963: 230), was a function of the relative autonomy of the Jesuit order *vis-à-vis* both the papacy and the Spanish state. As much as it emphasized the authority of its rectors, deans, and administrators, it also allowed—like other universities in Spanish colonies—for a remarkably strong participation of students in university governance.[50]

Two closely intertwined freedom were thus at play in Córdoba: that of ecclesiastic authorities to appoint and promote professors, establish

---

[48]Millicent Fawcett, a cofounder of Newnham College, served as NUWSS President from 1897 until the adoption in Parliament of the Representation of the People Act in 1918. In 1903, the more militant Women's Social and Political Union (WSPU) was formed. It adopted as its motto "Deeds not Words," echoing the watchword of "propaganda by deeds" adopted by the anarchist congress in London (1881).

[49]The first recipient of a Cambridge degree was the Queen Mother, who in 1848 received an honorary Doctorate of Law, her sixth from a British university.

[50]Four institutions of higher education were founded in Spanish colonies, all modeled on the Universidad de Salamanca (1218), which itself was inspired by the University of Bologna—the paradigmatic "republic of students": Regia y Pontificia Universidad de Santo Thomás de Aquino (the Royal and Pontifical University of St. Thomas Aquinas, 1538); Real y Pontificia Universidad de la Ciudad de los Reyes de Lima (the Royal and Pontifical University of the City of the Kings of Lima, 1551); and Real y Pontificia Universidad de México (the Royal and Pontifical University of Mexico (1551).

curricula, and so on, and that of students to engage in scholarly discussions and to participate meaningfully in university affairs. Squeezed out was the freedom of professors to teach and research, which, in other contexts, was very heart of academic freedom.

After the end of the civil wars (1810–1853), a peripheral iteration of the modern bureaucratic state began to take shape in Argentina. The federal district of Buenos Aires was established to facilitate the centralizing of administrative and financial functions; the occupation of national territory was structured around *encomiendas*, *reducciones*, *estancias*, and *latifundistas* (Zimmerman 1945); and the privileges as well as the obligations of citizenship were defined by legislation, including the Law of Residence (1902), the Law of Social Defense (1910), and the Sáenz Peña Law (1912), which extended suffrage to all males older than 18 years of age. A national system of knowledge production was constituted in which Napoleonic-style universities dedicated to the formation of civil servants were made to coexist with scholastic universities, in a manner reminiscent of England (de Figueiredo-Cowen 2002: 472).[51]

The Argentinian constitution of 1853 devolved power over matters of primary and secondary education to provinces (Spalding 1972: 33). In 1856, the organization of higher education was brought under the administrative control of the national government. In 1887, National Law 1597 (the so-called "Ley Avellaneda") granted Argentine universities autonomy to define their own hiring and disciplinary measures; determine the content of the programs of study and examinations; and manage internal affairs as they saw fit.[52]

The same year, the Collegium Maximum was nationalized, becoming the Universidad Nacional de Córdoba. Theological studies were eliminated, and a School of Exact, Physical, and Natural Sciences opened, along with a School of Medicine. Organizationally, the university came to be arranged around disciplinary faculties, each administered by authority of a dean, a vice-dean, and a *Consejo Directivo* composed of eight professors, four alumni, and four students (Walter 1968: 7). Defining the terms of

[51]By 1887, Argentina had two national universities: the Universidad Nacional de Córdoba, founded in 1613, and the Universidad de Buenos Aires, founded in 1821. In addition, there were two provincial universities that would soon be integrated in the national system of knowledge production: Universidad Provincial de La Plata (the Provincial University of La Plata), founded in 1897 and nationalized in 1905, and Universidad Provincial de Santa Fe (the Provincial University of Santa Fe), founded in 1899 and integrated in 1919 into the new Universidad Nacional del Litoral, with branches in Rosario, Paraná, and Corrientes. The Universidad Nacional de Tucumán (National University of Tucumán) was founded as a national university in 1914.

[52]The "*Ley Avellaneda*" remained "in effect until 1947, at which time President Juan D. Peron passed a new legislation to insure his personal control over the universities" (Walter 1968: 8).

the relationship between *facultades* was the *Consejo Superior*, made up of the deans of each faculties, five representatives of professors, and five of students (Walter 1968: 7). Holding executive power over that instance was a *Rector*, elected by a *Asamblea Universitaria* (University Assembly) made up of members of *Consejo Directivo* and *Consejo Superior* (Milanesio 2005: 551).

Students, at the Universidad Nacional de Córdoba, like others elsewhere in Argentina, occupied minority positions in the inner workings of the university. They were organized into faculty-based *centros de estudiantes* (student centers), which served as nodes of social and political activities (Millán 2007: 20) and as articulating instances with national and international organizations. There, students could develop a distinct sense of themselves and of their place in the world—political consciousness, in other words.[53]

As the Argentinian economy took an increasingly important place in the international division of trade and labor, an extensive infrastructure—railroad, meat-packing plants, refrigerated entrepots, stockyards, and piers.—led from the hinterland to the harbor cities of Rosario and Buenos Aires. This left Córdoba an increasingly remote center, unaffected by new ideas, "a cloister enclosed between ravines ... trapped and dammed, against everything."[54] The Universidad Nacional de Córdoba, "mirror[ing] the Catholicism and conservatism of its location" (Spalding 1972: 34) became a progressively anachronistic stronghold of clerical authority (Garberi and Navarro 2009: 6), its separateness simultaneously of reflection of the autonomy of religious orders—Franciscans took over the university after Carlos III expelled Jesuits from Spanish America in 1767—and a product of the influence of Córdoba's Catholic landowning families (Milanesio 2005: 505). This forced Córdoba's centros de estudiantes into clearer and more

---

[53]Most relevant for Argentinian students in the context of reforms were meetings of the National and International Congress of University Students in Bologna (1888); the International Federation of Students in Paris (1900) and Turin (1903); the International Congress of American Students (Montevideo, 1908), and congresses organized by the League of American Students (b. 1908) in Buenos Aires (1910) and Lima (1912). The Mexican revolution of 1910, World War I, and the Russian Revolution also fed a pervasive sense of context, which, as well as being relayed by specific instances, was also conveyed by novels, and by what could be termed the *zeitgeist* of the moment: "Faced with European civilization in crisis, the intellectual leadership of Europe was broken and there arose for the youth the vital need to save our people from the fate of the European people" wrote Gabriel de Mazo, a principal of the Córdoba movement, cited in Walter (1968; 27). Considering the development of student consciousness in Argentina, it is worth mentioning the importance of *Ideas* (b. 1916) the *El Ateneo Universitario*'s journal of ideas, organized and directed by student leader José María Sans as well as *Cultura*, published at the University of Córdoba itself.

[54]Faustino Sarmiento's book-length essay *Facundo: Civilización y Barbarie* (1845) is cited from translation in Abba and Streck (2021: 8).

political articulation of their interests, in opposition to the decadent casts of divinely appointed professors (Marsiske 2018: 198–201).[55]

The Córdoba reform movement began at the close of the 1917 academic year, when the Centro de Estudiantes de Medicina submitted a memorandum to the *Consejo Superior* and the National Minister of Justice and Public Education, José S. Salinas, to protest against the closing of boarding facilities at *Hospital de Clínicas* (Walter 1969: 247–48), considered essential both to the training of medical students (Garberi and Navarro 2009: 5) and to their collective life (Marsiske 2018: 202). Unacknowledged for three months, students ceased attending classes on March 14, with the support of the Centro de Estudiantes de Ingeniería—which the previous year had protested mandatory class attendance—and by the Centro de Estudiantes de Derecho, which had led a year-long strike against reform in the examination system in 1903 (van Aken 1971: 450). Mass demonstrations took place both inside university buildings and on the street; faculty premises were occupied; and consultative assemblies convened. To coordinate actions, students established a *Comité Pro-Reforma* (Pro-Reform Committee), which, by increments of quasi-daily assemblies, began giving political shape to a wide-ranging program of radical changes, including student participation in university councils and free class attendance.

On March 31, the Pro-Reform Committee held a mass rally in the city, attended by thousands of students. The following day, "professors faced almost completely empty classrooms," prompting the *Consejo Superior* to shut down the university. On April 11, Argentinian President Hipólito Yrigoyen mandated Attorney General José Nicolás Matienzo to mediate between students and the university administration. He arrived in Córdoba on April 16, insisting that "the normal functioning of the university be resumed." In a gesture of cooperation, students returned to class, which allowed the semester to end and Matienzo to go about his investigation unimpeded by protests. Quickly, he wrote a short report approving student demands for "periodic elections to council positions." On May 7, President Irigoyen, putting the report's recommendations to be in effect, "declared all administrative post in the University of Córdoba ... vacant."[56]

On June 15, forty-two of forty-five members of the *Asamblea Universitaria* met to elect a new Rector. Three candidates were considered: student-endorsed Enrique Martínez Paz, the Dean of Law; Conservative Professor Alejandro Centeno; and Antonio Nores, a staunch defender of clerical order, and member of the *Corda Frates*, a semisecret Catholic brotherhood. No candidate obtained the necessary majority in the first two rounds of voting. After the third round, Nores was declared the winner. Immediately, a thousand students invaded the meeting room where voting had been

[55] "Cast of professors" (*casta de profesores*) is from the *Manifiesto Liminar*'s condemnation of the interior minister José Nicolás Matienzo intervention in events at the University of Córdoba: "*la reforma Matienzo no ha inaugurado una democracia universitaria; ha sancionado el predominio de una casta de profesores.*"

[56] Unless otherwise referenced, citations are from Walter, *Student Politics in Argentina*, 43.

held. Claiming that Jesuits had manipulated voting, they expelled security guards and forced the *Asamblea Universitaria* to adjourn. Accompanied by the rough music of mingled whistles, shouting, curses, and chanting of anticlerical and anticonservative slogans, students threw rocks about, broke furniture, doors and windows, and vandalized paintings of clergy members. An occupation began and a strike was called. Outside the assembly hall, the pedestal of a bronze statue of Bishop Sanabria was covered in paint and an attempt was made to set fire to a Jesuit chapel. The offices of *Los Principios*, a Catholic newspaper, were vandalized. City authorities issued police edicts forbidding public manifestations (Milanesio 2005: 519).

The *Manifiesto Liminar de la Reforma Universitaria* (Liminar Manifesto) was the political expression of student's turn to action. Written on June 17 by recent Córdoba graduate Deodoro Roca and published four days later in *La Gaceta Universitaria*, it gave programmatic shape to students' demands for university autonomy; the reinstitution of full and effective student participation in university governance; a reform of the tenure system based on merit rather than seniority; the development of extension courses for workers; and free teaching (*docencia libre*). This latter notion, the *Manifiesto* defined broadly to include open admission and free tuition to qualified applicants; noncompulsory attendance (*estudios libres*); and freedom to choose courses unattached to individual professors—a freedom deemed essential to students' "right to think on our own" and for their "liberty to learn" (Milanesio 2005: 522).[57] Its *sine qua non* condition was a "truly subversive" (Millán 2007: 41–42) and perfectly relational understanding of the relationship between professors and students.

> If there is no significant connection (*vinculación espiritual*) between the ones who teach and the ones who learn, all teaching is hostile and therefore unfounded. All education is a long work of love for those who learn.[58]

---

[57]The *Manifiesto Liminar de la Reforma Universitaria* is widely available on the internet, notably from the website of University of Córdoba: https://www.unc.edu.ar/sobre-la-unc/manifiesto-liminar. Against the *Manifesto*, Friar Zenón Bustos y Ferreira, a principal of the arch-conservative *Unión Popular Católica Argentina*, issued on July 6 a proclamation condemning the movement in the strongest possible terms: "Cordoba has watched in amazement and without believing that the disorderly and sacrilegious manifestations it saw were a reality. ... It did not realize that the time had come to reap the bitter fruits of its painful neglect in leaving its children without discipline or culture or religious instruction. ... It has seen denied the coats of arms it had earned of high culture, of Catholic and Roman Argentina. She has felt threatened to lose them and she will lose them, if she does not wake up and undertake a reactionary movement against her neglect in the cultural, religious and moral education of her children." Ferreira's proclamation is cited from Garberi and Navarro (2009: 11).

[58]In the Spanish original, the quoted sentence reads: "*Si no existe una vinculación espiritual entre el que enseña y el que aprende, toda enseñanza es hostil y por consiguiente infecunda. Toda la educación es una larga obra de amor a los que aprenden.*" The phrase "vinculación spiritual" is usually translated quite literally as "spiritual connection," drowning student's anticlericalism in a mystifying formula. Translating the phrase as significant connection, draws on a more material sense of the term *spiritual*, in a manner that is more faithful to the *Manifiesto*'s legitimizing notions (Palcos 1926 [1920]).

In two short sentences: a most resonant declaration of *freedom in thinking* of scholars bound to self-defined of relation, collectively engaged in an always perfectible, necessarily critical and antidogmatic enterprise (Ingenieros 1920: 72).

On September 9, students began occupying the University of Córdoba, appointing themselves professors and choosing as deans of their respective faculties the presidents of the law, medical, and engineering Centro de Estudiantes. "Faced with such audacity, the forces of reaction intervened, and army and police detachments stormed the university, taking eighty-three leaders prisoner" (Garberi and Navarro 2009: 13). The rest of the students, they drove out of the building with the help of hired thugs (Milanesio 2005: 519). Relayed by the press (*La Vanguardia*, the socialist party newspaper published in Buenos Aires, and *La Voz del Interior* from Córdoba both supported students enthusiastically), news of police brutality provoked strong reactions. President Hipólito Yrigoyen—a pure product of recent reforms—responded by asking Minister of Justice and Public Education, José S. Salinas, to inquire.[59] On October 7, Salinas handed in his report, and five days later, President Yrigoyen signed into law a national decree incorporating almost all of the reformist demands.

Soon, the reform movement in Córdoba charged student movements at the University of Buenos Aires (1918), the National University of La Plata (1919–1920), the National University of the Littoral (1919), and the National University of Tucumán (1921). Outside Argentina, it was cited by student movements in Perú, Cuba, Chile, Colombia, Uruguay, and Guatemala and later in Paraguay, Brazil, Ecuador, Venezuela, México, and Bolivia (Tarazona and Lugos 2018).[60]

W. E. B. Du Bois in Atlanta (1897–1910, 1933–1944)

Voted into law during the second year of the American Civil War, as the Lincoln Administration was beginning to give shape to a national system of knowledge production—the National Academy of Sciences was established the following year—the first Morrill Act (1862) granted land for each state in the Union to establish publicly funded colleges and universities. After

[59]Among notable reactions against students were that of a group of "170 prominent Córdoba professors, lawyers, politicians, and businessmen" who on June 25 sent a declaration to President Irigoyen "deploring the actions of [reformers] and asking for a government intervention on behalf of the pro-Nores elements." A "Catholic women's group in Córdoba ... sent a similar message to Yrigoyen and made public their congratulations to the local legislators who had championed the Defense Committee stand." See Anon (1969a).

[60]A "Timeline of the Projections of the Córdoba University Reform in the student movements of Latin America (1919–1920)" can be found in Abba and Streck (2021: 15–16).

Reconstruction (1865–1877), the second Morrill Act (1890) provided funding for former Confederate states to establish separate institutions for Black students, lest race be eliminated altogether as a criterion for admissions and hirings.

In what we may term "historically white colleges and universities"—an underused phrase that draws attention to unproblematized whiteness (Bonilla-Silva and Peoples 2022)—academic freedom was an instituted principle. Drawing on the idea, articulated by the American Association of University Professors (AAUP), that academic work was essential to the development of the nation, it put forth an argument for the self-government of scholars, who were expected to conduct themselves in the public sphere with becoming modesty

> they should remember that the public may judge their profession and their institution by their utterances. Hence, they should at all times be accurate, should exercise appropriate restraint, should show respect for the opinions of others, and should make every effort to indicate that they are not speaking for the institution.[61]

In historically Black colleges and universities (HBCUs)—a consecrated, oft-acronymized term referencing the Civil Rights Act of 1964—academic freedom stayed an abstract, politically unarticulated idea; the AAUP did not desegregate until after the Second World War. Hindered in their research and teaching by lack of financial and institutional autonomy, and constrained in their ability to take place in the public sphere as full members of a learned profession by the prevailing sense that they were most useful when kept to their place as "negroes studying negroes" (Du Bois 1968: 228), Black scholars in HBCUs remained subjects of a more contingent, half-heartedly instituted, sort of academic freedom.

After completing undergraduate studies in history at Fisk University in Tennessee, W. E. B. Du Bois was admitted to Harvard University, where he studied history and philosophy, earning a second undergraduate degree in 1890. Having begun doctoral studies, he left for two years to study at Friedrich-Wilhelm University in Berlin on a scholarship from the John F. Slater Fund for the Education of Freedmen. Having completed a first draft of his dissertation—The *Suppression* of the African Slave-Trade to the United States of America, 1638–1870—he petitioned the university to advance to final examination before having completed the required three-year period. This petition was rejected on the grounds that demands for dispensation presented by foreigners "whose education significantly differ[s] from that usually found at German schools," were to be granted only "in quite special

[61]The citation is from the AAUP's 1940 Statement of Principles on Academic Freedom and Tenure, from the AAUP's own website: https://www.aaup.org/report/1940-statement-principles-academic-freedom-and-tenure.

and exceptional cases" (Mullen 2007: 88). Du Bois then returned to the United States, becoming in 1895 the first Black man to earn a PhD at Harvard.

Following a short stint at Wilberforce University—a Midwest outpost "dominated by the resident African Methodist [Episcopalian] bishop, a man of limited education, and by State politics" (Du Bois 1926: 229)—Du Bois was hired on the recommendation of the Philadelphia branch of the College Settlement Association as an "assistant in sociology"—an "unheard of title ... without office or teaching responsibilities"—at the University of Pennsylvania ... which at the time did not have a department of sociology (Lewis 1994: 179).[62] Tasked with conducting a study of the Black community of Philadelphia's Seventh Ward—the largest Black community in any northern city at the time—Du Bois worked with research assistant Isabel Eaton, with whom he lived in a "room over a cafeteria run by the College Settlement, in the worst part of the Seventh Ward" (Du Bois 1967: 37), gathering an astonishing compendium of quantitative and qualitative information on black life and race relations in Philadelphia (Back and Tate 2015: 3).

The result of this data gathering was *The Philadelphia Negro* (1899), a founding document of American sociology, most remarkable for its pioneering use of statistical methods (Zuberi 2004: 148) and for entwining a deeply situated mapping of the Seventh Ward community with foundational concerns for the transnationality of "those Africans whom two centuries of slave-trading [had] brought" to Philadelphia (Zuberi 2004: 150). Arguing that Black folks of the Seventh Ward could not be understood sociologically, even in the most situated dimensions of their collective lives, without consideration for the global structuring of race relations (Burawoy 2021: 550), Du Bois worked across the divide separating the inside of national social formations and the outside domain of world politics—what he called the "Great Near," "the always present but usually invisible structures of colonialism and racial capitalism" (Battle-Baptiste and Rusert 2018: 7).[63] In doing so, he challenged the core organizing principle of the colonial ordering of disciplines.

Unable to secure employment at the University of Philadelphia or elsewhere in historically white universities, Du Bois took a position at the University of Atlanta ("a common school ... called a university ... in the faith of what it was to be, and in accordance with the lines upon which it was

[62]The College Settlement Association was under the patronage of the Wharton School (Zuberi 2004: 149).

[63]*The Princess Steel* is a "little known speculative fiction" in which Du Bois, "weaves a tale about a black sociologist who stages a magnificent experiment on the top of a Manhattan skyscraper overlooking Broadway," using a *megascope* to view the "great Near"—"DuBois's term for the always present but usually invisible structures of colonialism and racial capitalism" (Battle-Baptiste and Rusert 2018: 7).

projected").[64] There, he founded the Atlanta Sociological Laboratory, "the first systematic and scientific program of collective sociological research in the United States" (Wright II 2002: 165).

In Atlanta—at "the center of the Cotton Kingdom" (Du Bois 1942: 106)—Du Bois met the most grotesque manifestation of Reconstruction violence. On the day Sam Hose was lynched, he was walking to a meeting with Joel Chandler Harris (he of the "Uncle Remus" stories), editor of the race-baiting *Atlanta Constitution*.[65] Informed that Hose had been caught and lynched, and that "some of his fingers were on exhibit at a butcher shop which [he] would pass on [his] way to town" Du Bois "turned about and went home" (Du Bois 1990: 44).

Hose's lynching was the wicked act of a racist crowd enabled by the complicit inaction of state officials. Accused of having killed his white landlord and raped the landlord's white wife—one of the *belles* of Newnan (Dray 2002: 4)—Hose, a farmhand, had been hiding for a fortnight in his mother's house. Betrayed by neighbors, he was captured and brought by train to Newnan jail. For fear that he would be caught by the searching mob before a reward could be cashed in, Hose's face was darkened and his bound hands hidden by the sleeves of an old raincoat (Dray 2002:9). As had been agreed by phone, Hose's betrayers surrendered him to the sheriff in exchange for a receipt guaranteeing that they would by paid their reward money. Immediately, the Sheriff turned Hose over to the mob. Former Georgia Governor William Gates Atkinson and Judge Freeman pleaded with the mob not to take action: "Do not stain the honor of this state with a crime such as you are about to perform" (Dray 2002: 11). A lynching was organized to take place on Old Troutman Field. Special excursion trains of the Atlanta and West Point Railroad brought so many spectators—perhaps 4,000—so quickly—in a matter of an hour—that police had to be called to control the excited crowd (Dray 2002: 13). Chained to a tree, Hose was "deprived of his ears, fingers and other portions of his body ... burnt and his body cut to pieces, with bits of his heart and liver hawked as souvenirs" (Tuttle 1973: 10). True to the *Constitution*'s prescient warnings—published when Hose was still at large—that "no law officer in his right mind would attempt to protect Hose from the mob" (Dray 2002: 5), police did not interfere. Indeed, apart from the speech of judge Freeman and governor Atkinson, there was an "almost complete lack of responsible intervention from high officials" (Dray 2002: 15). After the lynching, "there was no police investigation made of the crime scene, no evidence gathered, and Mattie Cranford [Hose's purported victim] was neither interviewed by any official or reporter nor examined by a physician" (Dray 2002: 8).

---

[64]Atlanta University sociologist T. N. Chase is cited here from his *Mortality among Negroes in Cities* (1896).

[65]After the lynching, Harris's editorial congratulated the mob on "having given the community general satisfaction" (Crowe 1969: 152).

Seven years after the lynching of Sam Hose, the Atlanta Riot took place. Triggered by the press—which, in days preceding events, had amalgamated "scattered and largely inconsequential incidents between Negro men and white women [into] an intolerable epidemic of rape" (Crowe 1969: 152)—a crowd of 10,000, mostly young white men armed with pistols and rifles, set out to beat every Black person in sight. They pulled some from segregated trolleys and buses, dragging others from the shops where they worked and attacked still others in hotel lobbies. The mob converged on the train station to assault Black porters (Williams 2006: 479) and ransacked Decatur Street, described in the press as "the breeding ground of Negro lust and crime" (Crowe 1969: 153). "In some portions of the streets ... the sidewalks ran red with the blood of dead and dying negroes" (Crowe 1969: 154–56). Again, officials acted helplessly and ineffectually. Mayor James Woodward—reporting "a demonstration of citizens"—asked, without effect, for police and fire units to intervene. The head of the police commission spoke to the crowd but was shouted down as "nigger lover"; the Fire Chief rode into Decatur Street "dramatically ... with all the city's hose carts trailing him," parting crowds that immediately reunified. A police line "perfunctorily held" a section of the mob until it didn't.[66] When Black folks began organizing in Brownsville near the University of Atlanta, threatening to transform what had begun as a racial massacre into a racial war (Godshalk 2006: 1), Fulton County police raided the community center where they were meeting. A shootout followed. Three thousand militiamen from the Georgia National Guard—"two cavalry troops and two batteries of machine guns"—were called "in an effort to restore order."[67] Three hundred community leaders, including university professors, were arrested and raids were conducted in Black homes and businesses "until every negro in the city ha[d] been disarmed" (Anon 1906).

Away in Alabama conducting research for the US Bureau of the Census, Du Bois returned to Atlanta in a hurry. Against long-held pacifist convictions, he purchased a shotgun; armed, he stood vigil, patrolling the campus of Atlanta University (Burns 2006: 174). On "bloody Saturday," he barricaded himself in his on-campus home, protecting his family (Lindsay 2013)

The Hose lynching and the Atlanta Riot had a profound impact on Du Bois. The former "seared" his soul: "something died in me that day" (Du Bois 1990: 44). The latter frightened him for his own safety and that of his family and for the irrelevance of his work: "there was no ... definite demand for scientific work of the sort that I was doing" (Dray 2002: 15). It also exposed political differences with Booker T. Washington's accommodationist politics,

[66]Citations are from Crowe (1969: 154–56).
[67]Anon (1906).

compounded the influence of philanthropies, and prepared the ground of the shunning of Du Bois from white sociology.[68]

Impeded in his ability to pursue scientific research (Du Bois 1968: 223–24), and silenced both by the carnage and by Washington's opportunism (Crowe 1969: 762), Du Bois resigned from Atlanta University in 1910, citing concerns that his presence would undermine the institution's ability to gather funding.

> I insist on my right to think and speak, but if that freedom is made an excuse for abuse of and denial of aid to Atlanta University, then with regret I shall withdraw
>
> (Du Bois 1968: 229)

"Freedom to think and act in unison" is a defining trait of Black sociology (Ladner 1998: 204). "One could not be a calm, cool, and detached scientist while Negroes were lynched, murdered, and starved."[69] In the first moment of Du Bois's professorial life, this freedom—more exacting and contingent than the contractual academic freedom being negotiated by the AAUP on behalf of white sociologists—was undercut by the banally evil inactions of a racist state given leverage by Atlanta University's lack of financial autonomy.

Leaving Atlanta University, Du Bois took a position as Director of Research and Publication for the National Association for the Advancement

---

[68]"Compelled" by its position "furthest down on the color-line frontier" to be most forceful in asserting its right to decide for itself whom it should admit regardless of race—and thereby to "disclaim any ideas of miscegenation"—Atlanta University was obliged by the peculiar circumstances of southern Reconstruction to defend its autonomy over admissions, a matter that Du Bois regarded as a "core matter" of academic freedom (Du Bois 1942: 110). Refusing on principle to deny admission to white students (in reality none applied), the university was deprived of state aid "under the stigma of refusing to 'cooperate' with the South in its educational policies" (Du Bois 1942: 111). This deprivation compounded the authority of philanthropies—principal among which was John D. Rockefeller's General Education Board (GEB), which before the First World War had "gained a virtual monopoly on education and philanthropy for southern Blacks" (Gasman 1999: 741). In effect, the GEB and lesser philanthropies—such as the Peabody and Slater Funds, the Daniel Hand Fund, and the Anna T. Jeanes Fund—who had come to "assume [in the South] what should have been the last-resort role of the federal government" (Levering Lewis 1994: 118) were supportive of Booker T. Washington's plans for the development of vocational training for Southern Blacks, marginalizing Du Bois's projects for the development of a Black *intelligentsia*. On this, see Anderson (1978: 378–79, 380). About the shunning of Du Bois in American sociology and the replacement of the Atlanta Laboratory by the Chicago School in the mythology of the discipline, it is worth noting that Robert Ezra Park, who became a leading figure of the "Chicago School," had earlier served as director of public relations of Booker T. Washington's Tuskegee Institute. He also acted as Washington's ghostwriter, his *nègre*, in French literary parlance. This relationship is explored in the fourth chapter of Morris (2107).

[69]Du Bois cited in Mullen (2007: 85).

of Colored People (NAACP)—which he had helped found. As editor of *The Crisis*, he benefitted from "the freedom of speech and criticism" afforded a researcher working in an institution "unfettered and unsubsidized [by the] vocational-studies complex"—Washington's Tuskegee machine, with support from northern philanthropies.[70]

As sociology was constituting itself into a white discipline, foreclosing any and all concerns with issue of races and the colonial ordering of the world (Barnor 2014: 143), the Atlanta Sociological Laboratory, suffering from neglect, allowed its annual conferences to lapse (Du Bois 1942: 113). Soon thereafter, the publication of its annual studies ceased, and the Laboratory itself closed (Wright II 2002: 171).

Du Bois rejoined Atlanta University in 1933, after having undergone "a gradual but enduring move to the left" informed by a visit to the Soviet Union and an encounter with Marxism (Burden-Stelly 2018: 181). In Atlanta, Du Bois wrote *Black Reconstruction*, a materialist retelling of the entwining of world ordering and situatedness, which, emphasizing the role of southern Blacks in their own liberation, challenged established scholarship. He also worked on two seminars: "Karl Marx and the Negro Problem" and "The Economic History of the Negro." Had these seminars been offered that they would have been the first to assign Marx's *Capital* and *The Communist Manifesto* as required readings and to "apply Marxism to the Negro problem in the US" (Burden-Stelly 2018: 185).

In February 1942, the Atlanta field office of the FBI began investigating Du Bois "for possible subversive activities" (Mullen 2007: 100). Two years later, 75 years old but "not ready to retire" (Yancy 1978), Du Bois was abruptly forced into retirement by Atlanta University President Rufus Clement, during an episode of infighting over the respect due a benefactor (Lindsay 2013). Thus ended the second moment of Du Bois's professorial career.

Once more out of university, Du Bois returned to the NAACP. Unfettered and unsubsidized, he coordinated a "special research" project on race relations and international affairs (Tuttle 1973: 22). He also engaged in Pan-African politics—becoming International President of the Pan-African Congress in 1945; in antinuclear activism—becoming Chairman of the Peace Information Center; and in anti-cold-war politics—standing as New York Senate candidate for the American Labor Party.

On February 16, 1951, Du Bois was indicted along with three Italian Communist Party (PCI) comrades under the Foreign Agent Registration Act of 1938 "on the flimsy charge of failing to register as an agent of a

[70]"Unfettered and unsubsidized" is from the Constitution of the Niagara movement, authored by Du Bois and William Monroe Trotter, the editor of the *Boston Guardian*. It is cited here from an article published in the *Oberlin Tribute* on the occasion of the movement's meeting August 31–September 2, 1908. https://www2.oberlin.edu/external/EOG/Niagara%20Movement/niagaramain.htm.

foreign power" (Burden-Stelly 2018: 196).[71] The trial lasted five days. Of all HBCU presidents "every one of which [he] had known and visited" only Charles Johnson of Fisk University spoke on Du Bois's behalf.[72] Shunned by scholars—"neglected" (Back and Tate 2015: 156), even "negated" (Green and Driver 1976)—Du Bois's professorial life was over.

In 1961, 95-year-old Du Bois became a member of the Communist Party. He renounced his citizenship and moved to Ghana where he continued work on his long-planned *Encyclopedia Africana*. He died in Accra on the evening of the Great March on Washington.

During the crisis of world ordering, sociology was made to move away from its "unproblematized acceptance" of race and racism (Hund and Lentin 2014: 14), and Du Bois was reinstated in the discipline—in his own terms, as both a scholar and an activist (Franklin 2015; Collins 2005). The first sign of his reinstatement was the establishment of "W.E.B. Du Bois Clubs" on American campuses during the 1960s (Tuttle 1973: 1). In 1973, *The Education of Black People* was republished by Monthly Review Press—a full four decades after having been accepted for publication and then shelved by the Board of Governors at the University of North Carolina Press (Mullen 2007: 89). In it, Du Bois presents an argument for academic autonomy rooted in his experience with the unsparing exigencies of Reconstruction, where Black people forever ran up against the color barrier.

> What the Negro needs to be educated "into the possibility of full citizenship in the modern world", he must largely teach himself; what he learns ... he must learn from his own people ... What is needed then, for any group of advancing people, is the COLLEGE-BRED COMMUNITY; for no matter how far the college may fail in individual cases, it is, after all, the center where knowledge of the past connects with the ideas of the future.[73]

---

[71]Specifically at issue was Du Bois's publicizing of the "Stockholm Appeal" petition, "a propaganda trick in the spurious 'peace offensive' of the Soviet Union" in the eyes of US Secretary of State Dean Acheson (Lanham 2017). Lisabeth Moos's report on Du Bois's indictment and trial, "describing the arrest, treatment, indictment, and court trial of W. E. B. Du Bois and his Peace Information Center associates " is available on the University of Massachusetts Amherst Libraries Special Collection and University Archives site: https://credo.library.umass.edu/view/full/mums312-b133-i327. The Stockholm appeal was an initiative of the World Peace Council, a Comintern concern. It was initiated by Frederic Joliot-Currie, cowinner with his wife Irène Joliot-Curie of the 1935 Nobel prize in Chemistry, a member of the French Communist Party.

[72]Du Bois is cited from Gasman (1999: 747). Du Bois was acquitted, as were all PCI defendants, but everyone's passport was temporarily confiscated. They were only returned eight years later, when the Supreme Court restored passport rights to all suspected communists. Charles Johnson himself was the subject of controversy over his firings in 1954 of professors Giovanni Lomani and Lee Loch, both accused of communist sympathies. In 1969 (five years after desegregation), the AAUP retroactively found Johnson, who had by then stepped down as Fisk University president, guilty of violating the principle of academic freedom.

[73]Citations are from « The College-Bred Community » written by Du Bois in 1910, cited in Aptheker (1975: 31).

Paul M. Sweezy versus New Hampshire (1954–1957)

Academic freedom in the United States is a political concept, never better defined than when asserted on behalf of titular professors bound to the mission of their universities. As a doctrine in law, it has only tentative standing derived from constitutional protection offered free speech, due process, and the right of assembly. It is, according to Nathan Adams, "a constitutional doctrine in shambles" (2021: 3); for J. Peter Byrne it is "a doctrine [which] floats in the law, picking up decisions as a hull does barnacles" (1989: 253).

It is only marginalized scholars who take actions that compel courts to clarify the judicial contours of academic freedom. How contacts and connections, linkages and interrelationships between peoples of the world are aligned is part of the conditions in which they do so and how significant that part varies with the broad dynamics of world ordering, with local circumstances, and with the relation between the two.

Cold war *exterminism* was the last chapter in the history of spatial fixing—the final blackmail of interstate disciplining, according to the Internationale Situationniste (IS, 1962), who considered nuclear families hunkering in nuclear bunkers the ultimate expression of the reduction of life's possibilities to mere survival. In the "military-industrial academic complex" (Giroux 2010: 19) that took form in this juncture, there was little room for the autonomy of reflexive instances, except where a narrowly defined sense of purpose gave it reason. Working at the Massachusetts Institute of Technology—"virtually [a] Pentagon university"—Chomsky was paradoxically freer to "be an open, outspoken, dissenting, intellectual and political activist" than he would have been at Harvard, where "the search for Communist infiltrators and spies was whispered about in every corridor."[74]

Educated at Harvard and the London School of Economics—in political economy, a discipline shunned by the colonial organization of knowledge—Paul M. Sweezy played in the years between the global crisis of the 1930s and the cold war a pivotal role in scholarly debates on matters of critical importance to Marxist theory: the transition from feudalism to capitalism; the crisis tendency of capitalism; the organization of modern corporations; and the historical development of capitalism in the United States and in the world. He was also a public intellectual, helping organize the Harvard Teachers' Union; volunteering to teach economics at the Samuel Adams School for Social Studies in Boston; getting involved in Henry Wallace's

[74]The first two quotes are from Chomsky (1997: 178–79). The third is from Nader (2017: 110).

1948 presidential run for the Progressive Party ticket in New Hampshire (his home state); and chairing the Committee in Defense of Carl Marzani.[75]

Despite a stellar publishing record and the very public support of Joseph Schumpeter, Sweezy was denied a professorial position at Harvard University, where he had established himself as a lecturer (Howard and King 2004: 433).[76] He resigned in 1948. Though "in constant demand as a guest lecturer," he never again held a full-time university position (Howard and King 2004: 413). In 1949, he cofounded *The Monthly Review*, a Marxist journal of extensive visibility (Albert Einstein's "Why Socialism" was published in the inaugural issue).

In January 1954, New Hampshire Attorney General Louis C. Wyman, authorized by the New Hampshire Subversive Activities Act of 1951, was given the mandate to inquire into subversive activities, with a view to dissolving "subversive organizations" and making "subversive persons" ineligible for employment by the state. In the course of his investigation, he subpoenaed lecturer Sweezy to answer questions relevant to his inquiry. Sweezy complied, meeting Wyman on January 5 and on June 3. Apart from denying membership in the Communist Party and ever having advocated the violent overthrow of the US government, he declined on constitutional grounds to answer questions related to his knowledge of the Progressive Party; to discuss the subject of a public lecture, "announced as a talk on socialism" (Uchitelle 2004), which he had given on March 22 at the University of New Hampshire (Hutchens and Mille 2023: 49); and to hand in his lecture notes (Simon 2000; Uchitelle 2004). In reaction, Attorney General Wyman petitioned the Merrimack County Supreme Court to hold Sweezy in contempt. Finding Wyman's questions relevant to his investigation, the court did hold Sweezy in contempt, a verdict he appealed on the grounds that his constitutionally guaranteed freedom of association had been infringed upon. Recognizing that it had indeed been the case, but finding the infringement justified by the State's interest in preventing a forcible overthrow of the government—and as such within the bounds of the Attorney General's mandate—the appellate court upheld the initial decision.

[75]Carl Marzani was convicted in June 1947 of having concealed his membership in the Communist Party of the United States of America. He was banned from US campuses, an interdiction, which, according to the City College's newspaper, "insult[ed] the student body by casting doubt on its ability to evaluate, analyze, and form decisions" (Anon 1947: 50).

[76]A comprehensive bibliography of Sweezy's work, excluding "Review of the Month" editorials, can be found in Howard and King (2004: 435–54).

Sweezy asked the US Supreme Court for a writ of *certiorari*. The issue was argued before the court on March 5, 1957, with Attorney General Wyman representing the State of New Hampshire and Yale Law Professor Thomas I. Emerson—a prominent First Amendment advocate—speaking for Sweezy.

Rendered on June 17, 1957, the Supreme Court's decision overturned Sweezy's conviction. Leaning on First Amendment protection of free speech and on Fourteenth Amendment protection of due process, Justice Warren, writing for the majority, faulted the New Hampshire legislature for having given the Attorney General a "sweeping and uncertain mandate," and he recognized that the state had "unquestionably" impinged on Sweezy's constitutionally protected rights. Giving those the widest berth possible, Justice Warren defined "liberties in the areas of academic freedom and political expression" to be particularly useful and necessary instances of free speech—"areas in which the government should be extremely reluctant to tread."

> The essentiality of freedom in the community of American universities is almost self-evident. No one should underestimate the vital role in a democracy that is played by those who guide and train our youth. To impose any strait jacket upon the intellectual leaders in our colleges and universities would imperil the future of our Nation. No field of education is so thoroughly comprehended by man that new discoveries cannot yet be made. Particularly is that true in the social sciences, where few, if any, principles are accepted as absolutes. Scholarship cannot flourish in an atmosphere of suspicion and distrust. Teachers and students must always remain free to inquire, to study and to evaluate, to gain new maturity and understanding; otherwise our civilization will stagnate and die.
>
> For society's good … inquiries into … problems [of interest for social scientists], speculations about them, stimulation in others of reflection upon them, must be left as unfettered as possible. Political power must abstain from intrusion into this activity of freedom, pursued in the interest of wise government and the people's well-being, except for reasons that are exigent and obviously compelling.[77]

In his concurring opinion, Justice Felix Frankfurter, citing ongoing events in South Africa—where apartheid was being instituted—considered even more broadly the dangers of "governmental intervention in the intellectual life of a university," thus laying the groundwork for a broader defense of academic freedom.

---

[77]*Sweezy v. New Hampshire*, 354 U.S. 234, 250 (1957) (Warren, C.J., plurality opinion). Except when otherwise noted, Supreme Court decisions are cited directly from *Justicia*, the Court's own website: https://supreme.justia.com/cases/federal/us/354/234/

> Progress in the natural sciences is not remotely confined to findings made in the laboratory. Insights into the mysteries of nature are born of hypothesis and speculation. The more so is this true in the pursuit of understanding in the groping endeavors of what are called the social sciences, the concern of which is man and society. The problems that are the respective preoccupations of anthropology, economics, law, psychology, sociology and related areas of scholarship are merely departmentalized dealings, by way of manageable division of analysis, with interpenetrating aspects of holistic perplexities. For society's good ... inquiries into these problems, speculations about them, stimulation in others of reflection upon them, must be left as unfettered as possible. Political power must abstain from intrusion into this activity of freedom, pursued in the interest of wise government and the people's well-being, except for reasons that are exigent and obviously compelling.[78]

"In a university" Justice Frankfurter further emphasized,

> knowledge is its own end, not merely a means to an end ... A university is characterized by the spirit of free inquiry, its idea being the ideal of Socrates [...] to follow the argument where it leads[79]

The Sweezy decision was "the first trenchant description of the legal rights of professors" and one of only a handful of key cold-war decisions on academic freedom rendered by the US Supreme Court (Byrne 1989: 256).[80] Throughout, the court expressed concern for abuses of congressional investigatory powers and ruled to uphold the autonomy of universities "to determine for [themselves] on academic grounds who may teach, what

---

[78] *Sweezy v. New Hampshire*, 354 U.S. 234, 262–63 (1957) (Frankfurter, J., concurring).
[79] *Sweezy v. New Hampshire*, 354 U.S. 234, 262–63 (1957) (Frankfurter, J., concurring).
[80] Two cases are considered to have played important roles in clarifying *Sweezy v. New Hampshire*. In *Adler v. Board of Education of City of New York* (1952), the Supreme Court considered the legality of a New York statute known as the Feinberg Law, designed to bolster civil service regulations preventing members of subversive groups—particularly the Communist Party—from teaching in public schools. The court upheld the Feinberg law. Writing for the majority, Justice Sherman Minton noted that, while individuals in the United States do have "the right under our law to assemble, speak, think and believe as they will," they do not have the "right to work for the State in the school system under their own terms." In *Keyishian v. Board of Regents the University of the State of New York* (1967), the Supreme Court struck down the *Adler* decision, invalidating regulations authorizing the removal of university faculty from public employment for "treasonable" or "seditious" utterances or acts, on the ground that they were impermissibly vague. Rosenthal (2021: 235).. Writing for the majority, Justice William Brennan Jr. took into account the "stifling and chilling impact of the New York law on faculty" (Adams IV 2021: 18). He also emphasized that the United States "is deeply committed to safeguarding academic freedom ... a special concern of the First Amendment, which does not tolerate laws that cast a pall of orthodoxy over a classroom." This decision is widely considered the clearest judicial statement of academic freedom (Hutchens and Mille 2023).

may be taught, how it shall be taught, and who may be admitted to study" (Rosenthal 2021:7).[81]

On April 25, 1958, the AAUP—that had not filed a brief in the Sweezy case (Byrne 1989: 291)—conferred its first Alexander Meiklejohn Award for Academic Freedom not to Paul Sweezy but to the president and trustees of the University of New Hampshire who had allowed him to address students in the interim period between the verdict of New Hampshire Superior Court and its overturning by the US Supreme Court (Anon 1958).[82]

Conclusion

At the beginning of the thirteenth century, Mongol control over Eurasian trade routes allowed for the proliferation of interactions between the *world-economies* of China, the *Dar al-Islam*, and Europe, creating in each conditions conducive to the relative autonomy of reflexive instances. This opened opportunities for scholars to push toward the instituting of relatively indeterminate relations of knowledge production. The "academy movement" in Southern Song China, the "madrasa movement" in late Abbasid *Dar al-Islam*, and the rush to incorporation of *studia generalia* during the European renaissance of the twelfth century were the local outcomes of their doings. Before *academic freedom*, these movements offer clear insight—drawn directly from scholar's own *praxis*—into *freedom in thinking* as a moral order.

Rather than multiplying interactions between peoples of the world, the world-system of territorial states that took form between the long sixteenth century and the latter half of the nineteenth century fixed them to places it organized hierarchically. Understood from its own epistemology—as if

[81]Concerns of the Supreme Court for the abuse of state authority were also conveyed in six other opinions rendered on the very same day as the *Sweezy* decision. On this, see Byrne (1989: 291).

[82]The AAUP's failure to intervene in the Sweezy case is coherent with the stance it took during the cold war. Though it often intervened in individual cases of dismissal, the AAUP, mindful of the widespread sentiment among US professors that Communists were not fit bearers of academic freedom, never issued any report on academic freedom in the context of cold war, and never took a public stance beyond reiterating the general principles contained in the 1915 "Declaration of Principle on Academic Freedom" and the 1940 "Statement of Principle on Academic Freedom" (Schrecker 1986: 94–95). A meeting of "twenty-five presidents of America's most prestigious universities" was organized under its auspices in New York on February 15, 1953, but it did not come close to making an argument for academic freedom as a stand-alone juridical right, referring to it instead as "an intellectual free enterprise" (Schrecker 1986: 13). Remarkably, academic freedom was not a notion that was ever invoked, either by Sweezy himself in his arguments to the New Hampshire Superior Court or by Thomas I. Emerson to the Supreme Court. A transcript of Sweezy's "Statement to the New Hampshire Attorney General" can be found in Simon (2000: 37–41). An audio recording of Emerson's argument in front of the Supreme Court is available from Cornell University's Legal Information Institute: https://www.oyez.org/cases/1956/175.

the world were indeed but an arrangement of units called nations, cultures and societies that could be conceptualized not as a whole but as a "sum of self-contained societies and cultures" (Wolf 1982: 302)—this fixing is most readily relatable to state- and empire-building. At the core, it defined what Nicos Poulantzas termed the state's general function of maintaining the unity of a social formation (Poulantzas 1982: 37)—of which the instituting of *academic freedom* would be part.

But if we conceive of the world as a whole—"a manifold, a totality of interconnected processes" (Wolf 1982: 5)—we understand the fixing of social relations as part and parcel of a broader process of world ordering. From this perspective, the state appears not as the condensation of nation-bound relationships of power—"the specific condensation of a power equilibrium" (Poulantzas 1978: 80)—but as an instance of world ordering. Entwined with "the male reproductive order of patriarchal monogamy ... the white economic order [and] the political order of empire" (McClintock 1995), it acted to organize and reproduce social relations not only at the level of national social formation but also in the world economy itself. In stride, *academic freedom* can be understood as part of the reproductive structure of world order as it took form in the late colonial period. Like the world-system of states and universities of which it is part, it too was organized into a hierarchy. At the core, where the autonomy of the university was a reflection of the sovereignty of the state (Praeg 2024: 356), *academic freedom* gave wide berth to the self-regulation of useful scholars; at the periphery, it functioned as a subjugating externality.

So broad were *academic freedom*'s terms of inclusion at the core of world ordering, so compelling the utilitarian fusion of professorial privileges and state- and empire-building, that it seemed as if there could be no more suitable expression of scholarly freedom than *academic freedom* itself. Professors and university administrators spoke in unison to define and defend it; the order of knowledge in and of the world seemed designed so that scholars, gathered in a free market of ideas, might trade under shelter of *academic freedom*.

Yet, looking into occasional moments when scholars' actions straddle the sanctioned boundaries of *academic freedom*, we recognize fleeting, sometimes inarticulate, even coarse assertions of scholarly relations—not as means to further state- and empire-building, nor for the advancement of knowledge or the valorization of colonies but in and for themselves. In the burning of books at Wartburg, we see a rough, performative, celebration of student power against the all-embracing, all-defining seizure of freedom in the name of the States needs. Though it was but a tiny happening involving only a handful of students, it is as telling a scholarly event as any medieval town and gown riot, student occupation, sit-in, or teach-in of the late 1960s, or, as we shall argue in Chapter 4, as the canceling of Angela David at Butler University, or pro-Palestinian encampments in summer 2024.

In the fight over degrees at Cambridge, we see not just an occurrence of women's campaign for recognition, but scholars opposing the arbitrariness of individual professors, bringing them—by way of what Ernesto Laclau and Chantal Mouffe (1985) would have called a struggle over a signifier—back into the folds of scholarly relations. In the reform movement at the National University of Córdoba, we see, through the critique of ecclesiastic appointments, the upholding of possibilities of a significant, unbound connection between scholars. In Du Bois's refusal to let himself be impressed into service as a "Negro studying Negroes," we see an assertion of scholarly indeterminacy as clear and eloquent as Chu Hsi's "Articles of Instructions" or Pierre Abelard's *Sic et Non*. In Sweezy's defense of the freedom "to inquire, to study and to evaluate, to gain new maturity and understanding," we see the refusal of a scholar to accept the subsumption of his autonomy to cold-war policing.

In the near-margins of *academic freedom*—at once enabled by and against it—we see small, situated acts that we understand to be part of the little tradition of scholarly practice, giving circumstantial shape to *freedom in thinking*.

1955–1975	US war in Vietnam
1960–1973	Worldwide wave of "antisystemic movements"
1964	Mississippi "Freedom Summer"
1964	**Free speech movement, UC Berkeley**
1965	Teach-ins, University of Michigan
1968	**Occupation movement, Paris**
1968	***Tlatelolco*** **massacre, Mexico**
12–27 October 1968	Oympic Games, Mexico
11–14 October 1968	Congress of Black Writers, Montréal
1968	**Rodney Riots, Kingston**
1969	**ANPO Protests**
1969	**Computer Center Incident, Sir George Williams University**
1969	**"McGill français," Montréal**

Timeline originated on behalf of the author by Alexandre Gravel.

3

The Crisis of Universities

The crisis of the world-system of universities was an integral part of the crisis of the matrix structure of world ordering.

In core countries, it was students who, charged by a sudden sense of global propinquity, animated antisystemic movements. Often dismissed as spasmodic reactions of restless youth to changes in study conditions (Cliff and Birchall, 1968: 214), as "[o]edipal revolt[s] of the sons against their fathers" (Barker 2008: 43–44), or as some kind of worldwide current "spread[ing] from campus to campus round the world, jumping like electrical sparks from terminal to terminal" (Harman 1988: 61), their doings are better understood as insurrections of a class of scholars that had occupied a subsidiary position in the old order of *academic freedom*. At a critical juncture when the manner in which linkages and relationships between peoples of the world had come to be organized seemed to be at play, they took actions that realized themselves as scholars.[1] This is what philosopher Edgard Morin (1969) called *faire université autrement* (doing university differently). At the periphery of the old world-system of states and universities, by contrast, the production of knowledge was always subsumed under coloniality and *academic freedom* never instituted as a distinct regime. The actions of students in this context remained inextricable part of broader struggles against subjugation.

Even when understood in relation to the broad process of world ordering, each situation belongs to itself; to recognize scholarly *praxis* in its own terms, we have to look into individual events.

*

[1]"Restless youth" evokes the title of a CIA report on the international student movement. A summary is available on the website of the CIA: https://www.cia.gov/readingroom/docs/LOC-HAK-1-2-21-4.pdf.

The Free Speech Movement, UC Berkeley (1964)

At UC Berkeley, the *locus classicus* of the New Left student revolt (Wallerstein 1973), the free speech movement began in the semester that followed the "Mississippi freedom summer" of 1964, with a protest against the administration's decision to forbid political activities on a narrow strip of land traditionally used by students to install tables, distribute leaflets, solicit contributions, and such activities. Both the proscription—overdetermined by fears that the resistance of marginalized Black people, having become stimulated by the "tricontinental revolution against European and U.S. hegemony" would take root in the white middle class—and protests—charged with a New Left sense of the global context of struggles—have to be understood as antagonistic expressions of the same awareness that social relations that had long been fixed and sheltered within the confined of social formations were suddenly being exposed to the ebb and flow of global movements.[2] Suddenly, Berkeley's students and administrators both looked uncomfortably toward a world of which the United States was becoming an unsure center.[3] Understanding themselves to be subjects in and of the world, students moved from representation to direct action. To deal with disruptions, university administrators adopted a more intransigent posture. "Berkeley's new rules," declared Dean Katherine Towle, "would be strictly enforced" (Barker 2008: 58).

"Almost immediately" (Lipset and Wolin, 1965), Berkeley students—many of whom had been freedom summer volunteers—installed tables in the forbidden area at the entrance of campus.[4] On September 30, police

---

[2]Malcom X is cited in Davis (2007: 293). It bears reminding that the civil rights movement began as an academic event. In February 1960, four Black students from the Greensboro Agricultural and Technical College in North Carolina sat down at the "whites only" lunch counter of the downtown Woolworth. Refused service, they continued to "sit in" all day, borrowing a tactic first used in the United States by Congress of Racial Equity (CORE) in 1947 (Boren 2013: 179). The following day, thirty Black students sat and were denied service. On the third day, nearly all of Woolworth's sixty-six seats were occupied by Black students. Still, they were denied service. The next week, sit-ins took place in nearby Winston, Salem, Durham, and Raleigh, where for the first time arrests took place. The first attempt to coordinate sit-ins took place on Easter weekend at Shaw University in Raleigh, North Carolina. Delegates from fifty-six southern colleges and high schools, representatives from the CORE and the Students for a Democratic Society (SDS) gathered. In 1964, the Student Nonviolent Coordinating Committee (SNCC) organized the "Mississippi Freedom Summer," taking predominantly white middle-class students into Mississippi to help with voter registration drives.

[3]This sentence paraphrases the opening of the Port Huron Statement, adopted by the SDS at their national convention meeting in Port Huron, Michigan, June 11–15, 1962: "We are people of this generation, bred in at least modest comfort, housed now in universities, looking uncomfortably to the world we inherit" (Students for a Democratic Society 2015: 2).

[4]Two central figures of the Berkeley free speech movement, Mario Savio and Steven Weissman, had just returned from Mississippi when Berkeley events got under way. Twenty-one freedom summer volunteers were enrolled at Berkeley that fall. Twelve were arrested in sit-in protests (Horn 207: 66).

cited eight students for political militancy. The following day, as a rally was to take place in protest of their suspension, police moved to arrest Jack Weinberg, a former Berkeley student who had set up a table to distribute leaflets from the Campus Congress of Racial Equality (CORE), in deliberate defiance of Berkeley's ban on on-campus political activities.[5] A little before noon, he was arrested for trespassing.

As his arrest was being announced by Dean of Student affairs, David Murphy, Weinberg addressed Berkeley students.

> WEINBERG: While we're waiting, can I tell you a little bit about the university … this knowledge factory we're all sitting here now.[6]
>
> [*There is a burst of laughter.*]
>
> WEINBERG: [I]t seems that certain … of the products are not coming out to standard specification. … We think, we talk, we discuss.

The arrival of a police car driven to Sproul Plaza for the purpose of taking Weinberg away interrupted the exchange. As officers moved to arrest Weinberg, he went limp, "in classic civil right style" (Heirich 1973). Then the crowd made itself into a subject: not an abstract interlocutor void of existence but a subject unto itself. Two hundred students, many "trained in the nonviolent exigencies of the civil rights movement" (Aptheker 2002), plumped down around the police car, chanting "release him, release him" (California Monthly Editors 1965), "[w]e're fighting for freedom, we shall not be moved," and the Star Spangled Banner (Heirich 1973).

Within an hour, a thousand students, charged with a sense of themselves as fighters in "a battle to change the nature of power" were blocking the police car (Adler 2002). Soon, there were several thousand (California Monthly Editors 1965). Surrounding them were 500 security guards and policemen from the university, Oakland and Alameda Counties, and the California Highway Patrol, as well as hundreds of "frat boy Freddie's" on rooftops, flicking cigarettes unto the crowd and threatening to muscle in (Heirich 1973).

The first person to address the crowd was civil rights activist Mario Savio, who did remove his shoes before climbing onto the roof of the police car (California Monthly Editors 1965: 111).

> SAVIO: We must really feel very very sorry for these poor policemen here you know. Good men. They're family men, you know. They have a job to do! That's right, they have a job to do.

---

[5]An exhaustive chronology of events, prepared by the editors of the *California Monthly* (Berkeley's alumni magazine) was published in California Monthly Editors (1965).

[6]Dialogues are excerpted from Heirich (1973: 145–50). "Knowledge factory" is a mocking reference to Clark Kerr's *The Uses of the University*, that would have been understood by everyone present. At the time, Kerr was president of the University of California system.

VOICES: Just like Eichmann

SAVIO: Yeah! Very good! It's very, you know, like Adolph Eichmann. He had a job to do. He fit into the machinery … We are asking the following.

After Savio, student body president Charles Powell spoke on behalf of due process. His plea did not sit well with the impetuous crowd.

POWELL: I'm Charlie Powell, ASUC president, and I'd like to try to serve somewhere in the in-between … let me speak for you. I will go to Dean Williams and Dean Towle and ask that this one boy, here, be allowed to go free.

VOICES: What about the other eight?

POWELL: I'll get to the others … all right?

VOICE: No!

POWELL: I ask you to give the Senate a week's time.

VOICE: You've got two more minutes.

Three hours later, it was agreed that Weinberg would be booked and immediately released on his own recognizance and that the university would not press charges. A committee representing students, faculty, and administration would be set up to settle all disputes over free speech (California Monthly Editors 1965). Twenty minutes later, Mark Savio spoke for the last time from the top of the police car: "Let us agree by acclamation to accept this document. I ask you to rise quietly and with dignity, and go home" (California Monthly Editors 1965: 118).

Thus did the inception moment of the American student movement come to a close. Six years later, the movement reached its tragic culmination at Kent State University, with the deaths of four students.[7]

[7]At Kent State, student protests were triggered by Richard Nixon's televised announcement—on April 30, 1970—that the war in Vietnam was being expanded into Cambodia. Again, the quick succession of events tells of settled relation suddenly upended. The morning after Nixon's speech (May 1 is not traditionally a day of celebration in the United States), some five hundred students gathered at Victory Bell on the Commons, a customary site for campus rallies. Speakers were heard and placards raised; a copy of the American constitution was symbolically buried. In the evening, students gathered in bars on nearby North Water Street for "the usual socializing." Around midnight, a "spontaneous anti-war rally" took shape on nearby streets. A small bonfire was lit, storefront windows were broken, a bank alarm went off, passing police cars were pelted with beer bottles. The mayor declared a state of emergency, teargas was used, and students pushed several blocks back to campus. The next morning, a thousand Ohio National guardsmen arrived to occupy the campus, making it appear like a military war zone. A crowd of hundreds gathered on the Commons, then headed toward student residences. Soon, 2,000 were marching. Crossing the Commons again, they came to surround the ROTC building, "an old wooden World War II barracks which was scheduled to be demolished." It was set on fire. Students and bystanders were pursued by police, stones were

The Occupation Movement, Paris (1968)

The events of May 1968 in Paris began in October 1966 in Strasbourg. During the Algerian war of independence (1954–1962), the Union Nationale des Étudiants de France (UNEF)—an "eminently prudent and respectable" organizer of *banquets* and *soirées* (Weisz and Weill 1983: 34)—had become a site of struggle unto itself (Monchablon 1988; Agacinski 2012). In every French university, communist, libertarians, Gaullists, Trotskyists, and Maoists contended to control it and to define terms of relationship between students and universities, and local and global issues. At the Université de Strasbourg, the local UNEF chapter—the Association Fédérative Générale des Étudiant.e.s de Strasbourg (AFGES)—was led by a group strongly influenced by the anti-Stalinist Socialisme ou barbarie group and the Internationale Situationniste (IS; 1957–1972), an "intensely transnational avant-garde brain trust" (Horn 2007: 8) openly supportive of Algerian independence (IS 1966a, 1966b); of the 1965 Watts riots in Los Angeles (Debord and Fillion 1954); and anticolonial struggles in Vietnam and Palestine (IS 1967).

At the beginning of the 1966 academic year, the AFGES posted a broadside for *Le Retour de la Colonne Durruti*—an antiauthoritarian comic strip—and it let it be known that its only program for the coming year was the dissolution of the association.[8] A general assembly was publicized for an indeterminate future. In November, the AFGES printed 10,000 copies of an Internationale Situationniste brochure—written for the most part by Mustapha Khayaty—which explicitly situated the poverty of students'

thrown. By Sunday, the campus was "fully occupied by Ohio National Guard troops." Ohio Governor James Rhodes—who was running for the US Senate on a law and order platform—vowed to use whatever force necessary to drive [protestors] out of Kent. Tear gas was fired from helicopters hovering overhead and guards dispersed the crowd. Some students were "bayoneted and clubbed by guardsmen." On Monday May 4, students again gathered on the Commons, "primarily [to] protest the presence of the Guard on campus. Ordered to disperse, they 'responded with jeers and chants'. A hundred guardsmen 'equipped with loaded M-1 rifles' moved to disperse them. Students ran away from the Commons to Blanket Hill. Guardsmen huddled briefly then marched back towards the Commons. Believing the episode to be over, 'many students began to walk to their next classes'. Then, 'about a dozen members of Troop G simultaneously turned around ... aimed and fired their weapons into the crowd' killing four and injuring nine." All were full-time students. Unattributed citations are taken from May 4 Task Force Students, 2010.

[8]Buenaventura Durruti was an important figure of the Spanish anarcho-syndicalist movement. During the civil war (1936–1939), he commanded the most important anarchist brigade fighting against the fascist insurrection.

situation in the global context and called for an immediate insurrection against the bureaucratic order of life.[9] It was distributed during the official opening ceremonies of the academic term that took place in the main assembly hall of the Palais Universitaire.

> Representatives of the Strasbourg elite, from the bishop to the prefect, from the general to University President Maurice Bayen … thus bec[a] me the first to read a brochure which, starting the next day, [was] also distributed at the doors of university cafeterias and all over campus.
>
> (Horn 2007: 13)

Immediately, the AFGES was placed under administrative control and its offices closed. The general assembly, which by this time had acquired quasi-mythical status, was canceled.

Two years after Strasbourg—with the UNEF more divided and French universities almost continuously disturbed by political movements—a heterogeneous group of students, later known as the Mouvement du 22 mars, occupied the upper floor the main administrative building of Nanterre University for a day, demanding the liberation of antiwar activists who had been arrested the previous day during street demonstrations "for the victory of the Vietnamese people against American imperialism."[10] On May 2, the administration of Nanterre University, facing the threat of further occupations, shut down the campus altogether and expelled six student leaders, including the main figures of the Mouvement du 22 mars. The following day, several hundred students gathered in protest in the courtyard of Paris-Sorbonne. University President Jean-Marie Roche asked police to clear the courtyard. When occupiers, having agreed to leave, were summoned to go to police headquarters for identity checks, a melee erupted. Cobblestones were thrown, police sticks were swung, and tear gas was used (Gilcher-Holtey 1999: 259).

The occupation began again the following day. Three thousand people—drawing spontaneously and playfully from a very Parisian repertory of action (Hazan 2015)—erected barricades around the Odéon theater and the Sorbonne. On May 6, they were 15,000. As numbers increased,

---

[9]Sometimes attributed to Internationale Situationniste principal Guy Debord, "De la Misère en milieu étudiant" was in fact mostly written by Mustapha Khayati. Immediately after the initial run of 10,000, 300,000 more copies of the text were immediately printed in six languages. Boucar-Victoire (2018). Over the next decade, a dozen translations were made and half a million copies printed (Horn 2007: 14). "On the Poverty of Student Life: Considered in Its Economic, Political, Psychological, Sexual, and Particularly Intellectual Aspects, and a Modest Proposal for its Remedy" is widely available in English.

[10]A full list of demands presented by the *Mouvement du 22 mars* was listed in a leaflet published in the March 29 edition of *Le Monde* newspaper.

barricades became context in themselves. On May 10, 20,000 people held a demonstration near the barricade. That evening, dozens of new barricades were raised on Boulevard Saint-Michel, rue Gay-Lussac, rue d'Ulm, and rue Saint-Jacques (Viénet 1968) in support of the release of students arrested earlier in the day and to demand the reopening of the Sorbonne as well as the withdrawal of police from the Latin Quarter.

> Helmeted students overturned hundreds of cars and trucks. Gas tanks were emptied to fill Molotov cocktails and the vehicles pushed into the streets as barricades. When the police charged, the students ignited the flimsy outer barricades and retreated behind a second, sturdier line. The police, perhaps rightly, considered everyone in the quarter their enemy. They beat anyone they could find in the streets, as well as any they could drag out of their apartments into the streets. [This was] the fiercest street-fighting since the Liberation of Paris in 1944.
>
> (Ehrenreich and Ehrenreich 1969: 82)

At two in the morning, when 6,000 Compagnies Républicaines de Sécurité (CRS) moved to bring barricades down, the war of position abruptly turned into a war of movement.[11] Students rushed out from behind barricades, hundreds of cars and motorcycles were burned, *pavés* and Molotov cocktails thrown, and shop windows smashed. Songs were sung that referenced wars in Algeria and Vietnam. Having borrowed their name from Congolese mercenaries and trained on the grounds of occupied Sorbonne, *katangais* actively engaged with police.[12] Soon, the rush of events was over: 200 CRS were injured, and 500 people had been arrested (B.G.A. 1968).

Wishing to benefit both from public antipathy toward police repression and from fears triggered by riotous movement of student (Viénet 1968), a coalition of unions called for a general day of strike for May 13. On that

[11]CRSs are a special permanent unit of France's Police Nationale. CRS has complete operational autonomy from other police corps and always acts away from home bases in answer to the demands of local *préfets*.

[12]The province of Katanga declared independence from the Democratic Republic of the Congo (DRC) in 1960, a move that was widely supported by internationalist and anti-imperialist movements. Katanga was reintegrated in the DRC in 1963. In Paris, a few dozen some students—unemployed youth and thug (*un ensemble de quelques dizaines de chômeurs et de voyous*) for Alain Touraine—posed as ex-mercenaries in the war between Katanga and the DRC (Touraine and Wieviorka 2018: 48). A short and rather comical training video of Paris's *Katangais* can be seen on the web site of the Institut National de l'Audio-visuel: http://www.ina.fr/video/AFE86001206/les-etudiants-de-la-nouvelle-nuit-des-barricades-a-l-evacuation-de-la-sorbonne-video.html.

day, a million people marched from Place de la République to Place Denfert-Rochereau (Blum 2012: 171), their orderly procession meeting with broad sympathy (Viénet 1968).

For a week after the first *nuit des barricades*, the movement spread through France, outpacing every effort—by the Parti communiste français, the Confédération générale du travail. and the Union nationale des étudiants français—to catch up, contain, and define events. Answering calls to leave the Latin Quarter and "go toward workers," students organized delegations (Maitron et al. 1968: 66). As a result, the occupation movement extended to the state-owned aircraft manufacturer Sud-Aviation in Nantes; Renault's factories in Cléon, Flins, Berliet, and Billancourt (France's largest manufacturing plant); Rhodiaceta (France's principal textile manufacturer, already made a *cause célèbre* by a documentary on the politics of occupation); Peugeot's factories in Montbéliard-Sochaux and Rhône-Poulenc; the Société nationale d'étude et de construction de moteurs d'aviation; and public buildings and hospitals.[13] Chemical and steelworks plants, rail transport, and postal services all ground to a halt. Furthermore, all manners of improvised sit-ins took place, involving professors and students, teachers, doctors and nurses, workers, and engineers (Castoriadis 1986).

By May 20, ten million workers were directly involved in the *mouvement des occupation*s or affected by it, and a general social strike—that old Sorelian myth—was becoming a realistic possibility (Viénet 1968). At the core of world order: a "total crisis ... absolute political emptiness" threatened to undo the organizations of social relations (Bartfeld et al. 1968).

Concerted efforts involving representatives of state and capital (the Conseil du Patronat Français most notably) as well as corporatist unions—the Confédération Générale du Travail, the Confédération française démocratique du travail, the Confédération générale des cadres—produced the reformist Accords de Grenelle, immediately put into effect by the Pompidou government. Minimum wage was increased, and days lost to strike by unionized workers were reimbursed in half.

Mired in politics, the *mouvement des occupations*, a creative opening for Alain Badiou (2008), soon gave way to defensive, procedural formulas, and ritualized forms of behavior, what in Deleuze and Guattari's (1980: 95) sense of the term are *mots d'ordre*—discursive utterances operating as commands that structure practice. A second, unspontaneous, *nuit des barricades* took place on June 10, and a third on June 12. Again, *pavés*

[13]The documentary on the Rhodiaceta strike in Besancon was titled *À bientôt, j'espère*. Directed by Chris Marker and Mario Marret, it was filmed in *cinéma-vérité* fashion during a factory occupation in March 1967 and released in spring 1968. During the events of May 1968, four Rhodiaceta factories were occupied: in Lyon-Vaise, Vénissieux, Saint-Fons, and Péage-du-Roussillon.

were thrown, cars burned, and windows smashed, though with a rehearsed, almost reified, sense of the moment (Badiou 2008). On June 14, the Odéon was evacuated. Having failed to create a "situation of no return" students resumed classes.[14]

The Tlatelolco Massacre (1968)

The Universidad Nacional Autónoma de México (UNAM) was founded in 1910, during the centenary of Mexican independence, as was beginning the revolution.[15] From its inception, it was conceived as a decentralized and formally autonomous assemblage of faculties—theology, canon law, medicine, engineering, arts—working, *dixit* its organic law, "to train professionals, researchers, university professors, and technicians useful to society; to organize and carry out research, especially pertaining to national issues and problems; and to disseminate as broadly as possible the fruits of culture."[16] Acknowledged in principle, the idea of academic self-government was only implemented after the general university strike of 1929 (Rhoads and Mina 2001: 336–37).

Under the presidency of Lázaro Cárdenas del Río (1934–1940), university enrollment and student militancy both increased, alongside state attempts to impress higher education into the service of state socialism. In the 1950s and 1960s, UNAM expanded, buoyed by "steady economic growth within a framework of political and financial stability."[17] State reliance on higher education for the training of bureaucratic functionaries increased the social ascendency of student organizations that worked alongside political organizations—most notably the Communist party of Mexico, which in 1966 created the Comité Nacional de Estudiantes Democráticos (CNED)—to organize demonstrations in support of Cuba after the revolution; against

---

[14]Badiou (2008); Deleuze and Guattari (1987), especially "Postulates of Linguistics." « Situations of no-return » is from *The Revolution of Everyday Life* (Vaneigem 2012) a translation of Vaneigem's *Traité de savoir-vivre à l'usage des jeunes générations* (1967), a defining situationist document.

[15]UNAM was built on the institutional heritage of the Real y Pontificia Universidad de México, founded in 1551 on the model of University of Valladolid (1241). Renamed the Universidad de México during the war of independence, it was closed as a center of corporatist privilege during the Second Mexican Empire (1864–1867), as higher education in Mexico was reorganized "with utilitarian zeal," around a network of institutes, colleges, and technical schools: "In this way, the system would produce the technical and professional experts that Mexico would need in its pursuit of progress" (Duncan 2001: 388, 400).

[16]UNAM's founding document is the Ley Orgánica de la Universidad Nacional Autónoma de México, from September 22, 1910. It is freely translated from https://www.diputados.gob.mx/LeyesBiblio/pdf/158.pdf.

[17]The quote is from a January 1968 *New York Times* article cited without further attribution by Kurlansky (2005: 521).

the American invasion of the Dominican Republic; against the war in Vietnam; and other such events.

After the May events in Paris—that "fascinated" Mexican students—the movement grew in aesthetical autonomy and political radicalness (Kurlansky 2005: 529).

"It all started" on July 23, 1968, with "the violent incursion of riot police (*granaderos*) into two vocational schools" under the pretext of breaking up a fight between working-class students of the Instituto Politécnico Nacional and middle-class students of UNAM-related preparatory school—such brawls were "something of a tradition" (Fox 2018). On July 26 the Federación Nacional de Estudiantes Técnicos (FNET) staged a protest march, which, while passing Alameda Park in downtown Mexico City, merged with a pro-Castro demonstration organized by the CNED. After engaging with police in front of the Palacio de Bellas Artes, students fled toward the old university quarters a few blocks away (Lempérière-Roussin 1989). Over the following few days, a nationwide spread across a remarkably diverse lot of institutions of higher learning, including UNAM, the Instituto Politécnico Nacional de México, the Colegio de México, the Universidad Iberoamericana (a private Jesuit university, affiliated with six others in a separate network), the Universidad La Salle, and the Benemérita Universidad Autónoma de Puebla (both private Catholic universities). On July 31, a *Consejo Nacional de Huelga* (CNH [National Strike Council) was established to coordinate occupations, articulate demands, and facilitate relationships with such instances as the *Coalición de Maestros* (Coalition of Teachers) and the *Agrupación* de *Intelectuales*, *Artistas*, *Periodistas y Escritores* (Committee of Intellectuals, Artists, Journalists and Writers). A *Manifiesto a la Nación* was subsequently issued, situating student demands within a broader critique of national politics highlighting "the profound inequalities in the distribution of income, ... the ever-increasing dependence of the Mexican economy on U.S. imperialism ... a development policy that essentially favors private capital, ... the irresponsibility of a government that avoids acting in benefit of the great majority of peasants and workers."[18] So widespread did the student movement become that, on August 1, UNAM rector Javier Barros Sierra himself marched at the head of an uncharacteristically orderly march in defense of university autonomy. Notably, this was the only episode in which demands related specifically to the self-government of scholars in Mexico were articulated apart from the broad movement of society.

At its August 9 general assembly, the CNH adopted a six-point list of demands, among which were freedom for political prisoners; the disbandment of *granaderos* ("a direct instrument of repression"); the repeal of article

[18]The *Manifiesto* is widely available on the internet. Here, it is translated freely from the website of Memoria Political de México: https://www.memoriapoliticademexico.org/Textos/6Revolucion/1968-M-CNH.html.

145 of the Penal Code—criminalizing "social dissolution," a measure introduced in 1941 to persecute strikers and protesters; the sacking of city police chiefs and officials responsible for repression; and compensation for the families of those killed or injured (Fox 2018). Wrapping academic freedom in the general freedom of the people, the CNH again rejected appeals for a return to normalcy in universities, issuing instead a strategic call to "win the street."

On September 1, as student demonstrations regularly attracted more than a hundred thousand people (Kurlansky 2005: 539), President Gustavo Díaz Ordaz Bolaños warned students that their irresponsibility would have consequences:

> We have been so tolerant that we have been criticized for our excessive leniency, but there is a limit to everything, and the irremediable violations of law and order that have occurred recently before the very eyes of the entire nation cannot be allowed to continue.
>
> (Kurlansky 2005: 540)

To reassure everyone that the upcoming Olympics—scheduled to be staged in part on UNAM's campus—would not be disturbed, President Díaz famously declared, "We will do what we have to" (Kurlansky 2005: 540).

On September 13, a silent march was held in protest against Díaz's authoritarianism. On the 18th, the army once again occupied UNAM's campus—a move, argued Interior Minister Luis Escheverría Alvarez, made necessary "because school buildings had been illegally taken over by political elements who were alien to the university's academic function."[19] "[T] o widespread outrage [the army] ransack[ed] labs and arrest[ed] students and professors" (Fox 2018: 7). Five days later, a pitched battle took place between students and police on the grounds of the Casco de Santo Tomás campus of the Instituto Politécnico Nacional.

On October 2—ten days before the opening of the Olympic games—10,000 high school and university students, answering the CNH invitation, occupied the Plaza de las tres Culturas. At 6:00 p.m., as the occupation was winding down, red and green flares lit up the sky (Fox 2018). Suddenly, police, regular soldiers, and soldiers belonging to the Batallón Olimpia of the Presidential guard—who had taken position in apartments buildings overlooking the Plaza since before the student's arrival—began firing indiscriminately into the crowd. As people attempted to flee, the Plaza was sealed by an estimated 5,000–10,000 soldiers and tanks—more than three hundred according to the special prosecutor's report—kept the plaza sealed (Doyle 2003). For an hour and a half, police and soldiers continued to rain bullets. Then they stopped. Three hours later, they resumed shooting for another half hour.

---

[19]*New York Times*, set 20, 1968, cited in Ecker (2009).

The Rodney Riots, Kingston (1968)

Possibilities for scholars to enter into relatively indeterminate, self-governed relations of knowledge production were contingent on their acceptance of interstate relations as the primary framework shaping relationships between peoples of the world—whether at the core of world ordering, where academic privilege was instituted on condition of usefulness, or at the periphery, where higher education functioned either as a tool of colonial extractivism or as part of developmental schemes.

This acceptance—a *sine qua non* condition of the colonial organization of knowledge production—was upset by the global sense of context born of the mid-twentieth-century crisis of world ordering. It is the clearest, most resonant expression was the "Black consciousness" movement, "fundamentally a racial movement undergirded by 400 years of slavery" (Adeleke 2017: 140).[20]

The Montreal Congress of Black Writers met at the Union Ballroom of McGill University, October 11–14, 1968.[21] It was not *stricto sensu* an academic congress, nor a literary affair in the usual sense of an event centered on the figure of the *auteur* (whom Roland Barthes had recently proclaimed dead) but, rather, a gathering of intellectuals engaged in political and intellectual work who, having "assumed the[ir] revolutionary responsibilit[ies]," were laboring to give epistemic and political shape to the broad movement of anticolonial peoples in the world (Adeleke 2017: 124). The atmosphere "was that of a religious revival spree" (Forsythe 1971: 63). Transnational before the term had entered common usage, it was an event simultaneously shaped by global happenings and deeply rooted in Montreal's Black community (Williams 1997: 118). While it lasted, Montreal stood at the center of the worldwide movement of Black consciousness (Austin 2007: 526).[22]

---

[20]Walter Rodney is cited by Tunde Adeleke from an unreferenced 1969 address at the University of the West Indies in Mona. In *The Grounding with My Brothers*, Rodney defined Black power as "a movement and an ideology springing from the reality of oppression of black peoples by whites within the imperialist world as a whole" (1969: 24). The term *Black consciousness* is used here in a broad, transnational manner coherent with Rodney's views. It encompasses political forms of consciousness born of "Black power" movements in the United States; antiapartheid struggles in South Africa; and decolonial struggles in Africa and the Caribbeans.

[21]"The Congress of Black Writers: Towards the Second Emancipation, The Dynamics of Black Liberation" was dedicated by organizers to the memories of Dr. Martin Luther King, Jr., killed in Memphis on April 4, 1968, and of Malcolm X, killed in New York on February 21, 1965.

[22]In Montreal-specific terms of reference, the Congress of Black Writers at McGill followed a more nationally centered conference titled "Problems of Involvement in Canadian Society with Special Reference to Black People," held at Sir George Williams University, October 4–6. Focusing on everyday problems and local instantiations of "Blackness," the Sir George Williams conference discussed, among other topics: "Problems of Unemployment, Mobility and Advancement in the Labour Force"; "Problems of Housing—Tendency for Formation of Physical and Social Ghettos"; "Political Social, and Cultural Alienation of the Black Man in Canadian Society"; and "The Economics of Black Power—Its Application to the Canadian Situation." See Forsythe (1971) and Mills (2010).

Born in British Guiana, Walter Rodney entered the University of the West Indies (UWI) at Mona, Jamaica, in 1960. Graduating with first-class honors in history, he earned a UWI scholarship to the University of London's School of Oriental and African Studies (SOAS), where he wrote his PhD dissertation: "A History of the Upper Guinea Coast, 1545–1800."[23] Upon graduation in 1966, he "quite naturally went to Africa" (Small 1969: 7), taking up position at the University of Dar es Salaam in Tanzania, where he organized "lectures and symposia about issues and challenges confronting Tanzania and other emerging post-colonial African states" (Adeleke 2017: 132). Confronted by the limits of his position as a foreigner, Rodney returned to Jamaica in 1968, taking up a position at UWI Mona, at that time "the pivot of the circulation and reproduction of ideas … relating to black dignity and respect" (Campbell 1980: 42).

In Jamaica, Rodney undertook to "ground" with ordinary people. "In nine months from January to October 1968, [he] traversed the Jamaican landscape with eloquence, fervour and dynamism, calling the oppressed black man to realize his state of dispossession and act upon it" (Gonsalves 1979:2). "He went to the middle-class clubs … he spoke to the less respectable groupings, all over urban areas, in the villages and towns outside Kingston" (Small 1969: 9).

> It might be in a sports club, it might be in a school room, it might be in a church, it might be in a gully. … They are dark, dismal places with a black population who have to seek refuge there. … I have spoken in what people call 'dungle', rubbish dumps, for that is where people live in Jamaica. I have sat on a little oil drum, rusty and in the midst of garbage, and some Black Brothers and I have grounded together.
>
> (Rodney 1969: 64)

Offering lessons to the masses, Rodney, by his own admission, learned more from them than they did from him (Adeleke 2017: 136), sharpening in the process his critique of Jamaica's petty-bourgeois nationalism. Closely monitored since his student days by Jamaican intelligence services—working in collaboration with Guyanese, US, and British counterparts—he came to be considered as "great [a] threat to the security of this land" as Home Affairs Minister Roy McNeill had ever known (West 2005).[24] The government of Hugh Shearer tried to have UWI administrators terminate

[23]A copy of Walter Rodney's dissertation can be found on the SOAS website: https://eprints.soas.ac.uk/31255/1/RodneyHistoryUpperGuineaCoast.pdf.

[24]McNeill is cited from a report presented to the House of Representatives by Prime Minister Hugh Shearer on October 17, 1968, in Gonsalves (1979: 12).

his contract of employment, a demand that was each time recused by UWI Vice-Chancellor Sir Philip Manderson Sherlock (Payne 1983: 165).

A few months after his return to Jamaica, Rodney was invited to the Montreal Congress of Black Writers by Roosevelt "Rosie" Douglas, who called his attention to "the fantastic outburst of the peoples of the world."[25] At the congress, Rodney made three presentations: "Grounding with my Brothers," a "Statement of the Jamaica Situation,"—a text coauthored with historian Robert Hill that "exposed the myth of the harmonious 'Out of Many, One People' multi-racial Jamaican society" (Austin 2018: 19)—and a talk on "African History in the Service of Black Liberation" (Austin 2013: 23).

The Congress of Black Writers ended on October 14. The following day, Rodney returned to Kingston, arriving at 2:20 p.m. As soon as his plane had landed, it was boarded by police, who ordered Rodney to remain in the cabin while other passengers left. Having never left the aircraft, he was sent back on the return flight to Montreal.

News that Rodney had been kept from reentering the country did not leak until 9:00 p.m. (Gonsalves 1979: 4). Immediately, UWI's Guild of Undergraduates called an emergency meeting in Mary Seacole Hall, "a promptness of response which [was] attributed to the example of student agitation in other parts of the world" (Girvan 1968: 59). Nine hundred students resolved that the very next morning they would take buses to the offices of the Minister of Home Affairs and the Prime Minister in Kingston to deliver petitions. After the meeting, guild principals wrote a pamphlet detailing instructions for the demonstration, which they framed as a protest in support of scholarly freedom and a challenge to the Shearer government. Students were prompted to obey marshals, wear academic gowns, behave in orderly fashion, and keep in their possession a damp rag for protection against tear gas (Gonsalves 1979: 5).

In the morning, buses did not arrive, and students took to marching in single file through the residential Saint Andrew neighborhood toward Kingston, six miles away. On Mona Road, they were met by police. Some students were stopped, and others were let through only to be stopped again, to be arrested, or once more allowed to go through. Guns, batons, and tear gas were used (Mills 2010: 239–40). Chased by police, marchers became runners; following many unplanned routes, they turned "the peaceful, middle-class thoroughfares of shopping centers and graceful old houses into a battleground" (Payne 1983: 166).

> Students invaded lawns, asking for the use of water taps for damping gowns and handkerchiefs. Fumes reached them there too, and suddenly, on these carefully tended lawns, as though responding to some supernatural

---

[25] Douglas's invitation letter to Rodney is cited here from West (2005: 4).

> command, students, gardeners, housewives and gentlemen of leisure were bent double, retching, and swearing and calling for water. Students jumped over barbed wire fences into open lots and gullies, half-blind, weeping and spitting and dribbling down their fronts like untrained children.
>
> (Payne 1983: 166)

By foot, car, and buses, students began arriving at the Ministry of Home Affairs around 10:00 a.m. A public meeting was held during which students were joined by residents, unemployed youth, "members of the lumpenproletariat" (Payne 1983: 167), and Rastafarians critical of "the conspicuous consumption and imitative nature of Shearer's petty bourgeois government" (Campbell 1980: 46). Speeches were made by Guild President Ralph Gonsalves to condemn "a serious breach of academic freedom" (Gonsalves 1979: 6) and by Patricia Rodney. Holding a placard that read: "Where is my husband?" she demanded that the Shearer government lift his ban (West 2005).

A clash erupted in front of the headquarters of the Bustamante Industrial Trade Union, an affiliate of the ruling Jamaica Labour Party. Stones and bottles were flung from both sides of the street. Throughout the evening and night, breakaway groups of unemployed youth and workers, animated less by the attack on Rodney's academic freedom than by the class and racial oppression he documented and acted against, "unleashed the pent-up anger and resentment of the country's dispossessed and disenchanted" (Austin 2018: 21). "The crowd, although headless, was not purposeless" (West 2005: 32). As they would have been by any global crowd acting in any dependent economy (Drainville 2015), signs of externality were targeted. Widely considered indigenous lackeys of British and American imperialism, "browns and mulattos" were taunted (Dupuy 1996), as were "Caucasian, … light-skinned Afro-Europeans, Jamaican, Chinese, and Afro-Chinese" (West 2005). "Fifty buses belonging to the foreign-owned Jamaica Omnibus Service were burnt or otherwise damaged" (Payne 1983: 167). Businesses owned by foreign investors were vandalized. Among targets were the Canadian Imperial Bank of Commerce, Barclays Bank, Bank of Canada and Montreal, Royal Bank of Canada, North American Life, Mexicana Airlines, Pan-American Airways, Woolworths, Bata Shoes, and the offices of Esso and Shell (Payne 1983: 167).

In the evening, Prime Minister Shearer made a short radio and television broadcast—an exceptional event in Jamaica in 1968—promising that he would have more to say the next day. On the 17th, he led debates in the House of Representatives. Again, his speech was broadcast. His tone left "no one in doubt that he wanted to raise the communist bogey of the cold war days"; he quoted at length a report from the government's security authorities that mentioned Rodney's student trips to Russia and Cuba and cast him as "a violent Black Power fanatic, an advocate of Castroite revolution, and a racist who proposed the destruction of white and brown-skinned people" (Gonsalves 1979: 17).

Students who had assembled at Mary Seacole Hall to view the broadcast called for a general meeting to take place the following day. On the morning of the 18th, the National Reserve was called into Kingston. Justices of the Peace and all owners of rifles in Kingston and St. Andrews were asked to assemble in support of the government (Gonsalves 1979). On campus, students found themselves "in a state of siege" (Gonsalves 1979: 17). "All classes were suspended and students, staff, and administrators mostly sat and talked among themselves" (Payne 1983: 170).

Two days later, Vice-Chancellor Sherlock addressed students. Emphasizing the political importance of the guild, he proclaimed a campus-wide ban on all meetings "not held by formal University bodies" (Gonsalves 1979: 21). He also announced that an emergency meeting of the University Council would be held on November 12 during which "security issues as they affect both staff and students" would be discussed. As well, plans for a "Code of Professional Conduct for Members of the Academic Staff" and a "Code of Behaviour for Students" were detailed. "The purpose of these two [codes] was to satisfy the West Indian governments that the University would put its house in order so as to prevent the University being used for subversive activities" (Gonsalves 1979: 21). That same evening, a joint committee of staff and students agreed to end protests on condition that police and army be removed from the vicinity of the university's campus (Gonsalves 1979: 20).

Thus did the Rodney riots end, with agreed-on terms of separation among scholars, state, and community.

After his expulsion from Jamaica, Walter Rodney returned to Montreal, where he wrote a long attack on the servility of the Shearer government:

> These men serve the interest of a foreign, white capitalist system and at home they uphold a social structure which ensures that the black man resides at the bottom of the social ladder.
>
> (Rodney 1969: 59)

Warned by Cuban intelligence of an imminent threat to his life, he soon left for Cuba, where he stayed from November 1968 to June 1969 (Austin 2013: 24). In 1969, he returned to the University of Dar el Salaam, where he wrote his most influential work, *How Europe Underdeveloped Africa* (1972). In 1974, Rodney left Tanzania for a professorial position in the History Department at the University of Guyana. However, upon arrival, the offer was rescinded by President Forbes Burnham, whose developmentalist regime allowed little autonomy for scholarly instances (Taylor 2020). Still, Rodney remained in Guyana, "to immerse himself in the daily struggles of the masses outside of academia" (Adeleke 2017: 413). In 1975, he cofounded the Working People's Alliance to challenge the hegemony of Burnham's People National Congress.

He was killed in June 1980 in Guyana by a car bomb believed to have been planted by Burnham's government (Dupuy 1996: 109).

ANPO Protests, Tokyo (1969)

The national system of knowledge production that took form in Japan during the Meji restoration (1868–1912) was built on "two almost parallel channels, wholly distinct in historical origins, founding ideals and financial security" (Smith 1970: 88). The first, geared toward state service, carried the heritage of Tokugawa Confucianism (Smith 1972: 7–8). At its endpoint were state-funded universities, such as Tokyo University (1886) and Kyoto University (1897), that taught "new elites including high-ranking bureaucrats, business leaders, and professional researchers who would define the thoughts of the majority of society" (Choi 2018: 91). The second channel, originating in professional and technical schools, led to privately funded universities, including Keio University (1858), Okayama University (1870), Nagoya University (1871), Hokkaido University (1876); Nihon University (1889), and Waseda University (1902), among others. These two distinct ensembles were organized into a national system of relatively autonomous and self-governed institutions by the University Law of 1918, which articulated an iteration of academic freedom tightly linked to state and empire building. Under this law, universities were granted *de facto* self-government (Marshall 2023: 55); professors were considered a highly ranked state bureaucrat, with a degree of operational autonomy commensurate with their position (Choi 2018: 97), the modalities of which could always be settled by gentlemanly discussion between administrators and professors (Marshall 1977a: 89). The Minister of Education habitually followed the recommendation of faculties in matters of hiring, promoting, and curriculum (Bartholomew 1988: 263). *Lernfreiheit*, the freedom to learn, had no standing in Meiji Japan.

As bureaucrats, faculty members were "strictly prohibited from public criticism of domestic or foreign policy," or even from participating in public debate (Marshall 2023: 60). This limitation on academic freedom was tested in the interwar years, as the Japanese university system expanded rapidly, buoyed by increases in the tuition revenues of private universities (Shimbori 1964: 206–32). One notable episode involved economist Tomizu Hiroto, dismissed from his professorship at the University of Tokyo for his advocacy for labor rights and social labor issues (Marshall 1977b).[26]

[26]Hiroto was soon rehired as a lecturer on irregular appointment, an act that did not require the approval of the Education Ministry.

Another was the "Seven Ph.Ds. Incident" (1921), involving a group of Japanese scholars who had returned from Germany with PhD degrees.[27] After engaging in public debates over Japanese foreign policy after the Russo-Japanese War (1904–1905), the seven wrote a series of memoranda calling on the Japanese government to resist further Russian penetration into Northern China, Manchuria, and Korea. Summoned by the Minister of Education, they refused to sign an oath of obedience to the Meiji Constitution emphasizing loyalty to the emperor as the supreme authority. In defense of these scholars, University of Tokyo professors signed a petition that made a familiar argument on behalf of *akademische freiheit*. "At the heart of the matter lies a great issue for our nation and the world: the independence of the university and the freedom of scholarship" (Marshall 2023: 8). "The independence of learning" argued University of Tokyo philosophy professor Inoue Tetsujirõ "is sacred" (Marshall 1977a: 91).

The student movement—rather than constituting itself in a political relation with the state, as it did for instance in Germany with the *Deutsche Studentenschaft* and in France with the *Union nationale des étudiants de France*—took form in Japan through a decentralized to-and-fro between in-campus protests (for dormitory privileges; against the arbitrary disciplining of students, etc.) and public protests against Japanese colonialism and American imperialism (Smith 1970: 90–93). In-campus protests were nourished by *garukens*: a widely used, wide-ranging, term that referenced student dormitories to describe all manners of student organizations, such as the *Shinjinkai* society (New Man Society) at the University of Tokyo, the *Todai Rodo Kumiai* (the Association of Laborers and Students) at Tokyo University, the *Kyodai Rodo Kumiai* at Kyoto University, and the *Kaitaku-sha* (the Society of Common Faith at Hosei University). At Waseda University, the most important *garukens* were the *Minshu Dõmei* (the People's League), the *Heimin Dõmei* (the Union of Common Men), the *Kaitaku-sha* (the Society of Pioneers), and the *Kensetsu Dõmei* (the Union of Builders).[28] In broader struggles, Japanese students often acted in concert with internationalist movements and organizations—most notably the Comintern (Smith 1970: 97). On every campus, the Japanese Communist Party (JCP; founded in 1925) was present. In a context overdetermined by the imperial state's desire to control both domestic social relations and relations between Japan and the rest of the world, this made students objects of special concern to authorities. When the Peace Preservation Law (1925) was adopted to punish members of any group threatening the integrity of imperial rule with longer prison terms, its privileged targets were student movements.

---

[27]"The Seven Ph.Ds." Incident is also known as "the Seven Hakushilin Incident," a term derived from the German word *habilitation*, itself derived from the French.

[28]The Japanese tern *garukan* comes from "garden." As the Japanese system of universities grew in the interwar years, it came to be used to evoke the sense of community and solidarity linking students in dormitories.

During the period of American occupation (1945–1952), it was the Supreme Command for the Allied Powers (SCAP) that stood at the intersection of domestic social relations and foreign affairs; the SCAP sought to integrate those into "the international political ambition of the United States" (Saruya 2012: 40). Social relations, it labored to recompose from above on the model of the American New Deal: the Peace Preservation Law was abolished; collective bargaining encouraged to regulate labor relations; women's suffrage was granted; and a parliamentary monarchy was instituted in place of imperial rule. To regulate social relations of knowledge production, the higher-education system was simultaneously expanded and consolidated through the creation of American-style multiversities in every prefecture.

It was in this context that *Zengakuren* (All-Japan League of Student Self-Governing Associations) was established (Usami 1968: 236).[29] From the onset, it too linked university-specific struggles—over the severity of entrance exams, the high cost of higher education, the participation of students in university governance, control of student halls, classroom overcrowding, and so forth—with broader struggles against American imperialism and the threat of nuclear proliferation. As *garukens* had been during the interwar period, Zengakuren became a privileged target of state repression. When relations with Vietnam and North Korea became strained, it was Zengakuren members who were the principal targets of the "Red-Purge" (Kiyota 1971; Krauss 1974).[30]

The American occupation of Japan formally ended with the signing of the Treaty of Mutual Cooperation and Security between the United States and Japan (known as ANPO from its Japanese acronym). The treaty was signed on September 8, 1951, the same day as the San Francisco peace treaty, and came into effect on April 28, 1952—an occasion that Zengakuren affiliates marked by organizing a ritual wake for Japan's independence. At the event's onset, a public address underscored the indissoluble link between academic freedom and national sovereignty:

---

[29] *Zengakuren* is a common abridgement of *Zen Nihon Gakusei Jichikai Sō Rengō* (literally All-Japan League of Student Self-Government). It was a loose federation rather than a political organization. At inception, it regrouped 300,000 students from 145 universities. A useful "Genealogy of the *Zengaruken* and its factions" can be found in Usami (1968: 234).

[30] The "Red Purge"—in reality a series of SCAP actions against all manners of left organizations in Japan—was initiated by General Douglas MacArthur after the 1952 May Day demonstrations, at the very end of American occupation. More than a million people throughout Japan participated. In Tokyo, 400,000 people gathered at the Meiji Shrine, the sacred site of the imperial family: "The anti-Americanism was blatant and rampant; twenty American cars were set on fire. Three unfortunate GIs who got caught up in the frenzy were thrown into the Imperial Palace moat and narrowly escaped a lynching" (Andrews, 2016: 30–31).

> We respectfully mourn the loss of Japan's independence! With the traitorous treaties and administrative agreement, Japan has become a colony. The Japanese people shall never be able to forget this day the 28th. ... All people are resolved never to forget this day the 28th, the day of humiliation, the day of darkness. We shall fight. We believe the nation's students will fight for peace instead of becoming slaves. ... We believe that the day of our victory is near. People of the nation. Crush the anti-Subversive Act of war and subservience! Protect campus self-governance and academic freedom!
>
> (Hasegawa 2019: 4)

As soon as it was signed, ANPO became an object of contention. In 1952 and 1953, students were actively involved in protests against the expansion of the Tachikawa airfield in Sunagawa, near Tokyo (Hasegawa 2019: 167–69). "The expansion of the runway, it was argued, would accommodate larger US jet bombers and be seen as an act of aggression by Japan's neighbors, China and Russia" (Andrews 2016: 20). Between 1954 and 1956, violent clashes between students and police repeatedly blocked land surveyors, eventually forcing the government to cancel plans for airport expansion (Hasegawa 2019: 167). When the government of Prime Minister Shigeru Yoshida attempted to push through the renewal of the ANPO Treaty, Zengakuren students joined in a broad coalition of antinuclear activists, trade unions, and left-wing parties—including the JCP and the Japanese Socialist Party—in "an all-out ... movement to abolish military ties with the United States" (Sunada 1969: 459).[31]

In January 1960, Bundo students helped organize a sit-in of several hundred students at Tokyo's Haneda airport, attempting to block Prime Minister Nobusuke Kishi from traveling to Washington, DC, to sign the new treaty (Usami 1968: 239).[32] Anti-ANPO protests reached a peak five months later. On June 4, 1960, more than 300,000 protestors clashed with police in front of the National Diet building in Tokyo, while several millions workers participated in a country-wide general strike (Saruya 2012: 3, 77). A week later, Zengakuren students immobilized the motorcade of White House Press Secretary James C. Hagerty, forcing him to escape by helicopter (Usami 1968: 239). Following that event, plans for a visit of President Dwight D. Eisenhower were canceled, and Prime Minister Nobusuku Kishi resigned (Tsuzuki 1970: 509). On June 15, just four days before the automatic ratification of the ANPO treaty, 5,000 students stormed the grounds of the Diet Building (Saruya 2012: 77). During protests, Bundo member Michiko

---

[31]By one account, twenty-two joint actions took place between April 1959 and July 1960 (Saruya 2012: 75).

[32]The Japanese Bundo (a term derived from the German *bundt*) was created in 1956 by anti-Stalinian student members of the CPJ. During anti-ANPO protests, it became the dominant political tendency within Zengakuren.

Kanba, a 22-year-old fourth-year student at the University of Tokyo, was killed by an armored car (Fuse 1969: 333).

To contain disturbances, the Central Council for Education advised the Japanese Education minister to encourage the development of "a new form of university ... which, while ensuring academic freedom, [would be] ready to accept the social requirements of the times and ... assume the responsibilities attendant on academic self-government" (Eisaku et al. 1970: 118). Under this plan, student organizations would be financed by tuition fees and membership would be made automatic ("check-off and union shop" in Fordist parlance). Links between student associations and "certain extra-mural organizations" would be severed, and "activities which disturb the intellectual atmosphere of freedom and tolerance required for education and research" would be banned.[33] Thus, half a century after the University Law of 1918, students in Japan would be free to learn—but only at the cost of severing their relationship with the general movement of society.

The "Global '68" worldwide wave of antisystemic movements, combined with the remarkable growth of Japan's economy, created favorable conditions for the emergence of a more autonomous and radical student movement—one closer in ways of being and struggling to New Left organizations in Europe and the United States (Tsurumi 1970).[34] Having faded after the resignation of Nobusuku Kishi, student movements reemerged with protests at Keio University in October 1965 and at Waseda University in June 1966. These were the first protests to be waged under the banner *Zenkyōtō* (All-Campus Joint Struggle Committees; Tsurumi 1970: 108). Although it did not replace Zengakuren as a federating instance, Zenkyōtō did define new ways of protest for students, to the point where its name became "a stand-in word for the whole student movement" (Andrews 2016: 87). Under Zenkyōtō's influence, the watchword of struggle changed from "stop the [ANPO] treaty revision" to "protect democracy"—a slogan that effectively linked student struggles for self-government to broader struggles against state authoritarianism (Saruya 2012: 81). *A contrario* of the separation wished-for by the Central Council for Education, students acted in the thick of protests, simultaneously moved by both campus-specific and global issues (Saruya 2012: 156). Regularly, they clashed with police, on campus or around train stations (Beer 1970).

On October 8, 1967, helmets and staves—previously used by students only in factional infighting—were, for the first time, used against police by students struggling to prevent Prime Minister Eisaku Sato from leaving at

[33]All citations are from the Central Council for Education Report to the Ministry of Education, as cited in Eisaku et al. (1970).

[34]Having grown three time as fast as Britain's or the United States' gross domestic products, Japan's gross domestic product was the third-largest in the world by the end of the 1960s. "Leisure industries boomed and mass production was generating consumption and wealth" (Andrews 2016: 77).

Haneda airport for South Vietnam (Tsurumi 1970: 109). This is customarily known as "the first Haneda incident" (Marotti 2015). A second took place a month later, when students gathered to prevent Prime Minister Sato from leaving for Washington (Steinhoff 2013).

In January 1968, students—again armed with helmets, shields, and staves—joined as many as 50,000 citizens in protest against the much-anticipated arrival of nuclear-powered attack aircraft carrier USS *Enterprise*, en route for the Gulf of Tonkin to participate in the Vietnam War (Usami 1968: 231). With hundreds of cameramen filming (Marotti 2009: 121), protestors engaged police and retreated from violent ripostes in the most spectacular fashion possible, on live television in prime time (Marotti 2009: 122). The same month, the student self-government association of the medical school of Tokyo University went on strike to protest unpaid internships (Tsurumi 1970: 107). This action triggered a wave of protests at medical schools nationwide, eventually involving nearly every university in the country (Saruya 2012: 196). In February, students joined with farmers protesting the seizure of land for the construction of the new Narita airport. In May, 10,000 students at Nihon University—a "stronghold of student power" (Tsuzuki 1970: 517)—went on strike against budgetary secrecy and corruption (Tsurumi 1970: 107). More than 3,000 were arrested (Fuse 1969: 330). On October 21, 6,000 Zenkyōtō students, joined activists from *Beheiren* (Japan National Student Federation Liaison Council) and Sōhyō (the General Council of Trade Unions of Japan), and participated in a massive "International Anti-War Unified Action Day." Rallies took place in thirty cities across the country. In Tokyo, demonstrators staged massive protests at the Japanese Defense Department, the Self-Defense Force Headquarters, and the US embassy. The Shinjuku railway station—a key transit hub for military equipment and fuel destined for Vietnam—became for a short time a "liberated zone" (Muto 2009). Students held it against police, acting for the first time under license of the Anti-Subversive Activities Control Act (Fuse 1969). Bloody battles were waged throughout the night (Nishio 1968; Omori 1970; Sunada 1969). At Haneda airport, as many as 20,000 unarmed and nonhelmeted demonstrators belonging to student groups and antinuclear social movements were assaulted by riot police (Marotti 2009).

On January 18, 1969, several thousand police in riot gear moved to dislodge several hundred Bundo-led students who for eight months had been occupying the Yasuda Auditorium of Tokyo University (Tsuzuki 1970: 501). "Using armored cars, tear gas and water cannon, they fought with students" for thirty-six hours; more than 600 students were arrested (Anon 1969b: 779). In February, classes were held, and entrance examinations conducted under heavy police surveillance. Four months later, with the university system paralyzed (Andrews 2016: 85) and street battles mobilizing a quarter of a million people—of whom as many as 470,000 were students

(Andrews 2016: 108)—the Central Council for Education advised the Minister of Education to place scholarly autonomy under probation. University administrations were given six months to resolve campus disputes before mandatory closures would be enforced. If disputes remained unsettled one year after closure, a new administration was to be appointed (Kiyota 1971: 20). To further clarify the limits of academic self-government, the government adopted the Orwellian-named "Act on Temporary Measures Concerning University Management" on August 7, which authorized the permanent presence of police on campuses; placed university budgets under control of state agencies; and forbade the use of university facilities for political gatherings (Kitamura 2019: 14).

The Computer Center Incident, Sir George Williams University (1969)

Rooted in YMCA educational outreach programs, Sir George Williams University in Montreal was of special significance for the city's anglophone lower-middle and working classes—"many of them holding day jobs, and attending school at night" (Williams 1997: 120)—as well as for working-class francophones without local access to higher education, and for Montreal's Caribbean population, which had grown following Britain's imposition of limits on immigration from West Indies countries (Greenidge and Gahman 2019: 32).[35]

On April 28, 1968, eight students—six from the West Indies and two from East and Southeast Asia—accused biology Professor Perry Anderson of "racial discrimination in grading and academic incompetence" (Mills 2010: 104).[36] In support of their petition, the students met with Dean of Students Affairs Magnus Flynn, who responded by setting up a committee composed exclusively of professors and administrators (Greenidge and Gahman 2019: 34), the representativeness of which was immediately questioned by students (Austin 2007: 530). During the following summer, "students were allowed to develop their bitterness which was to be intensified after the Black Writer's conference" (Kiven Tunteng 1973: 233).

[35]The British Nationality Act of 1948 was the first postwar measure limiting the rights of British subjects from the West Indies to settle in the UK. The Commonwealth Immigration act (1962) further tightened controls. In the same period, Canada was beginning to loosen is "white, if possible" immigration policies (only in 1953 was "climate unsuitability" dropped as a criterion for refusing immigrants; Williams 1997: 104). Sir George Williams University (1959) merged in 1974 with Loyola College (1896) to form Concordia University. On the importance of Sir George Williams University to Caribbeans in Montreal, see Austin (2018).

[36]The specific object of the petition was Physiology 431, "a compulsory course for students in biology and those wishing to pursue medical studies" (Cummings and Mohabir 2022: 4).

Committee hearings began with the new fall semester. Their slow pace making students feel that their complaint was not being taken seriously—an impression reinforced by the untimely promotion of Anderson from instructor to assistant professor—hearings became sites of protest unto themselves. Through the semester, sit-ins were held near the hearing room, and leaflets were distributed.

On January 29, 1969, the committee moved to dismiss all complaints of racism against Professor Anderson. In response, the complainants immediately walked out of the hearing room and proceeded toward the university's computer center on the ninth floor of the Henry F. Hall Building, accompanied by a diverse group of 200 students led by African-descended students and community activists. Principal among them was McGill student Rosie Douglass, one of the organizers of the Black Congress of Writers (Austin 2007: 531). Demands included that Dean Flynn's committee "be totally and publicly rejected"; that a meeting be convened between "university managers, Professor Anderson and students to settle the composition of [a new] hearing Committee"; that a "meeting with the administration take place in an environment free from all threats of reprisal and other punitive measures"; and that "due consideration be given to those Caribbean students who had lost months of study time due to their … devotion to the case" (Greenidge and Gahman 2019: 34).

For two weeks, students peacefully occupied the computer center, maintaining a constant presence through daily comings and goings. As negotiations with the university administration continued, "there was a lot of singing and dancing and calypso music to keep the spirits up" (Eber 1969: 27). In solidarity, hundreds of white students occupied the faculty club on the seventh floor of the building (Belgrave 1995: 127). In concord with the university administration, "some white boys … would come to the center and make sure the computers were in good shape, that the temperature was okay" (Bayne et al. 2021: 41–42).

On February 11, "news spread that a … settlement had been reached between the administration and the students to appoint a more representative committee" (Austin 2007: 531).[37] Feeling near "a big victory," many students exited the computer room, leaving a few behind to clean up the computer center until it was "all polished and shining" (Eber 1969: 31). However,

[37]According to a copy of the agreement, signed by the six original complainants and witnessed by their attorney but unsigned by university negotiators, the following had been agreed on: "students would withdraw from the computer center; a new committee would be established to hear charges against Professor Anderson that would be composed of « two nominees by black students … two from the other parties concerned, a fifth to be to be negotiated by all parties concerned … chosen and approved no later than February 15th"; and "that no violence will be directed towards professor Perry Anderson." The document is cited here from Butcher (1971: 93–95). The full text of "Document Signed by the six complainants and submitted to the Sir George Williams' Administration in the early morning hours of February 10" can be found in Eber (1969: 315–17).

students soon got word that the agreement had been rejected and that the administration would be calling in a riot squad (Greenidge and Gahman 2019: 35). Those still inside the computer center began to barricade themselves in.

At approximately 4:10 a.m. riot police arrived at the computer center, "their guns very visible on their swaggering hips" (Butcher 1971: 96). In the ensuing struggle, both police and students were sprayed with fire hoses. To signal what was happening to those outside, students threw a computer punch card out of ninth-floor windows, which fell to the ground "like large flakes of snow" (Austin 2007: 530). Someone set fire to the computer center. Soon, a hundred firefighters were battling a three-alarm blaze, while "onlookers on the streets below watched with alarm as smoke emerged from the building [and] less sympathetic members of the crowd began to chant « Let the Niggers burn ! » and « Montreal Alabama »" (Austin 2013: 26).

Ninety-seven protestors were arrested. According to Brenda Dash, it would have been "more like three hundred" had students not trusted that an agreement had been reached with the administration (Abraham and Dash 2022: 56). Many arrestees were "beaten and abused by the police upon arrest, and some had to be hospitalized" (Austin 2007: 531).[38]

The very next day, Professor Anderson was reinstated. A few weeks later, he was found not guilty of racism.

In the Caribbean, the Sir George Williams affair made headlines and provoked riots. During a goodwill tour of the region, Canada's Governor-General Roland Michener was confronted by hostile students at every stop. In Barbados, an effigy of Professor Anderson was symbolically buried on the Cave Hill campus of the University of the West Indies (Lumumba 1971: 179). In Trinidad, where the case had special resonance (Eber 1969: 20), protests "united various radical and progressive groups" (Belgrave 1995: 121). When ten Trinidadians were put to trial in Montreal for their involvement in the occupation, "the country was gripped by protests. … These protests spiraled into weeks of demonstrations against the government of Eric Williams, and … gave life to Trinidad's Black Power movement" (Austin 2007: 533).

In English Canada—"a country of very subtle racism" (Belgrave 1995: 120)—the computer center's occupation triggered a backlash against Black activists (Mills 2010: 12). "Across a wide spectrum of Canadian society, the barrage of racist behaviors and invectives that accompanied the crisis would not have disgraced white supremacists anywhere" (West 2021: 101). Echoing coverage of the Congress of Black writers—cast by the state-owned Canadian Broadcasting Corporation as "a thing of foreigners" (Austin 2013: 25)—taxpayers questioned the laxity of immigration law (Kealey et al. 2012). Some even demanded "the expulsion of all blacks from Canada" (Kiven Tunteng 1973: 234).

---

[38]Participants' narratives of events were gathered in a 2015 documentary film, titled *The 9th Floor*, written and directed by Mina Shum. It can be viewed from the website of the National Film Board: https://www.onf.ca/film/ninthfloor/.

In Québec, the occupation charged the struggle for self-determination with a "kind of kinetic connection and a common sense of purpose" with all colonized peoples (Austin 2013: 16). As had the Congress of Black Writers—held in Montreal the previous year—it animated ideas of a broad "nationalist front against colonial oppression" (Austin 2018: 3). That *Québécois* students mobilized in the vicinity of the courtrooms wearing "McGill français" buttons and distributing leaflets that proclaimed, *Nous les nègres blancs d'Amérique soutenons nos frères*; that during the occupation prominent nationalists canceled a scheduled "Québec week" to organize instead support for the movement; and the nationalist Confédération des Syndicats Nationaux called for the immediate release of all arrestees politicized linkages between antiracist struggle and *Québécois* nationalism (Mills 2010), giving resonance to the event (Kellough 2022: 27).[39]

On March 28—two months after the occupation of Sir George William's computer center—15,000 *nègres blancs* and their allies, charged by an anticolonial sense of the moment, marched from the Carré Saint-Louis—the cultural heart of Montreal's counterculture (Warren 2008: 97)—toward McGill University—the *sancto sanctorum* of Anglo-Saxon power. Chanting: *McGill aux ouvriers* (McGill to workers), *McGill français*, and *Université Populaire*, they made their way to Roddick Gate, the university's ceremonial entrance.[40] This was the largest demonstration in Québec since the end of the Second

[39]*Nègres Blancs d'Amérique* (literally, white negros of America) is the title of a book written by Pierre Vallières—a principal of the Front de Libération du Québec—and published in October 1968. Written "all-in-one-go ... after a twenty-nine day hunger strike" while Vallières was in his cell at the Tombs in New York, where he met Black Panthers activists, the book spoke of the place of *Québécois* among colonized people everywhere. Echoing *négritude* and Black consciousness movements, it emphasized race as a marker of oppression. This, of course, was common ground for activists present at the Congress of Black Writers, which had taken place in Montréal a few weeks before: "we need [had argued Walter Rodney] not be detained at the outset by what it means by 'Black' and 'White' ... these words are abstractions of the color names. 'Black' refers to those people in the world who lack economic power and who do not control their own destinies, i.e. the oppressed; and 'white' refers to the oppressors" Rodney (1969: 5). *Nègres Blancs d'Amérique* was published in English by Vallières (1971). Forty years later, it surfaced as a point of contention in English Canadian debates over academic freedom. In fall 2019, Condordia University Assistant Professor Catherine Russel was made to apologize for naming the book by its title and resumed teaching. The following summer, news anchor Wendy Mesley was suspended for her "careless" language after having referred to Vallières's book by its title. Mesley too apologized and later resigned from the Canadian Broadcasting Corporation. A year later, Haitian-born Danny Laferrière (a longtime Québec resident and the first Black writer elected to the Académie Française since Léopold Sédar Senghor) weighed in on the debate by emphasizing the importance of context: "En Haiti, le mot nègre signifie homme et, si on le bannit, on effacera du même coup la trace historique d'un peuple dont le bien le plus précieux est son histoire" (In Haiti, the word *nègre* means "man." Banishing it, we would be erasing the historical trace of a people whose most precious asset is its history). https://www.lepoint.fr/livres/dany-laferriere-et-le-mot-negre-16-01-2023-250500437.php#11.

[40]Roddick Gate is named in honor of Sir Thomas Roddick, who was commanded with the Most Distinguished Order of Saint Michael and Saint George for his service in the Militia Force during the 1885 North-West Rebellion against French-speaking métis.

World War. Waiting in anticipation were a hundred helmeted policemen and 3,000 English Canadians spectators "expect[ing] [hordes] of rabid separatists to burn McGill to the ground."[41] Army troops, the *Ottawa Citizen* had forewarned, were standing by, while Mounties themselves were ready to intervene—as they had time and again to defend colonial order against native unrest.[42] The whole of Montreal was said to be watching. Anarchy, alerted antinationalist newspaper *La Presse*, was threatening (La direction 1969).

But the meeting of *nègres blancs* and latter-day colonialists never amounted to an event. An hour after the march had arrived at Roddick gate, organizers announced that it had attained its goal; now it was time to disperse. And so the crowd did, obedient after all (Warren 2009: 503–4). As it withdrew, gathered anglophones performed their role in the colonial fable, singing "God save our Queen." *Nègres blancs* too performed according to their place in the colonial order of things and peoples: A few flags were burned and some firecrackers set off; a window was damaged at Eaton's department store—a well-known symbol of Anglo contempt for *Québécois* (Warren 2008: 99).

In fall 2020—fifty years after the occupation of the computer center—Concordia University (created in 1974 from the merger of Loyola College and Sir George Williams University) launched a task force on Anti-Black Racism. Two years after that, it acknowledged that "the university's actions and inactions were a stark manifestation of institutional racism" and apologized for its forty years of silence on what now demurely gets referred to as "the computer center incident."[43]

Conclusion

Buoyed by a sudden awareness of their "being in the world"—as full participants in what Alexander Trocchi famously termed the "invisible insurrection of a million minds"—students in core countries of the world-system of states moved beyond the subaltern positions they had occupied in the old regime of *academic freedom* to institute new relations of knowledge

[41]Mark Starowicz, "Terrorism in the Press. An Analysis of the Press Coverage of 'Operation McGill,'" *McGill Daily*, vol. 58, no. 88, 2 avril 1969, 6.

[42]"Mounties" is a colloquial term of endearment used by English Canadians for the Royal Canadian Mounted Police (RCMP). On their role in colonial policing in Canada, see Howe and Monaghan (2018).

[43]The final report of Concordia University's "President's Task Force on Anti-Black Racism" is available on the university's website: https://www.concordia.ca/provost/initiatives/task-force-anti-black-racism/apology-1969.html.

production.[44] In their most exalted moments, they created free and open universities. In Paris, a Université Autonome et Populaire was created; in Strasbourg, Montpellier, Grenoble, and Vincennes, there were Universités Libres; in London, an "Anti-University"; in Madrid and Barcelona, Universidades Autónomas; in Berlin, Munich, Hamburg, and Frankfurt, Kritische Universitäten; in Berkeley, New York, and many other cities in the United States, Free Universities; and in Copenhagen, a New Experimental College.[45] At Columbia University, the occupation of Hamilton Hall called itself "Malcolm X University." These inventions, Trocchi characterized as "our spontaneous university,"

> an "action university" in the sense in which the term is applied to the paintings of Kline *et al.* There were no examinations. There was no learning from ulterior motives. Students and teachers participated informally in the creative arts; every teacher was himself a practitioner—poetry, music, painting, sculpture, dance, pure mathematics, pure physics, etc.—of a very high order. In short, it was a situation constructed to inspire the free play of creativity in the individual and the group.[46]

More than merely an abstract appeal to the idea of the university, *faire université autrement* entailed the organizing of concrete, living, social relations of knowledge production. At the Université Autonome et Populaire in Paris, there were courses on Marxist philosophy, psychoanalysis, studies of repression, school and society, and the Vietnam War. At the Anti-University in London, there were lectures given by C. L. R. James, Robin Blackburn, Yoko Ono, Alex Trocchi, Allen Ginsberg, and Stokely Carmichael as well as seminars—held on second-floor rooms of a repurposed garage in working-class Shoreditch—on Black Power, the politics of small groups, the sociology

---

[44]Being in the world (*être au monde*) is borrowed from Alain Badiou who compared the occupation movement in Paris to "a birth into the world" in a 1969 interview (2009: 39–57). "Invisible insurrection of a million minds" references the title of an article written by Alexander Trocchi, a member of the Internationale Lettriste and later of the Internationale Situationniste—which had a strong influence on the politics and ideas of May 1968 in Paris. The text was originally published in the Scottish journal *New Saltire* and subsequently translated and published as "Technique du coup du monde" in *Internationale Situationniste*, no. 8 1963: 48–56. A full-length text can be found at: https://libcom.org/article/revolutionary-proposal-invisible-insurrection-million-minds-alexander-trocchi.

[45]In 1965 alone, more than fifty free universities were founded in the United States. By 1970, there were between 300 and 500 (Horn 2007: 197–99). For a comprehensive list, see B. Draves, *The Free University: A Model for Lifelong Learning* (Association Press, 1980).

[46]This paragraph, excerpted from Trocchi's "Invisible Insurrection," references goings on at Black Mountain College, an experimental liberal arts institution in North Carolina (1933–1957) renowned for its radical pedagogy as well as for the presence of Anni Albers, Ruth Asawa, John Cage, Buckminster Fuller, and others.

of revolution, and guerilla warfare. In Berlin, a high point of the occupation movement was a four-day symposium during which Herbert Marcuse was invited to discuss with students. In Vincennes, it was Jacques Lacan who spoke on psychoanalysis.

Everywhere, students—and some faculty—worked to define the terms of scholarly self-rule. In Paris, this work was coordinated by the student-led Commission Centrale Provisoire; in London on weekly meetings of faculty and students working under a banner that read: "Beware the pedagogical gerontocracy" (Rosenblatt 1967). Against exalted critiques ("No more dusty classes … no more examinations for trained monkeys, no more magisterial repression"), they regularized teaching and even organized examinations (in occupied Sorbonne, examinations were supervised by the Commission Centrale Provisoire).[47]

Sometimes belittled as "disorderly" affairs (Bell 1968), free, open, and critical universities were in fact remarkably conventional by scholarly standards in their attentiveness to living social relations of knowledge production. Seizing occasions offered by the crisis of world ordering, it was their own past as scholars that students cited; nothing they did would have been foreign to Chu Hsi or Pierre Abelard. And in the same manner that the academy movement in Southern Song China, the *madrasa* movement in late Abbasid *Dar al-Islam*, or the rush to incorporation of *studia generalia* in the European *world-economy* shows the relation between relative openness of world ordering and the opening of possibilities for scholars to institute relatively indeterminate social relations, so must the movement of students toward free, open, and critical universities be understood as expressing the possibilities of *praxis* opened up by the crisis of world ordering. At a critical juncture when structures of world order, unproblematized in *academic freedom*, suddenly seemed at play, subaltern scholars situated at the core of the world-system of states and universities acted against the regime of freedom that had governed their relations. In doing so, they returned to the freedom to which scholars' actions always return.

At the semi-periphery and periphery of the world-system, by contrast, the production of knowledge was decentered; *academic freedom* was an externality, and the struggles of scholars inseparable from the broader movement of society. In this context, the crisis of *world ordering* did not appear as a rupture, nor did it bring about a purposeful rush to *faire université*. Rather, it brought scholarly struggles into closer alignment

[47]The citation was freely translated from a manifesto distributed by "*La Sorbonne aux Étudiants*" committee cited in Maitron et al. (1968: 21).

with the general movement of society—against inequalities in Mexico, against the dispossessing ways of petty-bourgeois developmentalism in Jamaica, and so on.[48]

Seeing this difference prepares us to understand the reasons for current reifications. That *faire université* was pursued so intentionally at the core of world ordering in a moment of crisis reflects the centrality of freedoms instituted in universities in the old world-system of territorial states.

[48]Had I set out to historicize not what the contemporary discourse on *academic freedom* reifies but, rather, what it has always ignored, then the reader would have been led to see into a multitude of other situations at the periphery and semiperiphery when the struggles of scholars and the broader movement of society converged during the crisis of world ordering. In Czechoslovakia, the uprising of students was intertwined with broader struggles of civil society against monopoly control over power; in Yugoslavia, it was inseparable from opposition to bureaucratic authoritarianism; in Poland, student demands for the restoration of academic freedoms were wrapped up in broader demands for the abolition of censorship and for economic reform; in Pakistan, student struggles for what they sometimes called an "academic atmosphere" were folded in the broader battle against state authoritarianism; in Cairo, students—who had been given political standing during in the first years of the presidency of Gamal Abder Nasser, himself a former student leader during protests against British occupation—participated actively in mass mobilizations following Egyptian defeat in the Six-Day War; in Senegal, the movement of students that peaked with the occupation of the Université Dakar was intimately linked with the clandestine struggle of the Parti Africain de l'Indépendance against the government of Léopold Sédar Senghor, deemed subservient to foreign interests; in Tanzania students at the University of Dar es Salaam staged mass protests in 1966 against compulsory military service for high-school and university students, calling not for *academic freedom* but for socialism in Tanzania; in Côte-d'Ivoire, it was the authoritarian regime of President Houphouet-Boigny that students mobilized against; in Zaire, that of Mobutu Sese Seko; in Ethiopia, students at the University College of Addis Ababa simultaneously struck against increase in school fees and for the expulsion of American Peace Corps workers present on campus; and in Kenya, student mobilizations—triggered by Soviet Invasion of Czechoslovakia and the hanging of students in Rhodesia—were also folded with broader movement of society.

1996	*The New Knowledge Economy*, OECD
1998	"World Declaration on Higher Education for the 21st Century," UNESCO
2010	**Students riots, London**
2010–2013	**Long winter, Chile**
2012	***Printemps érable*, Québec**
2015	**Safe spaces at Yale and Mizzou**
2015–2016	**Rhodes Must Fall protests, South Africa**
2021	**The canceling of Angela Davis, Butler University**
1983–2022	**Strike movement, University of California**
2020–2023	**The State of Florida vs. Critical Race Theory**
2024	**Gaza solidarity encampments**

Timeline originated on behalf of the author by Alexandre Gravel.

4

A Global System of Knowledge Production

In the quarter-century since the Organisation for Economic Co-operation and Development's initial report on the new knowledge economy (OECD 1996), the production of knowledge in and of the world has increasingly been shaped by an ever-expanding, more coherent and purposeful *nebulae* of global, transnational, and international organizations made up of leftover colonial instances (the Association of Commonwealth Universities, the Agence Universitaire de la Francophonie, the Organización de Estados Iberoamericanos para la Educación, la Ciencia y la Cultura, the Associação das Universidades de Língua Portuguesa, the Goethe-Institut, etc.); multilateral organizations inherited from the old interstate system (the OECD, the United Nations Educational, Scientific and Cultural Organization [UNESCO], the World Bank, the World Trade Organization [WTO], etc.); state-based funding agencies (the Canadian Social Sciences and Humanities Research Council, the American National Science Foundation, the Dutch Centre for Higher Education, France's Centre national de la recherche scientifique, the British Council for Industry and Higher Education, India's Council of Scientific and Industrial Research, the Argentina's Consejo Nacional de Investigaciones Científicas y Técnicas [CONICET], and others); meeting places of capital (the Trilateral Commission, the Bilderberg meeting, the European Roundtable of Industrialists, etc.); watchdog organizations (the Middle East Forum, Campus Watch, the Hoover Institute, the Higher Education Policy Institute, etc.); professional networks (the Council for the Development of Social Science Research in Africa, the African Network of Scientific and Technical Institutions, etc.); private and semiprivate funding agencies (the Ford Foundation, the Gates Foundation, the Volkswagen Foundation; the Carnegie Foundation, the Open Society Foundation, the Mastercard Foundation, the Ribert Bosch Stiftung, the Phelps Stokes Fund, etc.); disciplinary associations (the Columbian Sociological Association, the International Studies Association, the International Association of Engineers, etc.); private think tanks (the State Policy Network, the Pioneer Institute, La foundation Concorde, the American Empire Institute, the Adam Smith Institute, the Institut Montaigne, the Fundación Fundación para el Análisis y los Estudios Sociales [FAES], the Freedom Centre, the Cato Institute, the Heritage Foundation, the American Trustees and Alumni, etc.); providers of market-ready courseware (Coursera, edX, UDA city, Blackboard, WebCT, etc.); regional associations (the Southern African Regional Universities Association, the Inter-University Council for East Africa, the Regional Universities Forum, the Ibero-American Network for the Accreditation and Quality of Higher education, etc.); and web-based networks (Academia, Anthology, ResearchGate, etc.).

In the *nebulae*, universities exist not as coordinating institutions of nationally bound systems of knowledge production—what they were in the old world order—but, more prosaically, as organizations in a world of organizations.

> an accelerator among others, a multiplier among others, a place of transition among others: [the university] is at work on every battlefront, and every battlefront engages and mobilizes it; it is a whirlwind within whirlwinds, no longer the eye of the storm.[1]

At a critical juncture when relations between peoples of the world are being flattened by *exterminism* and knowledge has taken on the fantastic appearance of solutions, the politics of usefulness—and with it possibilities for the autonomy of universities—gets defined not by the ability of scholars to put themselves forward as participant in the efficient management of state and empire but by how well they let totalizing notions of safety and security regulate the production of specific solutions (Rider 2009: 83). In this context, *academic freedom* is reduced to an organizational capacity, bound to the securing of social relations of knowledge production, and the very notion of scholarly indeterminacy becomes increasingly incredible.

Oft-referenced—in UNESCO's World Declaration on Higher Education for the Twenty-First Century, the German Academic Freedom Act (2007), the French *Loi relative à l'enseignement supérieur et à la recherche* (2013), the UK's Higher Education Freedom of Speech Act (2023), and others—the new organizational notion of *academic freedom* finds its clearest expression in the *Magna Charta Universitatum*, drafted in 1987 by "a small group of university leaders" (Observatory *Magna Charta Universitatum* 2022) and since endorsed by more than a thousand rectors

[1]Freely translated from Freitag (1998: 40–41, 45).

and university principals worldwide (Noorda 2021). In the sly manner of global governance (Drainville 1998), it leans on historical pretext—King John's 1215 Magna Carta, and the 900th anniversary of the University of Bologna—to assign new responsibilities:

> universities acknowledge that they have a responsibility to engage with and respond to the aspirations and challenges of the world and to the communities they serve, to benefit humanity and to contribute to sustainability.[2]

Henceforth privileged subjects of *academic freedom*, professors in core countries of the old world-system of states and universities have resisted impressment into *exterminism*'s endless problem-solving schemes by drawing on old Humboldtian ideas. Below their reifying discourses, they have also behaved in largely unassuming ways. Hiding in plain sight (Seyama 2020), speaking the metallic language of the new academic entrepreneurialism (Ball 2003), they have acted against imposed cadences (Moten and Harney 1999) and interminable assessment exercises; slowed down and acted lazily (Gildersleeve 2017); waited out "managerial fads" (Harvie 2004); invented strategies to manipulate journal impact factors (Cameron 2005); intentionally neglected obligations and deadlines (Barry et al. 2001); taken it upon themselves to modify or rewrite student-supervisor agreements (Harrison et al. 2010); and drawn on clichés of professorial absent-mindedness to skirt clerical duties (Anderson 2008) or wiggled out of administrative obligations (Macfarlane 2005). Sometimes slave drivers to themselves—a predisposition of professional academics that prolongs the pressures of intellectual work in neoliberal universities (Zeena and Marisol 2018: 223)—or struggling with mental health issues (Smith and Ulus 2020), they have let themselves burn out (Watts and Robertson 2011), killed themselves or each other, and sabotaged presence in other, more covert, ways.[3] To deflect speech codes and bibliometric exigencies, they have fabricated collaborations and cited themselves (Mott and Cockayne 2017; Fong and Wilhite 2017; Rodríguez-Ruiz 2009).

---

[2]The Magna Carta is cited from the website of the Magna Charta Universitatum Observatory: https://www.magna-charta.org/magna-charta/en/magna-charta-universitatum/mcu-1988.

[3]In the UK, attention to professorial suicide was focused by the death in 2018 of 48-year-old Malcom Anderson, an accounting lecturer and senior tutor at the Cardiff Business School, who killed himself by jumping out of his office window, leaving two notes behind. The first was addressed to his family. The second encouraged fellow lecturers to speak out against the workload and the "Big Brother environment" at Cardiff University. On this, see Deacon (2019). A special edition of *Accounting History Review* was dedicated to the memory of Professor Anderson (Chandler and Edwards 2019).

Students, for their part, have engaged in all manner of actions against the means and consequences of academic managerialism. They have occupied public places—the Student Union building at Bristol University, Bramber House at the University of Sussex, the Audimax Auditorium at the University of Vienna, the Mundet campus library at the University of Barcelona; held teach-ins at King's College, the London School of Economics, the Universitat Politècnica de Catalunya, and the Universitat Autònoma de Barcelona; organized demonstrations in Québec against tuition increases, in the UK against the casualization of academic labor, in France against increasingly selective admissions, and in Italy against Gelmini reforms; and waged strikes at the University of California for better wages, health benefits, and working conditions; at CUNY against spending cuts and new managerial practices; at NYU for bargaining rights; and at Humboldt University against the implementation of tuition fees. In the ludic manner of "antigloblization" protests everywhere (Drainville 2001), they have also called flash mobs—at Seattle University's Matteo Ricci College to protest the lack of diversity in the curriculum; at the University of California against cuts in funding; at Trent University against sexual violence on campus; at the University of Bologna against budget cuts—and crewed "book blocks"—in Rome against funding cuts; in Madrid and Barcelona against austerity measures; at University College London against tuition fee increases; and at the University of Heidelberg against the Bologna process.

Beneath collective actions, they too have acted in infrapolitical ways: skipping classes (Chircop 1997; Sever 2018); looking the other way when peers cheated (McCabe et al. 2001); sleeping and texting through lectures (Felder and Brent 2009); exploiting bibliographic software and search engines to fake references and inflate bibliographies (Banik 2014; Patel et al. 2011); using SMSs to cheat (Birchard 2006; Moran 2008); buying ready-made assignments from paper mills (Bartlett 2009); or relying on artificial intelligence (AI) machines to do their thinking. This, of course, has prompted myriad calls by university administrators to regulate AI in the name of academic integrity to defend the university's mission or uphold its responsibilities.

In every action of professors and students—no matter how tiny, singular, or mundane it may appear, or how little it is considered in reified discourses on *academic freedom—freedom in thinking* defines itself. To grasp this, we need to situate actions in relation to the little tradition of scholarly practice.

*

Student Riots, London (2010)

Protests against the rise in cap on tuition fees began in England "effectively overnight" (Younis 2011) after the abolishing of the Education Maintenance Allowance scheme.[4]

On November 10, 2010, a mass demonstration was jointly organized by the National Campaign Against Fees and Cuts (NCAFC), the National Union of Students (NUS), and the University and College Union (UCU). More than 50,000 students marched along a route preapproved by the Metropolitan Police Service (Gabbatt and Haynes 2010). Also taking part were representatives of the Labour Party, Plaid Cymru, the Green Party, the Socialist Workers' Party, the Socialist Party, the Young Communist League, and the Revolutionary Communist Group. In the fashion of the moment, a Facebook event had been created, images tweeted and Instagrammed, and demonstrators were in carnivalesque spirit.[5] Rude banners were held aloft (Helmet al. 2010), vuvuzelas—made popular during that summer's World Cup in South Africa—echoed through the crowd (Lewis and Vikram 2010), and mocking slogans were chanted:

> "no ifs, no buts—no education cuts"
> "they say cut back—we say fight back"
> "I say Tories—you say scum"
> "we're young, we're poor, we're not paying anymore."
>
> (Penny 2011)

As the procession was making its way passed the Houses of Parliament en route to the Tate Gallery—where UCU's general secretary, NUS's President, the Trade Union Congress's Deputy General, and other representatives were

---

[4]The Education Maintenance Allowance (EMA) had been introduced by the New Labour government in fall 2004 "to boost the number of young people from poor background staying in post-16 education" (Hyde 2023: 201). "Substantial reductions" to it were announced by the Liberal-Democrat coalition government in January 2011, before the scheme was abolished altogether in September 2011, and replaced by a bursary program administered by universities themselves. The report of the Independent Review of Higher Education and Student Finance (IRHESF) was published on October 12. Commissioned the previous year to "consider the balance of contributions between students, the taxpayers, employers and graduates to university funding in England" (Ibrahim 2014: 79), it marks a fundamental shift in thinking from education as "a public good, articulated through educational judgment and largely financed by public funds [to] a lightly regulated market in which consumer demand, in the form of student choice, is sovereign in determining what is offered by service providers (i.e. universities)" (Collini 2010: 24). The IRHESF report, titled "Securing a Sustainable Future for Higher Education," is available online: https://www.gov.uk/government/uploads/system/uploads/attachmentdata/file/422565/bis-10-1208-securing-sustainable-higher-education-browne-report.pdf.

[5]About the carnivalesque atmosphere of protests in the early days of the antiglobalization movement at the turn of the millennia, see Drainville (2001).

scheduled to speak—"a minority of idiots" (Gabbatt and Haynes 2010) split from the main contingent and moved to occupy the Conservative Party headquarters in Millbank Tower, half a mile down Abingdon street. Outside the building, a vigil was held and anarchist flags waved (Lewis and Vikram 2010). A bonfire was lit, and songs were sung. But soon, "students were pouring into the building and onto the roof. The mood was ugly and the police were struggling to cope" (Helm et al. 2010). A window was smashed (Ibrahim 2014: 84); office workers were evacuated; and closed-circuit TV cameras were ripped from the ceiling. Parts of the building were ransacked, and protesters fed bonfires with office furniture. For nearly an hour, "the violent rampage bore all the hallmarks of a riot" (Lewis et al. 2010). When a fire extinguisher was thrown from the roof of the building, the crowd on the ground responded by booing and then chanting in disapproval: "Stop throwing shit" (Gabbatt and Haynes 2010). A block away, across the Thames, students penned in a police kettle clashed sporadically with police. Thirty-five demonstrators were arrested and dispatched without fanfare to police stations throughout central London, where they were quickly processed and released (Gabbatt and Haynes 2010).

A fortnight later, on the eve of the student's second national march against cuts, Detective Chief Superintendent Adrian Tudway, recently appointed "National coordinator for domestic extremism," announced that protests against cuts in education would henceforth be the target of a national police intelligence operation (Gabbatt and Batty 2010). But again, "good natured, although very noisy" (Gabbatt and Batty 2010) parades took place in London and elsewhere throughout the UK. Again they were charged by a carnivalesque sense of happening; again Facebook events took place that were tweeted and retweeted; and there were instagrammed moments and rude chanting:

> "Fuck David Cameron"
> "Shame on you!"
> "Your job's next"
>
> (Gabbatt and Haynes 2010)

Confronted by students, London's Metropolitan Police—embarrassed by previous protests (Lewis and Dodd 2010)—responded in the zero-tolerance manner of antiglobalization policing elsewhere (Drainville 2015: 115). They deployed the strongest, most visible, contingent possible: not two hundred, but eight hundred officers, including mounted police (Gabbatt and Batty 2010). Midday, they drew from a new repertoire of neoliberal policing techniques, making a spectacle of authority (Mountz and Curran 2009; Policante 2013; Punch 2007; Sheptycki 1998). Marchers were corralled into a kettle on Whitehall—the symbolic axis of financial and government power. Intermittent clashes occurred along its perimeter at the point of contact with police. After about an hour, hundreds of students broke free from the kettle and began scattering throughout central London, pursued by police in what became a "game of cat and mouse." In rapid movement, a more fragmented and intent crowd engaged in "symbolic damage tactics" (Cammaerts 2013). Police vans were rocked back and forth, windows got smashed, rubbish bins upended, lawns pissed on, traffic cones thrown into the road, and bus shelters vandalized (Gabbatt and Batty 2010).

Protestors again clashed with police on November 30 and December 9, as occupations were going on in at least thirty university campuses (Trott 2014). Again, spectacular kettles, symbolic smears, and damages: a statue of Winston Churchill was defaced; a Christmas tree was set on fire; windows were smashed at the Treasury offices and Her Majesty's Revenue and Customs offices; and protesters cracked windows and threw paint. A Rolls Royce ferrying Prince Charles and the Duchess of Cornwall to the Royal Variety Performance at the London Palladium was blocked (Knight et al. 2013; Solomon and Palmieri 2011). The royal couple looked visibly shaken when they arrived at the Palladium, but later that evening, the Duchess had found resolve to quip drolly about the incident: "First time for everything" (Wintour and Watt 2010).

When police shot and killed Mark Duggan near Tottenham Hale station in North London, all manner of anitausterity protests—against police brutality, cuts public services, privatization, surveillance, housing inequality, and gentrification—fused into an insurgent movement radically about itself. In a radical moment fitting of Hegel's notion of the rabble—those outside organized social space, who could express their discontent only through "irrational outbursts of destructive violence" (Žižek 2011)—students were at the center of events (Hyde 2023).[6] They would be there again, weeks later, during the London iteration of the Occupy protests.

The Long Chilean Winter (2010–2013)

The commodification of higher education in Chile under the dictatorship of Augusto Pinochet (1973–1990) was folded in a broad authoritarian program aimed at the wholesale reinvention of society (Villalobos-

[6]Making the argument that shoplifting rioters were turning consumerist ideology against itself—realizing consumerism in oppositional ways—Žižek (2011) and Bauman (2011) reprised an argument initially made by Guy Debord about the 1965 Watts riot in Los Angeles: "The Los Angeles revolt is a revolt against commodity, against the world of the commodity and the worker-consumer hierarchically subjected to the measures of the commodity. … The looting … district manifested the crudest realization of the bastard principle 'To each according to his false needs,' the needs determined and produced by the economic system that the looting precisely rejects. But because this abundance is taken at its own word and no longer pursued in a ceaseless race of alienated labor true desires are expressed in playful affirmation—a potlatch of destruction." Freely translated from Debord (1966).

Ruminott 2012). Thirty-eight for-profit private universities were established; a new genus of technical schools was developed (Institutos Profesionales, Centros de Formación Técnica, etc.); and public funding that had been earmarked for research was put to the service of industry (Bellei 2005; Somma 2012). Capping reforms was the Ley Orgánica Constitucional de Enseñanza (LOCE; Constitutional Statutory Law of Education), which came into effect on March 10, 1990—the very last day of Pinochet's seventeen-year dictatorship. In redefining the role of the State from provider to regulator of higher education, LOCE suspended professor's contracts; dissolved faculty unions and student organizations; fragmented public universities into regional campuses; and transferred privileges of *academic freedom* to a newly appointed cadre class of "delegate-rectors" (Schwember and Bear 1981).

During the "transition period" (1990–2010), Chile's student population quadrupled—from about 250,000 to 1 million (Pousadela 2013). Touting "a new social contract between the state, the private sector and the universities" (Villalobos-Ruminott 2012: 12), successive Concertación governments labored, in governance fashion, to build consensus around the very same program that the Pinochet dictatorship had endeavored to impose. Having "merged with business and the military elite" (Ruiz 2012: 72), the bureaucratic state increased public funding in education and strengthened accreditation and quality control mechanisms—all the while leaving intact the neoliberal framework for higher education inherited from the dictatorship. The LOCE was not repelled; the state remained a mere regulator of higher education; and *academic freedom* stayed either an expression of the authority of delegate-rectors, or a by-product of the financial autonomy of educational investors.

The Penguin revolution of 2006 was the first major challenge to Chile's neoliberal framework for higher education. Initiated by the first generation of students born after the fall of Pinochet, it unfolded amid broader social unrest—antiextravtivism mobilizations; Mapuche resistances; strikes of public employees—in a context charged by a proximate sense of the global context of struggles—particularly informed by gas and water wars in Bolivia and by the *empresas recuperadas* movement in Argentina. Mobilizations began six months into Michelle Bachelet's first term as president of Chile, triggered by the announcement of an increase in fees for university selection tests (Prueba de Selección Universitaria [PSU]), amid rumors of changes to the *Pase Escolar* (PE; student transit pass) that would increase fees and limit preferential tariffs to two travels a day—diminishing students' autonomy in the most tangible fashion possible. In Santiago, public school students marched down Avenida Alameda, demanding the end of the LOCE; free access to the PSU and PE; and the rescinding of the *Jornada Escolar Completa*—a longer school day introduced in 1996, ostensibly to improve the quality of education. Loosely coordinated by a broad coalition of representative bodies—including the Coordinadora Nacional de Estudiantes Secundarios, the Centro de Alumnos del Instituto Nacional, the Asamblea Nacional Estudiantil, and the Asambleaj Coordinadora de Estudiantes Secundarios—the movement initially took the form of a series of orderly marches and sit-ins (Chovanec and Benitez 2008). Though spurred by the inertia of the Concertación government (Vogler 2007), it remained contained by representative bodies. But beginning on May Day, however, massive demonstrations across the country led to the occupation of public places and the closing of secondary schools (Ruiz 2012: 75). Police brutality escalated, drawing widespread condemnation, but President Bachelet offered no substantial engagement on educational reform—a subject she conspicuously avoided in her televised address on May 22 (Vogler 2007: 51). On May 30, a general strike shut down more than 250 schools in Santiago alone (Anon 2006). Tear gas was used, and students—as well as bystanders and journalists—were arrested in brutal, indiscriminate, fashion. After several weeks "during which the government either ignored the protests or criticized them as 'undemocratic' and violent" (Von Bülow and Bidegain Ponte 2015: 186), President Bachelet, on the evening of June 1, announced a package of non-negotiable measures including improved grants for university entrance exams; school meals and free bus passes for the neediest students; and the eventual rescinding of LOCE. A Consejo Asesor de Educación (Advisory Commission on Education) was also created.

On June 5, students took part in a day of strike that bore all the hallmarks of a celebration. Having successfully installed education reform "at the top of the political agenda" (Vogler 2007: 52), they returned to class the following week.

In December 2006, just days before the presentation of its report, student representatives—sixteen of eighty-two commission members—quit the Consejo "arguing that the text did not reflect their call for a clear and overall reform of the education" (Von Bülow and Bidegain Ponte 2015: 187). Still, the report was presented and subsequently used as a platform for extended negotiation between the Concertación government and the Alianza por Chile opposition. These negotiations culminated in 2009 with the replacement of the LOCE by a new Ley General de Educación (General Law of Education) that did not significantly alter the structure of Chilean higher education (Cabalin 2012: 223). Students and faculty organizations voiced their opposition, but they were unable to "reproduce the massiveness of the 2006 protests" (Von Bülow and Bidegain Ponte 2015: 187; Burton 2012: 45).

Sebastián Piñera's victory in the 2010 presidential election marked a return to ideological neoliberalism. Just as Pinochet's Renovación Nacional governments had been the most zealous implementor of "no-society" neoliberalism (Somma 2012), Piñera's Alianza por Chile sought to engineer the most faithful iteration of neoliberal governance. Charged by a global sense of context—informed by the Arab spring, the Indignados, and Occupy movements—students-led protests moved to more autonomous and radical forms of politics (Del Campo 2016: 179).

In March and April 2011, mass demonstrations were organized by the Federación de Estudiantes de la Universidad de Chile (University of Chile's Student Federation), with support from workers' organization (the Central Unitaria de Trabajadores de Chile, the Agrupación Nacional de Empleados Fiscale, and others); faculty members of public universities; and television personalities (Guzman-Concha 2012: 410). In every major city, students marched under broad slogans, folding demands for free education within broader calls for public ownership of domestic industries (Guzman-Concha 2012; Barrionuevo 2011). On June 16, more than 100,000 demonstrators took to the streets of Santiago—the largest demonstrations in the city since the end of the dictatorship (Bellei et al. 2014: 430).

As the movement expanded, the struggle over higher education became a vehicle through which popular dissatisfaction was articulated (Larrabure and Torchia 2015: 257). High schools and university students, parents, teachers, copper miners, and environmental and indigenous activists, coalesced into "a heterogeneous mass of citizens disgruntled with the political and economic system" (Somma 2012: 296). Becoming about itself, the crowd performed presence in the manner of global crowds elsewhere, "display[ing] a remarkable degree of tactical creativity" (Larrabure and Torchia 2015: 259).[7] In that as well students were at the forefront. Enacting strategies based on mass demonstrations and the occupation of schools and public places (Del Campo 2016: 182), they jogged around the presidential palace dressed up as superheroes; threw a beach party for Minister of Education Joaquín Lavin—who, attempting to discredit the movement, had sent students on winter vacations several weeks ahead of schedule; participated in *el gagazo*—a dance-a-thon set to the music of Lady Gaga—and *el besatón*—a mass-kissing marathon. On June 24, a flash mob of two hundred medical students reenacted Michael Jackson's *Thriller* video in front of the presidential palace (Del Campo 2016: 187).[8] Clad in ragged clothes, their faces pale and sunken, undead students wore tombstones around their necks to symbolize the debt that would follow them beyond the grave (Bush 2019).

On June 30, 2011, 100,000 people again marched in Santiago, as secondary school students occupied more than one hundred high schools, placing many under "the democratic management of teachers and students" (Larrabure and Torchia 2015). Laboring to contain the movement, President

---

[7]On global crowds and the moral economy of presence, see Drainville (2015).

[8]At the time of writing, a video of the event could still be found on the site of *Huffington Post*: http://www.huffingtonpost.com/2011/06/25/chile-thriller-protest-students-michael-jackson-dancen884531.html. About the carnivalesque sense of antiglobalization happenings, see Drainville (2001).

Piñera unilaterally announced five days later a Gran Acuerdo Nacional de la Educación (GANE; Grand National Agreement on Education)—a proposal that had not been discussed beforehand with any student organization. In continuity with the spirit of LOCE, GANE diminished the state as provider of higher education and expanded its role as regulator—most notably through the creation of a Superintendencia de Educación Superior (superintendency of higher education). Interest rates on state-backed student loan schemes were lowered; student rankings broadened in the name of accessibility; provisions were made for students to be included in quality-control mechanisms; funding was increased for voucher schools; and provisions were made for the legalization of for-profit universities. In response, the Confederación de Estudiantes de Chile published, on July 18, 2011, a *Bases de un acuerdo social por la educación chilena* (Draft Social Agreement for Education) and a companion *Manifiesto sobre la Educación Superior* (Manifesto on Higher Education), demanding respect for student organizations "through real participation and decision-making mechanisms" of "collegiate bodies that reflect the composition of the university community."[9]

In August 2011, the student movement in Chile gained breadth and resonance. "In support of the students, citizens from several neighborhoods in Santiago revitalized a type of protest utilized in the 1980s against the Pinochet dictatorship: they sounded a 'cacerolazo'—the coordinated banging of pots and pans" (Bellei et al. 2014: 431). President Piñera answered in a televised speech by broadening the terms of GANE's neoliberal inclusivity, offering students greater partnership in quality-assurance mechanisms—within a higher education system in which the private sector would play an even larger role (Von Bülow and Bidegain Ponte 2015: 188). In protests, thousands more marched down Santiago's Avenida Providencia toward the presidential palace. Borrowing from the repertory of antiglobalization policing, *carabineros* used tear gas to coral people into a spectacular kettle. A few hours into it, as people on balconies were banging pots and pans (Barrionuevo 2011), *carabineros* sought to compel movement where they had enforced immobility, and protesters reacted by occupying a place they had merely planned to traverse on their way to the palace. Barricades were set up, and water cannons and tear gas used, forcing students to leave Plaza Baquedano in disorderly fashion (BBC News 2011). In the rush to exit, La Polar, a department store recently exposed for having engaged in usury practices—a "paradigmatic revelation" for Alicia Del Campo (2016: 180)—was set ablaze and a television station briefly occupied (BBC News 2011). In unison, state actors and student representatives condemned violence (CNN Wire Staff 2011).

[9]The July 18 *Bases de un acuerdo social por la educación chilena* is cited, in translation, from the *Al Día* site: ps://brunner.cl/2011/07/documento-bases-de-un-acuerdo-social-por-la-educacion-chilena/.

On August 18, 2011, an estimated 50,000 students, dressed in raincoats and carrying umbrellas, vowed to fight "against the wind, the tide and the rain" (Délano 2011). Children, artists, teachers, and workers actively joined in demonstrations (Larrabure and Torchia 2015: 257).[10] Reacting to the breadth of support for students (Anon 2011), the Piñera government offered for the third time incremental changes to GANE. Again people marched in protests, and again the policing of place overdetermined events, as police moved into the Instituto Nacional José Miguel Carrera—the most prestigious humanities college in the country—to keep students from occupying it (Pousadela 2013: 689). A battle took place between students and police, ending with "1,394 arrests and the death of a 16-year-old [Manuel Gutiérrez Reinoso] hit by a bullet fired from a passing police car" (Pousadela 2013: 688).

Laboring to give shape to a situation beyond their control—in part for the role they had played in the betrayal of the Penguin revolution (Bellei and Cabalin 2013: 117; Von Bülow and Bidegain Ponte 2015: 188–90)—student representatives called for structural reforms. As Giorgio Jackson, then president of the Federación de Estudiantes de la Universidad Católica, suggested, the movement was proposing a change of paradigm (Del Campo 2016). On August 24, 2011, the Central Unitaria de Trabajadores ([CUT] National Workers' Union) called for a national strike. For that occasion, the CUT added demands for "free and quality education" to its usual list of "more traditional demands for better salaries, a new labor code, and an end to precarious jobs" (Larrabure and Torchia 2015: 258). In cities across the country, tens of thousands of people again marched in orderly fashion, demonstrating the breadth of support for education reform and signaling its increasing entanglement with wider struggles for social justice (Stromquist and Sanyal 2013: 166).

In the following months, state instances and representative organizations of workers and students made concerted efforts to regain control over the impolitic agitation of crowds. Minister of Education Joaquín Lavín—a prominent "Chicago boy" during the Pinochet period, and Rector of the for-profit Universidad del Desarrollo—was removed from his position. A constructive dialogue between "Educational Policy Stakeholders" was said to have begun (Bellei and Cabalin 2013; Villalobos-Ruminott 2012). At the General Assembly of the United Nations in September 2011, President Piñera described the student movement as having defended "a noble, big, beautiful, and legitimate cause" that his government also supported (Pousadela 2013: 688). The statement, widely understood as an attempt to reclaim discursive

[10]Marisa Von Bülow and Germán Bidegain-Ponte estimated that twenty-three marches were held in Chilean cities between May 2011 and September 2013 (2015: 188). For Christian Cabalin, it was thirty-six (Cabalin 2012: 114).

control over events, of course, contrasted with the continued deployment of repressive policing on the ground.

The long "Chilean winter" ended in December 2013 with the electoral victory of Nueva Mayoría, a broad coalition of center-left parties led by Michelle Bachelet, president for the second time.[11] During the campaign, she had stated her commitment to "advance decidedly toward universal gratuity" of higher education (Von Bülow and Bidegain Ponte 2015: 179). In her inaugural speech, she referenced her own experience to seal the terms of academic engagement:

> I know firsthand what public education can offer a person. I am a child of public education, and my commitment is that in Chile we all have the same opportunities, and I know firsthand what it means to fight for a free country, without authoritarian enclaves, where the majority is not vetoed by a minority.
>
> And we are going to carry out the government program that we have committed to you! And we are going to do so within a framework of dialogue with all the political and social forces. But a dialogue that has a clear objective, which is to advance in the fulfillment of the program.
>
> We have a national project that requires all views, without excluding anyone.[12]

Québec's Maple Spring (2012)

The provincial government of Québec is the only legislative body representing the francophone population in the Americas. The *modèle québécois* that took shape there during the "quiet revolution" of the 1960s was defined by (i) the nationalization of electricity companies (1962); (ii) the establishment of the Caisse de dépôt et placement du Québec (a state-run pension plan manager, 1965); (iii) the creation of a Ministry of Immigration distinct from that of the federal government (1965); and (iv) a protonational system of

---

[11]As the "Québec spring" of 2012 would be a year later, the "Chilean winter" was baptized by a foreign new media referencing the so-called Arab spring of 2011, a term "unintentionally coined" by political scientist Marc Lynch in an article in *Foreign Policy* that he made into a book (Lynch 2013). In Chile, it was *The New York Times*'s Alexei Barrionuevo (2011) who did the dubbing.

[12]President Bachelet's inaugural speech took place on March 11, 2014. It is cited here, in my own translation, from the web site of Archivo Michele Bachelet Jeria, Fondo Documental Administración 2014–2018: http://archivospresidenciales.archivonacional.cl/uploads/r/presidencia-de-la-republica-2/6/5/b/65be6d0656049878e281567478f0a1089b7d6751a53b92a37b196de678734c66/homearistotelesdocumentosComunicado1864.pdf.

knowledge production arranged around a public network of junior colleges and universities.[13]

In the *modèle québécois*, professors are represented by unions (except in anglophone McGill University, established during colonial rule), and students are organized into associations financed by dedicated dues drawn directly from tuition fees by university administrations. Both professors' unions and students' associations play roles akin to that of corporatist unions in Keynesian demand-management: They are privileged partners of the provincial state in the management of higher education (Gagnon 1960). As such, they were active participants in Québec's take on *academic freedom*.

One of the enduring legacies of Québec's quiet revolution is a relatively uncommodified system of higher education wherein reigns the *ancient régime* feel of a relatively independent community of mind and scholarly work.[14] From the beginning of the 1990s, however, neoliberalism in Québec labored to hitch this system to the production of "knowledge capital" (Gouvernement du Québec 2003, 2004).[15]

For the most part, early professorial opposition to the neoliberal reinvention of universities in Québec was expressed through political

---

[13]This section is revised from (Drainville 2013b). There were five universities in Québec at the time of the quiet revolution: McGill (1821), Bishop's (1836), Sir George Williams (1926), Université Laval (1852), and the Université de Montréal (1869). With the 1969 reform of education, a public network of Université du Québec was created. At inception it was made up of four local branches: the Université du Québec à Montréal, the Université du Québec à Trois-Rivières, the Université du Québec à Rimouski, and the Université du Québec à Chicoutimi. The Université du Québec en Outaouais was established in 1981, and the Université du Québec en Abitibi-Témiscamingue in 1983. Also part of Québec's public system of higher education are the Institut national de la Recherche Scientifique (1969), the École nationale d'administration publique, the Télé-Université (1972), and the École de technologie supérieure (1974). In Québec, junior colleges are called College d'Enseignement Collégial et Professionnel (Cégep), and eleven were created in the immediate aftermath of the quiet revolution: the Cégep de l'Abitibi-Témiscamingue, the Collège d'Ahunsic, the Cégep de Chicoutimi, the Collège Édouard-Monpetit, the Cégep de Jonquière, the Cégep Limoilou, the Collège Lionel Groulx, the Cégep de l'Outaouais, the Cégep de Rimouski, the Cégep de Sainte-Foy, and the Cégep de Valleyfield.

[14]"Community of mind and scholarly work" is cited from the Report of the Parent Commission (1967; Commission royale d'enquête sur l'enseignement dans la province de, Québec, and Alphonse-Marie Parent, *Résumé du rapport de la Commission royale d'enquête sur l'enseignement dans la province de Québec* [La Commission, 1967]), a defining document of the 1960s reform of higher education in Québec.

[15]Though modest by North American standards, tuition increases in Québec do serve as markers of the commodification of higher education before the spring of 2012. In 1990, the Parti Libéral government tripled fees, from the $540 per year that had been fixed by the Parent Commission twenty years previously, to $1,668/year. In October 1996, the social democratic government of the Parti Québécois announced plans to increase tuition fees by another 30 percent and enacted an increase in "associated costs" and "institutional fees." In 2003, the Parti Libéral government of Jean Charest, as part of its broad attack on the Keynesian *modèle québécois*, increased tuition fees again to $2,168/year. In 2010, the Charest government, still in power, imposed a tuition increase of $325/year for five years, to begin in fall 2013.

representations: in-house struggles against the reorganization of academic governance; the publication of scholarly critiques; jostling in trade paper (*Les Cahiers de l'Association Québécoise des Professeur.e.s d'Université* [*The Bulletin of the Canadian Association of University Professors*], etc.) and in a "house organ" such as *Le Devoir*—the newspaper of reference for serious public debates in Québec. Students, for their part, organized strikes, as they have throughout the (short) history of Québec's universities.[16] In 1986 and 1990, they struck in protest of fee increases. In 1996, the student movement, drawing inspiration and tactics from the Ejército Zapatista de Liberación Nacional's uprising, struck again over proposed increases in tuition fees. In 2005, a general strike of students—this time against cuts to the grant-and-loan system—ended on a compromise widely understood as a surrender of the student movement.

In fall 2010, the Parti Libéral government summoned all partners in education to a grand summit on the future of universities, where the funding of all institutions of higher education, and their contribution to the development of Québec, would be discussed in the context of the new knowledge economy. The Sommet sur le financement des universités opened on December 6, with a foreboding discourse of the finance minister on the necessity to solve the financial crisis of universities. It ended the same day with professors' unions and students' associations walking out in protest.

Three months later, the governing Liberal Party adopted a budget announcing a sharp increase in tuition fees (75 percent over five years), along with a broad restructuring of university financing around private research. A new "Fund for University Excellence and Performance" was established, a full quarter of which was earmarked as seed money to encourage private donations.[17]

In the year-and-a-half that followed, information sessions were held, discussions organized, position papers written, and summer schools set up—all under the guidance of students' associations.

On February 13, 2012, a broad coalition of students' associations called for an unlimited general strike against the government's plans.[18] In the days and weeks that followed, students' associations gathered in general

---

[16]The first student strike in Québec took place as soon as the new system of Cégeps and universities was put in place. In October 1968, Cégep students, moved by May events in Paris, struck in favor of broadening the provincial grant-in-aid system and to hasten the creation of a second francophone university in Montréal (what would become the Université du Québec network). In 1974 and 1978, Cégep and university students struck against a new general aptitude test seen to curtail public access to higher education in favor of broadening the grant system.

[17]On this, see Éric Martin and Simon Tremblay-Pepin, *Faut-il vraiment augmenter les frais de scolarité ? Huit arguments trompeurs sur la hausse* (Institut de recherche et d'informations socio-économique, 2011).

[18]The 2012 strike was organized jointly by four student organizations: the Coalition large de l'association pour une solidarité syndicale étudiante (Classé); the Fédération étudiante collégiale du Québec (FecQ); the Fédération étudiante universitaire du Québec (FeuQ); and the Table de concertation étudiante du Québec (TaCEQ).

assemblies to vote on whether to join the strike. By mid-March, three-quarters of the province's university and college students had joined the movement. Thus began what would become the most significant season of social protest in Québec's modern history: the so-called *Printemps érable* (Maple Spring).[19] For the first time, a strike in Québec would be waged by students whose entire run through the school system had been shaped by the ways of the new knowledge economy, against the most ambitious attempt to commodify it further.

As the student movement gained strength, the Parti Libéral government kept shunning students, breaching—through its inaction—a social contract at the heart of the *modèle québécois*. It remained aloof as mobilizations grew, content to let courts arbitrate. As a result, hundreds of judicial injunctions were issued, compelling professors to hold classes despite the strike.[20]

On April 20, the Liberal government held the Plan Nord summit to signal its intent to open to mineral-rich territories north of the forty-ninth parallel to extractive industries. With a thousand students protesting outside, Prime Minister Charest quipped drolly to the assembled representatives of the mining industry that the students seemed "so very keen to get in." Egged on by the jocularity of the crowd, he followed suit with an improvised punchline—a thinly veiled allusion to labor camps that spoke volumes of his scorn for students: "I will find them jobs in the North far from here."[21] Three days later, students in Montreal held their first nightly march through

---

[19]Wishing to nod knowingly to the sap of maple trees, which begins to flow in the springtime, and to the Arab spring but succeeding only in evoking a colonial idea of *Québécois* as French-Canadians (it is, after all, a maple leaf that appears on the Canadian flag), France's media—*Le Monde* in particular—popularized the term *Printemps érable* to capture events. On this, see the blog of semiology student, René Lemieux, "Brève traductologique sur le caractère parodique de la grève étudiante, du 'printemps érable' aux manifestations de casseroles" (2012) at *Trahir*. http://trahir.wordpress.com/2012/05/28/lemieux-parodie/

[20]In a typical occurrence, an undergraduate course in anthropology was held on April 3 at Université Laval, under judicial duress following an injunction issued by Judge Bernard Godbout of the Québec Superior Court on behalf of Laurent Proulx. Proulx, a former soldier in Afghanistan taking elective courses to qualify for admission into the law program, had argued against everyone (the university itself, the university-wide students' association, the professors' union, the lecturers' union, the social sciences students' association, and the anthropology students' association) that his individual right to an education had been violated by a collective decision of the general assembly of anthropology students to join the province-wide strike movement. Escorted to his classroom by security forces, Professor Martin Hebert, scheduled to lecture on conflict resolution, turned judicial obligations into pedagogical opportunity. With security guards and media at the door lending something of an "occupation" feel to proceedings and assembled students behaving very much in the fashion of the moment (with "Up Twinkles" indicating approval and "Down Twinkles" disapproval), he drew on Quakers and Graeber and leaned on invited colleagues to give soldier Proulx a proper lesson on the give-and-take of academic relationships.

[21]Videos of the Charest speech at the Salon du Plan Nord are easily found on the internet. See for instance: http://www.youtube.com/watch?v=qXg6zHPaMEM.

the city (Asselin 2012). The crowd's chant echoed its indignation: *Cha-rest de-hors, on va-t'rouver une jobbe dans l'nord* (Charest be out! We'll find you a job up north).

On April 27, the government extended an offer so meager it could only have been received by students' associations as a deliberate gesture—one that underscored their destitution from privileged interlocutor of the state to mere clients boycotting a state-tendered commodity.[22] "A little insulting" as it was—according to Fédération étudiante universitaire du Québec (FEUQ) president Martine Desjardins—the offer was nonetheless dutifully brought to general assemblies, where it was overwhelmingly rejected.

On May 18, 2012, the Charest government adopted an emergency act bearing a distinctly Orwellian title, *Loi permettant aux étudiants de recevoir l'enseignement dispensé par les établissements de niveau postsecondaire qu'ils fréquentent* (Law enabling students to receive instruction from the postsecondary institutions they attend). By it, the winter semester was suspended, the right of peaceful assembly was restricted to gatherings of fifty people or fewer, and—perhaps most significantly—the funding of students' associations made contingent on the compliance of leaders. Professors were threatened with liability for the content of their courses and all other public utterances concerning the strike movement—tweets included, as education minister Michèle Courchesne emphasized (Lamarre 2012).

Immediately, the Loi was denounced by the Québec Bar Association as prejudicial to the constitutional rights of Quebeckers. On May 20, Classé launched its Arrêtez-moi quelqu'un (Someone arrest me) website, inviting people to post portraits of themselves online, holding signs vowing to disobey the new law. More than 3,000 people responded in the weeks that followed. At this critical juncture, the quite quotidian—often playful—nature of their performance spoke eloquently of radical ordinariness. Some held hastily printed pictures of Mahatma Gandhi or Martin Luther King Jr, and others wore playful costumes. Many posted with their cats and dogs. One woman dressed up as Rosie the Riveter. People posed alone or with friends, many in their kitchen—a privileged site of *québécois* sociability. Separately and simultaneously, at home in the world, they participated in the largest act of civil disobedience in Québec history.

Within days, the emblematic red square of the student movement had been carried on the red carpet at the Cannes film festival by the crew of Xavier Dolan's film *Laurence Anyways*—which won the Queer Palm for best LGBT film—and on the set of *Saturday Night Live* by Montreal-based Arcade Fire. Amnesty International, the Canadian Civil Liberties Associations, and the UN's Human Right's Commission made their concerns known, while Anonymous launched "Operation Québec," a concerted cyberattack on the

[22]The offer tendered to students was to spread tuition hikes over seven rather than five years and in the process to up fees from $1,625 to $1,778.

websites of the Liberal Party, the Ministry of Education, and the Montreal police. In New York, Berlin, Madrid, Taiwan, London, and Paris, students marched in defense of Quebeckers' right to demonstrate, an agitation picked up by news services around the globe and immediately relayed to Quebeckers by local media.

Quite in a rush, the fight over tuition fees became constitutive of a totality in movement—its momentum outpacing everyone's capacity to define or contain it. Gaining in numbers and resonance, public demonstrations became radically about themselves, in the eyes of both participants and police. People banged on casseroles, and news was made of blogs tracking the inchoate movement of crowds. The most prosaic questions far removed from any questions related to higher education came to shape public discourse: "Where is the crowd now?" "Where is it heading?" and "Where are the police?"

Applying tactics developed to deal with antiglobalization protests (Sagar 2011), police across Québec kettled-in protesters. Night after night, crowds made up of individuals guilty only of crimes of presence were toyed with in cat-and-mouse fashion; until, as if on a whim, police interrupted the movement they had provoked to trap the crowd in place. Those caught were made to wait, as time and not movement, became the measure of police power. After having been displayed, people were arrested and sent—hands tied behind their back—to waiting buses and driven around before being charged with minor traffic violations.

The Parti Libéral government called for negotiations to resume on May 27. For three days, student leaders met with the education minister. Unwilling to compromise on tuition increase, a matter of principle the minister said, the government offered students another measly concession: the yearly rise in tuition fees could be reduced by $35 a year. Again, the offer was rejected by general assemblies. On May 31, the government walked out of negotiations.

As summer approached, Anonymous released a video threatening to upset the upcoming Formula 1 Grand Prix—by far the biggest tourist event in Montreal. On June 3 the director of the "Just for Laughs Festival," which billed itself as the largest comedy festival in the world, appealed to reason and called for a meeting student representatives. It was agreed that an off-festival benefit would be held. In exchange, students would refrain from disturbing the official festival. On the first day of the Grand Prix, 3,000 people took part in a naked demonstration. Of raw life standing against political reductions, there can be few clearer images than that of 3,000 people in underwear protesting a government's intransigeance.

A local event overdetermined by a global sense of happenings, the *Printemps érable* could only find resolution outside of itself. On August 1, Premier Charest called a general election to be held on September 4—the very day classes were due to resume in universities. The campaign was as short as is legally allowed in Québec and as unfocused as summertime politics can be. Indeed, it was hardly question of higher education at all. Even Léo Bureau-Blouin—the very visible spokesperson of the Fédération étudiante collégiale du Québec (FECQ), now candidate for the Parti Québécois—drowned issues related to the *Printemps érable* in aseptic references to youthful desires for change.

On September 4, the long *printemps érable* ended with the election of the Parti Québécois. Student returned to class—some to finish courses that had been interrupted by the strike, and others to begin a new term. On the day she was sworn in as Premier, Parti Québécois leader Pauline Marois promised to abrogate the Loi permettant aux étudiants; to cancel tuition increases, which had already appeared on student invoices; and to hold another summit on the financing of higher education in the age of the new knowledge economy.[23]

At the Université du Québec en Outaouais, teach-ins took place under the gaze of surveillance cameras installed over the summer in departments where students had voted in favor of the strike.

"Safe Spaces" at Yale and Mizzou (2015)

The idealization of universities as "academic villages" (what Thomas Jefferson called the University of Virginia in his 1825 commencement speech) and the commodification of the "college experience"—sold wholesale to parents as safe and welcoming—combine to give higher education in the United States the allure of a distinct, almost familial realm where social conflicts and issues can be staged without risk, under the watchful eye of administrations, understood until the mid-1960s to be acting in *loco parentis* (in lieu of parents). In the age of exterminism, such staging has sometimes led to the recasting of conflicts over knowledge production as struggles over "safe space." In oft-told tales, two paradigmatic figures get pitted against each other. On one side stands the Student—imagined as inherently vulnerable, or else mocked as a coddled figure hiding from "scary ideas … with coloring books, cookies and Play-Doh" (Barrier et al. 2016). On the other side are Professors and Administrators, figured as guardians of the university's truth function. In their imagined encounter, a detached sort of freedom, having little to do with any real-life social relations, appears to be at stake.

Considering two recent events—one situated at the core of the old regime of *academic freedom* and the other at its periphery—we can see, beyond abstracting discourses, how notions of safe space get invoked strategically by students to claim a measure of autonomy from the exterminist reinvention of social relations of knowledge production and by university administrations to foreclose scholarly relations.

[23]The Sommet sur l'enseignement supérieur du Québec took place February 25–26, 2013.

Black Lives Matter (BLM) emerged in July 2013 as "an ideological and political intervention" that was also a Twitter hashtag (Garza 2014; Ross 2015). In 2014, the phrase moved from social media to the streets and came "to signify a movement" (Freelon et al. 2016). Not a platform or an organization per se but, rather, an idea of life itself circumstantially embodied when and where it was most threatened: in Florida after the killing of Trayvon Martin; in Ferguson Missouri after that of Michael Brown; in New York City after Eric Garner was killed by the NYPD; in Cleveland after Tamir Rice was shot, and others. In 2015, BLM gained coherence as a movement "with political aims [and] policy demands" (Ross, 2015; Eligon 2015b). A policy platform took shape, a ten-point program was put forth, and reports issued on BLM's behalf—most notably by Campaign Zero on the use of body cameras by police. Candidates vying for the Democratic presidential nomination began to be interpellated on what came to be recognized as "BLM issues."

As BLM concerns crossed over to the campuses of privileged, historically white universities, they were transmuted into performative protests against racial signifiers: place and building names, statues, effigies, institutional designations, and so on. At Princeton, students, led by the Black Justice League, demanded that the Woodrow Wilson School of Public and International Affairs be renamed. At Harvard, they opposed the use of the term *masters*, evocative of slavery, to designate college deans, and they asked that the law school change its seal—derived from a slaveholder's coat of arms. At the University of North Carolina at Chapel Hill, students asked trustees to rename Saunders Hall (honoring Ku Klux Klan leader William L. Saunders). At Oberlin College of Arts and Science ("the ideal laboratory in which to ... design the world we want" according to the university's website), students questioned the authenticity of food at Afrika Heritage House and complained that sushi and *bánh mì* served at the school's cafeteria made "a mockery of cultural cuisine" (Heller 2016). At Brandeis, #concernstudents2015 occupied administrative offices in support of demands "for an increase in the number of full-time Black faculty in all departments ... curriculum that would increase racial awareness, annual diversity workshops for faculty, more black school counselors and students, and an office that would investigate student complaints against faculty and staff" (Ransom 2015). At Yale, students demanded that Calhoun College—named for the vice-president of John Quincy Adams and Andrew Jackson, a graduate of Yale College, who famously defended slavery as an act of providence bringing Black and white people together as masters and slave—be renamed (Boyce 2020).

On October 27, 2015—a few days before Halloween, an important date on the activities calendar of US universities—Yale's Intercultural Affairs Committee sent an e-mail asking students to avoid wearing "culturally unaware and insensitive" costumes that could offend minority students.

Specifically, it advised students to steer clear of outfits "that included elements like feathered headdresses, turbans or blackface" (Foundation for Individual Rights in Education [FIRE], 2015b). In courteous Yale fashion, struggles for racial justice were played out: Students wrote emails to complain of university intrusion on their rights of free speech or in support of wider interdictions, slogans were written on bathroom walls, and articles published in the student papers. Wishing to put matters in perspective, Erika Christakis, professor of early childhood education and associate master of Silliman College, wrote an open letter in defense of academic autonomy that explicitly referenced the tradition of universities as "safe space[s] not only for maturation but also for a certain regressive, or even transgressive, experience."

> Pretend play is the foundation of most cognitive tasks, and it seems to me that we want to be in the business of encouraging the exercise of imagination, not constraining it. I suppose we could agree that there is a difference between fantasizing about an individual character vs. appropriating a culture, wholesale.... But then I wonder what is the statute of limitations on dreaming of dressing as Tiana the Frog Princess if you aren't a Black girl from New Orleans? Is it okay if you are eight, but not 18? I don't know the answer to these questions; they seem unanswerable. ... American universities ... it seems, they have become places of censure and prohibition. And the censure and prohibition come from above, not from yourselves ... Have we lost faith in young people's capacity—in your capacity—to exercise self-censure, through social norming, and also in your capacity to ignore or reject things that trouble you.[24]

In response, Yale students accused Christakis and her husband Nicholas—also a Yale "master"—of failing to create a safe space for Silliman residents. Some demanded that they both resign or be fired (FIRE 2015c; Friedersdorf 2015). On November 5, a brief encounter took place that would almost certainly have gone unnoticed had it not been recorded and uploaded to YouTube by Greg Lukianoff, president of FIRE. Gathering around Nicholas Christakis in Silliman's central courtyard, a few students pressed him to apologize for his wife's email. Unwilling to do so, Nicholas apologized instead "for causing pain." As his wife had, he spoke in defense of an idea of academic freedom rooted in older notions of *Lehrfreiheit*. Triggered, students berated Christakis, calling him "disgusting" and shouting at him to "shut up" (Pies 2016; Wang and Wang 2015). With the students' principled outrage spent, the gathering soon fizzled out.

To make amends, Christine and Nicholas Christakis welcomed Silliman students into their home (Master's house) a few days later. Also present

[24]Cited from Foundation for Individual Rights in Education (FIRE 2015a).

were Dean of Yale College Jonathan Holloway, as well as other university administrators. "I have disappointed you," said a contrite Professor Christakis, admitting to a broken heart, "and I'm really sorry. ... I have the same beliefs that you do. ... I'm genuinely sorry to have disappointed you. I've disappointed myself" (Stanley-Backer, 2015a). On November 9, several hundred students—some reports estimated more than a thousand—took part in a well-ordered "March of Resilience" organized by Next Yale, an alliance of Yale students of color and supporters. Framed as a response to Christakis's Halloween-costume email but also to a series of other incidents—including allegations of racial exclusion at the Sigma Alpha Epsilon fraternity—the march brought students from the Afro-American Cultural Center, through campus, ending at the Sterling Memorial Library (named for a Gilded Age corporate lawyer and mega-donor, John William Sterling). A few days later, another procession delivered a petition to the campus residence of University President Peter Salovey—at the quite uncivil hour of midnight (Stanley-Backer 2015b). Appearing alongside his wife on the doorstep of their home, Salovey stood silently as women from Next Yale presented their demands: the hiring of more professors of color across faculties; curriculum changes; the creation of a multicultural center; and the removal or renaming of offensive symbols (Shimer and Wang 2015).

Thanking petitioners, President Salovey pledged a prompt response:

> I feel incredibly strongly that there is no place for racism at Yale. ... I respect what you're trying to accomplish. ... We'll be in touch.
>
> (Stanley-Backer, 2015b)

Days later, President Salovey announced a series of measures to address protesters' concerns, "including more resources for hiring diverse faculty, the creation of a center for the study of race, increased funding for minority student centers, and more support for students in need" (Cole 2016). He also announced that Yale would name two new residential colleges after Anna Pauline Murray, "an advocate for women's rights and African American rights and Benjamin Franklin ... a slave owner who changed ways and became the president of the Abolitionist Society in Philadelphia" (Cole 2016).

By contrast, BLM issues, instead of being reinvented performatively to be settled symbolically, arrived whole at the University of Missouri, where they were lingered unresolved.[25]

The University of Missouri was founded in 1839, when Missouri was a slave state. In 1862, it was designated as the state's land-grant institution under the Morrill Act. Black students were first admitted in 1950—a full

---

[25]I am grateful to Scout Hudson, former editor-in-chief of the *Maneater* for sharing her thoughts on Mizzou's situation. She is, of course, not responsible for what I understood of them.

twelve years after the Supreme Court, following a lengthy battle, finally recognized Lloyd L. Gaines's right to study medicine (Lewis and Barnes 2022: 111). The first Black faculty members were hired in 1969. To this day, it remains a predominantly white university, with Black students making up a relatively small minority of students.[26]

At Mizzou, racial tensions are "woven into the fabric of everyday life" (Eligon 2015a). Rather than being acted out, they manifest themselves in more ordinary, almost private encounters: "I was approached by a white man in a white truck with a confederate flag very visible and proudly displayed. … He leaned out his window … Not only did he spit at me, he called me the n-word and gave me the finger."[27] They also surface in coarse public gestures, ranging from the pinning of the picture of a Black woman's lynching to the door of a Black woman's dorm room (Eligon and Péres-Peña 2015) to the strewing of cotton balls about the Gaines/Oldham Black Culture Center (Sawey and Schrader 2015).

Protests at the University of Missouri–Columbia campus began in August 2015, a year after BLM protests in Ferguson—a suburb of St. Louis, two hours away. Earlier that year, the Department of Justice had released its report condemning the Ferguson police for systematic violations of African Americans' constitutional rights. They were prompted by the university administration's announcement that it would stop paying health insurance for graduate teaching and research assistants (Eligon and Péres-Peña 2015).[28] Though not in itself race-based, this measure had unequal impact on white and Black students. As BLM protests were happening on college campuses across the United States (Larkins 2019), Mizzou's graduate assistants joined forces with antiracist students and took the first steps toward forming a union. Faced with system-wide opposition, the university administration reversed course.

On September 11, Payton Head, the President of the Missouri Students Association, was racially harassed as he walked home (Miller 2015). The following day, he posted on Facebook:

---

[26]The University of Missouri is a four-campus system: the University of Missouri–Columbia (the historic heart of the system, colloquially known as "Mizzou," founded in 1839); the University of Missouri–Kansas City (1933); the University of Missouri–St. Louis (1963); and the Missouri University of Science and Technology in Rolla (founded in 1870 as the Missouri School of Mines and Metallurgy). In 2015, it reported 2,544 Black and/or African American students, making up roughly 7 percent of its student population.

[27]Quotes are from University of Missouri Professor Cynthia Frisby (2015).

[28]Protests in Ferguson began on August 9, 2014, when Michael Brown, an unarmed Black teenager, was killed by a white officer of the Ferguson Police Department. They lasted until mid-August 2015, when the US Department of Justice (DOJ) issued a report condemning the Ferguson Police Department for having systematically violated African American constitutional rights. The DOJ's *Investigation of the Ferguson Police Department* is available from its website at https://www.justice.gov/sites/default/files/opa/press-releases/attachments/2015/03/04/fergusonpolicedepartmentreport.pdf

> Last night as I was walking through campus, some guys riding on the back of a pickup truck decided that it would be okay to continuously scream N——at me. … I really just want to know why my simple existence is such a threat to society.[29]

On October 5, members of the Legion of Black Collegians (LBC) were rehearsing a play on Mel Carnahan quadrangle when "an inebriated white male [called them] n——s." (Miller 2015). Police were called to the scene, but matters went no further. Five days later, "with the LBC abuse still fresh in their minds," eleven African American students interrupted in Mizzou's homecoming parade—a historically white space (Lewis and Barnes 2022: 104).[30] Led by graduate student Jonathan Butler, who had taken part in BLM protests in nearby Ferguson, the eleven "strode out in front of the car, locking arms, clad in black shirts with a red, green, and black power fist" (Lewis and Barnes 2022: 104). Soon, they were surrounding the "gleaming red convertible" in which University of Missouri President Timothy M. Wolfe—a corporate executive that had been brought to Mizzou on a cost-cutting mandate—and his wife were seated, perched atop the back seat and waving at the crowd. "We will be here until we are heard," Butler shouted into his megaphone "and our people are protected, and they feel safe on this campus." Mirroring the car driver's attempts to edge forward, the group held its ground until officers from the Columbia Police Department "pushed them out of the way, threatening to arrest them and rattling cans of pepper spray in their faces" (Miller 2015).

On October 20, student activists from "Concerned Student 1950"—who had been meeting since Payton Head's Facebook post—issued a set of demands. They called on Timothy Wolfe to issue a written apology; for "the University of Missouri to meet the Legion of Black Collegians' demands"; for mandatory "diversity training [to be] established on campus"; for the University of Missouri to create and enforce a comprehensive racial awareness and inclusion curriculum across all campus departments and units; for a strategic plan be devised to "increase retention rates for marginalized students, sustain diversity curriculum and training, and promote a safer and more inclusive campus"; and for greater representation for minorities among the university's teaching staff (Tracy and Southali 2015).[31]

---

[29]Posted by Payton Head on Monday, October 12, 2015, cited in Miller (2015).

[30]"Homecoming" is a peculiarly American tradition celebrating the symbolic return of alumni to their *alma mater*. As such, it is a key moment in fundraising efforts. Mizzou was among the first universities to celebrate homecoming in 1910, by playing "Dixie," the unofficial anthem of Secessionists defenders of slavery, while a white-only fraternity unfurled their flag (Lewis and Barnes, 2022: 112). This particular homecoming tradition endured until 1989.

[31]In March 2016, "Concerned Students 1950" was made the object of a documentary film, titled *Field of Vision*, directed by Adam Dietrich and Varun Bajaj and available on YouTube: https://www.youtube.com/watch?v=fxJLvMxVFdQ.

Four days later, someone drew a swastika with human feces on a bathroom wall of Gateway Hall, a student residence (Teoh and Wynn 2015). This was the second such act that year (Larkins 2019: 12). Concerned not only by the act itself but also by the apparent indifference of the university administration to student safety in general ("Mizzou doesn't give a damn about its Black students"), CS1950 students met again with President Wolfe.[32] After the meeting, they released a statement deploring that Wolfe had "not mention[ed] any plan of action to address the demands or help us work together to create a more safe and inclusive campus."[33]

The following Monday, Jonathan Butler tweeted out that he would go on hunger strike until President Wolfe resigned (Miller 2015). In support, a spontaneous tent camp formed on Mel Carnahan quadrangle (Schroeder 2017: 325).

On November 7, five days into Butler's hunger strike, thirty players from the University of Missouri's football team linked arms in support (Tracy and Southali 2015), vowing to boycott all football-related activities until President Wolfe had stepped down or was removed (Rhoden 2015). Athletic Director Mark Rhoades and head coach Gary Pinkel held a press conference to declare their support for the players. Standing together so publicly, Black players and white coaches alike leveraged visibility: Had they been ignored and the upcoming game against Brigham Young University forfeited, it would have been a "disaster" for Mizzou, both financially and for the recruitment of Black athletes (Rhoden 2015).[34] The same day, CS1950 students started a Change.org petition asking for President Wolfe to step down and for all future University of Missouri presidents and chancellors to be selected by "a collective of students, staff, and faculty of diverse backgrounds" (Brewer 2018: 292).[35] Echoing previous statements, CS1950 students also demanded a 10 percent increase in African American faculty and staff by the

---

[32]The citation is from E. Gallion and T. Oide, "Protests Remind Students, Faculty that 'Racism Lives here,'" cited by Larkins (2019: 8).

[33]The citation is from K. Kovacs. "Protestors Say Talks with President Wolfe Did Not Achieve Resolution," cited in Larkins (2019: 12).

[34]Three intertwined elements of context are crucial to understanding the importance of players' and coaches' action: (i) football is a critical source of revenue for the University of Missouri, as it is for all universities that are member of the National Collegiate Athletic Association. Had the Tigers' game against BYU's Cougars been canceled, then the University of Missouri would have had to forfeit a million dollars in penalties and incur substantial loss in revenues (Eligon and Pérez-Peña 2015: ii). Approximately 76 percent of the student body self-identified as white. In the state of Missouri as a whole, Blacks and/or African Americans comprised 12.5 percent of the total population according to the Missouri Census Data Center (Larkins 2019). Though only 7 percent of Mizzou students are Black, half of the football team is, including well more than two-thirds of the 2015 scholarship class (Rhoden 2015; Gleeson 2015: iii). Coach Gary Robin Pinkel was the winningest coach in the history of Mizzou's Tigers. In "a move [that] shocked the college football world" he announced his retirement a few days after his press conference, before season's end (Tracy 2015).

[35]Within forty-eight hours, the petition had—by its sponsor's own account—garnered seventy-one hundred signatures (Lu 2015).

2017–2018 academic year; a ten-year plan to increase the retention rate of minority students; sustained diversity training; and measures to promote a safer and more inclusive campus (Lu 2015).

Spontaneously, a "safe zone" formed around the encampment. "We need to relax and gather our thoughts," said a Black graduate student identified only as "Mr. Senior" by a white reporter, who ended the interview with a scornful homily:

> time to go out there and start earning a living -paying some taxes, start getting a house and a car and all that good stuff like me.[36]

On the morning of Monday November 9, with Mizzou's student government again demanding President Wolfe's resignation, it was announced that classes would be canceled for two days in favor of teach-ins on race relations. Calling themselves "Concerned Faculty," professors published a statement in support of students and declared their intention to participate in future CS1950 actions.

> We, the concerned faculty of the University of Missouri, stand in solidarity with the Mizzou student activists who are advocating for racial justice on our campus and urge all MU faculty to demonstrate their support by walking out on Monday, November 9 and Tuesday November 10, 2015, along with other allies such as the Forum on Graduate Rights[37]

In a subsequent tweet, "Concerned Faculty" encouraged faculty and students to visit the student campsite on Carnahan quadrangle and demonstrate support.

> the more faculty on Carnahan Quad tomorrow, the better. Hold class, have office hours, grade papers, listen, help

Amid speculation that he would soon be ousted by the University of Missouri's Board of Curators, President Wolfe resigned later the same day (Eligon and Péres-Peña 2015).

That afternoon, the briefest attempt at defending a safe space took place. To shield the encampment, CS1950 and allies linked arms, forming a line that was soon met by student journalist Tim Tai, who had stepped forward from a group of assembled reporters. Chanting "Hey, hey, ho, ho, reporters have got to go," CS1950 students and allies blocked him out. Against the students' demand, Tai invoked his constitutional rights: "I am documenting this for a national news organization. … the First Amendment protects your right to be

[36]Cited from the Dietrich and Bajaj documentary.

[37]"Concerned faculty" tweets are cited from H. Stolze, "Concerned Faculty Cancels Class" (Larkins 2019: 14).

here and mine" (Huguelet and Victor 2015). As the encounter was becoming a situation unto itself, Greek Life and Leadership Assistant Director Janna Basler—identifying herself as "1950"—summoned Tai: "You need to back off right now." The line pushed forward, and Tai was made to retreat.

In the empty space behind the mêlée, *College Fix* contributor Mark Schierbecker, identifying himself as "media," asked to speak to Assistant Professor Melissa Click (Kristof 2015). Repeating Basler's line, Professor Click admonished Schierbecker: "You need to get out." When he refused—"No I don't"—Professor Click, who is white, turned toward Black students observing events from a distance. Agitated by the situation and moved by her "best intentions" (Click 2016), she hollered for support,

> Who wants to help me get this reporter out of here? I need some muscle over here.
>
> (Huguelet and Victor 2015)[38]

The brief moment over, the University of Missouri returned to life much as it had been. Jonathan Butler resumed eating, and football players returned to practice (Péres-Peña and Hauser 2015). On November 10, an anonymous caller phoned in a threat—soon echoed on Yik Yak—to the Gaines/Oldham Black Culture Center:

> I'm going to stand my ground tomorrow and shoot every Black person I see.
>
> (Nero 2015)[39]

Dixit Henri Lefebvre: "In the space of power, power does not appear as such; it hides under the 'organisation of space'. It elides, it evades, it evacuates" (Lefebvre 1981: 376). Counterpower, for its part, sometimes

[38]A video of the event is available at: https://www.nytimes.com/2015/11/10/us/university-missouri-protesters-block-journalists-press-freedom.html. The following day, Melissa Click cut ties with the journalism school, keeping her contractually limited appointment in the department of communications. In March 2016, the department decided not to renew her contract, a decision that led the American Association of University Professors to launch an investigation.

[39]Yi Yak is a public, anonymous, location-based message board popular with college students. "Stand Your ground" is a reference—that everyone at the University of Missouri would have understood—to the case of neighborhood watch coordinator George Zimmerman, accused of killing of Trayvon Martin, an unarmed 17-year-old African American. Initially arrested for the killing, Zimmerman was released a few hours later under the State of Florida's Stand Your Ground statute, first adopted in 2005. After review of the case, Zimmerman's trial on the charge of second-degree murder took place in June 2013 and ended with his acquittal. In February 2015, the US Department of Justice decided not to prosecute Zimmerman for hate crimes. Happening eight years before the murder of George Floyd by Minneapolis police, protests over the killing of Martin—which occurred in more than one hundred US cities—marked the beginnings of a wave of protests against racial violence in the United States.

reveals itself in the deliberate instituting of counterspaces. In contemporary universities, the encounter between the two is overdetermined by exterminist attempts to foreclose scholarly relations. At Yale—a place of privilege where distant dangers are performed—struggles over safeness were played out and then settled in ways consistent with world ordering. At Mizzou—as exposed by the murder of Michael Brown as the University of Atlanta after the lynching of Sam Hose—an awkward safe space was momentarily instituted, allowing scholars to take a step back from the order of the world and gather their thoughts. Then it disappeared.

Rhodes Must Fall, University of Cape Town (2015)

With the idea of a peaceful transition as their go-to legitimizing notion, African National Congress (ANC) governments held the building of postracial capitalism in South Africa in a state of suspension for two decades—facilitating the admission of the Black majority into existing institutions without substantially altering the racial framework inherited from the apartheid period. In higher education, they increased Black students' access to universities while forever postponing the building of "a truly national system of education and training" capable of "redress[ing] past inequalities and [of] transform[ing] the higher education system to serve the new social order."[40] Thirty years after the Universities Amendment Act (1983), and twenty years after the election of the first ANC government (1994), South African universities remained organized in a "very white, middle-class, Eurocentric" system (Everatt 2016: 133).[41]

Owing to structural adjustment programs, post-apartheid ANC governments also cut university funding, further disadvantaging historically Black institutions (Badat and Sayed 2014). In a more open, increasingly market-based system bent on transforming knowledge "into a marketable product, rated, bought and sold by standard units, measured, counted and reduced to staple equivalence by impersonal, mechanical tests" (Mbembe 2016: 30), Black students enrolled proportionally less in institutions of higher education (Hendricks 2018: 27); they continued

[40]The July 1997 Education White Paper, titled "A Programme for the Transformation of Higher Education," is cited in Fiske and Ladd (2004: 207).

[41]The Universities Amendment Act (1983) was the first measure of transition away from the apartheid race-based organization of universities. Colloquially known as the "Quota Act," it allowed historically white universities to admit Black students in limited numbers, "so as not to disturb the established pattern of the population structure of the [admitting] institution" (Behr 1987: 4).

to pay a relatively higher cost for doing so; and their studies remained longer and less certain (Hodes 2017). The best students sought admission into better-endowed, higher-ranked white universities, turning them into privileged sites of struggles over the modalities of the transition (Fiske and Ladd 2004: 214).

The University of Cape Town (UCT) was founded in 1829 as the South African College, "a superior kind of high school [which] also prepared students for matriculation" (Stimie and Geggus 1972: 24). It became a degree-granting university in 1874 and, in 1928, moved to Groote Schuur in the suburb of Rondebosch, on a terrain bequeathed by arch-imperialist Cecil Rhodes. It remained an open university until the Extension of University Education Act (1959) brought all South African universities under the principle of "self-determination for each population group within its own sphere" (Behr 1987: 3). Taking advantage of the principle of "academic-non-segregation," UCT leaned on its ties to the international community of scholars to secure relative autonomy from the apartheid state (Fiske and Ladd 2004: 204). It retained some freedom to decide for itself whom to hire, whom to admit, and how to go about articulating an integrated learning environment with a racially ordered society (Stimie and Geggus 1972). In the 1980s, the number of Black students at UCT increased—especially in programs not offered in historically Black universities (Mabokela 1997: 3–4). As a result, campus-based protests came to be articulated more tightly then in other white universities with broader social protests against apartheid. This linking led police to invade the UCT campus in 1987. By the 2010s, Black students had been in majority at UCT for more than a decade (Mabokela 1997: 3), yet in its structure and functioning, the university remained "the whitest institution in the whitest city" (Cini 2019: 950). "Of 256 professors, 147 [were] white, ... 10 black, seven colored, 17 Indian and 69 other nationalities" (Govender 2016).[42]

On March 9, 2015, political science student Chumani Maxwele—consciously referencing recent protests from activists in the nearby township of Khayelitsha (Robins 2014a, b) and perhaps also drawing from the broader tradition of dirty protest against colonial rule (O'Keefe 2012; Collins 2008)—"picked up one of the buckets of shit that sat reeking on the kerbside" and hurled its contents at the "brooding" statue of Cecil Rhodes ("chin resting on fist, a scroll in his left hand"), demanding that it be removed from

[42]The continuous underrepresentation of Black students in historically white universities is an object of much scholarly attention. For a brief survey of the literature, see Breetzke and Hedding (2018).

campus (Hall 2015).[43] As students chanted "One settler, One bullet" in rude defiance of official nonracialism (Maylam 2005: 567), Maxwele emphasized his performance with a rhetorical appeal to collective memory

> This poo that we are throwing on the statue represents the shame of black people. By throwing it on the statue we are throwing our shame to white affluence. ... there is no collective history here—where are our heroes and ancestors?[44]

On March 11, UCT's Student Representative Council issued a formal statement condemning the failure to rid the campus of Rhodes's statue as "symptomatic of the lack of transformative actions being taken by the institution" (Schmahmann 2016: 90). Two days later, students began gathering on Jammie Plaza, in the heart of what heritage scholar Nick Shepherd referred to as "the last Rhodesian Landscape" in South Africa.[45] On March 20, students broke into Bremner Building, the administrative center of the university and an important site of student protest during the Mafeje affair (Phillips 2019: 284), renaming it Azania House, "the black-consciousness inspired name that people used during apartheid as

---

[43]The statue under which UCT students gathered was commissioned in the early 1930s by the Rhodes National South African Memorial Committee and installed on campus in the midst of what Maylam (2005) in *The Cult of Rhodes* termed the "second wave" of Rhodes commemorations, when "the links between the white settler minority in Southern Rhodesia and the British in South Africa needed affirmation as the legitimacy and survival of the settler state depended on this racial and economic relationship" (Phimister 1988). The statue is "a 1.5 times life-size bronze statue in a similar pose as that of Auguste Rodin's *The Thinker*. [It] has Rhodes seated with a map in one hand, a symbol of his dream of empire, with his 'imperial gaze' on the landscape below the hills" (Knudsen and Andersen 2019: 242). Engraved on the statue's pedestal is an excerpt from Rudyard Kipling's "The Song of Cities" specifically referencing Cape Town, amid a dozen other paragraphs pertaining to cities in the British Empire: "I dream my dream; by rock and heath and pine; of empire to the northland; Ay, one land from lion's head to line." The statue was a focal point of protest before Rhodes Must Fall movement. On the occasion of UCT's 150th anniversary in 1979, antiapartheid protesters covered it in pink paint in protest against perceived wasteful expenditures (Knudsen and Andersen 2019: 248) and Schmahmann (2016: 96). This protest was perhaps referenced by Maxwele, who wore a pink safety hat as he threw the bucket of feces. During Heritage Day in 2007, students adorned the statue with paraphernalia linked to the widely supported Johannesburg football team, the Kaizer Chiefs. In May 2014, UCT organized a forum to debate the removal of the statue. "[A] Intervention to the sculpture ... took place on the eve of the event. The words 'Remember Marikana' were painted across its pedestal, and a stylized figure wearing a blanket and represented with an outstretched arm stenciled on it."

[44]Maxwele is cited from Ndelu (2017b: 64) and from Holmes and Loehwing (2016: 1219).

[45]"Jammie Plaza" is a UCT colloquialism for Jameson Plaza, named after Leander Starr Jameson, a Professor of Natural History at the University of Edinburgh who became a close associate of Rhodes, serving as Managing Director of the British South Africa Company and Prime Minister of the Cape Colony. Nick Shepherd is Professor of African Studies and Archeology at UCT. He is cited in Knudsen and Andersen (2019: 241).

an alternative name for a liberated South Africa" (Naicker 2016: 54).[46] A safe space by another name (and frequent site of student occupations), it "functioned as the headquarters for all radical activity on the UCT campus" during protests (Naicker 2016: 54).[47]

For three weeks, students gathered on Jammie Plaza, singing, drumming, and dancing. "About a hundred students sleep[t] overnight in Azania house" (Schmahmann 2016: 91). Rhodes's statue was tagged with graffiti, its body at times covered in garbage bags, and its nose sanded off with an angle grinder (Mortlock 2015). On March 27, the statue was boarded up pending final decision on its removal. On April 8, the University Council voted in favor of removing it altogether from UCT's upper campus. The following day—merely a month after Maxwele's dirty protest—it was lifted by a backhoe loader, put on a flatbed truck, and driven off campus as selfie-taking students intoned songs of struggles and toyi-toyied with varying degrees of enthusiasm and malaise according to where they would have stood in the apartheid order of people. Those who would have been classified as Black clapped hands and chanted, "One Settler, One Bullet"; others who would have been white thronged around shouting, "Rhodes must fall" in English but not "*uRhodes kufanele awe*" in Xhosa or "*Rhodes o swanetse awe*" in Tswana (Hill 2015).

To write that Maxwele's throwing of feces triggered a "wave" of student protest in South Africa would accurately highlight the breadth and energy of "Rhodes Must Fall" protests, but it would draw undue attention to a single moment in a movement that—as fulgurant as it was—drew on prior protests on and off campus and transformed itself as it grew. Each episode of protest belonged to itself, to the wider movement of students,

[46]The "Mafeje affair" was a *cause célèbre* in apartheid South Africa. After completing his undergraduate studies at UCT, Archie Mafeje (1936–2007), a Black South African, went on to Cambridge University where he wrote a PhD thesis on "Social and Economic Mobility in a Peasant Society: A Study of Commercial Farmers in Buganda." In August 1967, Mafeje applied for a Senior Lecturer position at UCT and was offered the job. The offer was rescinded after pressure from Minister of National Education Jan de Clerk. This led to significant protests by UCT administrators, professors, and students who marched *en masse* and held sit-ins and teach-ins (Plaut 2010). Defending academic autonomy, they leaned on a separation that Mafeje himself questioned: "the whole thing is so superficial ... the student ... talking about this university autonomy business. But do they think they can have a free university in a society that is not free. ... suppose I had been allowed to join the faculty of Cape Town University would they have protested against the fact that I would be forced to live off the campus? ... that I would have to have a permit to stay in Cape Town? So long as I can sit with them for a few hours a day in the university canteen, many of them would call that academic freedom." Mafeje is cited here, from an interview given to *The Guardian*'s Jonathan Steele. On this, see also Phillips (2019: 218).

[47]On the first day of the academic year 2016, UCT students constructed yet another safe space, the starkness of which reflected the intwining of academic struggles and broader struggles against the exclusion of Black people. The structure, made of corrugated iron, wood, and iron nails, was erected at the top of the steps leading to Jameson Hall. It was named "Shackville," in "an overt intertextual reference to the Sharpeville massacre of March 21, 1960, in which sixty-nine unarmed protestors were killed by police for demonstrating against passbooks laws" (Oxlund 2016: 9). It was demolished by police and private security.

and to broader struggles for inclusion and equality in South Africa. In the fashion of the moment, each begot its own Twitter (now X) hashtag: At Stellenbosch University (*#OpenStellenbosch*) students shouted down Wim de Villiers on the day he was being installed as vice-chancellor (Peterson 2015), and they staged protests against the continued use of Afrikaans as a teaching language. At Rhodes University—a large "oppressively white" university situated in a small Black town in the middle of the Eastern Cape (the poorest province in South Africa)—students staged demonstrations and sit-ins against the slow pace of transformation and the lack of inclusiveness. They demanded that the name of their university be changed; that gender violence ended (*#patriarchymustfall*); and curricula decolonized (Adebajo 2020).[48] At the University of the Witwatersrand in Johannesburg (*#witsfeesmustfall*), students protested a proposed hike in tuition fees; the subjection of women *(#Imbokodolead*); and the privatization of service jobs (*#Outsourdcingmustfall*). They blocked access to campus (*#witsshutdown*), forcing the cancelation of all classes (*#witshasshutdown*).[49] For three days, students were in full control of the university—a "revolutionary moment" for Wits Professor David Dickinson (Oxlund 2016: 7). At the University of Pretoria, students demanded that competence in Afrikaans language be removed as a condition for employment (*#AfrikaansMustFall*, *#UPRising*). For the first time since the end of apartheid era, they marched to the House of Parliament, protesting against the rising cost of university fees (Hodes 2017: 140). Stones were flung at policemen in riot gear, tires set alight, and green paint hurled at the statue of iconic *voortrekker* Paul Kruger (Holmes and Loehwing 2016; Maclean 2015).

Having begun in historically white universities, the *#Mustfall* movement soon charged struggles in historically Black universities, which had been rendered more vulnerable by postapartheid neoliberal reforms (Hodes 2017: 140). At the Cape Peninsula University of Technology (*#FreeDecolonisedEducation!*, *#EndOutsourcing!*, *#FreeRegistration*) students protested against poor infrastructures, the poverty of financial aid, and the payment of registration fees. Singing historic songs of struggle, they forced the shutdown of all operations (Ndelu 2017a). At the University

---

[48]In the second year of the struggle, the names of eleven men allegedly guilty of rape were circulated on social media (*#RUReferencelist*). A crowd of students gathered at the student center and marched together to the male students' residences "with the intention of rounding up the listed students. Three of the students on the list were apparently rounded up by the crowd of students, who threatened to take matters into their own hands" (Meth 2017: 100).

[49]*Imbokodo* is an isiZulu word, meaning "rock," which was used with reference to *Wathint'abafazi, wathint'imbokodo, uzakufa! Ubobhasopa*! (You strike women, you strike a rock, you will be crushed!) a battle cry of South African Women linked to a women's march on Union Buildings in Pretoria on August 9, 1956, against a broadening of Pass Laws to include women. For a broad overview of protests at the University of the Witwatersrand, see Desai (2018). At the moment of writing, it was available on Vimeo on demand: https://vimeo.com/ondemand/everythingmustfall. Professor Dickinson is cited from the documentary, at 18:44.

of the Western Cape, students graffitied "BEING BLACK IS SHIT!!!" on the walls of administrative offices and "BIKO LIVES" on the walls of a university residence (Maringira and Gukurume 2017: 36). At the University of the Free State, they unbolted a bronze statue of apartheid President Charles Robberts Swart (*dit* blackie) and threw it in a nearby pond (Merwe and Reenen 2016). At the University of South Africa—an Open-Distance e-Learning institution (ODEL) based in Johannesburg—students mobilized against outsourcing. At Nelson Mandela Metropolitan University in Port Elisabeth, they clashed with police, "who used gas and rubber bullets to force control of the situation" (Oxlund 2016: 8). At the University of KwaZulu-Natal's Howard College Campus in Durban, they mobilized around a wide-ranging list of concerns and demands: rejection of changes to the online application system of National Student Financial Aid Scheme; rejection of planned increases in tuition fees; cancelation of all student debts; construction of proper facilities for students living with disabilities; the immediate expulsion of racist lecturers; full reporting of all rape on campus; and details of ways to protect students against rape and other gender-based violence (Kujeke 2017: 88). A statue of King George V was splashed with white paint. Its head was covered in a knitted Rastafarian-colored beanie and a message hung around its neck that read: "END WHITE PRIVILEGE" (Schmahmann 2016: 92). Unattributed citations printed on A4 paper were plastered on the statue—perhaps a reappropriation of scholarly referencing or an attempt to reanimate a sense of history numbed by the legitimizing discourses of the postapartheid rainbow state coalition:

> The white race is the chosen race and blacks will work for us forever.
> Our identity, our statues, our heritage and no one can remove them.
> We rule universities as whites and all of the blacks are our servants
> (Wilson 2001)

In a reappropriation of their own, Professors made themselves "Professors of Protest." In the process, they defined the university as a relatively autonomous site of critical relations:

> If it means that we offer a space for free and critical dialogue about academic and financial exclusion; if it means decolonising the curriculum; if it means fighting, teaching and writing for social justice; if it means we put our bodies between students and security services to defend the right of our students to register their dissatisfaction, alienation and marginalisation; and, finally, if it means we defend the public university as a space for critical dialogue and exchange, then we are, proudly, Professors of Protest.[50]

[50]Settler et al., Letter: The "Professors of Protest" at UKZN Respond to the M&G's Story (2016), http://mg.co.za/article/2016-10-07-00-letters-to-the-editor-october-7-to-13-2016, accessed February 5, 2017, cited in Kujeke (2017: 92).

At Bristol University, student protests focused on Wills Tower, named after Henry Overton Wills III—a university founder and financial backer associated by tobacco trade to slavery in the Americas.[51] At Oxford University—where many UCT graduates pursue further studies (Chigudu 2020: 307)—protests centered on a statue of Cecil Rhodes hover[ing] out of plain sight above a doorway on the front of Oriel College's Rhodes Building on busy High Street, occupying "a position of simultaneous invisibility and hypervisibility. It is an always present, shaping political, economic and cultural force, but goes unnamed and unseen" (Gebrial 2018: 27).[52] On November 6, 2015, "300 students occupied the square outside Oriel College chanting in call-and-response fashion—'Rhodes Must Fall! Take it Down!'" (Chigudu 2020: 303). "Inconvenient questions" were raised about Oxford's imperial past, and a petition demanding the statue's removal was submitted (Chigudu 2020: 303). Chancellor Chris Patten balked, framing protests as part of a broader attack on free speech and exhorting students to read Karl Popper's *The Open Society*—"the most important book for any undergraduate" (Newsinger 2016: 2).[53] Echoing events across the Black Atlantic, Oxford students—who prior to the Rhodes Must Fall protests had held solidarity marches and teach-ins in support of BLM protests in Ferguson (Gebrial 2018: 32)—chanted "black staff matters" in protest of outsourcing at Oxford.

Hopping and skipping from campus to campus—everywhere the same and different—*#RhodesMustFall* protests acquired in motion the allure of a political movement. Called "fallism" (Ahmed 2019; Ndelu 2017b; Mabasa 2017; Heffernan 2018), it was taken to be the thing of "fallists"

---

[51]The citation is from https://www.thebristorian.co.uk/publichistory/thewillsfamilyandsmoking.

[52]Oriel College is where Cecil Rhodes studied and where he composed *Confession of Faith*, his ode to Anglo-Saxon racial expansion: "I contend that we are the finest race in the world and that the more of the world we inhabit the better it is for the human race." It is also where, in 1891, he sought inspiration for the building of a university on the very site where UCT would move its main campus in 1928 (Maylam 2005: 63) and where the Rhodes Chair in Race Relations was established in 1953. His statue was installed in 1932, two years before the UCT statue was erected in the midst of a bicontinental "spate of Rhodes monument-erecting" (Maylam 2005: 58).

[53]Patten, who was imperial Governor of Hong Kong when the island was retroceded to China after a century and a half of British rule, also invited students unhappy with conditions at Oxford, to "go to China" (Espinoza 2016: 1, 8). His impolitic rebuke found many scholarly echoes, most notably in a statement by a group of academics led by University of Canterbury Professor Frank Furedi ("students who are offended by opposing views are perhaps not yet ready to be at university"), and in a *Times* interview with Oxford Professor Nigel Biggar who reframed Rhodes's imperialism as a belief "in the modernity and progress that the British empire of his time represented" (Khan 2015). "More jarring" still was a commentary from Cambridge Professor, Mary Beard in the *Times Higher Education Supplement* arguing that RMF Oxford was "a dangerous attempt to erase the past" and suggesting that minority students be empowered to look at the statue with "a cheery and self-confident sense of un-batterability" (Mary Beard, "Mary Beard Says Drive to Remove Cecil Rhodes Statue from Oxford University Is a 'Dangerous Attempt to Erase the Past'," *The Independent*, December 22, 2015).

(Chinguno et al. 2017; Headley and Kobe 2017; Herwitz 2022). Seeing it as a moment in the little tradition of scholarly struggles, we see students in South Africa acting at the intersection of local struggles to deracialize social relations of knowledge production and neoliberal attempts to bring what UCT Professor of Anthropology Francis B. Nyamnjoh (2020) called "convivial scholarship" beyond the limits of South Africa's suspended revolution.

"Convivial scholarship" might appear as a call to reconciliation—perhaps even an attempt to placate or contain the Rhodes Must Fall moment. But recognized for its ethical commitment to the "mutually responsive, reciprocal engagement ... of student-and-teacher" (Beyer 2023: xvi), and for its emphasis on the inherent incompleteness of social relations in knowledge production—"in convivial scholarship, there are no final answers, only permanent questions and ever-exciting new angles of questioning"—it can be recognized as an attempt to delineate the possible autonomy of South African universities. "Confront[ing] and humbl[ing] the challenge of over-prescription, over-standardization, over-routinization, and over-prediction ... especially those that seek to ... oversimplify the social realities of the people, places and spaces it seeks to understand and explain," it defines *freedom in thinking* in a particular moment in the transition between South African apartheid and neoliberal world ordering.[54]

The Canceling of Angela Davis (2021)

Understood as a political event, the canceling of Angela Davis's Zoom talk at Butler University in Indiana on April 1, 2021—titled "Joint Struggle and Collective Liberation: A conversation with Angela Davis"—was an inconsequential, almost mundane incident in the life of a militant who, for more than half a century, has been animated by the ideal of "the indivisibility of justice" (Cholshi 2019).

> I support Palestinian political prisoners just as I support current political prisoners in the Basque Country, in Catalunya, in India, and in other parts of the world[55]

In this context, Davis appears in familiar guise. She is "Angela the red"—as *Time* magazine called her when it made her its woman of the year in 1971 (Gore 2011: 204n74 ; a "symbol of the struggle for Black liberation, anticapitalism and feminism" (Goffman 1964); a latter-day reembodiment of that figure on those FBI's Wanted posters; an "emotionally unstable, sexual siren" (Roman 2020); a Deleuzean thing of libido (Kaplan 2012);

[54]Citations are from Nyamnjoh (2020: 5, 27).
[55]Angela Davis, cited in Cholshi (2019).

that cameo-like profile on countless signs carried during the Manifestation pour la liberation d'Angela Davis in Paris.[56] She is an agitator on campus, a troubling, foreign presence.

When seen instead as a moment in the history of social relations of knowledge production, the canceling of Professor Davis's talk sheds light on what is at stake in the rise of *academic freedom* as an organizational concept. Here, she appears not as "pop-cultural reference point" (Goffman 1964) but as a scholar among scholars. She is a Brandeis-and-Sorbonne–educated professor of philosophy who worked with Theodor Adorno at the Institut für Sozialforschung in Frankfurt, and with Herbert Marcuse in Paris and San Diego (Davis 2014); a "good sociologist and philosopher" (Langer 1974); author and coauthor of many academic books (Davis 1981, 1983, 1990, 1994, 1999, 2012, 2016) and articles in peer-reviewed journals (Davis 1996, 2000, 2003, 2004, 2013, 2018). What was at stake in the canceling of her talk is not the indivisibility of justice—and thus the unity of all struggles against injustices—but, rather, the possibility for scholars to step back from political interpellations and enter into relatively indeterminate, self-defined, relations with one another (George 2020).

Long overdetermined by the power of the Israel lobby in US universities (Mearsheimer 2015; Butler 2006), the "Palestinian exception" to academic freedom (Bangstad 2025; Fúnez-Flores 2024) served as a proving ground for the capacity of university administrations to foreclose scholarly debate well before October 2023 (Langen 2008). To see more clearly into this, we might consider the censuring of Tariq Ramadan at the University of Notre Dame (2004); of Norman G. Finkelstein at DePaul University (2007); of Terri Ginsberg at North Carolina State University (2008); of Steven Salaita at the University of Illinois at Urbana–Champaign (2014); of Omar Barghouti's campus speaking tour (2019); and of Rabab Abdulhadi at San Francisco State University (2020). We might also recall more ordinary events: the scrutiny and disciplining of Joseph Massad, George Saliba, and Hamid Dabashi at Columbia University (2004–2005); the suspension of Students for Justice in Palestine (SJP) at Northeastern University (2014); the tolerated disruptions of guest lectures by Ali Abunimah at the University of Michigan (2015) or Kristian Davis Bailey at Stanford (2014); the momentary canceling at UC Berkeley of a student-led course on "Palestine: A Settler Colonial Analysis" (2016); Fordham University's refusal to recognize SJP as a student organization (2016), and so on. At stake in all these events is the ability of scholars to disenclave what Edward Saïd (1992) termed "the Question of Palestine" beyond the narrow terrain on which it is confined by the US system of knowledge production (Riemer 2016).

[56]The Manifestation pour la liberation d'Angela Davis, which took place in Paris on November 13, 1970, was the largest demonstration in the city since the end of occupation movement. It went from the headquarters of the Communist party to the Place de la Bastille, "the revolutionary heart of the city" (Kaplan 2012: 211).

The episode at Butler University follows in direct continuity with these previous events; its rapid unfolding underscores how swiftly *academic freedom* can be made to operate once recast as an organizational concept.

Answering in part the administration crackdown on pro-Palestinian activism on campus—a high-point of which was a push to adopt resolutions embracing the International Holocaust Remembrance Alliance's censuring definition of antisemitism (Arria 2020)—the Butler's Student Government Association (SGA) Diversity, Equity and Inclusion Board—endorsed by the Gender and Sexuality Studies Department and the Hub for Black Affairs and Community Engagement—reached out on December 6, 2020, to Gotham Artists, the agency representing Professor Davis (Early and Stratton 2021). She signed her contract on January 9, 2021, and preparations began for the Zoom event. On March 15, an advertisement designed by SGA's marketing and communication team was posted on social networks and sent out to the media (Early and Stratton 2021), making the event known outside SGA circles. Immediately, Butler's administration began pulling "policies left and right," invoking "never enforced regulations"—according to SGA president chair Roua Daas (2021)—to force the cancelation of the event.

Butler's administration did not ban the talk outright. In true governance fashion, it engaged SGA principals in narrow, precircumscribed, behind-the-scenes negotiations, impressing on them only those the reasons—framed as procedural and financial—why it would be unreasonable to honor the invitation extended to Professor Davis, never allowing talks to spill into broader question of censorship or to threaten the university's long-standing embargo on the question of Palestine. The key policy invoked was a regulation requiring prior approval for outside speakers before they could be publicly invited on campus. Though this regulation—created after the October 2019 "Boycott and Safe Protesting 101" seminar and art show on activism—had never been enforced before (Early and Stratton 2021), Butler's administration framed the SGA's failure to comply with it as a violation of established process, shifting financial and organizational risk squarely onto the SGA (Jaschik 2021). At issue was the honorarium owed to Davis, a five-figure sum that the SGA would have been obliged to cover in full had the university withdrawn institutional backing, together with ancillary expenses for promotion and technical support (Jaschik 2021).

Beyond monetary issues, the administration's language—emphasizing that "established processes weren't followed" and that "funding for the program ... was neither discussed nor authorized by the SGA student senate"—conveyed a veiled threat that SGA officers might themselves be exposed to contractual liabilities and that future budget allocations might be jeopardized if they proceeded (Herron 2021). Such risks were hardly abstract: Davis was represented by Gotham Artists, and contracts negotiated through external agencies typically contain cancelation clauses that, once deadlines pass, expose signatories to financial penalties (Early and Stratton 2021).

On the evening of March 29—two days before the (virtual) visit of Davis was to take place, and only a few hours before contractual guarantees were set to take effect—the SGA, compelled to act as the agent of its own compliance, wrote to rescind its invitation, putting an end of any possibilities for Butler scholars to meet with Professor Davis—even virtually, even for the briefest unit of time—to think for themselves about the goings-on in Palestine.[57] Answering critiques in the most depoliticizing manner possible, Butler's administration later claimed that the event—which it labeled a meeting with Ms., not Professor, Davis—had been postponed by the student government itself because "established processes weren't followed for this substantial expenditure of student activity fees" (Herron 2021).

The University of California Academic Labor Movement (1983–2022)

Contingent—adjunct, casual, contractual, midlevel, non–tenure-track, and temporary—faculty is a pure product of cognitive capitalism (Boutang 2007).[58] Indispensable to the proper functioning of contemporary universities (American Association of University Professors [AAUP] 2022; McNaughtan et al. 2017: 9), it is largely invisible from any Humboldtian understanding of academic freedom (Gappa and Leslie 1993). It constitutes a class of scholars who are neither professors nor students—and yet both at once—which aspires to, but cannot claim, the freedom to research, teach, or learn. What autonomy it has can only be wholly derived from that of the organization that employs it, and whatever intellectual indeterminacy it may desire stands at odds with its subservient position in the production of knowledge. Academic strikes are a product of the situation in which it finds itself.

Strikes, of course, were part of the original repertory of scholarly actions. The 1299 *cessasio* in Paris was a strike (*grève*), arguably the first in the

[57]"[A] few scholars meeting for a brief unit of time" alludes to "Sur le passage de quelques personnes à travers une assez courte unité de temps," a script written by Guy Debord, a founder of the Internationale Situationniste, on the alienating reduction of everyday life in the society of the spectacle and the possibilities of constructed situations (Debord 1978). It is also the title of a short experimental film he made, available on YouTube: https://www.youtube.com/watch?v=mHLrzhk745c

[58]*Midlevel faculty* is a term used in Germany to refer to "an ill-defined intermediate layer of scientists employed by universities, who are neither students nor full professors. Some of the members of this status group are still in the process of completing a Ph.D. program ... others are post-docs, and some are teaching or research fellows or coordinate research projects" (Gallas: 2018: 92 n1). A fifty-word-long list of terms used for contingent faculty in the United States is cited in Worthen and Berry (1999) and reproduced in the introduction to Berry (2005).

modern sense of the term (Gorochov 2012).[59] Once professors and students became privileged subjects of *academic freedom*, however, striking fell out of practice in universities—half-a-century after it had replaced "machine-wrecking, rioting and the destruction of property in general" in the world of labor (Hobsbawm 1952: 58). After the First World War, Fordism installed itself as a hegemonic mode of social regulation at the core of world ordering (Aglietta 1979). Strikes became a more regulated, less disruptive part of the repertory of workers' actions, but academic strikes remained exceedingly rare. Tenured and organized into professional associations (the AAUP; the Association of University Teachers; the Deutscher Hochschulverband, etc.), professors did not view themselves as employees but as professionals in mission-driven institutions. Commensurate with their standing in society, they favored representation over action. Students, for their part, remained confined in eminently prudent and respectable associations (the Union Nationale des étudiants de France, the American Student Union, the Deutsche Studentenschaft, etc.). Even when faced with frontal attacks—by the fascist state in Germany or during the McCarthy era in the United States—scholars in general did not strike back. Rather, they shrunk into complicit inactions (Schrecker 1986).

Only with the emergence of managerial universities did scholars in the core of the old world-system of states and universities reacquaint themselves with the practice of striking—often by joining unions not traditionally connected in higher education: the Communication Workers of America (CWA) at the State University of New York; the State, County and Municipal Employees Union (SCMEU) at the University of Wisconsin; the Vereinte Dienstleistungsgewerkschaft (US Trade Union, *ver. di*) in Germany; the National Association of Teachers in Further and Higher Education (NATFHE) in Britain; the Canadian Union of Public Employees (CUPE) in Canada, and others.

---

[59]*Grève* is the French word for strike. The word comes from the Old French *gravele*, itself derived from the Vulgar Latin *grava* and is attested from the ninth century. In twelfth-century Paris, it referred specifically to the *place de la grève*, a gravelly beach on the banks of the Seine used to load and unload merchandises, as an informal marketplace, and, occasionally, for public executions. There, workers waited in the hope of being hired. If a worker was unhappy with his employer, he could leave and return to the *grève*; if it was the employer who was dissatisfied, he could leave the worker stranded on the *grève*—in effect abandoning him to the whims of an unregulated market. In 1229, Paris's *studium generale* gathered on the *place de la grève* before they left the city. When the creation of universities became folded in the process of state-building, more modern *grèves* were organized in defense of scholarly privileges—giving the word an academic connotation that it retained in France until the beginning of the eighteenth century, at which point it began to refer more broadly to work stoppage (Douët d'Arcq 1844). The term *strike* in English originates from this period. It is customarily understood to have appeared with the 1768 London protests of coal heavers and sailors, who lowered the topsails of transport ships ("strike the sails" in nautical parlance), rendering them motionless before dropping anchor.

A notable chapter in the recent history of academic strikes—that led to "perhaps the most dramatic victory that graduate labor organizers have achieved"—took place in the University of California (UC) system, the largest public university system in the United States (Discenna 2001: 2). It began in spring 1983 when students at UC Berkeley sought recognition of collective bargaining rights. On August 15, 1984, California's Public Employees Relations Board (PERB) ruled that Berkeley students could indeed be considered employees of the university under California's Higher Education Employer-Employee Relations Act (HEERA). As such, they could begin the unionization process and seek affiliation.[60] United Auto Workers (UAW) Local 2865—the first union to represent graduate students in a US public university—was created as a result of this decision (Ethnic Studies Graduate Collective 2020: 560). Over the next decade and a half, it spearheaded unionization drive throughout the UC system (Singer 1999: 41).[61]

Following the end of the affiliation process, campus-specific actions took place at UC Berkley (1998, 2007, 2009), UC Davis (2001), UC Santa Cruz (2005), UC San Diego (2010), and UC Riverside (2012). In April 2014, strike authorization votes were held simultaneously across all ten UC campuses, and a first system-wide strike began on April 23, 2014. It lasted for a week, until an agreement was reached between UAW Local 2865 and the UC administration. The two-year collective agreement addressed issues related to wages, health benefits, and working conditions—including family leave, workload issues and job security—for teaching assistants, tutors, and readers. It did not, however, address the issue of *academic freedom*, implicitly regarded as a privilege of tenured faculty or of the UC administration. That agreement was renewed and expanded in fall 2016, with additional gains in wages and working conditions. In fall 2019, graduate employees at UC Santa Cruz withheld grades in support of demands for a living wage (Gilich and Boardman 2022). In the context of a near-Fordist labor regime, this was the equivalent of a wild-cat strike (Ethnic Studies Graduate Collective 2020:

---

[60]The PERB is a quasi-judicial arbitration body headed by political appointees. The 1984 ruling, made by Democrat appointees, was overturned in 1989 when a Republican-appointed PERB ruled that teaching assistants at UC Berkeley could not be in fact be considered employees of the university under the HEERA because their work was a part of their educational process and not essential to the mission of the university. This decision was upheld by a state appellate ruling in 1992. Three years later, a Democrat-appointed PERB again ruled that readers, tutors, and teaching associates at UC San Diego were indeed eligible for collective bargaining rights. See Singer (1999). The university's appeal was rejected in 1998. All PERB decisions are available on its website. https://perb.ca.gov/about/perb-functions/; https://perb.ca.gov/decisions/decision-search/#gsc.tab=0&gsc.q=1989&gsc.sort=

[61]UAW-affiliated unions obtained membership cards from a majority of graduate employees at UC Davis (1999), UC Irvine (1999), UC Los Angeles (1999), UC Riverside (1999), UC San Diego (1999), UC Santa Barbara (1999), UC Santa Cruz (1999), UC San Francisco (1999), and UC Merced (2007).

559). Seventy-four students were fired for this action. They did not regain their position until UAW 2856 settled a charge of unfair labor practice on their behalf (Gilich and Boardman 2022: 109).

In March 2020, a general assembly of UC Berkeley students began to organize in solidarity with UC Santa Cruz students. Students in seventeen departments declared themselves "strike ready" (Ethnic Studies Graduate Collective 2020: 560), and a wave of grading strikes spread across campus, beginning with the Department of African American and Diaspora Studies. Demands were put forth for the reinstatement of all fired UC Santa Cruz students; cost-of-living allowances; the demilitarization of UC police; and the elimination of single-semester appointments for lecturers. The COVID-19 pandemic put an end to this collective effort:

> Now the university itself would be blockaded, not by strikers but by its own administration. Zoom, the videoconferencing platform, had been deployed just weeks earlier as strike-breaking technology. The university of quarantine would free Zoom of this stigma, refashioning it as a means of providing the "essential" service of education in a crisis. Armed by Zoom, the campus could be blockaded without a drastic disruption in tuition-generative university operations
>
> (Evans et al. 2020: 3)

The next UC-wide strike began on November 14, 2022. Again, it was organized by UAW Local 2865—alongside UAW Local 5810, representing postdoctoral scholars. Involving some 48,000 graduate student workers, postdoctoral researchers, and academic researchers across all ten UC campuses, it became the largest labor action in the history of the UC system.[62] For six weeks, pickets were set up on UC campuses, and solidarity actions organized. The strike ended in December 23, with a new contract providing significant wage increases for postdoctoral and academic researchers, improved benefits, paid parental leave, childcare subsidies, and protections related to workload and job security. Again, no mention was made of academic freedom.

In its first iteration, *academic freedom* was a particular set of privileges and obligations ascribed to scholars whose usefulness to state and empire afforded them a measure of relative autonomy and discipline-bound indeterminacy. Professors enjoyed the freedom to teach and research and students to learn. Between them a free market of ideas was instituted. In its second iteration, *academic freedom* lords over the travails of scholars. Increasingly organized as a labor movement, contingent scholars meet workplace issues not with demands for *academic freedom* (a mirage to casualized academic

[62]At the time of the UC strike, "the UAW represented around 80,000 academic workers in the U.S." (Wright 2023: 68).

labor) but with more prosaic demands for indeterminacy.[63] Acting in the folds of concrete struggles in defense of concrete possibilities, they resolve in their own practice the insoluble dilemma of freedom and necessity, lending circumstantial shape to *freedom in thinking*.

The State of Florida versus Critical Race Theory (2020–2023)

Between the Civil War and the First World War, scholarly freedom in the United States was apportioned unequally along racial lines. In white universities, a regime of freedom was instituted that allowed professors follow their calling "with dignity and independence," free to govern themselves in their own manner and to enjoy "freedom of extramural utterance and action."[64] In Black universities, the freedom of scholars was made contingent on the brutal vagaries of Reconstruction politics and the ordinary workings of a segregated system of knowledge production.

After *Brown v Board of Education* (1954), desegregation brought a more insidious iteration of the same color line into universities. Historically white universities remained sites of hegemonic whiteness. Black professors—though formally integrated in the instituted order of freedom—remain exposed, "in the Academy, but not of the Academy" (Bell 1985: 392); fragilized by disciplinary marginalization and lack of collegial support (Martin et al. 2019: 3); flat objects of microaggressions—"a form of systemic, everyday racism used to keep those at the racial margins in their place" (Yancy 2018). Ontologically haunted about "nigger moments" (Anderson 2011), they remained doubly conscious bearers of a more contingent sort of academic freedom.[65] In historically Black universities an increasingly diverse

---

[63]The first citation is from Winn (2015: 2) and the second from Ross (2009: 25).

[64]Citations are from the AAUP's "Declaration of Principles on Academic Freedom and Academic Tenure," (1915) available from the AAUP site, at: https://www.aaup.org/NR/rdonlyres/A6520A9D-0A9A-47B3-B550-C006B5B224E7/0/1915Declaration.pdf.

[65]"Nigger moment" is a shocking phrase that invites the blanket use of prudish euphemisms and the prudent placing of asterisks. It is my position that such strategies, commendable in the consideration they express, efface the very violence that the reappropriation of assaultive terms seeks to highlight, censuring critique. Borrowed by Elijah Anderson from the African American vernacular, the term should be situated within the broad context defined by *négritude* and Black consciousness movements. When Franz Fanon wrote of a colonial administrator coming face-to-face with the *colonisé* and addressing them in *petit nègre*, effectively saying, "You, stay where you are," or when James Baldwin of a lone policeman on a street corner grumbling, "Why don't you niggers stay uptown where you belong?," to an adolescent on his way to the public library, they write not of Black or African American moments, but of "nigger moments." Underlining the connection between everyday transactions and the wider order, the term allows for a "racially informed sociological imagination" to develop (Pérez Huber and Solorzano 2015).

lot of professors shared in the structural fragility of underfinanced, poorly endowed institutions with little autonomy (Gasman 2009, 2010).

The roots of critical race theory (CRT) can be traced to the Critical Legal Studies movement, which began to take form at Harvard Law School in the early 1980s around efforts to perennialize the teachings of Professor Derek Bell, who had left Harvard to become dean of the University of Oregon School of Law.[66] Faced with Harvard's refusal to have Bell's courses taught by a new minority hire, the Black Law Student Association's and the Third World Coalition ("made up of representatives from all the students-of-color organizations") set up an alternative course based on Bell's *Race, Racism and American Law* (Bell 1973).[67] At inception, CRT was a broad referent, rooted in a shared understanding that race is a social construct and a collective commitment to engage in "studying and transforming the relationship among race, racism, and power" (Delgado and Stefancic 2023: 3). It was comparable—in the breadth of its theoretical referents and scope of its engagement—to such frameworks as orientalism or transmodernity, with which it shares deep affinities (Bell 1995: 898).

On July 8, 1989, a workshop on "New Developments in Critical Legal Studies" was held at the University of Wisconsin–Madison (Crenshaw 2002). This was not the founding event of CRT as a theoretical proposition—how could something as wide-ranging and dialectically constituted as an epistemological framework be considered to have been born of any single event—but it did mark a moment of its instrumentalization.

Feeling that the "New Developments" did not fully capture their critical ambitions, CRT principals "made what essentially amount[ed] to a marketing decision":

> We jettisoned the generic title and sought something more provocatively substantive. … If we were going to give this inchoate thing a name, let it be a proper sign on the intellectual landscape: Critical Race Theory. … So the name Critical Race Theory, now used as interchangeably for race scholarship as Kleenex is used for tissue, was basically made up, fused together to mark a possibility.
>
> (Crenshaw 2002: 1360–61)

After the police murder of George Floyd on May 25, 2020, and the introduction by the College Board of a new two-year pilot project to develop

---

[66]The "Critical Legal Studies" movement is itself rooted in the American Legal Realist Movement of the 1930s (Haines 1987). At the time of Bell's leaving, there were sixty tenured law professors at Harvard. "All but one were men, and only one was Black" (Fortin 2021).

[67]The citation is from Crenshaw (2002: 1350).

an AP African American History course—CRT swiftly transmuted from a decade-old theoretical proposition into an object of political dispute.[68]

On July 8, 2020, journalist Christopher F. Rufo was alerted by an employee of the city of Seattle's Office of Civil Rights of alleged issues with the city's antibias training. Recognizing a political opportunity, Rufo quickly published two short articles in the *City Journal*, a concern of the Manhattan Institute (Wallace-Wells 2021).[69] In "Cult Programming in Seattle" Rufo denounced the deep-seated cultic indoctrination within the Office of Civil Rights, accusing it of engaging in the explicit promotion of segregationist principles, group-based guilt, and race essentialism (Rufo 2020a). In "White Fragility Comes to Washington," he bemoaned the rapid expansion of "the toxic principles of critical race theory, race essentialism, and neo-segregationism" (Rufo 2020b). Denouncing the mandatory pledging of federal employees—"at the Treasury Department, the Federal Reserve, the Federal Deposit Insurance Corporation, the Consumer Finance Protection Bureau, the National Credit Union Association ... the Office of the Comptroller"—to "allyship amid the George Floyd tragedy," he warned of a long struggle to come "against the diversity-industrial complex," and

[68]The College Entrance Examination Board (CEEB) was founded at Columbia University in 1899 by representatives of twelve private white universities—no Morrill Act university or college was involved—to rationalize admissions into elite universities and to broaden the social foundations of American meritocracy. CEEB testing began in 1926 with the Scholastic Aptitude Test, a psychological examination derived from intelligence tests administered to sailors and soldiers during World War I. It was soon administered on behalf of the CEEB by the Educational Testing Services (ETS), founded in 1933 under the leadership of Harvard Dean Henry Chauncy. In 1993, the test was renamed the Scholastic Assessment Test, reflecting a shift toward subject-based learning. Four years later, Scholastic Assessment Test was rebranded as a free-standing acronym: SAT. The Law School Admission Test (LSAT), designed specifically to measure the skills deemed necessary to the study of law, was introduced in 1948; the Graduate Management Admission Test (GMAT), designed for business schools, was introduced in 1954; and the Practice SAT (PSAT) in 1959. The Advanced Placement (AP) test, designed to shepherd high-achieving high school graduates toward the best colleges, was first administered in 1955. From its inception, it was supported by the Advanced Placement Program, which offered students the opportunity to participate in college-level classes and thereby showcase both intellectual capacity and motivation to learn. The National Merit Scholarship Qualifying Test (NMSQT), introduced in 1971, is distinct from SAT, PSAT, and AP examinations. It functions as a qualifying test for the National Merit Scholarship and is said to "provides firsthand practice for the SAT." Accuplacer, introduced in 1985, is a basic-skills computer-assisted placement test. More recent College Board innovations include the College Level Examination Program (CLEP), introduced in 2018 to allow student to take classes in which they earn college-level credit, and SpringBoard, a "pre-Advanced Placement program" designed for learners of all ages—"including highschoolers, college students, homeschooled students, adults, senior citizens, children, and exceptional toddlers." A century and a quarter after its founding, the College Board benefits from a near-monopoly in the scholarly exams and surveillance market. In 2023, it administered fee-paying test to almost one million students.

[69]The Manhattan Institute was founded in 1973 as the International Center for Economic Policy Studies by Ronald Reagan's CIA director William Casey and Anthony Fisher, libertarian businessman who also founded the Institute of Economic Affairs (1971) and the Atlas Network (1981).

called on President Trump to issue an executive order banning federal agencies from teaching "the toxic principles of critical race theory, race essentialism, and neo-segregationism" (Rufo 2020b).

Invited on Fox's *Tucker Carlson Tonight* on August 17 and September 2, Rufo argued, fusing phrases from his two *City Journal* articles, that "the cult of critical race theory ... has pervaded every aspect of the federal government [becoming] in essence, the default ideology of the federal bureaucracy" (Miller et al. 2023: 71). The FBI, which had labeled BLM "Black Identity Extremists" as early as 2017, was now said to be holding weekly seminars on intersectionality. Evoking the ghosts of Angela Davis and Herbert Marcuse, Rufo declared CRT an existential threat to the United States (Wallace-Wells 2021).[70]

Once again, the phrase *critical race theory* was instrumentalized, this time by political opponents.

> We have successfully frozen their brand ... and [we] are steadily driving up negative perceptions. ... Critical race theory is the perfect villain [i]ts connotations are all negative to most middle-class Americans, including racial minorities, who see the world as 'creative' rather than 'critical,' 'individual' rather than 'racial,' 'practical' rather than 'theoretical" most opportunely it is not ... an externally applied pejorative [but] the label the critical race theorists chose themselves.
>
> (Wallace-Wells 2021)

President Trump was watching Rufo on *Tucker Carlson Tonight*, as did three million Americans most evenings. His reaction came instantly, in the form of a rapid-fire of tweets (Cineas 2020). The following morning, Rufo received a call from Trump's Chief of Staff Mark Meadows, inviting him to the White House: "He saw your segment on 'Tucker' last night, and he's instructed me to take action" (Wallace-Wells 2021). On September 5, Trump tweeted *a propos* of CRT: "This is a sickness that cannot be allowed to continue. Please report any sightings so we can quickly extinguish!" (Cineas 2020). The next day, Rufo flew to Washington to assist in drafting an executive order limiting how contractors providing federal diversity seminars could talk about race. Days later, as the campaign against CRT consumed Twitter every morning and Fox News every night (Wallace-Wells 2021), the Director of the Office of Management and Budget sent a memo to denounce the "divisive, false, and demeaning propaganda of the critical race theory movement." Diversity trainings and CRT were immediately suspended in federal government agencies.[71]

[70]The interview available on the Fox website: https://www.foxnews.com/politics/chris-rufo-race-theory-cult-federal-government and https://www.foxnews.com/us/chris-rufo-one-man-war-race-theory.

[71]The "2020 Statement on White House Memo Barring Federal Agencies from Race-Related Trainings" is widely available on internet. It is cited here from the UNC's College of Arts and Science site: https://history.unc.edu/2020/09/statement-on-white-house-memo-barring-federal-agencies-from-race-related-trainings/.

On September 22, 2020, President Trump signed into law Executive Order 13950, prohibiting the teaching in federal workplaces of "destructive" and "malign[ment]" ideologies "grounded in hierarchies based on collective social and political identities" (Miller et al. 2023).[72] On November 2, he signed Executive Order 13958, establishing the "1776 Commission" to promote patriotic interpretations of US history (Wise 2020).[73]

The swift action of the federal government triggered a cascade of state-level initiatives assimilating CRT to racial discrimination and censuring diversity training for "inflaming divisions on the basis of sex, race, ethnicity, religion, color [or] national origin."[74] Within months, an "Ed scare" had taken shape that was no less censuring than the cold-war era "Red scare" (Friedman 2022). According to PEN America, proposals had been introduced in forty-one states—and laws passed in fifteen states—to ban teaching of divisive concepts and of ideas that "individuals, by virtue of sex, race, ethnicity, religion, color, or national origin, are inherently responsible for actions committed in the past by other members of the same sex, race, ethnicity, religion, color, or national origin."[75]

In Florida, the State Board of Education voted in June 2021 to prohibit schools from teaching CRT altogether (Schwartz 2023).[76] On 15 December, Governor Ron DeSantis—citing egregious examples of CRT and "woke corporate training"—announced a legislative proposal to "give

[72]Executive Order 13950 "Combating Race and Sex Stereotyping" is cited from the presidential document collection of the *Federal Register* of the National Archives. https://www.federalregister.gov/documents/2020/09/28/2020-21534/combating-race-and-sex-stereotyping.

[73]Executive order 13958 is cited from the website of UC Santa Barbara's "The American Presidency Project": https://www.presidency.ucsb.edu/documents/executive-order-13958-establishing-the-presidents-advisory-1776-commission. Executive Order 13950 was revoked by Executive Order on President Joe Biden's first day in office. The "1776 Report," which enjoins educators to "reject any curriculum that promotes one-sided partisan opinions, activist propaganda, or factional ideologies that demean America's heritage, dishonor our heroes, or deny our principles," was filed on January 2021. Tracing the origins of critical theory to Italian Marxist Antonio Gramsci and the Frankfurt school, it singles out Critical Race Theory, "a variation of critical theory applied to the American context," both for its emphasis on racial divisions and for its promotion of "fundamental social transformation," deemed "significant to its intellectual content." The 1776 Report, Trump's answer to the *New York Times* 1619 Project, is cited here from the website of the White House Archives. https://trumpwhitehouse.archives.gov/wp-content/uploads/2021/01/The-Presidents-Advisory-1776-Commission-Final-Report.pdf.

[74]Maryland councilman Nathan Volke, who introduced an anti–critical-race-theory bill in October 2021, is cited from Pappoe (2022).

[75]On this, see PEN's Index of Educational Gag Orders, https://pen.org/issue/educational-censorship/ (last visited December 1, 2022). Idaho's Code 33-138 "Dignity and Nondiscrimination in Public Education" is cited from the official website of the Idaho Legislature, consulted on April 21, 2023: https://legislature.idaho.gov/statutesrules/idstat/title33/t33ch1/sect33-138/

[76]*Education Week* maintains a listing of State-level initiatives to ban teaching of critical race theory: http://www.edweek.org/leadership/map-where-critical-race-theory-is-under-attack/2021/06.

businesses, employees, children and families tools to fight back against woke indoctrination."[77] The "Individual Freedom Act" (colloquially known as the "Stop W.O.K.E. Act"—"Stop Wrongs Against Our Kids and Employees") was adopted by the Florida Legislature in "the waning days of the 2022 legislative session" (Schwartz 1970: 6) and signed into law on April 22, 2022. Among other provisions, it amended the Florida Civil Rights Act, the Florida Educational Equity Act, and Florida's statutory provisions for the professional development of educators.

This drawing of political lines increased opportunities for Christopher Rufo—now described in publicities as "a conservative journalist who specializes in critical race theory, gender ideology, and the capture of America's institutions"—to intervene on the public space, leaving the College Board—always an object of criticism—with little option but to capitulate or face widespread abandonment of its programs.[78] On the first of February 2023 (the beginning of Black History Month)—less than a semester into its planned two-year pilot project, before students and professors had had a chance to give any feedback—the board announced a revised framework for its AP African American studies course: a "capitulation" according to the *National Review* (Kurtz 2023). The course itself was maintained, but authors were removed and the study of contemporary events and issues—including BLM, the mass incarceration of Black people, queer life, and the debate over reparations—was demoted. They are no longer part of the exam but simply offered as options for research project (Hartocollis and Fawcett 2023).

---

[77]Cited from https://www.flgov.com/2021/12/15/governor-desantis-announces-legislative-proposal-to-stop-w-o-k-e-activism-and-critical-race-theory-in-schools-and-corporations/

[78]Expanding alongside the US system of knowledge production, the CEEB/CB—an intermediate agency with little autonomy from governing instances—was always an object of critique. For example, see Crouse (1988); Klein (1930: 373–76); Philip Cox, "Testing and the High School Curriculum," *Educational Research Bulletin* 9, no. 8 (1930): 188–93; and Albert Longley, "Standardized Testing in the Secondary Schools," *Journal of Educational Research* 16, no. 5 (1927): 321–27. Critics denounced the poor quality of its evaluations, its biases against minority students and students from underprivileged backgrounds (Atkinson 2009), and its tendency to "virtually nationalize America's high schools in violation of cherished principles of local control" (Kurtz 2014). In the 2010s, the CB was criticized for its revised AP US History course, developed under guidance of NYU historian Thomas Bender, whose *A Nation Among Nations: America's Place in World History* (Hill and Wang, 2006), 573–74, links the history of the United States with world events, making Americans "think about their history from a global perspective" (Cayton 2006: 573–74). Deemed to subsume American exceptionalism to "cosmopolitan, 'transnational' sensibilities" (Kurtz, *Lost History*), and by that to endorse "hatred of America ... and the promotion of social justice activism and the welfare state" (David Randall, *The Disappearing Continent: A Critique of the AP U.S. History Framework* [National Association of Scholars, 2020], 15), it was attacked by notable think tanks, among them: the Jack Miller Center for Teaching America's Founding Principles and History; the Alexander Hamilton Institute for the Study of Western Civilization; and the National Association of Scholars (which initiated the "1620 Project" to counter the *New York Times*–led "1619 Project").

More rapidly than the lynching of Sam Hose and the Atlanta Riot had forced W. E. B. Du Bois out of Atlanta University, a movement that "came from nothing" (according to Rufo himself) exposed how contingent the possibilities are for scholars to take a step back and think about the racial ordering of the world (Wallace-Wells 2021).

Gaza Solidarity Encampments (2024)

Three years after the canceling of Angela Davis's talk at Butler University, war in Gaza further curtailed the ability of US scholars to meet relatively apart from political injunctions and engage in relatively autonomous and self-defined relations of knowledge production. Again, two iterations of *academic freedom* came into conflict—one allowing a measure of scholarly indeterminacy and the other, an organizational concept intent on containing scholarly relations. Nowhere was this meeting more charged by a global sense of the moment than in historically white universities.

The foreclosing of scholarly possibilities began as it had before, with Congress signaling that the limits of academic autonomy had been reached. Just as Lee Overman's "Senate Subcommittee on German and Bolshevik Propaganda" did during the Red Scare that followed the Bolshevik Revolution, and as Joseph McCarthy's "Senate Permanent Subcommittee on Investigations" did during the cold war, Congresswoman Virginia Foxx's "House Committee on Education and the Workforce" called scholars forth to account publicly for what they were making of their freedom in exacting circumstances. On December 5, 2023, political scientist Claudine Gay, law scholar Liz Magill, and molecular biologist Sally Kornbluth were sat before Congress. What distinguished the events of that day from McCarthy's and Overman's hearings was the positionality of scholars being interpellated. It was not as titular bearers of professorial privileges that professors Gay, Magill, and Kornbluth were brought to testify before Congress but as administrators: Claudine Gay as president of Harvard University, Liz Magill as president of the University of Pennsylvania, and Sally Kornbluth as president of the Massachusetts Institute of Technology. What representatives questioned—and what university presidents defended—was not the professorial freedom to teach, research, and make public utterances, nor students' freedom to learn, but the organizational capacity to contain scholarly debates.

In the days, weeks, and months that followed, the pressure induced by congressional hearings played out differently in different universities. At the University of Pennsylvania, Magill faced an immediate attack of students and wealthy donors—led by hedge-fund billionaires Marc Rowan and Bill Ackman (Sorkin et al. 2024). She resigned on December 9, the day after Republican members of Congress called for her firing (and those of presidents Gay and Magill). At Harvard, Gay also faced a revolt of donors—a significant happening in an institution that relies on philanthropy for 45 percent of annual revenues, and especially fraught as it came on the heels of a very public controversy over race-based affirmative action programs (settled by the Supreme Court in favor of plaintiffs in June 2023). Dr. Gay resigned on January 2, 2024. At MIT—a science-based university less swayed by ideological controversies *dixit* Noam Chomsky (Chomsky 1997: 178–79)—Kornbluth weathered the storm.

On February 29, Congresswoman Foxx's Committee live-streamed a "Roundtable with Jewish Students Impacted by Antisemitism."[79] Nine carefully selected students were invited to testify about their experience with antisemitism on campus: Shabbos Kestenbaum, founder and president of Harvard University's Divinity School Jewish Student Association and lead plaintiff against the university in a case alleging "pervasive and severe antisemitism"; Noah Rubin, former copresident of the University of Pennsylvania's Israel Public Affairs Committee; Talia Khan, president and cofounder of the MIT Israel Alliance; Eden Yadegar, president of Students Supporting Israel at Columbia University; UC Berkeley student Hannah Beth Schlacter, "recognized for her local, national, and international leadership in the Jewish community"; Joe J. Gindi, a member of Rutgers University's Chancellor's Advisory Council on Jewish Life; Kevin Feigelis, founder of Stanford University's "Blue and White Tent—a novel and visible approach to combating antisemitism on college campuses"; Yasmeen Ohebsion, president of the Movement to Address Antisemitism at Tulane University; and Jacob Khalili, president of the Cooper Union and "an active member of the downtown Manhattan Jewish community."[80] Echoing Foxx's charge against "mealy-mouthed, spineless college leaders," they spoke in unison about feelings of insecurity and lamented universities' lack of concern for their physical and emotional safety.[81]

On April 17, Columbia University President Nemat "Minouche" Shafik—unavailable in December—answered in turn Congress's call. A career administrator rather than a professor, she had been appointed as president of Columbia University a year previously after having occupied several administrative positions—at the London School of Economics, the Bank of England, the World Bank, and the International Monetary Fund.[82]

---

[79]A video recording of the event is available on YouTube: https://www.youtube.com/watch?v=qrW4BQGz1AA.

[80]All citations are taken from the Committee's website: https://edworkforce.house.gov/calendar/eventsingle.aspx?EventID=410200.

[81]Virginia Foxx is cited in Kelley (2024).

[82]An Oxford trained economist, Nemat Shafik served as adjunct professor at Georgetown University (1989–1994) and as visiting professor at the University of Pennsylvania (January–June 1996), but she never did hold position as titular professor before embarking on her administrative career. She was appointed president of Columbia University on July 1, 2023. At the time of writing, she had been appointed as chair of the Victoria and Albert Museum.

In the same venue where presidents Gay, Kornbluth, and Magill—all titular professors—had wavered unconvincingly between different iterations of academic freedom—exposing themselves to the ire of committee members—President Shafik expressed in the least ambiguous manner possible her intent to uphold organizational responsibilities. In a move reminiscent of McCarthy-era denunciations, she "named names" of professors under investigation for alleged violations of the university's antidiscriminatory regulation (Saul 2024). She promised to fire those professors, in spectacular violation of professional norms of academic freedom (Otterman 2024b). Furthermore, she told Foxx's Committee, two student groups (Students for Justice in Palestine and Jewish Voice for Peace) had already been suspended and a visiting professor barred. Decreed President Shafik: he "will never work at Columbia again" (Fandos et al. 2024).

The following day, a Palestinian solidarity encampment that had been set up in previous days on the steps of Columbia's Low Memorial Library was raided by campus police assisted by NYPD officers, some in riot gear (Rosman 2024). The camp, President Shafik contended, presented a "clear and present danger to the substantial functioning of the university," creating "an harassing and intimidating environment for many of our students" (Blinder 2024). It was destroyed and a hundred students were arrested. Teach-ins about to begin were canceled (Otterman 2024c).

As quickly as the camp had been dismantled, it went up again, initiating what can only be understood as a springtime of pro-Palestinian encampments on US campuses. In quick order, encampments were set up at the Massachusetts Institute of Technology (April 21), UC Berkeley (April 23), New York University (April 24), Tufts (April 24), the City University of New York (April 25), the University of California Los Angeles (April 25), Northwestern University (April 25), Yale (April 28), and University of Connecticut (April 27), among others. At the University of Chicago, a minivillage of tents went up (April 29) on the Main quadrangle, steps away from the president's office.[83]

Encampments were also set up in universities outside the United States, inviting comparisons with "Global '68": at the American University in Cairo (April 22), the University of Sydney (April 23), the Institut d'études politiques in Paris (April 24), the Sorbonne (April 25), McGill University in Montreal (April 27), the University of Tokyo (April 27), the University of British Columbia (April 29), the University of Valencia (April 29), Oxford (May 6), Cambridge (May 6), the University of Liverpool (May 6), the University of Amsterdam (May 6), and the Free University of Berlin (May 7), among others.

---

[83]In all, more than 500 protests occurred in the United States in summer 2024, resulting in the arrest of more than 3,000 students and faculty (Darian-Smith 2025).

Crowded tents on campus lawns and handmade placards featuring watermelon slices defined the aesthetics of the day; "trust and mutual care"—the perfect opposite of the exterminist blackmail—defined its ethos (Aiden 2024).[84] As all tent cities do, student encampments simultaneously displayed "characteristics of permanence and temporariness" (Avnon et al. 2018)—the blending of these opposites under police gaze evoking both the enduring contingency of Palestinian refugee camps—the oldest of which are as old as the Nakba itself—and the permanent sense of alertness fostered by Israel's systematic destruction of Palestinian centers of education—what Maya Wind, borrowing from Abu-Rabia-Queder, called the "checkpoint mentality" (Wind 2024: 106).

Understood as political events, student encampments were spontaneous inventions that answered the performative showing of congressional authority with evocation of fragility. A spectacular showing of police force brought them to an end. At Columbia, police again dismantled the camp, committing in the process yet another "unprecedented assault on student rights" (Saul 2024). At the University of Chicago—a flashpoint of recent debates on academic freedom (for the Report of the Commission on Freedom of Expression)—police in riot gear pulled tents down.[85] In the same "unhinged" manner (Lennard 2024), police broke up student encampments at Northeastern University (April 27), Yale (30 April), CUNY (April 30), University of Connecticut (April 30), NYU (May 5), Harvard (May 10), UCLA (May 2), USC (May 5), MIT (May 10), UC Berkeley

[84]An exception to the aesthetics of student encampments: at the New School in New York, a faculty encampment was established on March 6 in the lobby of the University Center building on Fifth Avenue. The only professorial encampment, it was also the only sheltered from inclement weather.

[85]The University of Chicago appointed Robert J. Zimmer as head of the Commission on Freedom of Expression in October 2014, and its report was released in January 2015. Bowing to Supreme Court allowances for censorship of "fighting words"—"which by their very utterance inflict injury or tend to incite an immediate breach of peace"—see Schroeder (2017: 332); the commission recommended regulations to curtail "disruptive conduct and behavior," that is, behavior that "substantially obstructs, impairs, or interferes with the teaching, study, research, or administration functions of the university." In August 2016, Dean of Students John Ellison followed through with an open letter addressed to incoming students underlining the university's commitment to "freedom of inquiry and expression." He informed students that the university did not support "trigger warnings"—"the suddenly ubiquitous cautions, often on syllabi, about topics covered in the class"—nor "condone the creation of intellectual 'safe spaces' where individuals can retreat from ideas and perspectives at odds with their own." See Johnson (2017: 39) and McShane and Highsmith (2016: 4). Ellison's letter to students was accompanied by a book written by University of Chicago professor John Boyer, in *Academic Freedom and the Modern University: The Experience of the University of Chicago* (University of Chicago Press, 2016), as noted in Luis Vivanco, "Trigger Warnings and Academic Freedom," *Chronicle of Higher Education*, August 2016. The "Report of the Committee on Freedom of Expression" is available from the University of Chicago, https://freeexpression.uchicago.edu/sites/freeexpression.uchicago.edu/files/FOECommitteeReport.pdf (accessed November 8, 2016).

(May 15), and Tufts (May 15). In total, more than 3,000 students—and perhaps as many as 4,000—were arrested on more than fifty campuses in the United States between the end of April and the end of May 2024. At Rutgers, the encampment ended on May 2, with a negotiated settlement dramatically announced an hour before a university-imposed deadline, as police were standing by and professors had begun forming a line to protect students.

In Berlin, Lausanne, Geneva, and Zurich, police also intervened in spectacular manner. At the University of Amsterdam, police used a bulldozer to break up the student encampment. More than a hundred students were arrested. In Canada, the parameters of political acceptability are defined by the Charter of Rights and Freedoms. Entrenched in the constitution, it grants broad interpretative powers to the Supreme Court. In this context, the end of student encampments could only begin with the spectacle of judicial authority. At McGill University in Montreal, two students citing feelings of insecurity asked the Québec Superior Court for a temporary injunction ordering students to move their encampment at least one hundred meters away from university buildings and, thus, off campus and unto the public street, where they infringe on municipal bylaws (Hanes 2024). They were rebuked by the court,

> The court is of the opinion that the balance of inconveniences leans to the side of the protesters, whose freedom of expression and of peaceful assembly would be seriously affected. … The evidence of harm to the students … is rather limited, arising more from subjective worries and discomfort rather than precise and serious worries for their safety.[86]

Citing "security, safety and public health risk" and "fierce verbal exchanges" between protesters and counterprotestors, McGill's administration took it upon itself to follow suit, filing its own petition. Again, the Superior Court refused to grant a temporary injunction, citing a lack of urgency.[87] McGill's administration petitioned the court once more, this time asking for the camp to be permanently banned. For a third time, the court refused. On July 10, private security guards in riot gear—from SIRCO, a private security firm—surrounded at a distance by Montreal's municipal police and provincial police—some on bicycles or horseback, bulletproof vests, dogs, and drones—closed off McGill's campus. Bulldozers and CAT machinery razed the encampment; "workers in high-visibility vests [then] used a front loader and a backhoe to clear the tents, signs and tarps left by the protesters" (Jones and Lapierre 2024).

---

[86]Québec Superior Court Justice Chantal Massé is cited from https://www.cp24.com/news/court-rejects-students-request-for-injunction-against-mcgill-university-encampment-1.6869516.

[87]https://www.cbc.ca/news/canada/montreal/mcgill-injunction-request-1.7202366

Looking into encampments as scholarly events, we understand the actions of students and professors to be giving shape to a familiar idea of knowledge relations: *faire université autrement* not through occupation, *tumultus*, or *cessatio* but through a collective act of presence. Acting, students in encampments sometimes cited their own past: At Oberlin College, a "People's College" was established and teach-ins took place—on "Technology and apartheid" by software engineer Laith Abad (Wallerstein and Shinozaki 2024), on the Nakba by historian Hala Marshood; on the political economy of occupation by economist Shir Hever; and on water justice by Muna Daani and Lamis Q'demat, among others. At the University of Chicago, a "Popular University for Gaza" was established. At the University of Amsterdam, "Al Aqsa University"—named for a university destroyed in Palestine—hosted a program that included classes on Liberation theology and the climate justice movement. At McGill, a "Popular University of Gaza" was established where Rula Abisaab Jurdi gave a lecture on "Anti-Zionism and Jewish and Islamic Histories of Resistance," and historian Robin D. G. Kelley lectured on "The Longue Durée of Palestinian Resistance: From 1948 to the Present." At the Dominicus Kerk in Amsterdam, anthropologist Maya Wind (2024) detailed the complicity of Israeli universities with the apartheid state, the military occupation of Palestine, and the systematic destruction of Palestinian educational institutions. At the University of Ottawa, sociologist Nahla Abdo (2024) spoke on anticolonial and anti-imperialist feminism, on the Nakba, and on genocide. References to "scholasticide" (attributed to Oxford Professor Karma Nabulsi [Mhamdi 2024]); "settler colonialism," "decolonization," "epistemicide," "genocide" everywhere filled the air, giving coherence to a rough *curriculum* of authors and books instituted not from above by popes and state agencies but, from within, by the praxis of scholars at a particular moment.

Encampments, for the most part, involved students who might otherwise have had few occasions "to experience what a non-vulgar, non-pragmatic, non-instrumentalized university is like," whose horizons were simultaneously broaden and narrowed by the hyperconnectiveness of the network world and the constant threat of police intervention.[88] *Faire université autrement* in such dire circumstances could only bring the most fleeting, evocative reenactment of scholarly dialectics

> the best social movements do what great poetry always does: transport us to another place, compel us to relive horrors and, more importantly, enable us to imagine a new society.
>
> (Kelley 2022)

[88]Giroux (2015) citing Bauman and Donskis (2013).

Graduation ceremonies—*initium* in Latin; *commencement* in English; *diplomfeirer* in German; *cérémonie de remise des diplômes* in French; *ceremonia de graduación* in Spanish—have served as legitimizing moments for European universities since medieval times (Destemberg 2009). They simultaneously sanction the knowledge conferred upon graduating students and the power of the institutions doing the conferring. In the context of the neoliberal university, they also validate the ability of an organization to stage the closing of what one Columbia parent described as "a full graduation experience" (Fahy and Greene 2024).

At Columbia, the main graduation ceremony was postponed, then cancelled, and then broken up into smaller ceremonies to be held in each of Columbia's nineteen colleges (Otterman 2024a). These smaller events provided occasions for further retellings and instrumentalizations: One self-described Zionist student complain of the injustice of being deprived of the full college experience; some students walked across the stage wearing black-and-white *kaffiyehs*; others unfurled small Palestinian flags. The valedictorian of Columbia College, the university's main undergraduate school, held up a sign that said "Divest" as she walked around the stage (Otterman 2024b). At the University of Michigan, some students wore *kaffiyehs* over their graduation gowns; at Indiana University, students walked out during remarks by school President Pamela Whitten; at Ohio State University, Northeastern, and Duke students also walked out, some chanting "Free Palestine." At McGill, graduation was moved from the main campus to the cavernous Bell Centre (Hanes 2024).

At Berkeley, the chancellor opened her remarks by acknowledging the participation of students in an encampment that had been raided by her authority: "They feel passionately about the brutality of the violence in Gaza," she said. "I, too, am deeply troubled by the terrible tragedy." As she spoke, students in the stands rose with signs reading, "Divest," and they began to chant: "Hey hey, ho ho, the occupation has got to go" and "U.C. divest." When Associated Students of the University of California (ASUC) president Sydney Roberts rose to speak, she too was drowned out by chanting. Bowing to Berkeley's own tradition, she acknowledged: "This wouldn't be Berkeley without a protest."

Conclusion

Contemporary world-ordering labors to fix social relations not to place—as did the old world-system of territorial states—but to endless problem-solving, processes defining best practices bound by what International Monetary Fund Managing Director Michel Camdessus called "the widespread acceptance of a set of general propositions about the most effective way of achieving sustainable growth."[89] Forever beckoning solutions to all manners of global dangers, problems, and insecurities, it subsumes the politics of usefulness to the exigencies of global reproduction, narrowing the possibilities of struggles for autonomy.

"Global civil society"—a pure product of global governance's attempts at depoliticizing social relations (Drainville 2004)—is *exterminism*'s stalking horse; "global knowledge society" is its extension into the domain of knowledge production. It is a functional assemblage of organizations striving to produce "knowledge-based capital" (OECD 2013) of which the university, owing to its historic importance, remains a significant, though increasingly indistinguishable, part—a site among others for the reproduction of capital (Readings 1996).

Everywhere, the making of a global knowledge society is made to compose with conditions inherited from past world orders. In countries at the core of the old system of territorial state, these conditions include the old regime of *academic freedom*. Herein lies the source of current reifications: As privileged bearers of old and new notions of freedom clash one with the other, everyone and their foe find legitimizing notions in ever more abstract, detached notions of *academic freedom* that come to mean everything and its opposite. Professors who are professionally engaged in the pursuit of teaching and researching and in the collegial management of universities, lean on archaic notions of *akademische freiheit* to defend acquired rights, obligations, and privileges. And, just as intently, a new class of professor-managers—'uncertain of their place in the new order of knowledge [they] absorb without conscious effort the globally-defined mission of universities' (Giroux 2014: 8)—cloak their foreclosing of scholarly possibilities by invoking responsibilities incumbent on the defenders of *academic freedom*.

Beneath discourses, actually existing scholars act in situations made smaller by the depth of *exterminism*'s burrowing into social relations of knowledge production. At times, they are moved to *faire université*. The Melbourne Free University (2010–), the Free University Auckland Aotearoa (aka The University Without Condition, 2012), the People's Free University of Saskatchewan (2002), the Université Populaire de Caen (2002–2018), the Birmingham Free University (2014+), and the Free University of Sheffield (2016), among others, all offered (or are still offering) courses, seminars,

[89]The restructuring of Eastern European economies after the end of the cold war was a testing ground for global governance. It brought about an unprecedented level of collaboration between core regulatory agencies (the World Bank, the OECD, the Bank for International Settlements, the International Monetary Fund, etc.). The citation is taken from Michel Camdessus, "Opening Address," in *Central and Eastern Europe: Roads to Growth* (International Monetary Fund and the Austrian National Bank, 1992), 16.

and workshops on authors—Marx, Spinoza, Deleuze, Heidegger, and so on—and subjects—economics, morals, history, politics, poetry, music, mathematics, literature, wars, and so on—that would not have been out of place in free, open, and critical universities created during the mid-twentieth-century crisis of world ordering, in outreach programs and popular universities of the late nineteenth, or indeed in scholastic universities, academies, and *madrasas* created in the period of Mongol control over Eurasian trade routes.

More broadly concerned with "those forms of social life that expand our collective possibilities beyond the scrooge of capitalism," some creations have deliberately moved to link scholars' practice with the general movement of society, in effect directly confronting the utilitarian separation at the heart of the regime of *academic freedom*.[90] Rooted in the occupation of London's Millbank Tower, the University for Strategic Optimism (2010–2013) considered itself a "horizontal tendency" rather than an institution (Hope 2014). It organized performative occupations "in banks ... supermarkets, and libraries" and "flash lectures" to expose the "insidious neoliberal 'logics' employed by capitalist 'elites' to justify mutating the education system into a factory [and to] disassemble normative understandings of the rights and allowances that the architectures of the private sphere coerce us to embody and perform" (Latimer et al. 2011: 275). In like spirit, the Copenhagen Free University (2001–2007)—housed in the flat of founders Henriette Heise and Jakob Jakobsen—existed as "an artist-run institution dedicated to the production of critical consciousness and poetic language."[91] Against "the invasion of our life by the abstract calculations of capitalist valorization [and] the sheltered space of normalizing universities," it organized as a "subversively porous" place where "at the intersection between social and aesthetic politics, freedom and responsibility, life, work and the role of the artist," a creative "leakage between being in the university and outside the university" (White 2003: 24) could be enacted.[92] The Informal University (2010–) radicalized porousness further by existing not as a place at all but as an open space in which resources, information, and knowledge could be produced and

---

[90]The citation is taken from the website of the Provisional University: https://provisionaluniversity.wordpress.com/about-2/.

[91]See Robert J. Podesva, "Phonation Type as a Stylistic Variable: The Use of Falsetto in Constructing a Persona," *Journal of Sociolinguistics* 11, no. 4 (2007): 478, citing Henriette Heise and Jakob Jakobsen, *Copenhagen Free University Information: 17 Theses on Knowledge Production*, http://www.copenhagenfreeuniversity.dk/theses.html (accessed November 1, 2006).

[92]See Joe Berry, Helena Worthen, Beverly Stewart, and Mickey Tiegland, *Contours of Change: The Story of Unionism in Higher Education* (AAUP, 2002), cited in Tyler Wall, "Notes on the Politics of the Police," *Social Justice* 41, no. 2 (2015): 8; citations from Copenhagen Free University, http://www.copenhagenfreeuniversity.dk

shared "in the spirit of emancipation" (Informal university n.d.-a). Likewise, the Manoa Free University (Vienna 2003), the Free Floating Faculty (New York City 2001), and the University of Openness (London 2002) organize screenings, *colloquia*, seminars, workshops, and summer camps where intellectual work is done "with drinks and music," as if heeding Adorno's enjoinder that "only a cunning intertwining of pleasure and work leaves real experience still open" (Informal university n.d.-b). The Silent University (2012–), which presents itself not as a formal institution but as a solidarity-based platform for knowledge exchange situated between contemporary art and pedagogy, designed to enable refugees and other marginalized individuals to share their expertise and skills (Malzacher et al. 2016). Born in Barcelona of the convergence "of a series of highly heterogeneous collectives and individuals without much passion for unifying fusion," the Universidad Nomáda (2001) is a "political laboratory open and in process, which enables the collective production of new theoretical paradigms."[93] In "rupture with the scientific research, the production and transmission of knowledge, the cultural and artistic practices domesticated by the State or the market," the Université tangeante (Strasbourg, 2001–?) existed only as a nonentity ("*une université zero*") that sought nothing more than to embody radically noninstitutional, autonomous "forms of life, exchanges, knowledge and enjoyment" (Université Tangeante/Tangential University n.d.). Against "the academic speed-up," the Slow/Free University of Warsaw (2010) is "a nomadic center of interdisciplinary studies, critical reflection, and independent thinking about art and society."[94] Against appropriations, the Edu-Factory collective sees universities as

> the terrain on which to rethink the actuality of revolution after its classical forms have been definitively exhausted.
>
> (Edu-Factory Collective 2009)

Full of insurgent bluster and immanent certitudes, such inventions are easily dismissed as grandiloquent *beaux gestes* having little to do with the patient rigors of scholarly work or else ignored altogether—as indeed they have been in scholarly debates on *academic freedom*. Yet, seen in the light of the little tradition of scholarly action, they show a familiar attentiveness to maintaining the intrinsic possibilities of—"dialectical" for Abelard, "dialogical" for Freire, "convivial" for Nyamnjoh—relations of knowledge production. At a critical juncture when reproduction is being globally integrated and struggles over the possibility of standing relatively apart

[93]Translated freely from the Universidad Nomada's website: https://sindominio.net/unomada/present.html.

[94]The citation is taken from the website of the Slow/Free University of Warsaw: https://indexfoundation.se/etc/slow-free-university-of-warsaw-pedagogies-of-space

from the order of the world are taking place on ever smaller, more dispersed terrains, scholars, simultaneously forced to defend the smallest positions and charged by a deepening sense of being in the world—what Zaki Laïdi called our "global phenomenology" (Laïdi 1998, 2000)—return to indeterminacy. How they do so—attuned to the contingency of world ordering—invites us to think beyond *academic freedom*, about the relationship between *freedom in thinking* and freedom in acting in the world.

Conclusion: Freedom in World Ordering Now

To contain social relations, contemporary *exterminism* has, for half a century, leaned on totalizing notions of safety to reach more deeply into the fabric of existing societies than *world ordering* ever did, inducing a myriad of specific, deeply situated resistances that are difficult to apprehend, both in themselves and as a whole. To counter dispersion all sorts of *globish* subjects, movements, and beings–the "People of Porto Alegre," the "global justice movement," the dispossessed, the 99 percent, the *indignados*, and so on—have been imagined as existing in, of, and for themselves, ever busy making another world possible.[1] There, in the leveled distance, would lie an elysian domain of freedom that can only be reached by reining in the inchoate agitation of the multitude (Drainville 2005). Thus, discipline has become the answer to discipline, blinding us to the very real freedom that might be being born in the down-to-earth actions of concrete, historical human beings.

Having burned away the illusion of *academic freedom*, are we better equipped to see beyond such reification?

We might begin by acknowledging how often social forces resisting the ways and consequences of neoliberal world ordering are understood to be enacting a "politics of the commons" (Klein 2001; Federici and

[1]The term *globish*, first introduced by Robert McCrum in *The Story of English* (1986), was popularized by former IBM executive Jean-Paul Nerrière in *Parlez Globish* (2004). It labels a simplified language, with straightforward syntax, bereft of idioms, reduced to little more than fifteen hundred words—enough to allow communication between non-native speakers. Deliberately codified and prescriptive, it stands in relation to contemporary world ordering much as trade English—ad hoc, used for commercial negotiations—stood in relation to mercantile world ordering. Writing of globish subjects, I want to underscore both the plastic verisimilitude of cosmopolitan subjects born of the present context, and their estrangement from the places where the many live as many, which deprives them of the essential quality of subjecthood. This argument is developed in the introduction to Drainville (2013a).

Linebaugh 2018). In step, analyses of struggles against the new knowledge economy—when they have looked beyond titular professors defending guild privileges—were commonly framed as efforts to defend academic commons (Ballantyne 2022; Erdem 2020; Szadkowski 2019).

Such appeals carry the significance of a Sorelian myth: They are expressions of a will to act (Jennings 1999: xiii).

But commons, of course, is *praxis* before politics. Purposely entered into, and dependent "on customs, memory, and oral transmission for the maintenance of its norms" (Linebaugh 2014: 14), commoning—and the freedom inherent to it—was always embedded in situated practices and more visible to itself in relation to its outsides, especially in moments when existing ways of being and struggling suddenly found themselves exposed. Freedom, *dixit* David Graeber, "has to be in tension with something, or it's just randomness" (Graeber 2015: 192). In central and northern Italy in the twelfth century, it was the need to expand and protect harbors, secure trading rights, organize markets, validate currencies, and construct ships that gave form to freedom in the urban *comuni*—what Max Weber termed the city-commune (Weber 2019: 158, 226ff). "Urban franchises were primarily 'liberties' for trade: freedom of movement, property and contract, etc." (Jones 1997: 32). However, it was struggles against landed powers, popes, and emperors; the expansion of Mediterranean trade; and the ongoing wars between city-states and against the Ottoman Empire that made merchant families, *compagnie*, guilds, militias, popular assemblies, and civic officials give political shape to that which Dante Alighieri celebrated as *libertas communis* (Shaw 2016: 178). In manorial England, "a long strip was most convenient for a plow drawn by a lumbering, cumbrous team of oxen ... so individual families had to join together ... and having joined together ... they naturally apportioned the units of ploughed land on a basis of equal shares."[2] These arrangements defined commoning as *praxis* and made possible a quotidian, vernacular sort of freedom. *Dixit* Gerrard Winstanley: "true freedom lies where a man receives his nourishment and preservation, and that is in the use of the earth" (Maddison 2010: 36). But it was the world being turned upside down by mercantile expansionism that made Winstanley's Diggers struggle in the name of commons, making it "one of the master notions of English political life" (Watts 2015: 208). In nineteenth-century Paris, neighborhood solidarities gave substance to communal relationships to the city (Harvey 2004: 84, 259), but it was Haussmann's radical transformations of it into "a model capital city that would glorify the Empire" (Gould 1995)—a metropolitan ode to "the worldly and spiritual rule of the bourgeoisie" wrote Walter Benjamin (1968)—and the Prussian siege following France's defeat in the 1871 war,

[2]The citation is from Joan Thirsk's Preface to the third edition of Charles Stuart Orwin and Christabel Susan Lowry Orwin's *The Open Fields* (Clarendon Press, 1938), vii.

that gave political shape to the Commune (Gould 1995: 27). In Jamaica's maroons, hoeing, planting, and weeding had to be done on difficult terrains. There—"within a demarcated social space that allows for the enactment of subversive speech acts, gestures, and social practices" (Roberts 2019a: 4)—runaway slaves could cultivate a workaday sort of freedom (Bledsoe 2017). But it was the proximity of plantations that charged relations in Maroon communities with a performative sort of freedom (Wilson 2009) and the fall of sugar prices following the end of Napoleonic wars—combined with increased competition from more productive plantations elsewhere—that transformed Maroon into strategic positions from which rebellions could be organized in the name of freedom (Blackburn 2011). *Obshchinas* were defining institutions of Russian peasant society. There, land was collectively held and periodically redistributed among household on the basis of need, and governance was organized around collective assemblies, supporting a customary sort of freedom. But it was Alexander II's commodification of communal land (Mironov 1985) that made them objects of reference for Narodniks as well as for the First International (Kimball 1973). Reconstruction violence made urban ghettos little worlds unto themselves, where could be found the everyday sort of freedom W. E. B. Du Bois wrote about in *The Souls of Black Folk* (Du Bois 1967). But it was what Malcom X called the "tricontinental revolution against European and U.S. hegemony" (Davis 2007) that transformed ghettos into sites of struggles and made Black Panthers articulate a more political notion of freedom.

> We Want Freedom. ... We believe that Black people will not be free until we are able to determine our destiny. ... We Want An End to the Robbery By the Capitalists of Our Black Community. ... We Want Decent Housing Fit For The Shelter of Human Beings ... We believe in an educational system that will give to our people a knowledge of self. ... We believe we can end police brutality in our Black community by organizing Black self-defense groups that are dedicated to defending our Black community from racist police oppression and brutality. ... We Want All Black People When Brought to Trial To Be Tried In Court By A Jury Of Their Peer Group Or People From Their Black Communities.
>
> —*What We Want, What We Believe,*
> Huey P. Newton, Bobby Seale Black Panther Party

Contemporary world ordering has not abolished the separation between the inner space where freedom is embedded in custom-bound practices and the outer domain of worldly interconnections—in tension with which freedom becomes an object of politics—but it has worked to empty the relation between the two of transformative possibilities.

Claiming eminent necessity to safeguard an abstract thing it has called the "Global Commons," it has instituted global, radical reiterations of what

Karl Polanyi, in *The Great Transformation*, termed "bad freedoms"—"the freedom to exploit one's fellows ... to make inordinate gains without commensurable service to the community ... to keep technological inventions from being used for public benefit ... to profit from public calamities secretly engineered for private advantage"—all the while ensnaring social forces to practical-inert reason by confining them to false, preemptively foreclosed situations.[3] Thus—by what David Harvey (2003) called the global "enclosing of the commons"—have social forces been simultaneously dispossessed of inherited riches and of the ability to recognize themselves as subjects.

Struggling against "new enclosures" (Duarte-Abadía et al. 2023), social forces have acted in ways to re-embed relations. Contemporary uses of the term *commoning* emphasize this grounding, lending an earthly allure to all sorts of distinct struggles—"from indigenous peoples' demands for a return ... of common land and the practices that make its use possible, to the software designers ... demanding that their creations become part of a larger human pool of communication and creativity accessible to all, to the environmentalists who [are] demanding the transformation of the atmosphere, the oceans and the remaining large-scale forests into a common, democratically regulated" (Caffentzis 2004). Emphasizing the localness of commoning, such use tends to overlook precisely what historicizing *freedom in thinking* invites us to consider: the constitutive, dialectical relation between situated actions and the structure of world order. Reaching deeply and intently into the folds of all social relations, contemporary world ordering had brought social forces engaged in the defense of situated ways of being to bypass the order of scale that had been instituted in the old world-system of states and become active in the world itself (Kenny 2006: 21).[4] Looking for like groups to exchange with and draw from and for

---

[3]The safeguarding the global commons has become a legitimizing trope of global governing agencies. A sense of its pervasiveness can be gleaned even from a cursory glance at the World Bank's Open Learning Campus initiative (World Bank OLC Course): https://www.worldbank.org/en/olc/course/57633. In "A Tale of Two Conferences," George Caffentzis points to the Indiana University Digital Library of the Commons—that contains "almost 40,000 titles of articles and books ... [dealing], in one way or another, with the commons"—as an indicator of how ubiquitous references to the commons have become (Caffentzis 2004). Another sign was the 2009 co-awarding of the Nobel Prize in Economics to Elinor Ostrom, whose work stresses the necessity to manage commons well enough for commonality to be reproduced, and to Oliver E. Williamson "for his analysis of economic governance." https://www.nobelprize.org/prizes/economic-sciences/2009/illustrated-information/. Karl Polanyi's *The Great Transformation* is cited from Harvey (2007: 36).

[4]On "scale jumping"—"a vital strategy to gain power or influence in a multiscalar relational organization of networks of governance,"—see Tomiak (2016: 13). See also Eric Swyngedouw, "Scaled Geographies: Nature, Place, and the Politics of Scale," in *Scale and Geographic Inquiry: Nature, Society, and Method*, ed. Eric Sheppard and Robert McMaster (Blackwell, 2004), 129–53; and Eric Swyngedouw, "Neither Global nor Local: 'Glocalization' and the Politics of Scale," in *Spaces of Globalization: Reasserting the Power of the Local*, ed. Kevin R. Cox (Guilford Press, 1996), 137–66.

tactical as well as strategic relations to build (Drainville 2013a), they "grope their way uncertainly into a dimly perceived world, discovering and creating the rule as they go along" (Morris-Suzuki 2000). In doing so, they rekindle all manners of contacts and connections, linkages and interrelationships that had been bent out of shape by being fixed to place. Therein—in the active reestablishment of human bonds—lies a global, vernacular sort of freedom that is at once consequence and cause of human self-realization. Like *freedom in thinking*, it is not an ideal sitting at the end of political rainbows but a living *praxis* defined in actions—no matter how tiny, mundane, or inconsequential they may seem, at times even to those who are most concerned by them—taking place in situations, amid the ordering of the world.

This book is the product of the very freedom it labors to historicize. As I put the final touches to it, it is fast becoming more difficult for scholars everywhere to stand apart from the prevailing order of the world to ask how that order came about and how to transform it. However much this may appear on the surface to be the works of a maverick US president drawing justification for his war on *academic freedom* from a peculiarly US tradition of anti-intellectualism (Hofstadter 1964)—what Isaac Asimov more bluntly called "a cult of ignorance" (Asimov 1980)—it is a development overdetermined by the structural conditions of world ordering. Fifty years after the Trilateral Commission et al. began articulating a global strategy out of the mid-twentieth-century crisis of world ordering, we are, it seems, still suspended between an old world order that will not die and a new one that cannot be born. Each makes a particular concept of freedom its watchword. That of the old world-system of states—defended in its morbid phase by authoritarian governments and parties—is rooted in an excluding, vengeful rapport to national traditions. That of contemporary world ordering subsumes all freedoms to the exigencies of working toward the reproduction and intensification of global accumulation. It is the oil that lubricates the engine of global appropriation.

Wedged between totalitarian tendencies, reflexive instances are being stripped of any possibility for autonomy. Nowhere is this more evident than in the United States, the last hegemon of the old state-system. There, spectacular attacks on scholars and universities—the showy firing of faculty, the sudden suspending of funding, the theatrical deployment of police on campus, the tossing of books in parking lot dumpsters, the arrests of foreign students by hooded officers in the streets, the public casting of professors as enemies of the state (*dixit* Vice President J. D. Vance to the National Conservative conference [Bumiller 2025]), and the ransoming of universities for cause of presumed antisemitism—are being underwritten by defiant, at times almost clownish, displays of unknowledge regarding the very real dangers, problems, and challenges that contemporary *exterminism* exploits to subsume all social relations of knowledge production to a depoliticizing process of problem-solving. These conditions have made it necessary to defend freedom as it was instituted—as *academic freedom*—thereby entrapping professorial discourse in rearguard defense of inherited privileges—furthering deepening estrangement from contingent faculty and graduate students who form the bulk of academic labor, as well as from the broader movement of people engaged in resisting the ways and consequences of contemporary world ordering. Seeing into the little tradition of scholarly actions, we are instead invited to see beyond corporatist reflexes, toward a more political understanding of the indivisibility of freedom.

REFERENCES

American Association of University Professors (AAUP). 1915. *Declaration of Principles on Academic Freedom and Academic Tenure. Report of the Committee on Academic Freedom and Academic Tenure*. AAUP.

American Association of University Professors (AAUP). 2022. *The Annual Report on the Economic Status of the Profession, 2021–22*. AAUP.

Abba, Maria Julieta, and Danilo Romeu Streck. 2021. "The 1918 Córdoba Reform and University Internationalization in Latin America." *História da Educação*, 25(E102256): 1–32.

Abdel-Latif, Sara. 2020. "The Development of a Sufi Anti-Curriculum: Politics of Knowledge and Authority in Classical Islamic Education." In *Knowledge and Education in Classical Islam: Religious Learning between Continuity and Change* (2 vols), edited by Hinrich Biesterfeldt and Sebastian Günther, 637–67. Brill.

Abdo, Nahla. 2024. "Israel's Settler Colonialism and the Genocide in Gaza." *Studies in Political Economy* 105 (1):94–106.

Abraham, Christiana, and Brenda Dash. 2022. "'I Won't Take Bail Until We All Get It': Gender, Black Power, 1960s Student Activism and the Sir George Williams Affair—An Interview with Brenda Dash." *TOPIA: Canadian Journal of Cultural Studies* 44 (1):48–66.

Abu-Lughod, Janet L. 1991. *Before European Hegemony: The World System* AD 1250–1350. Oxford University Press.

Adams, Nathan A. IV. 2021. "Resolving Enmity between Academic Freedom and Institutional Autonomy." *Journal of College and University Law* 46 (1):1–70.

Adebajo, Adekeye. 2020. "A Crumbling Legacy." *Times Literary Supplement*, August 6. https://ipatc.joburg/facing-up-to-woodrow-wilsons-true-legacy/

Adeleke, Tunde. 2017. *Africa in Black Liberation Activism: Malcolm X, Stokely Carmichael and Walter Rodney*. Taylor & Francis.

Adler, Margo. 2002. "My Life in the FSM: Memories of a Freshman." In *The Free Speech Movement: Reflections on Berkeley in the 1960s*, edited by Robert Cohen and Reginald E. Zelnik, 111–28. University of California Press.

Agacinski, Daniel. 2012. "Comment la guerre d'Algérie a politisé le milieu étudiant." *Cahiers du GRM*https://doi.org/10.4000/grm.258.

Aglietta, Michel. 1979. *A Theory of Capitalist Regulation: The US Experience*. New Left Books.

Ahmed, Abdul Kayum. 2019. *The Rise of Fallism:# RhodesMustFall and the Movement to Decolonize the University*. Columbia University.

Aiden, Will. 2024. "A New Jewishness Is Being Born before Our Eyes." *The Nation* May 10.

Al-Faruque, Muhammad. 1987. "The Development of the Institutions of Madrasah and the Nizamiyyah of Baghdad." *Islamic Studies* 26 (3):253–63.

Al-Khalili, Jim. 2011. *The House of Wisdom: How Arabic Science Saved Ancient Knowledge and Gave Us the Renaissance*. Penguin.

Alatas, Syed Hussein. 2000. "Intellectual Imperialism: Definition, Traits, and Problems." *Asian Journal of Social Science* 28 (1):23–45.

Algeriani, Adel Abdul-Aziz, and Mawloud Mohadi. 2017. "The House of Wisdom (Bayt al-Hikmah) and Its Civilizational Impact on Islamic Libraries: A Historical Perspective." *Mediterranean Journal of Social Sciences* 8 (5):179.

Althusser, Louis. 2014. *On the Reproduction of Capitalism: Ideology and Ideological State Apparatuses*. Verso Trade.

Anderson, Elijah. 2011. *The Cosmopolitan Canopy: Race and Civility in Everyday Life*. W. W. Norton & Company.

Anderson, Gina. 2008. "Mapping Academic Resistance in the Managerial University." *Organization* 15 (2):251–70.

Anderson, James D. 1978. "Northern Foundations and the Shaping of Southern Black Rural Education, 1902–1935." *History of Education Quarterly* 18 (4):371–96.

Anderson, Robert D. 2004. *European Universities from the Enlightenment to 1914*. Oxford University Press.

Andrews, William. 2016. *Dissenting Japan: A History of Japanese Radicalism and Counterculture from 1945 to Fukushima*.Oxford University Press.

Anievas, Alexander, and Kerem Nişancıoğlu. 2015. *How the West Came to Rule: The Geopolitical Origins of Capitalism*. Pluto Press.

Anon. 1896. "Degrees for Women at Cambridge." *The British Medical Journal* 1 (1838):741–42.

Anon. 1897a. "Cambridge Degrees for Women." *The British Medical Journal* 1 (1888):608–9.

Anon. 1897b. "Cambridge Refuses Degrees for Women." *Daily News* (Friday, May 21).

Anon. 1906. "3,000 Georgia Troops Keep Peace in Atlanta: Soldiers Disarming Negroes in All Parts of the City." *The New York Times*, September 25.

Anon. 1946. "Burning More Books." *The New York Times*, Wednesday, May 15, 20.

Anon. 1947. "Unwelcome Guests." *Time* 50 (25): 50.

Anon. 1969a. "A Brief Triumph for Student Power" *Minerva* 7 (4):783–812.

Anon. 1969b. "Continuing Disorder in Japanese Universities." *Minerva* 7 (4):778–83

Anon. 2006. "250 establecimientos se pliegan a paro nacional, según asamblea." *El Mercurio*. https://www.emol.com/noticias/nacional/2006/05/30/220641/250-establecimientos-se-pliegan-a-paro-nacional-segun-asamblea.html.

Anon. 2011. "Movilizaciones: recuperar la sensatez." *El Mercurio*, 17 August.

Applebaum, Wilbur. 2000. *Encyclopedia of the Scientific Revolution from Copernicus to Newton*. Garland.

Aptheker, Bettina. 2002. "Gender Politics and the FSM: A Meditation on Women and Freedom of Speech." In *The Free Speech Movement: Reflections on Berkeley in the 1960s*, edited by Robert Cohen and Reginald E. Zelnik, 129–39. University of California Press.

Aptheker, Herbert. 1975. *The Education of Black People: Ten Critiques by W.E.B. Du Bois 1906–1960*. Monthly Review Press.

Arendt, Hannah. 2009. "Prologue." In *Responsibility and Judgment*, edited by Hannah Arendt, 3–17. Schocken.
Aroca, Alberto Cordero. 2017. "Centenario de la Reforma Universitaria de Cordoba 1918–2018." *Boletín de la Academia Nacional de Historia* 96 (198):45–61.
Arria, Michael. 2020. "Butler Students Win BDS Victory Amid Attacks From Pro-Israel Critics" *Mondoweiss*, October 22.
Arrighi, Giovanni, Terence K. Hopkins, and Immanuel Wallerstein. 1989. *Antisystemic Movements*. Verso.
Aschheim, Steven E. 2012. *At the Edges of Liberalism: Junctions of European, German, and Jewish History, Palgrave Studies in Cultural and Intellectual History*. Palgrave Macmillan.
Ash, Mitchell G. 1997. "Introduction." In *German Universities Past and Future: Crisis or Renewal?*, edited by Mitchell G. Ash, vii–xx. Berghahn Books.
Ashby, Eric. 1966. *Universities: British, Indian, African. A Study in the Ecology of Higher Education*. Weidenfeld and Nicolson.
Asimov, Isaac. 1980. "A Cult of Ignorance." *Newsweek*, January 21, 19.
Asselin, Olivier. 2012. "Carré rouge. Le destin politique d'une forme colorée." *Theory & Event* 15 (3 [Supplement]).
Asztalos, Monica. 1992. "The Faculty of Theology." In *A History of the University in Europe*, edited by Walter Ruëgg, 409–42. Cambrige University Press.
Atkinson, Richard C., and Saul Geiser. 2009. "Reflections on a Century of College Admissions Tests." *Educational Researcher* 38 (9):665–76.
Austin, David. 2007. "All Roads Led to Montreal: Black Power, the Caribbean, and the Black Radical Tradition in Canada." *The Journal of African American History* 92 (4):516–39.
Austin, David. 2013. *Fear of a Black Nation: Race, Sex, and Security in Sixties Montreal*. Between the Lines.
Austin, David. 2018. "The Dialect of Liberation." In *Moving against the System: The 1968 Congress of Black Writers and the Making of Global Consciousness*, edited by David Austin, 1–77. Pluto Press.
Avnon, Dan, Julien Bauer, Corinne Blackmer, Gabriel Brahm, Shlomo Dubnov, Ronnie Fraser, Janet Freedman, Larissa Benita Klazinga, Jeffrey Kopstein, and Martin Kramer. 2018. *Anti-Zionism on Campus: The University, Free Speech, and BDS*. Indiana University Press.
B.G.A. 1968. "Les négociations tardives avec les étudiants ayant échoué la police prend d'assaut soixante barricades la C.G.T., la C.F.D.T. et la F.E.N. lancent un appel à la grève générale lundi 367 blessés, 460 interpellations, 188 voitures endommagées." *Le Monde*, 13 May.
Back, Les, and Maggie Tate. 2015. "For a Sociological Reconstruction: W.E.B. Du Bois, Stuart Hall and Segregated Sociology." *Sociological Research Online* 20 (3):155–66.
Backman, Clifford R. 2009. *The Worlds of Medieval Europe*. 2nd ed. Oxford University Press.
Badat, Saleem, and Yusuf Sayed. 2014. "Post-1994 South African Education: The Challenge of Social Justice." *The Annals of the American Academy of Political and Social Science* 652 (1):127–48.
Badiou, Alain. 2008. "Mai 1968 à la puissance quatre." *À Babord*, 24 (April/May.
Badiou, Alain. 2009. *L'hypothèse communiste*. Nouvelles éditions Lignes.

Bains, Paul. 1997. "Subjectless Subjectivities." *Canadian Review of Comparative Literature/Revue Canadienne de Littérature Comparée* 24 (3):511–28.

Balandier, Georges. 1951. "La situation coloniale: approche théorique." *Cahiers internationaux de sociologie* 11:44.

Balazs, Etienne, and Arthur F. Wright. 1964. *Chinese Civilization and Bureaucracy: Variations on a Theme*. Yale University Press.

Baldwin, James. 1959. "Letter from the South: Nobody Knows My Name." *The Partisan Review* 26 (1):72–93.

Baldwin, James. 1962. *The Fire Next Time*. Dell.

Ball, Stephen J. 2003. "The Teacher's Soul and the Terrors of Performativity." *Journal of Education Policy* 18 (2):215–28.

Ballantyne, Neil. 2022. "Scholarly Publication, Open Access and the Commons." *Critical and Radical Social Work* 10 (3):469–83.

Bangstad, Sindre. 2025. "The Palestine Exception to Academic Freedom and the IHRA Definition of Antisemitism." *The Journal of Imperial and Commonwealth History* 53, no. 3: 689–700.

Banik, Gouranga. 2014. "Perceptions Regarding Cheating among CM and AEC Students." Paper presented at 2014 ASEE Annual Conference & Exposition, Indianapolis, Indiana.10.18260/1-2--22911

Barker, Colin. 2008. "Some Reflections on Student Movements of the 1960s and Early 1970s." *Revista Crítica de Ciências Sociais* 81:43–91.

Barnor, Hesse. 2014. "Racism's Alterity: The After-life of Black Sociology." In *Racism and Sociology*, edited by Wulf D. Hund and Alana Lentin, 141–74. LIT Verlag Munster.

Barreira, Irlys Alencar Firmo. 1999. "Le redécouverte du Brésil par la 'Caravane de la Citoyenneté': Rituels et symboles politiques à l'occasion de la campagne électorale de 1994." *L'homme et la société* 132–33 (2–3):195–215.

Barrier, Jeff, Antonio Bustos, John Calvert, Christian Chalstrom, and Shiloh Chambers.2016. *Safe Spaces for Dangerous Ideas: The Case for Intellectual Diversity on Campus*. Heterodox Academy

Barrionuevo, Alexei. 2011. "With Kiss-Ins and Dances, Young Chileans Push for Reform." *The New York Times*, August 4.

Barry, Jim, John Chandler, and Heather Clark. 2001. "Between the Ivory Tower and the Academic Assembly Line." *Journal of Management Studies* 38 (1):88–101.

Bartfeld, D., Le Gal, J. M., and Zagnoli, N. 1968. "Edgar Morin, Claude Lefort, Jean-Marc Coudray, Mai 1968: la brèche: premières réflexions sur les événements." *L'Homme et la société* 9 (1):247–51.

Bartholomew, James R. 1988. "Japanese Modernization and the Imperial Universities, 1876–1920." *The Journal of Asian Studies* 37 (2):251–71.

Bartlett, Thomas. 2009. "Cheating Goes Global as Essay Mills Multiply." *Chronicle of Higher Education* 55 (28): A1.

Bary, Wm. Theodore de. 1989. "Chu Hsi's Aims as an Educator." In *Neo-Confucian Education: The Formative Stage*, edited by Wm. Theodore de Bary, 186–218. University of California Press.

Battle-Baptiste, Witney, and Britt Rusert. 2018. *WEB Du Bois's Data Portraits: Visualizing Black America*. Chronicle Books.

Bauman, Zygmunt. 2011. "The London Riots–on Consumerism Coming Home to Roost." *Social Europe Journal* 9 (8). https://www.social-europe.eu/2011/08/the-london-riots-on-consumerism-coming-home-to-roost

Bauman, Zygmunt, and Leonidas Donskis. 2013. *Moral Blindness: The Loss of Sensitivity in Liquid Modernity*. John Wiley & Sons.

Bayen, Maurice. 1973. *Que sais-je? Histoire des universités*. Presses universitaires de France.

Bayne, Clarence, Brenda Dash, Philippe Fils-Aimé, and Nancy Warner. 2021. "Fifty Years Ago: Reflections on the Sir George Williams University Protests." In *The Fire That Time*, edited by Ronald Cummings and Nalini Mohabir, 33–46. Black Rose Books.

BBC News. 2011. Chile Police Break Up Student Protest in Santiago. August 4. https://www.bbc.com/news/world-latin-america-14412646

Beer, Lawrence W. 1970. "Japan, 1969: 'My Homeism' and Political Struggle." *Asian Survey* 10 (1):43–55.

Behr, A. L. 1987. "South African Universities Today: Perceptions for a Changing Society." *South African Journal of Higher Education* 1 (1):3–10.

Belgrave, Valerie. 1995. "The Sir George Williams Affair." In *The Black Power Revolution of 1970: A Retrospective*, edited by Selwyn Ryan and Taimoon Stewart, 119–33. The University of the West Indies.

Bell, Daniel. 1968. *The Reforming of General Education: The Columbia College Experience in Its National Setting*. Anchor Books.

Bell, Derrick. 1973. *Race, Racism, and American Law*. Little, Brown.

Bell, Derrick. 1985. "Strangers in Academic Paradise: Law Teachers of Color in Still White Schools." *USFL Rev*. 20:385–95.

Bell, Derrick A. 1995. "David C. Baum Memrial Lecture: Who's Afraid of Critical Race Theory." *University of Illinois Law Review* 1995 (4):893–911.

Bellei, Cristian. 2005. "The Private-Public School Controversy: The Case of Chile." Conference on Mobilizing the Private Sector for Public Education, October.

Bellei, Cristian, and Cristian Cabalin. 2013. "Chilean Student Movements: Sustained Struggle to Transform a Market-Oriented Educational System." *Current Issues in Comparative Education* 15 (2):108–23.

Bellei, Cristián, Cristian Cabalin, and Víctor Orellana. 2014. "The 2011 Chilean Student Movement against Neoliberal Educational Policies." *Studies in Higher Education* 39 (3):426–40.

Benda, Julien. 2003. *La trahison des clercs* Grasset.

Benjamin, Walter. 1968. "Paris–Capital of the Nineteenth Century." *New Left Review* 1 (48):77–88.

Berkeley, George. 1725. *A Proposal for the Better Supplying of Churches in Our Foreign Plantations*. H. Woodfall.

Berkey, Jonathan P. 1995. "Tradition, Innovation and the Social Construction of Knowledge in the Medieval Islamic Near East." *Past and Present* 146 (1):38–65.

Berkey, Jonathan P. 2007. "Chapter 2. Madrasas Medieval and Modern: Politics, Education, and the Problem of Muslim Identity." *Schooling Islam: The Culture and Politics of Modern Muslim Education*, edited by Robert W. Hefner and Muhammad Quasim Zaman, 40–60.Princeton University Press.

Berkey, Jonathan Porter. 1992. *The Transmission of Knowledge in Medieval Cairo: A Social History of Islamic Education*. Princeton University Press.

Bernstein, Alan E. 1978. "Magisterium and License: Corporate Autonomy against Papal Authority in the Medieval University of Paris." *Viator* 9:291–308.

Beyer, Jeff. 2023. "Foreword." In *Decolonizing the South African University: Towards Curriculum as Self Authentication*, edited by Oscar Koopman and Karen J. Koopman, vii–xvii. Palgrave Macmillan/Springer.

Bhabha, Homi K. 1992. "Freedom's Basis in the Indeterminate." *October* 61:46–57.

Birchall, Frederick T. 1933. "Nazi Book-Burning Fails to Stir Berlin." *The New York Times*, Thursday, May 11, 1, 12.

Birchard, Karen. 2006. "Cheating Is Rampant at Canadian Colleges." *The Chronicle of Higher Education* 53 (8):A53.

Birt, Robert E. 2002. *The Quest for Community and Identity: Critical Essays in Africana Social Philosophy*. Rowman & Littlefield.

Blackburn, Robin. 2017. Revisiting the Transition to Capitalism Debate. *Almanack* 17:465–75.

Blasi, Paolo, Nuria Sanz, and Sjur Bergam. 2002. "The Idea of Europe through the History of Universities: The European Dimension as University Heritage in the Past, Today, and in the Future." *The Heritage of European Universities*:103–10.

Bledsoe, Adam. 2017. "Marronage as a Past and Present Geography in the Americas." *Southeastern Geographer* 57 (1):30–50.

Blinder, Alan. 2024. "Campus Protests. Universities Make Arrests, or Deals, to Protect Commencement Events." *The New York Times*, May 10, 11.

Bloch, Marc, and Étienne Bloch. 1995. *Histoire et historiens*. Armand Colin.

Blum, Françoise. 2012. "Sénégal 1968: révolte étudiante et grève générale." *Revue d'histoire moderne et contemporaine* 59 (2):144–77.

Bol, Peter K. 1992. *"This Culture of Ours": Intellectual Transitions in T'ang and Sung China*. Stanford University Press.

Bonilla-Silva, Eduardo, and Crystal E. Peoples. 2022. "Historically White Colleges and Universities: The Unbearable Whiteness of (Most) Colleges and Universities in America." *American Behavioral Scientist* 66 (11):1490–504.

Boren, Mark Edelman. 2013. *Student Resistance: A History of the Unruly Subject*. Routledge.

Bostick, Theodora. 1980. "The Press and the Launching of the Women's Suffrage Movement, 1866–1867." *Victorian Periodicals Review* 13 (4):125–31.

Boucar-Victoire, Kévin. 2018. "*Le « scandale de Strasbourg »: l'origine trop méconnue de Mai 1968*." Le Media Press, 18 mai 2022.

Boutang, Yann Moulier. 2007. *Le capitalisme cognitif: la nouvelle grande transformaton*. Éditions Amsterdam.

Boxill, Bernard R. 1992. *Blacks and Social Justice*. Rowman & Littlefield.

Braithwaite, Lloyd. 1958. "The Development of Higher Education in the West Indies." *Social and Economic Studies* 7 (1):1.

Brambilla, Elena. 2009. "Lycées et Université impériale. Innovations éducatives en France et influence sur l'instruction des élites en Italie (1789–1814)." *Rives méditerranéennes* 32–33 :97–119.

Braudel, Fernand. 1984. *Civilization and Capitalism, 15th–18th Century*. Vol. III: *The Perspective of the World*. Translated by Sian Reynolds. Collins.

Breetzke, Gregory D., and David W. Hedding. 2018. "The Changing Demography of Academic Staff at Higher Education Institutions (HEIs) in South Africa."

Higher Education: The International Journal of Higher Education Research 76 (1):145–61.

Brenner, Robert. 1976. "Agrarian Class Structure and Economic Development in Pre-Industrial Europe." *Past and Present* 70 (1):30–75.

Brentjes, Sonja. 2018. *Teaching and Learning the Sciences in Islamicate Societies (800–1700)*. Brepols Publishers.

Brewer, Rose M. 2018. "Capitalism, Racism, and the Neoliberal University: The Case of the University of Missouri (Mizzou)." In *Teaching Economic Inequality and Capitalism in Contemporary America*, edited by K. Haltinner and L. Hormel, 291–99. Springer.

Browning, Oscar. 1887. "The University Extension Movement at Cambridge." *Science* 2075, (9):61–63.

Buell, Paul D., and Francesca Fiaschetti. 2018. *Historical Dictionary of the Mongol World Empire*. Rowman & Littlefield.

Bumiller, Elisabeth. 2025. "Trump Battles Academia, but Especially the Ivy League" *The New York Times*, May 4.

Burawoy, Michael. 2021. "Decolonizing Sociology: The Significance of WEB Du Bois." *Critical Sociology* 47 (4–5):545–54.

Burbank, Jane, and Frederick Cooper. 2010. *Empires in World History: Power and the Politics of Difference*. Princeton University Press.

Burden-Stelly, Charisse. 2018. "W.E.B. Du Bois in the Tradition of Radical Blackness: Radicalism, Repression, and Mutual Comradeship, 1930–1960." *Socialism and Democracy* 32 (3):181–206.

Burke, Peter. 2013. *Social History of Knowledge: From Gutenberg to Diderot*. John Wiley & Sons.why

Burns, Rebecca. 2006. *Rage in the Gated City: The Story of the 1906 Atlanta Race Riot*. University of Georgia Press.

Burton, Guy. 2012. "Hegemony and Frustration: Education Policy Making in Chile under the Concertación, 1990–2010." *Latin American Perspectives* 39 (4):34–52.

Bush, Daniella Wittern. 2019. "Their Dissidence Remains: Lessons from the 2011 Chilean Student Movement." In *Sustainable Tools for Precarious Times*, edited by Natalie Alvarez, Claudette Lauzon, and Keren Zaiontz, 69–93. Springer.

Butcher, LeRoi. 1971. "The Anderson Affair." In *Let the Niggers Burn: The Sir George Williams University Affair and Its Caribbean Aftermath*, edited by Dennis Forsythe, 76–110. Black Rose Books/Our Generation Press.

Butler, Judith. 2006. "Israel/Palestine and The Paradoxes of Academic Freedom." *Radical Philosophy* 135:8–17.

Byrne, J. Peter. 1989. "Academic Freedom: A 'Special Concern of the First Amendment'." *The Yale Law Journal* 99 (2):251–340.

Cabalin, Cristian. 2012. "Neoliberal Education and Student Movements in Chile: Inequalities and Malaise." *Policy Futures in Education* 10 (2):219–28.

Caffentzis, George. 2004. "A Tale of Two Conferences: Globalization, the Crisis of Neoliberalism and Question of the Commons." Alter-Globalization Conference, San Miguel de Allende, Mexico, August 9, 2004 https://www.globaljusticecenter.org/sites/default/files/pdfs/A%20tale%20of%20Two%20Conferences.pdf.

California Monthly Editors. 1965. "Chronology of Events: Three Months of Crisis." In *The Berkeley Student Revolt: Facts and Interpretations*, edited by Seymour Martin Lipset and Sheldon S. Wolin, 99–199. Anchor Books.

Cameron, Brian D. 2005. "Trends in the Usage of ISI Bibliometric Data: Uses, Abuses, and Implications." *Portal: Libraries and the Academy* 5 (1):105–25.

Cammaerts, Bart. 2013. "The Mediation of Insurrectionary Sÿmbolic Damage: The 2010 UK Student Protests." *The International Journal of Press/Politics* 18(4):525–48

Campbell, Horace. 1980. "The Rastfarians in the Eastern Caribbean." *Caribbean Quarterly* 26 (4):42–61.

Cardozier, V. R. 1968. "Student Power in Medieval Universities." *Journal of Counseling and Development* 46 (10):944–48.

Castoriadis, Cornelius. 1986. "Les mouvements des années soixante." *Pouvoirs: Revue française d'etudes constitutionnelles et politiques* 39:107–16.

Cavanagh, Edward. 2016. "Corporations and Business Associations from the Commercial Revolution to the Age of Discovery: Trade, Jurisdiction and the State, 1200–1600." *History Compass* 14 (10):493–510.

Cayton, A. 2006. "Putting the United States in Its Place Thomas Bender, A Nation Among Nations: America's Place in World History." *Reviews in American History* 34 (4):573–80.

Chaffee, John W. 1982. "To Spread One's Wings: Examinations and the Social Order in Southeastern China during the Southern Song." *Historical Reflections / Réflexions Historiques* 9 (3):305–32.

Chaffee, John W. 1985a. *The Thorny Gates of Learning in Sung China: A Social History of Examinations*. Cambridge University Press.

Chaffee, John W. 1985b. "Chu Hsi and the Revival of the White Deer Grotto Academy, 1179–1181 A.D." *T'oung Pao* 71 (1):40–62.

Chamberlain, Michael. 2002. *Knowledge and Social Practice in Medieval Damascus, 1190–1350*. Cambridge University Press.

Chamberlin, William Henry. 1946. "Bigger and Better Book Burnings." *Wall Street Journal*, May 24.

Chan, Wing-Tsit, ed. 1963. *A Source Book in Chinese Philosophy*. Princeton University Press.

Chandler, Roy, and John Richard Edwards. 2019. *Malcolm Anderson 1970–2018: His Academic Career*. Taylor & Francis.

Chapoulie, Jean-Michel, and Jean-Pierre Briand. 2019. *Les collèges du peuple: l'enseignement primaire supérieur et le développement de la scolarisation prolongée sous la Troisième République* Presses universitaires de Rennes.

Chapron, Emmanuelle. 2014. "Des livres « pour l'usage de l'École royale militaire »: choix pédagogiques et stratégies éditoriales (1751–1788)." *Histoire, économie et société* 33e année (1):3–16.

Charle, Christophe. 2018. *La République des universitaires (1870–1940)*. Média Diffusion.

Chartier, Roger. 1982. "Espace social et imaginaire social: les intellectuels frustrés au XVIIe siècle." *Annales. Histoire, Sciences Sociales* 37 (2):389–400.

Chase, T. N. 1896. *Mortality among Negroes in Cities.*Atlanta University Press.

Chase-Dunn, Chris, and Barry Gills. 2003. "Understanding Waves of Globalization and Resistance in the Capitalist World-System." *Social Movements and Critical Global(ization) Studies* 12.

Chigudu, Simukai. 2020. "Rhodes Must Fall in Oxford: A Critical Testimony." *Critical African Studies* 12 (3):302–12.

Chinguno, Crispen, Morwa Kgoroba, Sello Mashibini, Bafana Nicolas Masilela, Boikhutso Maubane, Nhlanhla Moyo, Andile Mthombeni, and Hlengiwe Ndlovu. 2017. *Rioting and Writing: Diaries of Wits Fallists*. Friedrich Ebert Stiftung Johannesburg.

Chircop, Denise. 1997. "Voting with Their Feet: Students and Absenteeism." In *Inside/Outside Schools: Towards a Critical Sociology of Education in Malta*, edited by R. G. Sultana, 353–74. Publishers Enterpirses Group Ltd.

Choi, Jamyung. 2018. "The Hegemony of Tokyo Imperial University and the Paradox of Meritocracy in Modern Japan." *The Journal of Japanese Studies* 44 (1):89–116.

Cholshi, Niraj. 2019. "Angela Davis Says She's 'Stunned' after Award Is Revoked over Her Views on Israel." *The New York Times*, January 8.

Chomsky, Noam. 1997. "The Cold War and the University." In *The Cold War and the University*, edited by Noam Chomsky, David Barsamian, and Howard Zinn, 171–95. New Press.

Chouillet, J. 1985. "Un projet de réforme de l'Université au dix-huitième siècle: le Plan d'une Université de Denis Diderot pour l'Impératrice de Russie (1775)." In *Mélanges de la Bibliothèque de la Sorbonne*, edited by André Gouron, 47–58. Bibliothèque de la Sorbonne.

Chovanec, Donna M., and Alexandra Benitez. 2008. "The Penguin Revolution in Chile: Exploring Intergenerational Learning in Social Movements." *Journal of Contemporary Issues in Education* 3 (1): 39–57.

Cineas, Fabiola. 2020. "Critical Race Theory, and Trump's War on It, Explained." *Vox*, 24 September.

Cini, Lorenzo. 2019. "Disrupting the Neoliberal University in South Africa: The FeesMustFall Movement in 2015." *Current Sociology* 67 (7):942–59.

Clark, Christopher. 1996. "The Wars of Liberation in Prussian Memory: Reflections on the Memorialization of War in Early Nineteenth-Century Germany." *The Journal of Modern History* 68 (3):550–76.

Click, Melissa. 2016. "Melissa Click: What Would Our World Be Like if No One Ever Took a Chance?" *The Washington Post*.

CNN Wire Staff. 2011. Tear Gas Flies during Chilean Student Protests.

Cobban, Alan B. 1971. "Medieval Student Power." *Past and Present*, 53: 28–66.

Cliff, Tony and Birchall, Ian 1968. *France: The Struggle Goes On*. Socialist Review Publishing Co. Ltd.

Cobban, Alan B. 2017. *The Medieval English Universities: Oxford and Cambridge to c1500*. Taylor & Francis.

Cohen, Bernard S. 1996. *Colonialism and Its Forms of Knowledge: The British in India*. Princeton University Press.

Cohn, Samuel. 2012. "The 'Modernity' of Medieval Popular Revolt." *History Compass* 10 (10):731–41.

Cole, David. 2016. "Race on Campus: A Conversation with Yale President Peter Salovey." *The New York Review of Books*, April 29.

Collini, Stefan. 2017. *Speaking of Universities*. Verso Books.

Collins, John. 2008. "'But What if I Should Need to Defecate in Your Neighborhood, Madame?': Empire, Redemption, and the 'Tradition of the Oppressed' in a Brazilian World Heritage Site." *Cultural Anthropology* 23 (2):279–328.

Collins, Patricia Hill. 2005. "Black Public Intellectuals: From Du Bois to the Present." *Contexts* 4 (4):22–27.
Collins, Randall. 2009. *The Sociology of Philosophies*. Harvard University Press.
Commission on Global Governance. 1995. *Our Global Neighborhood*. Oxford University Press.
Contat, Michel, and Michel Rybalka. 1976. *Sartre on Theatre*. Translated by Frank Jellinek. Pantheon Books.
Coutin, André. 1969. *Huit siecles de violence au quartier latin*. Stock.
Crenshaw, Kimberlé Williams. 2002. "The First Decade: Critical Reflections, or a Foot in the Closing Door." *UCLA Law Review* 49:1343–72.
Cressy, David. 2005. "Book Burning in Tudor and Stuart England." *The Sixteenth Century Journal* 36 (2):359–74.
Crouse, James, and Dale Trusheim. 1988. *The Case against the SAT*. University of Chicago Press.
Crouter, Richard. 2005. "A Proposal for a New Berlin University." In *Friedrich Schleiermacher: Between Enlightenment and Romanticism*, edited by Richard Crouter, 140–68.Cambridge University Press.
Crowe, Charles. 1969. "Racial Massacre in Atlanta September 22, 1906." *The Journal of Negro History* 54 (2):150–73.
Crozier, Michel, Samuel P. Huntington, and Joji Watanuki. 1975. *The Crisis of Democracy*. New York University Press.
Crum, Steven J. 1991. "Colleges before Columbus: Mayans, Aztecs and Incas Offered Advanced Education Long before the Arrival of Europeans." *Tribal College* 3 (2): 14.
Cummings, Ronald, and Nalini Mohabir. 2022. "Protests and Pedagogy: The Legacies of Caribbean Student Resistance and the Sir George Williams Protest, Montreal 1969." *TOPIA: Canadian Journal of Cultural Studies* 44 (1):1–24.
Curran, Charles E. 1990. *Catholic Higher Education, Theology and Academic Freedom*. University of Notre Dame Press.
Daas, Roua. 2021. "Letter to the Editor: Students Demand Answer, Ation." *The Butler Collegia*, March 30 https://thebutlercollegian.com/2021/03/letter-to-the-editor-students-demand-answers-action/.
Dardess, John W. 2002. *Blood and History in China: The Donglin Faction and Its Repression, 1620–1627*. University of Hawai'i Press.
Darian-Smith, Eve. 2025. "Policing the University: A Global Trend." *Revista de Direito Econômico e Socioambiental* 16, no. 2: 1–10.
Daun, Holger, and Reza Arjmand. 2018. *Handbook of Islamic Education*. Springer.
Davies, Emily. *The Higher Education of Women*. Alexander Strahan, 1866.
Davis, Angela Y. 1981. "Rape, Racism and the Capitalist Setting." *The Black Scholar* 12 (6):39–45.
Davis, Angela Y. 1983. *Women, Race and Class*. Vintage.
Davis, Angela Y. 1990. *Women, Culture and Politics*. Vintage.
Davis, Angela Y. 1994. "Afro Images: Politics, Fashion, and Nostalgia." *Critical Inquiry* 21 (1):37–45.
Davis, Angela Y. 1996. "Incarcerated Women: Transformative Strategies." *Black Renaissance* 1 (no. 1): 20–34.
Davis, Angela Y. 1999. *Blues Legacies and Black Feminism: Gertrude "Ma"Rainey, Bessie Smith, and Billie Holiday*. Vintage.

Davis, Angela Y. 2000. "Women and Capitalism: Dialectics of Oppression and Liberation." In *The Black Feminist Reader*, edited by Joy James and T. Denan Sharpley-Whiting, 146–82.

Davis, Angela Y. 2003. "Race and Criminalization: Black Americans and the Punishment Industry." In *Criminological Perspectives: Essential Readings*, 2nd ed. edited by Eugene McLaughlin, John Muncie, and Gordon Hughes, 146–82. Sage Publications.

Davis, Angela Y. 2004. "Public Imprisonment and Private Violence: Reflections on the Hidden Punishment of Women." In *Frontline Feminisms*, edited by Marguerite Waller and Jennifer Rycenga, 2–17. Routledge.

Davis, Angela Y. 2012. *The Meaning of Freedom: And Other Difficult Dialogues*. City Lights Publishers.

Davis, Angela Y. 2013. "Critical Refusals and Occupy." *Radical Philosophy Review* 16 (2):425–39.

Davis, Angela Y. 2014. "Marcuse's Legacies." In *Herbert Marcuse*, edited by Douglas Kelnner, 43–50. Routledge.

Davis, Angela Y. 2016. *Freedom Is a Constant Struggle: Ferguson, Palestine, and the Foundations of a Movement*. Haymarket Books.

Davis, Angela Y. 2018. "The Past, Present, and Future of Assata's Message." *WSQ: Women's Studies Quarterly* 46 (3):232–34.

Davis, Mike. 2007. "Malcom More Than Ever." In *In Praise of Barbarians: Essays against Empire*, edited by Mike Davis, 291–94. Haymarket Books.

Davy, Marie-Madeleine. 1931. "La situation juridique des étudiants de l'université de Paris au XIIIe siècle." *Revue d'histoire de l'Église de France* 17 (76):297–311.

de Crespigny, Rafe. 1991. "The Three Kingdoms and Western Jin: A History of China in the 3rd Century AD." *East Asian History* 1 (1):1–37.

de Figueiredo-Cowen, Maria. 2002. "Latin American Universities, Academic Freedom and Autonomy: A Long-Term Myth?" *Comparative Education* 38 (4):471–84.

De Weerdt, Hilde. 2020. *Information, Territory, and Networks: The Crisis and Maintenance of Empire in Song China*. Brill.

Deacon, Thomas. 2019. "'My Husband Worked So Hard… There Was No Sign He'd Do Anything Like This… but Then He Killed Himself'." *Wales Online*, 21 February. Accessed 21 August 2022.

Debord, G. E., and Jacques Fillion. 1954. "Résumé 1954." *Potlatch*, 14: 63.

Debord, Guy. 1966. "Le déclin et la chute de l'économie spectaculaire-marchande." *Internationale Situationniste* No. 10: 3–11.

Debord, Guy. 1978. "Sur le passage de quelques personnes à travers une assez courte unité de temps." In *Oeuvres cinématographiques complètes,1952–1978*, edited by Guy Debord, 15–32. Champ Libre.

Del Campo, Alicia. 2016. "Theatricalities of Dissent: Human Rights, Memory, and the Student Movement in Chile." *Radical History Review* 2016(124):177–91.

Délano, Manuel. 2011. "Los estudiantes chilenos rechazan la reforma propuesta por el Gobierno." *El Pais*, August 19.

Deleuze, Gilles, and Félix Guattari. 1980. *Mille Plateaux*. Les Éditions de Minuit

Delgado, Richard, and Jean Stefancic. 2023. *Critical Race Theory: An Introduction*. NYU Press.

Deng, Kent G. 2013. *Demystifying Growth and Development in North Song China, 960–1127*. Department of Economic History, London School of Economics.

Desai, Rehad. 2018. *Everything Must Fall..*

Destemberg, Antoine. 2009. "Un système rituel? Rites d'intégration et passages de grades dans le système universitaire médiéval (XIIIe–XVe siècle)." *Cahiers de recherches médiévales* 18: 113–32.

Dewey, John, Jo Ann Boydston, and Larry A. Hickman. 2003. "*The Collected Works of John Dewey, 1882–1953 (2nd release). Electronic edition.*" InteLex Corporation. https://www.nlx.com/collections/133.

d'Irsay, Stephen 1933. *Histoire des universités françaises et étrangères des origines à nos jours*. A. Picard.

Didier, Béatrice. 1995. "Quand Diderot faisait le plan d'une université." *Recherches sur Diderot et sur l'Encyclopédie* 18 (1):81–91.

Discenna, Thomas Andrew. 2001. "Apprenticed or Exploited: Critical Rhetoric and the Yale Grade Strike." P.h.D., Communication (Rhetoric), Wayne State University.

Doüet d'Arcq, Louis. 1844. "Émeute de l'université de Paris en 1453." *Bibliothèque de l'École des chartes* 5 (1):479–89.

Doyle, Kate. 2003. *Tlatelolco Massacre: U.S. Documents on Mexico and the Events of 1968*. National Security Archive.

Drainville, A. C. 2015. "The Moral Economy of Global Crowds: Egypt 1977, Brazil 2013." *New Global Studies* 9 (2):101–24.

Drainville, André C. 1994. "International Political Economy in the age of Open Marxism." *Review of International Political Economy* 1 (1):105–32.

Drainville, André C. 1998. "The Fetishism of Global Civil Society: Global Governance, Transnational Urbanism and Sustainable Capitalism in the World Economy." In *Transnationalism from Below*, edited by L. E. Guarnizo M. P. Smith, 35–63. Transaction Publisher.

Drainville, André C. 2001. "On the Relevance of the Avant-Garde." *Telos* 120:49–72.

Drainville, André C. 2003. "Critical Pedagogy for the Present Moment: Learning from the Avant-Garde to Teach Globalization from Experiences." *International Studies Perspectives* 4 (3):231–49.

Drainville, André C. 2004. *Contesting Globalization: Space and Place in the World Economy*. Routledge.

Drainville, André C. 2005. "Beyond Altermondialisme: Anti-Capitalist Dialectic of Presence." *Review of International Political Economy* 12 (5):884–908.

Drainville, André C. 2013a. *A History of World Order and Resistance: The Making and Unmaking of Global Subjects*. Routledge.

Drainville, André C. 2013b. "Present in the World Economy: Québec's Students in the Springtime." *Globalizations* 10 (6):785–801.

Drainville, André C. 2016. "A Struggle of Civilization against Barbarim: About Universities as Autonomous Zones." *Globalisation, Societies and Education* 14:447–65.

Drainville, André C. 2021. "Gatherings of Academic Crowds as World-Historical Events." In *University on the Border: Crisis of authority and precarity*, edited by Vasu Reddy, Siseko H. Kumalo, and Lis Lange, 41–96. Sun Press.

Draper, Hal. 1977. *Karl Marx's Theory of Revolution. Vol. II: The Politics of Social Classes*. NYU Press.
Dray, Philip. 2002. *At the Hands of Persons Unknown: The Lynching of Black America*. Random House.
Du Bois, W. E. B. 1926. "Negroes in College." *Nation*, 122: 228–32.
Du Bois, W. E. B. 1942. "The Cultural Missions of Atlanta University." *Phylon* (1940–1956) 3 (2):105–15.
Du Bois, W. E. B. 1967. *The Philadelphia Negro*; 1899 reprint edition. Schocken Books.
Du Bois, W. E. B. 1968. *The Autobiography of W.E.B. Du Bois: A Soliloquy on Viewing My Life from the Last Decade of Its First Century*. International Publisher.
Du Bois, W.E. B. 1990 [1944]. "My Evolving Program for Negro Freedom." *Clinical Sociology Review* 8 (1):27–57.
Duarte-Abadía, Bibiana, Rutgerd Boelens, and Emerson Buitrago. 2023. "Neoliberal Commensuration and New Enclosures of the Commons: Mining and Market–Environmentalism Governmentalities." *Territory, Politics, Governance* 11 (7):1480–500.
Duncan, Robert Henry. 2001. "For the Good of the Country: State and Nation Building during Maximilian's Mexican Empire, 1864–1867." (Ph.D., History, University of California,Irvine, UMI Number: 3018696).
Dupuy, Alex. 1996. "Race and Class in the Postcolonial Caribbean: The Views of Walter Rodney." *Latin American Perspectives* 23 (2):107–29.
Early, Bridget and Meghan Stratton.. 2021. "Angela Davis, and the Bureaucracy That Cancelled Her." *The Butler Collegian*, April 21. https://thebutlercollegian.com/2021/04/angela-davis-and-the-bureaucracy-that-cancelled-her/.
Eber, D. H. 1969. *The Computer Center Party*. Tundra Books.
Ecker, R. L. 2009. "*The Tlatelolco Massacre in Mexico*." The Ron.
Editors. 2017. "Chinese Philosophy". In *Encyclopedia Britannica*.
Editors. 2018. Shāfiʿī. In *Encyclopaedia Britannica*. https://www.britannica.com/topic/Shafiiyah: Accessed 6 December 2023.
Edu-Factory Collective. 2009. "All Power to Self-Education." In *Towards a Global Autonomous University*, edited by Edu-Factory Collective, 18–32. Autonomedia
Ehrenreich, Barbara, and John Ehrenreich. 1969. *Long March, Short Spring: The Student Uprising at Home and Abroad*. Monthly Review Book.
Eisaku, Satō, Fukuda Takeo, Sakata Michita, and Noda Takeo. 1970. "Coping with student disorder in Japan." *Minerva* 8:116–35.
El-Hibri, Tayeb. 2021. *The Abbasid Caliphate: A History*. Cambridge University Press.
Eligon, John. 2015a. "At University of Missouri, Black Students See a Campus Riven by Race." *The New York Times*, November 11.
Eligon, John. 2015b. "One Slogan, Many Methods: Black Lives Matter Enters Politics." *The New York Times*, 18 November.
Eligon, John, and Richard Péres-Peña. 2015. "University of Missouri Protests Spur a Day of Change." *The New York Times*, November 9.
Elman, Benjamin A. 1989. "Imperial Politics and Confucian Societies in Late Imperial China: The Hanlin and Donglin Academies." *Modern China* 15 (4):379–418.

Ephrat, Daphna. 1993. "The Sunni 'Ulama' of 11th-Century Baghdad and the Transmission of Knowledge: A Social History." (PhD diss., History and Middle Eastern Studies, Harvard University).

Ephrat, Daphna. 2000. *A Learned Society in a Period of Transition: The Sunni "Uama" of Eleventh Century* State University of New York Press.

Erdem, Esra. 2020. "Free Universities as Academic Commons." *The Handbook of Diverse Economies*, edited by J. K. Gibson-Graham and Kelly Dombroski, 316–22.

Espinoza, Javier. 2016. "Don't like Rhodes? Go to China, says Patten." *The Daily Telegraph*January 14: 1, 8.

Ethnic Studies Graduate Collective, University of California, Berkeley. 2020. "COLA, COVID, and 50/500 Years of Struggle: A Dispatch from the University of California, Berkeley, Wildcat Strike." *Critical Times* 3 (3):559–65.

Evans, Gabe, Nick Mitchell, and Taylor Wondergem. 2020. "Scenes from the Wildcat Strike. A Documentary History." *Critical Ethnic Studies* 6 (2): https://manifold.umn.edu/read/ces0602-wildcat-strike/section/1c1f5d90-5075-44c0-9fdd-d45b6a7ee7e9.

Evans, Stephen. 2002. "Macaulay's Minute Revisited: Colonial Language Policy in Nineteenth-Century India." *Journal of Multilingual and Multicultural Development* 23 (4):260–81.

Everatt, D. 2016. "Standing on the Shoulders of the Giants? Successive Generations of Youth Sacrifice in South Africa." In *FeesMustFall. Student Revolt, Decolonisation and Governance in South Africa*, edited by S. Booysen, 126–47. WITS University Press.

Eyck, F. Gunther. 1955. "The Political Theories and Activities of the German Academic Youth between 1815 and 1819." *The Journal of Modern History* 27 (1):27–38.

Fahy, Claire, and Connor Michael Greene. 2024. "How Parents of College Seniors Are Reacting to Campus Disruptions." *The New York Times*, May 7.

Fandos, Nicholas, Stephanie Saul, and Sharon Otterman. 2024. "Columbia's President Tells Congress That Action Is Needed Against Antisemitism." *The New York Times*, April 17.

Fanon, Frantz. 1952. *Peau noire, masques blancs*. Éditions du Seuil.

Fanon, Frantz. 1961. *Les Damnés de la terre*. François Maspéro.

Felder, Richard M. and Rebecca Brent. 2009. "Active Learning: An Introductions." *ASQ Higher Education Brief* 2 (4):1–5.

Federici, Silvia. 2004. *Caliban and the Witch: Women, the Body, and Primitive Accumulation*. Autonomedia.

Federici, Silvia, and Peter Linebaugh. 2018. *Re-Enchanting the World: Feminism and the Politics of the Commons*. PM Press.

Fichte, Johann Gottlieb. 1847 (1794). *The Vocation of the Scholar*. John Cgapman.

Finan, Victoria. 2013. "A Brief History of Student Protest: From 'No Women at Cambridge' in 1897 to 'Cops off Campus' in 2013." *The Independent*, 11 December. https://www.independent.co.uk/student/news/a-brief-history-of-student-protest-from-no-women-at-cambridge-in-1897-to-cops-off-campus-in-2013-8997569.html.

Fındıklı, Burhan. 2022. "Rethinking Ancient Centers of Higher Learning: Madrasa in a Comparative-Historical Perspective." *British Journal of Educational Studies* 70 (2):129–44.

Finn, Mike. 2022. "Academic Freedom in the Modern British University: A Historical Perspective." In *Handbook on Academic Freedom*, edited by Rille Raaper, Richard Watermeyer, and Mark Olsse, 18–36. Edward Elgar.

Foundation for Individual Rights in Education (FIRE). 2015a. "Email from Erika Christakis: 'Dressing Yourselves,' Email to Silliman College (Yale) Students on Halloween Costumes." https://www.fire.org/research-learn/email-erika-christakis-dressing-yourselves-email-silliman-college-yale-students

Foundation for Individual Rights in Education (FIRE). 2015b. "Email from the Intercultural Affairs Committee." https://www.thefire.org/research-learn/email-intercultural-affairs-committee.

Foundation for Individual Rights in Education (FIRE). 2015c. "Yale University: Protesters at Yale Threaten Free Speech, Demand Apologies and Resignations from Faculty Members Over Halloween Email."https://www.fire.org/cases/yale-university-protesters-yale-threaten-free-speech-demand-apologies-and-resignations

Fishburn, Matthew. 2008. *Burning Books*.. Palgrave Macmillan.

Fiske, Edward B., and Helen F. Ladd. 2004. *Elusive Equity: Education Reform in Post-Apartheid South Africa*. Brookings Institute Press.

Fong, Eric A., and Allen W. Wilhite. 2017. "Authorship and Citation Manipulation in Academic Research." *PLoS One* 12 (12)e0187394.

Forsyth, James. 2013. *The Caucasus: A History*. Cambridge University Press.

Forsythe, Dennis. 1971. "The Black Writers Conference: Days to Remember." In *Let the Niggers Burn: The Sir George Williams University Affair and Its Caribbean Aftermath*, edited by Dennis Forsythe, 57–76. Black Rose Books/Our Generation Press.

Fortin, Jacey. 2021. "Critical Race Theory: A Brief History." *The New York Times*, November 8.

Foucault, Michel. 1997. *Il Faut Défendre la Société: Cours au Collège de France (1975–1976)*. Gallimard, Seuil.

Foucault, Michel. 2012. "*Il faut défendre la société: Cours au Collège de France (1975–1976)*," edited by François Ewald, Alessandro Fontana and Mauro Bertani. Association pour le Centre Michel Foucault. https://monoskop.org/images/9/99/Foucault_Michel_Il_faut_defendre_la_societe.pdf.

Fox, Lorna Scott. 2018. "Impunity Reigns: The Tlatelolco Massacre of 1968: What Happened and What It Means for Mexico." *TLS: Times Literary Supplement* (6026):5–8.

Franklin, V. P. 2015. "The Power to Define: African American Scholars, Activism, and Social Change, 1916–2015." *The Journal of African American History* 100 (1):1–25.

Freelon, Deen, Charlton D. McIlwain, and Meredith D. Clark. 2016. *Beyond the Ashtags: #Ferguson, #Blacklivesmatter and the Online Struggle for Offline Justice*. Center for Media and Social Impact. School of Communication, American University.

Freitag, Michel. 1998. Le naufrage de l'université: Et autres essais d'épistémologie politique. Nota Bene.

Friedersdorf, Conor. 2015. "The New Intolerance of Student Activism." *The Atlantic*, November 9.

Friedman, Jonathan. 2022. "Goodbye Red Scare, Hello Ed Scare." *Inside Higher Ed*. https://www.insidehighered.com/views/2022/02/24/higher-ed-must-act-against-educational-gag-orders-opinion

Friese, Heidrun, and Peter Wagner. 1998. "More Beginnings than Ends. The Other Space of the University." *Social Epistemology* 12 (1):27–31.

Frisby, Cynthia. 2015. "From Readers: MU faculty member shares stories of racism." *Columbia Missourian*, November 8. https://www.columbiamissourian.com/from_readers/from-readers-mu-faculty-member-shares-stories-of-racism/article_69d9487c-8644-11e5-910b-238aa5321294.html.

Fuchs, Ralph F. 1963. "Academic Freedom. Its Basic Philosophy, Function, and History." *Law and Contemporary Problems* 28 (3):431–46.

Fúnez-Flores, Jairo I. 1924. "The Coloniality of Academic Freedom and the Palestine Exception." *Middle East Critique* 33 (3):465–85.

Fuse, Toyomasa. 1969. "Student Radicalism in Japan: A 'Cultural Revolution'?" *Comparative Education Review* 13 (3):325–42.

Gabbatt, Adam, and David Batty. 2010. "Second Day of Student Protests - How the Demonstrations Happened." *The Guardian Online*, 24 November.

Gabbatt, Adam, and Jonathan Haynes. 2010. "Demo 2010 Student Protests - Live Coverage." *The Guardian Online*. https://www.theguardian.com/uk/blog/2010/nov/10/demo-2010-student-protests-live.

Gagnon, Gabriel. 1960. "Démocratiser l'université par l'action étudiante." In *L'idée d'université: Anthologie des débats sur l'enseignement supérieur au Québec de 1770 à 1970*, edited by Claude Corbo, 255–58. Les Presses de l'Université de Montréal.

Gallas, Alexander. 2018. "Precarious Academic Labour in Germany: Termed Contracts and a New Berufsverbot." *Global Labour Journal* 9 (1). https://doi.org/10.15173/glj.v9i1.3391

Gally, Michèle. 1987. "Le chant et la dispute (song and dispute)." *Argumentation* 1 (4):379–95.

Gappa, Judith M., and David W. Leslie. 1993. *The Invisible Faculty: Improving the Status of Part-Timers in Higher Education*. Jossey-Bass.

Garberi, Carlos D., and Rodrigo A. Navarro. 2009 "El Movimiento Estudiantil y la Reforma de 1918." Paper presented at the XII Jornadas Interescuelas/Departamentos de Historia, Departamento de Historia, Facultad de Humanidades y Centro Regional Universitario Bariloche, Universidad Nacional del Comahue, San Carlos de Bariloche.

Gardner, Daniel K. 1984. "Principle and Pedagogy: Chu Hsi and The Four Books." *Harvard Journal of Asiatic Studies* 44 (1):57–81.

Garza, Alicia. 2014. "A Herstory of the #BlackLivesMatter Movement." accessed October 7. https://news.northseattle.edu/sites/news.northseattle.edu/files/blacklivesmatter_Herstory.pdf.

Gasman, Marybeth. 1999. "Scylla and Charybdis: Navigating the Waters of Academic Freedom at Fisk University during Charles S. Johnson's Administration (1946–1956)." *American Educational Research Journal* 36 (4):739–58.

Gasman, Marybeth. 2009. "Historically Black Colleges and Universities in a Time of Economic Crisis." *Academe*95 (6): 26–28.

Gasman, Marybeth. 2010. "Five Lessons for Campus Leaders: Academic Freedom, Shared Governance, and Tenure at an Historically Black University." *Change: The Magazine of Higher Learning* 42 (6):54–57.

Gaudemar, Jean-Paul de. 1980. *Usines et ouvriers: Figures du nouvel ordre productif*. François Maspéro.

Gaudiosi, Monica M. 1987. "Influence of the Islamic Law of Waqf on the Development of the Trust in England: The Case of Merton College." *University of Pennsylvania Law Review*. 136 (4):1231–62.

Gebrial, Dalia. 2018. "Rhodes Must Fall: Oxford and Movements for Change." In *Decolonising the University*, edited by Gurminder K Bhambra, Dalia Gebrial, and Kerem Nişancıoğlu, 19–36. Pluto Press.

George, Nelson. 2020. "Angela Davis Still Believes America Can Change." *The New York Times*, October 19, 2020. https://www.nytimes.com/interactive/2020/10/19/t-magazine/angela-davis.html?searchResultPosition=3.

Gernet, Jacques. 1999. *Le monde chinois* 4. éd., rev. Armand Colin.

Gibert, Julie S. 1994. "Women Students And Student Life At England's Civic universities before the First World War." *History of Education* 23 (4):405–22.

Gilbert, Joan E. 1980. "Institutionalization of Muslim Scholarship and Professionalization of the 'ulamā'in Medieval Damascus." *Studia Islamica* 52:105–34.

Gilcher-Holtey, Ingrid. 1999. "May 1968 in France: The Rise and Fall of a New Social Movement." In 1968: The World Transformed, edited by Carole Fink, Philipp Gasset, Getlef Junker, and Gerard Beaulieu, 253–77. Cambridge University Press.

Gildersleeve, Ryan Evely. 2017. "The Neoliberal Academy of the Anthropocene and the Retaliation of the Lazy Academic." *Critical Methodologies* 17 (3): 286–93.

Gilich, Yulia, and Tony Boardman. 2022. "Wildcat Imaginaries: From Abolition University to University Abolition." *Critical Times* 5 (1):109–20.

Gill, Stephen, 1993. "Epistemology, Ontology and the 'Italian School'." In *Gramsci, Historical Materialism and International Relations*, edited by Stephen Gill, 21–48. Cambridge University Press.

Gilman, D. C. 1867. "Our National Schools of Science", *The North American Review*, 105, no. 217:495–520.

Gimpel, Jean. 1975. *La révolution industrielle du Moyen Âge*. Éditions du Seuil.

Gindberg, Terri. 2017. "They Shoot Tenure, Don't They? How I Crossed the Borders of Acceptable Academic Discourse on Holocaust Film and the Question of Palestine, and Never Came Back." In *We Will Not Be Silenced: The Academic Repression of Israel's Critics*, edited by William I. Robinson and Maryam S. Griffin, 36–52. Pluto Press.

Giroux, Henry. 2010. "Academic Unfreedom in America: Rethinking the University as a Democratic Public Sphere." In *Academic Freedom in the Post-9/11 Era*, edited by Edward J. Carvalho and David B. Downing, 19–41. Pallgrave.

Giroux, Henry A. 2014. *Neoliberalism's War on Higher Education*. Haymarket Books.

Giroux, Henry A. 2015. "Neoliberalism's War on Higher Education." *Límite. Revista Interdisciplinaria de Filosofía y Psicología* 10:5–16.

Girvan, Norman. 1968. "After Rodney—The Politics of Student Protest in Jamaica." *New World Quarterly* 4 (3):50–68.

Glahn, Richard von. 1993. "Community and Welfare: Chu Hsi' Community Granary in Theory and Practice." In *Ordering the World: Approaches to State and Society in Sung Dynasty China*, edited by Robert P Hymes and Conrad Schirokauer, 221–54. University of California Press.
Gleeson, Scott. 2015. "Missouri Football Players to Boycott until President Tim Wolfe Resigns." *USA Today*, November 8.
Gluckman, Max. 1940. "Analysis of a Social Situation in Modern Zululand." *Bantu Studies* 14 (1):1–30.
Gluckman, Max. 1958. "Analysis of a Social Situation in Modern Zululand,." In *The Rhodes-Livingstone Papers*. Manchester University Press.
Godshalk, David Fort. 2006. *Veiled Visions: The 1906 Atlanta Race Riot and the Reshaping of American Race Relations*. University of North Carolina Press.
Goffman, Erving. 1964. "The Neglected Situation." *American Anthropologist* 66 (6): 133–36.
Gonsalves, Ralph. 1979. "The Rodney Affair and Its Aftermath." *Caribbean Quarterly* 25 (3):1–24.
Gooding-Williams, Robert. 2011. *In the Shadow of Du Bois: Afro-Modern Political Thought in America*. Harvard University Press.
Gordon, Lewis. 1996. *Existence in Black: An Anthology of Black Existential Philosophy*. Routledge.
Gordon, Lewis. 2020. *Freedom, Justice, and Decolonization*. Routledge.
Gordon, Lewis R. 2014. "Black Existentialism." In *Critical Theory to Structuralism*, edited by David Ingram, 199–219. Routledge.
Gore, Dayo F. 2001. *Radicalism at the Crossroads: African American Women Activiss in the Cold War*. NYU Press.
Gorochov, Nathalie. 2009. "Les maîtres parisiens et la genèse de l'Université (1200–1231)." *Cahiers de recherches médiévales et humanistes/ Journal of medieval and humanistic studies* 18:53–73.
Gorochov, Nathalie. 2012. *Naissance de l'université: les écoles de Paris d'Innocent III à Thomas d'Aquin (v. 1200–v. 1245)*. Honoré Champion Éditeur.
Goscha, Christopher E, and Agathe Larcher. 2016. "Aux origines du républicanisme vietnamien." *Vingtième siècle. Revue d'histoire* 131(3):17–35.
Gould, Roger V. 1995. *Insurgent Identities: Class, Community, and Protest in Paris from 1848 to the Commune*. University of Chicago Press.
Gouvernement du Québec. 2003. *Commission de l'éducation sur la qualité, l'accessibilité et le financement des universités Québec*. Éditeur du Québec.
Gouvernement du Québec. 2004. *L'importance d'une main-d,oeuvre compétente, spécialisée et disponible pour le développement des entreprises*.Éditeur du Québec.
Govender, Prega. 2016. "There Still Aren't Enough Black Professors, Despite University Transformation Attempts." *Mail and Guardian*, 11 July. https://mg.co.za/article/2016-07-11-there-still-arent-enough-black-professors-despite-university-transformation-attempts/.
Graeber, David. 2015. *The Utopia of Rules: On Technology, Stupidity, and the Secret Joys of Bureaucracy*. Melville House.
Green, Dan S., and Edwin D. Driver. 1976. "WEB DuBois: A Case in the Sociology of Sociological Negation." *Phylon* 37 (4):308–33.

Greenidge, Adaeze, and Levi Gahman. 2019. "Roots, Rhizomes and Resistance: Remembering the Sir George Williams Student Uprising." *Race and Class* 61 (2):27–42.

Grendler, Paul F. 2004. "The Universities of the Renaissance and Reformation." *Renaissance Quarterly* 57 (1):1–42.

Griffin, Ben. 2020. "The Rising Tide: Women at Cambridg since 1869." *The Year: The Annual Review of Girton College Cambridge 2019–2020*, 41–46.

Grosfoguel, Ramón. 2011. "Racismo epistémico, islamofobia epistémica y ciencias sociales coloniales." *Tabula Rasa* 14: 341–55.

Grosfoguel, Ramón. 2013. "The Structure of Knowledge in Westernized Universities: Epistemic Racism/Sexism and the Four Genocides/Epistemicides of the Long 16th Century." *Human Architecture: Journal of the Sociology of Self-Knowledge* 11 (1):73–90.

Grüttner, Michael. "German Universities under the Swastika." In *Universities under Dictatorship*, edited by John Connelly and Michael Grüttner, 75–113. Penn State Press, 2005.

Gu, Jianmin, Xueping Li, and Lihua Wang. 2018. *Higher Education in China*. Springer.

Guha, Ramachandra. 2007. "Crucibles of Modernity." *India International Centre Quarterly* 34 (3/4):2–19.

Guillerme, André. 1989. "Les ingénieurs et la Révolution." *Les Annales de la Recherche Urbaine* 43:71–84.

Günther, Sebastian. 2022. "Knowledge and Learning in Baghdād." In *Baghdād*, edited by Isabel Toral Jens Scheiner, 473–520. Brill.

Gutas, Dimitri. 2012. *Greek Thought, Arabic Culture: The Graeco-Arabic Translation Movement in Baghdad and Early'Abbasaid Society (2nd–4th/5th–10th c.)*. Routledge.

Guzman-Concha, Cesar. 2012. "The Students' Rebellion in Chile: Occupy Protest or Classic Social Movement?" *Social Movement Studies: Journal of Social, Cultural and Political Protest* 11 (3–4):408–15.

Hacking, Ian. 1982. "Biopower and the avalanche of printed numbers." *Humanities in Society* 5 (3–4):279–95.

Haines, Andrew W. 1987. "Critical Legal Studies Movement and Racism: Useful Analytics and Guides for Social Action or an Irrelevant Modern Legal Scepticism and Solipsism, The." *William Mitchell Law Review* 13 (4):685–736.

Hajnal, Peter. 1989. *The Seven Powers Summit: Documents from the Summits of Industrialized Countries*. Kraus International Publications.

Hall, A. Rupert. 1959. "The scholar and the craftsman in the scientific revolution." In *Critical Problems in the History of Science*, edited by Marshall Clagett, 3–23. University of Wisconsin Press.

Hall, Martin. 2015. The Symbolic Statue Dividing a South African University. *BBC News*, March 25.http://www.bbc.com/news/business-31945680,.

Hamburger, Max. 1959. "Aristotle and Confucius: A comparison." *Journal of the History of Ideas* 20(2): 236–49.

Hanes, Allison. 2024. "Universities Walk a Tightrope as Protesters Hunker Down." *The Gazette*, May 24. https://montrealgazette.com/opinion/columnists/allison-hanes-protests-part-of-montreals-lifeblood.

Hargreaves, John D. 1973. "The Idea of a Colonial University." *African Affairs* 72 (286):26–36.

Haring, Clarence Henry. 1963. *The Spanish Empire in America*. Harcourt, Brace and World.

Harman, Chris. 1988. *The Fire Last Time: 1968 and After*. Bookmarks.

Harrison, Liz, Sioux McKenna, and Ruth Searle. 2010. "'I Won't Be Squeezed into Someone Else's Frame': Stories of Supervisor Selection." *Acta Academica: Critical Views on Society, Culture and Politics* (1):175–200.

Hartocollis, Anemona, and Eliza Fawcett. 2023. "The College Board Strips Down Its A.P. Curriculum for African American Studies." *The New York Times*, February 1. https://www.nytimes.com/2023/02/01/us/college-board-advanced-placement-african-american-studies.html.

Harvey, David. 1985. "The Geopolitics of Capitalism." In *Social Relations and Spatial Structures. Critical Human Geography*, edited by D. Gregory and J. Urry, 128–63. Springer.

Harvey, David. 2003. "The 'New' Imperialism: Accumulation by Dispossession." *Socialist Register* 40:63–87.

Harvey, David. 2004. *Paris, Capital of Modernity*. Routledge.

Harvey, David. 2007. *A Brief History of Neoliberalism*. Oxford University Press.

Harvie, David. 2004. "Commons and Communities in the University: Some Notes and Some Examples." *The Commoner* No. 8: 1–10. https://thecommoner.org/wp-content/uploads/2020/06/David-Harvie-Commons-and-Communities-in-the-University.pdf

Harwarth, Irene, Elizabeth DeBra, and Mindi Maline. 1997. *Women's Colleges in the United States: History, Issues, and Challenges*. Diane Publishing.

Hasan, Ahmad. 1966. "AL-Ṣhaf'i's' Role in the Development of Islamic Jurisprudence." *Islamic Studies* 5 (3):239–73.

Hasegawa, Kenji. 2019. *Student Radicalism and the Formation of Postwar Japan*. Palgrave Macmillan.

Haskins, Charles Homer. 1955 (1927). The *Renaissance of the Twelfth Century*. Harvard University Press.

Haskins, Charles Homer. 1965 (1923). *The Rise of Universities*. Cornell University Press.

Hayhoe, Ruth. 1994. "Ideas of Higher Learning, East and West: Conflicting Values in the Development of the Chinese University." *Minerva* 32 (4):361–82.

Hayhoe, Ruth. 2001. "Lessons from the Chinese Academy." In *Knowledge across Cultures: A Contribution to Dialogue Among Civilizations*, edited by Julia Pan and Ruth Hayhoe, 323–47. Comparative Education Research Centre.

Hazan, Eric. 2015. *A History of the Barricade*. Verso Books.

Headley, Selena, and Sandiswa L. Kobe. 2017. "Christian Activism and the Fallists: What about Reconciliation?" *HTS: Theological Studies* 73 (3):1–11.

Heffernan, Anne. 2018. Fees Must Fall: Student Revolt, Decolonisation, and Governance in South Africa/As By Fire: The End of the South African University. *South African Historical Journal* 70(2): 434–39

Heidegger, Martin, Karsten Harries, and Hermann Heidegger. 1985. "The Self-Assertion of the German University: Address, Delivered on the Solemn Assumption of the Rectorate of the University Freiburg the Rectorate 1933/34: Facts and Thoughts." *The Review of Metaphysics* 38 (3):467–502.

Heirich, Max. 1973. *The Spiral of Conflict: Berkeley, 1964*. Columbia University Press.

Heller, Nathan. 2016. "The Big Uneasy: What's Roiling the Liberal-Arts Campus?" *The New Yorker* (May 30).

Helm Toby, Mark Townsend, and Anushka Asthana. 2010. "Student Protests Set Stage for Winter Wave of Unrest." *The Guardian*, November 14.

Hendricks, Cheryl. 2018. "Decolonising Universities in South Africa: Rigged Spaces?" *International Journal of African Renaissance Studies - Multi-, Inter- and Transdisciplinarity* 13 (1):16–38.

Herron, Arika. 2021. "Angela Davis Event at Bulter Postponed or Canceled? Students Allege Censorship Flap." *The Indianapolis Star* March 31 https://www.indystar.com/story/news/education/2021/03/31/angela-davis-event-butler-university-students-allege-censorship/4818627001/.

Herwitz, Daniel. 2022. "Negotiating Offence of Fallist Proportion: Cecil Rhodes and the Removal of University of Cape Town's Statue." *Third Text* 36 (6):631–50.

Hill, Christopher. 1972. *The World Turned Upside Down*. Viking.

Hill, Goeff. 2015. "Rhodes to Understanding." *The Zimbabwean*. April 20. https://www.thezimbabwean.co/2015/04/rhodes-to-understanding/

Hillenbrand, Carole. 2022. "The Al-Mustanṣiriyya Madrasa in Baghdad and Its Founder, Al-Mustanṣir." In *The Historian of Islam at Work: Essays in Honor of Hugh N. Kennedy*, edited by Letizia Osti and Maaike van Berkel, 320–39. Brill.

Ho, Ping-ti. 1976. *The Ladder of Success in Imperial China: Aspects of Social Mobility, 1368–1911*. Da Capo Press.

Hobsbawm, E. J. 1952. "The Machine Breakers." *Past and Present* 1(1):57–70.

Hodes, R. 2017. "Briefing Questioning 'Fees Must Fall'." *African Affairs* 116 (462):140–50.

Hofstadter, Richard. 1964. *Anti-Intellectualism in American Life*. Knopf.

Hofstadter, Richard, and Walter P. Metzger. 1955. *The Development of Academic freedom in the United States*. Columbia University Press.

Holmes, Carolyn E., and Melanie Loehwing. 2016. "Icons of the Old Regime: Challenging South African Public Memory Strategies in# RhodesMustFall." *Journal of Southern African Studies* 42 (6):1207–23.

Hongbo, Deng. 2009. "A General History of the Research on Chinese Academies (1923–2007)." *Frontiers of Education in China* 4 (1):133–58.

Hope, Dorian. 2014. "UfSO Timeline 2010–2013." *University for Strategic Optimism*. https://universityforstrategicoptimism.wordpress.com/ufso-timeline-2010-2013/.

Horn, Gerd-Rainer. 2007. *The Spirit of '68: Rebellion in Western Europe and North America, 1956–1976*. Oxford University Press.

Horn, Michiel. 1998. *Academic Freedom in Canada: A History*. University of Toronto Press.

Horton, Dave, Paul Rosen, and Peter Cox. 2016. "Men, Women and the Bicycle: Gender and Social Geography of Cycling in the Late-Nineteenth Century." In *Cycling and Society*, edited by Dave Horton, Paul Rosen, and Peter Cox, 153–77. Routledge.

Howard, M. C., and J. E. King. 2004. "The Economic Contributions of Paul Sweezy." *Review of Political Economy* 16 (4):411–56.

Howe, John. 1988. "The Nobility's Reform of the Medieval Church." *The American Historical Review* 93 (2):317–39.

Howe, Miles, and Jeffrey Monaghan. 2018. "Strategic Incapacitation of Indigenous Dissent: Crowd Theories, Risk Management, and Settler Colonial Policing." *The Canadian Journal of Sociology* 43 (4):325–48.

Hsi, Chu. 1991. *Further Reflections on Things at Hand: A Reader*. Translated by Allen Wittenborn. University Press of America.

Hu, Yongguang. 2011. "Cultivating Merit: The Three Hall System in Late Northern Song, 1070–1121." Ph.D., History, State University of New York at Binghamton (3472866).

Huang, Shuguang. 2020. "Confucian Culture and the Institutional Reform of Chinese Schools." In *Encyclopedia of Educational Philosophy and Theory*, edited by M. A. Peters. Springer.https://doi.org/10.1007/978-981-287-532-7_714-1

Huguelet, Austin, and Daniel Victor. 2015. "'I Need Some Muscle': Missouri Activists Block Journalists." *The New York Times*, November 9. nytimes.com/2015/11/10/us/university-missouri-protesters-block-journalists-press-freedom.html.

Huizinga, Johan. 1956. *The Waning of the Middle Ages*. Doubleday Anchor books.

Hund, Wulf D., and Alana Lentin. 2014. "Editorial." In *Racism and Sociology*, edited by Wulf D. Hund and Alana Lentin, 7–22. LIT Verlag.

Hussain, Amjad. 2013. *A Social History of Education in the Muslim World: From the Prophetic Era to Ottoman Times*. Ta-Ha Publishers.

Hutchens, Neal, and Vanessa Mille. 2023. "Florida's Stop WOKE Act: A Wake-Up Call For Academic Freedom." *Journal of College and University Law* 48 (1):35–69.

Hyde, Suzanne. 2023. "The England August 2011 Riots: An Exploration of Emergent Narratives and Counter-narratives." Ph.D. Philosophy, University of Brighton.

Ibn-baṭṭūṭa, Muḥammad Ibn.2016. The Travels of Ibn Battūta A.D. 1325–1354, translated by, Hamilton A. R. Gibb, and C. F. Beckingham. Routledge.

Ibrahim, Joseph. 2014. "The Moral Economy of the UK Student Protest Movement 2010–2011." *Contemporary Social Science* 9 (1):79–91.

İhsanoğlu, Ekmeleddin. 2023. *The Abbasid House of Wisdom: Between Myth and Reality*. Taylor & Francis.

Informal University. n.d.-a. "About Us." https://www.jackie-inhalt.net/aboutus.html.

Informal University. n.d.-b. "Praxis." https://www.jackie-inhalt.net/praxis.html.

Ingenieros, José. 1920. *La Universidad del Porvenir*. Ciirculo Médico Argentino/Centro Estudiantes de Medecina.

Internationale Situationniste (IS). 1962. "Géopolitique de l'hibernation." *Internationale Situationniste* No. 7: 3–10.

Internationale Situationniste (IS). 1966a. "Addresse aux révolutionnaires d'Algérie et de tous les pays." *International Situationniste* No, 10:43–49.

Internationale Situationniste (IS). 1966b. "La lutte de classes en Algérie." *International Situationniste* No. 10: 12–21.

Internationale Situationniste (IS). 1967. "Deux guerres localea." *Internationale Situationniste* No. 11:13–22.

Islahi, Abdul Azim. 2018. "The Role of Women in the Creation and Management of Awqāf: A Historical Perspective." *Intellectual Discourse* 26 (2): 1025–46.

Jaschik, Scott. "Why Isn't Angela Davis Appearing at Butler University?" *Inside Higher Ed*, April 1, 2021.
James, Edmund Janes. 1905. "The Function of the State University." *Science* 22 (568):609–28.
Jarausch, Konrad H. 2012. "The Sources of German Student Unrest 1815–1848 [1974]." *Historical Social Research/Historische Sozialforschung. Supplement* 24:80–114.
Jardine, Lisa. 2000. *Ingenious pursuits: Building the scientific revolution*. Anchor.
Jennings, Jeremy. 1999. "Introduction." In *Sorel: Reflections on Violence*, edited by Jeremy Jennings, vii–xxii. Cambridge University Press.
Jessop, Bob, and Henk Overbeek. 2019. *Transnational Capital and Class Fractions*. Routledge.
Johnson, K. C. 2017. "Safe Spaces and Defending the Academic Status Quo." *Academic Questions*, 30 (1): 39–46.
Jolivet, Jean. 1977. "Abélard entre chien et loup." *Cahiers de civilisation médiévale* 20 (80):307–22.
Jones, David R. 1985. "Governing the Civic University." *History of Education Quarterly* 25 (3):281–302.
Jones, H. S. 2018. "The English Civic Universities: Endowments and the Commemoration of Benefactors." In *Dethroning Historical Reputations: Universities, Museums and the Commemoration of Benefactors*, edited by JillPellewand Lawrence Goldman, 25–34.. University of London.
Jones, P. J. 1997. *The Italian City-State: From Commune to Signoria*. Clarendon.
Jones, Sabrina, and Matthew Lapierre. 2024. McGill Dismantles Pro-Palestinian Encampment, Ending Months-Long Protest on Campus. *CBC News*.
Jorgensen, Joseph G., and Eric R. Wolf. 1970. "Anthropology on the Warpath in Thailand." *The New York Review of Books* 15 (19):26–35.
Kaplan, Alice. 2012. *Dreaming in French: The Paris Years of Jacqueline Bouvier Kennedy, Susan Sontag, and Angela Davis*. The University of Chicago Press.
Karady, Victor. 1998. "La république des lettres des temps modernes." *Actes de la recherche en sciences sociales* 121 (1):92–103.
Kealey, Gregory S., Lara Campbell, and Dominique Clément. 2012. *Debating Dissent: Canada and the Sixties*. University of Toronto Press.
Kelley, D. G. 2024. "UCLA's Unholy Alliance." *Boston Review*, May 18.
Kelley, Robin D. G. 2022. *Freedom Dreams: The Black Radical Imagination*. Beacon Press.
Kellough, Kaie. 2022. "Fire in the Mainframe: The Sir George Williams Computer Center Occupation of 1969 as Narrative." *TOPIA: Canadian Journal of Cultural Studies* 44 (1):25–32.
Kenny, Deborah Anne. 2006. "Anatomies of the Subject: Spinoza and Deleuze." Ph.D., Queen Mary, University of London.
Khan, Shehad. 2015. "Universities 'Are Killing Free Speech', Says Group of Leading Academics." *The Independent* (19 December).
Kibre, Pearl. 1948. *The Nations in the Mediaeval Universities*: Mediaeval Academy of America.
Kibre, Pearl. 1954. "Scholarly Privileges: Their Roman Origins and Medieval Expression." *The American Historical Review* 59 (3):543–67.
Kibre, Pearl. 1962. *Scholarly Privileges in the Middle Ages*. Mediaval Academy of America.

Kim, Ki-Seok, and Sung Sik Kim. 2013. "A Historical Comparison of Intellectual Renaissance in the East and the West." *Comparative Education* 49 (1):16–27.

Kimball, Alan. 1973. "The First International and the Russian Obshchina." *Slavic Review* 32 (3):491–514.

Kitamura, Yuto. 2019. "Background and Context of Education System in Japan." *Education in Japan: A Comprehensive Analysis of Education Reforms and Practices*, edited by Yuto Kitamura, Toshiyuki Omomo, and Masaaki Katsuno, 1–21.

Kiven Tunteng, P. 1973. "Racism and the Montreal Computer Incident of 1969." *Race* 14 (3):229–40.

Kiyota, Minoru. 1971. "Recent Japanese Student Movement (1968–69): Its Impact on Educational Reform." Twentieth Annual Midwest Conference on Asian Affairs, Madison, Wisconsin, October 29–31.

Klein, Arthur J. 1930. "Colleges, Universities, and Graduate Schools." *Educational Publications* 1:50.

Klein, Naomi. 2001. "Reclaiming the Commons." *New Left Review* 9:81–89.

Knight, Stephen, Michael Goold, and Emily Elliott. 2013. "New Threat to the Right to Protest: Stephen Knight on the New Arrest Tactic to Include Legal Observers and Michael Goold and Emily Elliott on an Important Victory in the High Court against the Met Police and Its Kettling Actions." *Socialist Lawyer* (No. 65):14–17.

Knudsen, Britta Timm, and Casper Andersen. 2019. "Affective Politics and Colonial Heritage, Rhodes Must Fall at UCT and Oxford." *International Journal of Heritage Studies* 25 (3):239–58.

Koehler, Benedikt. 2014. *Early Islam and the Birth of Capitalism*. Lexington Books.

Krauss, Ellis S. 1974. *Japanese Radicals Revisited; Student Protest in Postwar Japan*. University of California Press.

Kristof, Nicholas. 2015. "Mizzou, Yale and Free Speech." *The New York Times*, November 11. https://www.nytimes.com/2015/11/12/opinion/mizzou-yale-and-free-speech.html.

Kuhn, Dieter. 2011. *The Age of Confucian Rule: The Song Transformation of China* Harvard University Press.

Kujeke, Muneinazvo. 2017. "Violence and the #FeesMustFall Movement at the University of KwaZulu-Natal." In *# Hashtag: An Analysis of the# FeesMustFall Movement at South African Universities*, edited by Malose Langa, 83–96. Centre for the Study of Violence and Reconciliation.

Kuran, Timur. 2001. "The Provision of Public Goods under Islamic Law: Origins, Impact, and Limitations of the Waqf System." *Law and Society Review* 35(4):841–98.

Kuran, Timur. 2005. "The Absence of the Corporation in Islamic Law: Origins and Persistence." *The American Journal of Comparative Law* 53 (4):785–834.

Kurlansky, Mark. 2005. *1968: The Year that Rocked the World*. Random House.

Kurtz, Stanley. 2015. "Sorry, Still No American Exceptionalism in APUSH." *National Review Online*, https://www.nationalreview.com/corner/sorry-still-no-american-exceptionalism-apush-stanley-kurtz/.

Kurtz, Stanley. 2014. "A Hard Left for High-School History: The College Board Version of Our National Story." *National Review* 66 (20). https://www.nationalreview.com/magazine/2014/11/03/hard-left-high-school-history/

Kurtz, Stanley. 2023. "College Board Capitulates on African-American Studies … Maybe." *National Review*, 25 January.

La direction. 1969. "Le glissement vers l'anarchie." *La Presse*, February 14, 4.

Laclau, Ernesto, and Chantal Mouffe. 1985. *Hegemony and Socialist Strategy: Towards a Radical Democratic Politics*. 2nd edition. Verso.

Ladner, Joyce A. 1998. *The Death of White Sociology: Essays on Race and Culture*. Black Classic Press.

Laïdi, Zaki. 1998. "Les imaginaires de la mondialisation." *Esprit* (246):85–98.

Laïdi, Zaki. 2000. *La mondialisation comme phénoménologie du monde*. Centre de recherche et d´action sociales.

Lamarre, Thomas. 2012. "Outlaw Universities." *Theory & Event* 15 (3 (Supplement)).

Langen, Roger. 2008. "The Butterfly in the Classroom: Academic Freedom and the Labour Movement." *Briarpatch* 37 (7):32–37.

Langer, Elinor. 1974. "Angela Davis." *New York Times Book Review*, 27 October, Section 7, 5.

Lanham, Andrew. 2017. "When W. E. B. Du Bois Was Un-America." *Boston Review*, January 13.

Lapenson, Bruce P. 2013. "Race and Existential Commitment in James Baldwin." *Philosophy and Literature* 37 (1):199–209.

Lapidus, Ira M. 1975. "The Separation of State and Religion in the Development of Early Islamic Society." *International Journal of Middle East Studies* 6 (4):363–85.

Larkins, Emma L. 2019. "'The Struggle Continues': An Analysis of the Concerned Student 1950 Demands at the University of Missouri." Masters of Arts, Women, Gender, and Sexuality Studies, Oregon State University.

Larrabure, Manuel, and Carlos Torchia. 2015. "The 2011 Chilean Student Movement and the Struggle for a New Left." *Latin American Perspectives* 42 (5):248–68.

Latimer, Charlotte, Christopher Collier, Jaideep Shah, Katherine Burrows, Matthew Woodcraft, and Saoirse Fitzpatrick. 2011. "Creative Subversions: A Politics beyond Representation in the UK." *Qui Parle: Critical Humanities and Social Sciences* 20 (1):271–78.

Laulan, Robert. 1957. "Pourquoi et comment on entrait à l'École royale militaire de Paris." *Revue d'Histoire Moderne et Contemporaine* 4 (2):141–50.

Lawrie, Alexandra. 2014. "The University Extension Movement." In *The Beginnings of University English*, edited by Alexandra Lawrie, 56–85. Springer.

Le Goff, Jacques. 1986. *La Bourse et la vie: Economie et religion au Moyen Age*. Hachette.

Le Goff, Jacques. 1991. *Pour un autre moyen âge*. Gallimard.

Le Goff, Jacques. 2009. *The Birth of Europe*. John Wiley & Sons.

Le Goff, Jacques. 2013. *Les intellectuels au moyen âge*. Seuil

Le Strange, G. 2018 (1900). *Baghdad during the Abbasid Caliphate: From Contemporary Arabic and Persian Sources*. Taylor and Francis.

Lee, Sukhee. 2013. "Cooperation and Tension: Revisiting Local Activism in the Southern Song Dynasty." *Harvard Journal of Asiatic Studies* 73 (1):43–82.

Lee, Thomas Hong-Chi. 1985. *Government Education and Examinations in Sung China*. The Chinese University Press/St.Martin's Press.

Leerssen, Joep. 2011. "Viral Nationalism: Romantic Intellectuals on the Move in Nineteenth-Century Europe." *Nations and Nationalism* 17 (2):257–71.

Lefebvre, Henri. 1981. *La production de l'espace*. 2nd ed. Éditions Anthropos.

Legrandjacques, Sara. 2019. *Former des élites pour l'Asie coloniale. Empires coloniaux, éducation et mobilités étudiantes (Inde-Indochine, fin XIXe siècle–1940)*. Cluj University Press.

Leitner, Helga, and Byron Miller. 2007. "Scale and the Limitations of Ontological Debate: A Commentary on Marston, Jones and Woodward." *Transactions of the Institute of British Geographers* 32 (1):116–25.

Lempérière-Roussin, Annick. 1989. "Le mouvement de 1968 au Mexique." *Vingtieme siecle. Revue d'histoire* 23:71–82.

Lennard, Natasha. 2024. "I've Covered Violent Crackdowns on Protests for 15 Years. This Police Overreaction Was Unhinged." *The Intercept*, May 1. https://theintercept.com/2024/05/01/nyc-gaza-college-protests-police-outside-agitators/.

Levine, Emily J. 2021. *Allies and Rivals: German-American Exchange and the Rise of the Modern Research University*. University of Chicago Press.

Levy, Reuben. 1928. "The Nizamiya Madrasa at Baghdad." *Journal of the Royal Asiatic Society of Great Britain and Ireland* 2:265–70.

Lewis, A. F., and Kelcea Barnes. 2022. "Racism Lives Here: Queering the Neoliberal University Campus through Choreopolitical Antiracist Activism." In *Politics as Public Art: The Aesthetics of Political Organizing and Social Movements*, edited by M. Zebracki and Z. Z. McNeill, 96–115. Taylor & Francis.

Lewis, David Levering. 1994. *W. E. B Du Bois: Biography of a Race, 1868–1919*. 1st Owl Book edition. Henry Holt.

Lewis, Paul, and Vikram Dodd. 2010. "Met Admits Policing of Student Protest Was 'An Embarrassment." *The Guardian Online*, 10 November.

Lewis, Paul, Matthew Taylor, Adam Gabbatt, and Rachel Williams. 2010. "Police Caught out by Peaceful Student Protest that Turned Violent." *The Guardian*, November 10.

Lewontin, R. C. 1997. "The Cold War and the Transformation of the Academy." In *The Cold War and the University: Toward an Intellectural History of the Postwar Years*, edited by Noam Chomsky, Richard C. Lewontin, David Montgomery, et al, 1–34. The New Press.

Li, Jun. 2018. "Chinese Model of Higher Education." In *Encyclopedia of Educational Philosophy and Theory*, edited by Michael A. Peters, 1–7. Springer.

Liard, Louis. 1890. *Universités et facultés*. Armand Colin.

Lindholm, Charles. 1999. "Justice and Tyranny, Law and the State in the Middle East." *Journal of the Royal Asiatic Society* 9 (3):375–88.

Lindsay, Dsvid. 2013. "W.E.B. Du Bois's Legacy Deferred." *Atlanta Magazine*.

Linebaugh, Peter. 2014. *Stop, Thief!: The Commons, Enclosures, and Resistance*. PM Press.

Lipset, Seymour and Sheldon S. Wolin, eds. 1965. *The Berkeley Student Revolt: Facts and Intepretations*. Anchor Books.

Lipietz, Alain. 1987. *Mirages and Miracles: The Crises of Global Fordism*, translated by David Macey. Verso.

Liu, James T. C. 1973. "How Did a Neo-Confucian School Become the State Orthodoxy?" *Philosophy East and West* 23 (4):483–505.

Liu, William Guanglin. 2015. *The Chinese Market Economy, 1000–1500*. SUNY Press.

Lott, Tommy L. 2000. *The Idea of Race*.Hackett

Lowenthal, Leo, and Carol Hamilton. 1987. "Caliban's Legacy." *Cultural Critique* 8:5–17.

Lu, Alicia. 2015. "What Is Concerned Student 1950?" *Bustle*, November 9. https://www.bustle.com/articles/122575-what-is-concerned-student-1950-the-university-of-missouri-peaceful-protests-were-led-by-a-standout.

Lumumba, Carl. 1971. "The West Indies and the Sir George Williams Affair: An Assessment." In *Let the Niggers burn: The Sir George Williams University affair and its Caribbean aftermath*, edited by Dennis Forsythe, 144–92. Black Rose Books/Our Generation Press.

Lutz, Rolland Ray. 1976. "'Father' Jahn and his Teacher-Revolutionaries from the German Student Movement." *The Journal of Modern History* 48 (2):1–34.

Lynch, Marc. 2013. *The Arab Uprising: The Unfinished Revolutions of the New Middle East*. Public Affairs.

Lyons, Jonathan. 2010. *The House of Wisdom: How the Arabs Transformed Western Civilization*. Bloomsbury Publishing USA.

Mabasa, Khwezi. 2017. "The Rebellion of the Born Unfrees: Fallism and the Neo-Colonial Corporate University." *The Strategic Review for Southern Africa* 39 (2): 94–116.

Mabokela, Reitumetse Obakeng. 1997. "The Evolution of Admissions and Retention Policies at an Historically White South African University." *Journal of Negro Education* 66 (4):423–33.

Macfarlane, Bruce. 2005. "The Disengaged Academic: The Retreat from Citizenship." *Higher Education Quarterly* 59 (4):296–312.

Maclean, Ruth. 2015. "South African War on Colonial Past Escalates." *The Times Africa*, April 13.

Maddison, Ben. 2010. "Radical Commons Discourse and the Challenges of Colonialism." *Radical History Review* 2010(108):29–48.

Maitron, Jean, Michelle Perrot, and Madeleine Rebérioux, eds. 1968. *La Sorbonne par elle-même: mai-juin, 1968*. Editions Ouvrières.

Mak, K. T., and A. Ramaprasad. 2003. "Knowledge Supply Network." *The Journal of the Operational Research Society* 54 (2):175–83.

Makdisi, George. 1961. "Muslim Institutions of Learning in Eleventh-Century Baghdad." *Bulletin of the School of Oriental and African Studies* 24 (1):1–56.

Makdisi, George. 1970. "Madrasa and University in the Middle Ages." *Studia Islamica* 32:255–64.

Makdisi, George. 1981. *The Rise of Colleges: Institutions of Learning in Islam and the West*. Edinburgh University Press.

Makdisi, George. 1989. "Scholasticism and Humanism in Classical Islam and the Christian West." *Journal of the American Oriental Society* 109 (2):175–82.

Malinowski, Bronislaw. 1939. "The Present State of Studies in Culture Contact: Some Comments on an American Approach." *Africa* 12 (1):27–48.

Malzacher, Florian, Ahmet Öğüt, and Pelin Tan. 2016. *The Silent University: Towards a Transversal Pedagogy*. Sternberg Press.

Man, A. Varsity. 1897. "Why We Declined to Give Women Degrees." *The Sketch*, June 2, 206.

Mannoni, O. 1950. *Psychologie de la colonisation*. Édition du Seuil.

Marenbon, Joihn. 1997. *The Philosophy of Pierre Abelard*. Cambridge University Press.
Marga, Andrei. 2006. "The Cultural Legitimacy of the European University." *Higher Education in Europe* 31 (4):425–438.
Marginson, Simon. 2011. "Higher Education in East Asia and Singapore: Rise of the Confucian Model." *Higher Education* 61 (5):587–611.
Maringira, Godfrey, and Simbarashe Gukurume. 2017. "'Being Black' in #FeesMustFall and #FreeDecolonisedEducation: Student Protests at the University of the Western Cape." In *# Hashtag: An analysis of the# FeesMustFall Movement at South African Universities*, edited by Malose Langa, 33–48. Centre for the Study of Violence and Reconciliation.
Marotti, William. 2009. "Japan 1968: The Performance of Violence and the Theater of Protest." *The American Historical Review* 114 (1):97–135.
Marotti, William. 2015. "The Art of the Everyday as Crisis: Objets, Installations, Weapons, and the Origin of Politics." *Boundary* 2 42 (3):79–96.
Marsha, L. Richmond. 1997. "'A Lab of One's Own': The Balfour Biological Laboratory for Women at Cambridge University, 1884–1914." *Isis* 88 (3):422–55.
Marshall, Byron K. 1977a. "Professors and Politics: The Meiji Academic Elite." *Journal of Japanese Studies* 3 (1):71–97.
Marshall, Byron K. 1977b. "The Tradition of Conflict in the Governance of Japan's Imperial Universities." *History of Education Quarterly* 17 (4):385–406.
Marshall, Byron K. 2023. *Academic Freedom and the Japanese Imperial University, 1868–1939*. Universityof California Press.
Marsiske, Renate. 2018. "'La juventud desinteresada y pura': el movimiento estudiantil en la Universidad de Córdoba, Argentina, 1918." *Perfiles educativos* 40 (161):196–215.
Marston, Sallie A., John Paul Jones III, and Keith Woodward. 2005. "Human Geography without Scale." *Transactions of the Institute of British Geographers* 30 (4):416–32.
Martin, Lori Latrice, Biko Mandela Gray, and Stephen C. Finley. 2019. "Endangered and Vulnerable: The Black Professoriate, Bullying, and the Limits of Academic Freedom." *Journal of Academic Freedom* 10:1–21.
Martin, William Alexander Parsons. 1880. *Hanlin Papers: Essays on the Intellectual Life of the Chinese*. Kelly and Walsh.
Mason, Paul. 2013. *Why It's Still Kicking Off Everywhere: The New Global Revolutions*. Verso Books.
May, Timothy. 2013. *The Mongol Conquests in World History*. Reaktion Books.
May 4 Task Force Students. 2010. "Chronology." *May 4 Task Force*. https://web.archive.org/web/20160120124016/http://www.m4tf.org/chronology.html.
Maylam, Paul. 2005. *The Cult of Rhodes: Remembering an Imperialist in Africa*. David Philip Publisher.
Mazón, Patricia M. 2000. "'Fräulein Doktor': Literary Images of the First Female University Students in Fin-de-Siècle Germany." *Women in German Yearbook: Feminist Studies in German Literature and Culture* 16 (1):129–50.
Mazón, Patricia M. 2003. *Gender and the Modern Research University: The Admission of Women to German Higher Education*, 1865–1914. Stanford University Press.

Mbembe, Joseph Achille. 2016. "Decolonizing the University: New Directions." *Arts and Humanities in Higher Education* 15 (1):29–45.

McCabe, Donald L., Linda Klebe Trevino, and Kenneth D. Butterfield. 2001. "Dishonesty in Academic Environments: The Influence of Peer Reporting Requirements." *The Journal of Higher Education* 72 (1):29–45.

McClintock, Anne 1995. *Imperial Leather: Race, Gender and Sexuality in the Colonial Contest*. Routledge.

McCoy, Meredith, Roopika Risam, and Jennifer Guiliano. 2021. "The Future of Land-Grab Universities." *Native American and Indigenous Studies* 8 (1):169–75.

McMichael, Philip. 2000. *Development and Social Change: A Global Perspective*. Pine Forge Press.

McNair, Grace Elizabeth. 1898. *The Relations of the Students and Citizens at Paris, 1200–1350*. University of Wisconsin–Madison.

McNaughtan, Jon, Hugo A. García, and Kim Nehls. 2017. "Understanding the Growth of Contingent Faculty." *New Directions for Institutional Research* 2017 (176):9–26.

McShane, Michael, and Michael Highsmith. 2016. *Moving Mizzou Forward: Reform Ideas from around the Nation*. Show-Me institute.

McWilliams-Tullberg, Rita. 2014. "Women and Degrees at Cambridge University, 1862–1897." In *A Widening Sphere: Changing Roles of Victorian Women*, edited by Martha Vicinus, 117–45. Routledge.

Mearsheimer, John. 2015. "Israel and Academic Freedom." In *Who's Afraid of Academic Freedome*, edited by AkeeliBilgrami and Jonathan R. Cole, 316–33. Columbia University Press.

Menand, Louis, Paul Reitter, and Chad Wellmon. 2017. "Introduction to Humboldt's Texts." In *The Rise of the Research University: A Sourcebook*, edited by Louis Menand, Paul Reitter and Chad Wellmon, 105–8. University of Chicago Press.

Merwe, J. C. van der, and Dionne van Reenen. 2016. *Transformation and Legitimation in Post-Apartheid Universities: Reading Discourses from "Reitz"*. The Institute for Reconciliation and Social Justice/Sun Press.

Meth, Oliver. 2017. "#FeesMustFall at Rhodes University: Exploring the Dynamics of Student Protests and Manifestations of Violence." In *# Hashtag: An Analysis of the# FeesMustFall Movement at South African Universities*, edited by Malose Langa, 83–97. Centre for the Study of Violence and Reconciliation.

Mhamdi, Ridha. 2024. "Beyond the Blockade: Exploring Research Outputs in the Gaza Strip." https://www.10.21203/rs.3.rs-4417530/v1

Mies, Maria. 1986. *Patriarchy and Accumulation of a World Scale: Women in the International Division of Labour*.Zed.

Milanesio, Natalia. 2005. "Gender and Generation: The University Reform Movement in Argentina, 1918." *Journal of Social History* 39 (2):505–29.

Millán, Mariano. 2007. *El movimiento estudiantil argentino: Historias con presente*, edited by Mariano Millán, Pablo Augusto Bonavena, and Juan Sebastián Califa. Ediciones Cooperativas.

Miller, Michael E. 2015. "Black Grad Student on Hunger Strike in Mo. after Swastika Drawn with Human Feces." *The New York Times*, November 6. https://www.washingtonpost.com/news/morning-mix/wp/2015/11/06/black-grad-student-on-hunger-strike-in-mo-after-swastika-drawn-with-human-feces/.

Miller, Vanessa, Frank Fernandez, and Neal H. Hutchins. 2023. "The Race to Ban Race: Legal and Critical Arguments against State Legislation to Ban Critical Race Theory in Higher Education." *Missouri Law Review* 88 (1):61–106.

Mills, C. Wright. 1960. "Letter to the New Left." *New Left Review* 1 (5):18–23.

Mills, C. Wright. 1969. *Sociology and Pragmatism: The Higher Learning in America*. Oxford University Press.

Mills, Sean. 2010. *The Empire Within: Postcolonial Thought and Political Activism in Sixties Montreal*.McGill-Queen's Press-MQUP.

Ming-kin, Chu. 2020. *The Politics of Higher Education: The Imperial University in Northern Song*. Hong Kong University Press.

Minot, Jacques. 1991. *Que sais-je? Histoire des universités françaises*.Presses Universitaires de France.

Mironov, Boris. 1985. "The Russian Peasant Commune after the Reforms of the 1860s." *Slavic Review* 44 (3):438–67.

Mohamed, Ahmed Fathi Korani, and F Korani. 2015. "Between Dictators and Scholars: Institutions and Methods of Teaching in Medieval Islam." *Journal of Islamic Studies and Culture* 3 (1):34–41.

Monchablon, Alain. 1988. "Syndicalisme étudiant et génération algérienne." *Bulletins de l'Institut d'Histoire du Temps Présent* 10 (1):119–29.

Moran, Caitlin. 2008. "Cellphones, Handy Tools for Emergency Alerts, Could Be Used for Cheating during Tests." *Chronicle of Higher Education* 55 (7). https://www.chronicle.com/article/cellphones-handy-tools-for-emergency-alerts-could-be-used-for-cheating-during-tests/

Morgan, David O. 1986. "The 'Great Yāsā of Chingiz Khān'and Mongol Law n the Īlkhānate." *Bulletin of the School of Oriental and African Studies* 49 (1):163–76.

Morin, Erdard. 1969. *La Rumeur d'Orléans*. Éditions du Seuil.

Morris-Suzuki, Tessa. 2000. "For and Against NGOs." *New Left Review Second ser* (No. 2):63–84.

Mortlock, Monique. 2015. Security Beefed Up at Rhodes Memorial. *EWN Eyewitness News* http://ewn.co.za/2015/09/21/Security-beefed-up-Rhodes-Memorial.

Motani, Nizar A. 1979. "Makerere College 1922–1940: A Study in Colonial Rule and Educational Retardation." *African Affairs* 78 (312):357–69.

Moten, Fred, and Stefano Harney. 1999. "The Academic Speed-Up." *Workplace: A Journal for Academic Labor* No. 4: 23–28.

Mott, Carrie, and Daniel Cockayne. 2017. "Citation Matters: Mobilizing the Politics of Citation toward a Practice of 'Conscientious Engagement'." *Gender, Place and Culture* 24 (7):954–73.

Mougeot, Christelle. 2002. "Les apports de l'économie de l'information et des incitations à l'analyse des corporations artisanales médiévales." Ph.D. diss., Université Nancy.

Mountz, Alison, and Winifred Curran. 2009. "Policing in Drag: Giuliani Goes Global with the Illusion of Control." *Geoforum* 40 (6):1033–40.

Mullen, Bill V. 2007. "Blacklist Redux: WEB Du Bois and the Price of Academic Freedom." *Social Text* 25 (1):85–103.

Mullett, Michael A. 2014. *Martin Luther*. Routledge.

Munby, Julian. 2007. "Oxford: The Medieval University and the Town." In *Les universités et la ville au Moyen Âge*, edited by Jacques Verger, Patrick Gilli, Daniel Le Blévac, 55–62. Brill.

Musa, Aisha Y. 2007. "Al-Shāfiʿī, the Ḥadīth, and the Concept of the Duality of Revelation." *Islamic Studies* 46 (2):163–97.

Muto, Ichiyo. 2009. "Japan, Student Movements." In *The International Encyclopedia of Revolution and Protest*, edited by Immanuel Ness, https://doi.org/10.1002/9781405198073.wbierp0820. Blackwell Reference Online.

Nader, Laura. 1997. "The Phantom Factor: Impact of the Cold War on Anthropology." In *The Cold War and the University*, edited by Noam Chomsky, David Barsamian, and Howard Zinn, 107–46. New Press.

Naicker, Camalita. 2016. "From Marikana to# feesmustfall: The Praxis of Popular Politics in South Africa." *Urbanisation* 1 (1):53–61.

National Research Council. 1995. "History and Overview of the Land Grand College System." In *Colleges of Agriculture at the Land Grant Universities: A Profile, Edited by Committee on the Future of the Colleges of Agriculture in the Land Grant University System*, 1–18. National Academies Press.

Nawas, John A. 1994. "A Reexamination of Three Current Explanations for al-Maʾmun's Introduction of the Miḥna." *International Journal of Middle East Studies* 26 (4):615–29.

Ndelu, Sandile. 2017a. "A Rebellion of the Poor':1 Fallism at the Cape Peninsula University of Technology." In *# Hashtag: An Analysis of the# FeesMustFall Movement at South African Universities*, edited by Malose Langa, 13–32. Centre for the Study of Violence and Reconciliation.

Ndelu, Sandile. 2017b. "'Liberation Is a Falsehood': Fallism at the University of Cape Town." In *# Hashtag: An Analysis of the# FeesMustFall Movement at South African Universitie*s, edited by Malose Langa, 58–82. Centre for the Study of Violence and Reconciliation.

Neggaz, Nassima. 2020. "Al-Karkh: The Development of an Imāmī-Shīʿī Stronghold in Early Abbasid and Būyid Baghdad (132–447/750–1055)." *Studia Islamica* 114 (3):265–315.

Nelson, Susan E. 2000. "Catching Sight of South Mountain: Tao Yuanming, Mount Lu, and the Iconographies of Escape." *Archives of Asian Art* 52:11–43.

Nero, Amanda. 2015. "Missouri Legislative Black Caucus '100 Percent Supportive of Students Seeking Change'." *Columbia Missourian*, November 10. https://www.columbiamissourian.com/news/state_news/missouri-legislative-black-caucus-percent-supportive-of-students-seeking-change/article_400d466e-87e4-11e5-bcb6-67c814229cf3.html.

Newsinger, John. 2016. "Why Rhodes Must Fall." *Race and Class* 58 (2):70–78.

Nishio, Harry K. 1968. "Extraparliamentary Activities and Political Unrest in Japan." *International Journal* 24 (1):122–37.

Noorda, Sijbolt. 2021. "A New Magna Charta Universitatum." *International Higher Education* No. 107:5–6.

Norwood, Stephen H. 2009. *The Third Reich in the Ivory Tower: Complicity and Conflict on American Campuses*. Cambridge

Nourrisson, Paul. 1928. *Histoire légale des congrégations religieuses en France depuis 1789*. Recueil Sirey.

Novikoff, Alex J. 2013. *The Medieval Culture of Disputation*. University of Pennsylvania Press.

Nowotny, Helga. 1991. "Knowledge for Certainty: Poverty, Welfare Institutions and the Institutionalization of Social Science." In *Discourses on Society: The Shaping of the Social Science Disciplines*, edited by Peter Wagne, 23–41. Kluwer Academic Publishers.

Nwauwa, Appollos. 1993. "The British Establishment of Universities in Tropical Africa, 1920–1948: A Reaction against the Spread of American "Radical" Influence." *Cahiers d'Études africaines* 33(130):247–74.

Nyamnjoh, Francis B. 2020. *Decolonizing the Academy: A Case for Convivial Scholarship*. Basler Afrika Bibliographien.

O'Keefe, Theresa. 2012. "Power, Body Politics and Dirty Protest." Presented at the Jailers, Prisons, and Prisoners seminar series, Centro de Investigacao e Estudos de Sociologia, Lisbon.

O'Rourke, Kevin; Findlay Ronald 2007. *Power and Plenty: Trade, War, and the World Economy in the Second Millennium*. Princeton University Press.

Observatory Magna Charta Universitarium. 2022. "History." https://www.magna-charta.org/about-us/hystory.

Organisation for Economic Co-Operation and Development (OECD). 1996. *The Knowledge-Based Economy*. OECD.

Organisation for Economic Co-Operation and Development (OECD). 2013. *Supporting Investment in Knowledge Capital, Growth and Innovation*. OECD.

Omori, S. 1970. "June 1970." *Japan Quarterly* 17 (4):383–92.

Östling, Johan. 2018. *Humboldt and the Modern German University: An Intellectual History*. Lund University Press.

Otterman, Sharon. 2024a. "After Weeks of Protests, Columbia Cancels Main Commencement Ceremony." *The New York Times*, May 6. https://www.nytimes.com/2024/05/07/nyregion/college-protests-parents.html.

Otterman, Sharon. 2024b. "Columbia Faculty Group Passes No-Confidence Resolution Against President." *The New York Times*, May 16. https://www.nytimes.com/2024/05/16/nyregion/president-shafik-columbia-faculty-vote.html?searchResultPosition=1.

Otterman, Sharon. 2024c. "Columbia Sends In the N.Y.P.D. to Arrest Protesters in Tent City." *The New York Times*.

Outlaw Jr. Lucius T. 2005. *Critical Social Theory in the Interests of Black Folks*. Rowman & Littlefield Publishers.

Oxlund, Bjarke. 2016. "# EverythingMustFall: The Use of Social Media and Violent Protests in the Current Wave of Student Riots in South Africa." *Anthropology Now* 8 (2):1–13.

Palcos, Alberto. 1926 (1920). "La Reforma Universitaria y el Problema Educacional." In *La Reforma Universitaria*, edited by Federacion Universitarià de Buenos Aires/Circulo Medico Argentino, 49–59. Imp Ferrari.

Paletschek, Sylvia. 2001. "The Invention of Humboldt and the Impact of National Socialism: The German University Idea in the First Half of the Twentieth Century." In *Science in the Third Reich*, edited by Margit Szollosi-Janze, 37–58. Berg

Panitch, Leo, and Colin Leys. 2001. *The End of Parliamentary Socialism: From New Left to New Labour*. Verso.

Panofsky, Erwin. 1951. *Gothic Architecture and Scholasticism*. New American Library.

Pappoe, Yvette N. A. 2022. "Unpacking the Mystery of Critical Race Theory." *What's Up? Media*. https://whatsupmag.com/culture/unpacking-the-mystery-of-critical-race-theory/#:~:text=Critical%20race%20theory%20(CRT)%20is%20an%20academic%20theoretical%20approach%20to,at%20institutional%20and%20structural%20levels.

Patel, Ahmed, Kaveh Bakhtiyari, and Mona Taghavi. 2011. "Evaluation of Cheating Detection Methods in Academic Writings." *Library Hi Tech* 29 (4):623–40.

Payne, Anthony. 1983. "The Rodney Riots in Jamaica: The Background and Significance of the Events of October 1968." *The Journal of Commonwealth and Comparative Politics* 21 (2):158–74.

Pedersen, J.; Rahman, Munibur; Hillenbrand, R. 2009. "Madrasa." In *Encyclopaedia of Islam*, edited by T. Bianquis P. Bearman, C. E. Bosworth, E. van Donzel and W. P. Heinrichs., 1123–25. Brill Online.

Pehlivan, Necmettin, and Hadi Ensar Ceylan. 2022. "Old Rivalry, Eternal Friendship: The Story of an Opponent-al-Fuṣūl in the ʿilm al-naẓar." *Methodos: Savoirs et textes* https://doi.org/10.4000/methodos.9505.

Peiss, Kathy Lee 2019. *Information Hunters: When Librarians, Soldiers, and Spies Banded Together in World War II Europe*. Oxford University Press.

Penny, Laurie. 2011. "Inside the Millbank Towrd Riot." In *Fight Back: A Reader on the Winter of Protest*, edited by Dan Hancox, 66–70. Open democracy.net.

Péres-Peña, Richard, and Christine Hauser. 2015. "University of Missouri Professor Who Confronted Photographer Quits Journalism Post." *The New York Times*, November 2015. https://www.nytimes.com/2015/11/11/us/university-of-missouri-names-law-professor-to-diversity-post.html?searchResultPosition=1.

Pérez Huber, Lindsay, and Daniel G. Solorzano. 2015. "Racial Microaggressions as a Tool for Critical Race Research." *Race Ethnicity and Education* 18 (3):297–320.

Perkin, Harold. 1984. "The Historical Perspective." In *Perspectives on Higher Education: Eight Disciplinary and Comparative Views*, edited by Burton R. Clark, 17–56. University of California Press.

Peterson, Carlo. 2015. "'Poo Man' Pitches up to Spoil Ceremony." *Cape Times*, April 30, 5, E1.

Phillips, H. 2019. UCT *Under Apartheid: From Onset to Sit-In, 1948–1968*. Fanele.

Phimister, Ian R. 1988. *An Economic and Social History of Zimbabwe, 1890–1948: Capital Accumulation and Class Struggle*. Longman.

Piché, Claude. 2007. "Fichte, Schleiermacher et W. von Humboldt: sur la création de l'Université de Berlin." *Historia Philosophiae: hommage à Alexis Philonenko*:117–41.

Piché, David, Claude Lafleur.1999. *La condamnation parisienne de 1277, Sic et non*. Librairie philosophique J. Vrin.

Pies, R. 2015. "Campus Protests, Narcissism, and the Dearth of Civility." *Psychiatric Times*, 33 (2). https://www.psychiatrictimes.com/view/campus-protests-narcissism-and-dearth-civility

Plaut, Martin. 2010. "South African Student Protest, 1968: Remembering the Mafeje Sit-In." *History Workshop Journal*. 69 (1):199–250

Polastron, Lucien X. 2009. *Livres en feu: Histoire de la destruction sans fin des bibliothèques*. Folio Essais.

Policante, Amedeo. 2012. "Of Cameras and Balaclavas: Violence, Myth, and the Convulsive Kettle." In *Situating Global Resistance*, edited by Lara Montesinos Coleman and Karen Tucker, 63–77. Routledge.

Poulantzas, Nicos. 1978. *L'Etat, le pouvoir, le socialisme*. Presses Universitaires de France.

Poulantzas, Nicos. 1982. *Pouvoir politique et classes sociales*. François Maspero.

Pouly, Marie-Pierre. 2007. "La promotion d'un savoir utile dans l'ordre scolaire français de la Troisième République. Le cas des langues étrangères." *Cahiers de la recherche sur l'éducation et les savoirs* 6:119–34.

Pousadela, Inés M. 2013. "Protest and Proposal, Participation and Representation: the Chilean Student Movement, 2011–12." *Development in Practice* 23 (5–6):685–700.

Praeg, Leonhard. 2024. "Just Thinking." In *The Routledge Handbook for Global South Studies on Subjectivities*, edited by Susanne Goumegou and Georgina Cebey, 352–63. Routledge India.

Press, Steven Michael. 2009. "False Fire: The Wartburg Book-Burning of 1817." *Central European History* 42 (4):621–46.

Punch, Maurice. 2007. *Zero Tolerance Policing*. Policy Press.

Raina, D. 2011. "Institutions and Knowledge: Framing the Translation of Science in Colonial South Asia." *Asiatische Studien - Études Asiatiques* 65 (4): 945–67.

Ransom, Jan. 2015. "Brandeis Students Say Campus Lacks Racial Diversity." *Boston Globe*. November 22. https://www.bostonglobe.com/metro/2015/11/22/brandeis-students-occupy-building-protest-lack-racial-diversity/I1yUrfTbEpFdyW2ilajvJM/story.html

Rashdall, Hastings. 1824. *The Universities of Europe in the Middle Ages*. MacMillan & Co. (Oxford).

Ray Lutz, Rolland. 1971. "The German Revolutionary Student Movement, 1819–1833." *Central European History* 4 (3):215–41.

Readings, Bill. 1996. *The University in Ruins*. Harvard University Press.

Reitter, Paul, and Chad Wellmon. 2016. "Introduction." In *Friedrich Nietzche Anti-Education: On the Future of Our Educational Institutions*, edited by Paul Reitter and Chad Wellmon. New York Review Books.

Remley, William L., and Nicole G. Albert. 2013. "Le Juif et le Colon. Figures Psychologiques Chez Jean-Paul Sartre et Frantz Fanon." *Diogene* 241(1):58–79.

Rhoads, Robert A., and Liliana Mina. 2001. "The Student Strike at the National Autonomous University of Mexico: A Political Analysis." *Comparative Education Review* 45 (3):334–53.

Rhoden, William C. 2015. "University of Missouri Football Players Exercise Power in Racism Protest." *The New York Times*, November 8. https://www.nytimes.com/2015/11/09/sports/ncaafootball/missouri-football-players-exercise-power-in-racism-protest.html.

Riché, Pierre, and Jacques Verger. 2006. *Des nains sur des épaules de géants: Maîtres et élèves au Moyen Âge*. Tallandier.

Rider, Sharon. 2009. "The Future of the European University: Liberal Democracy or Authoritarian Capitalism?" *Culture Unbound* 1 (1):83–104.

Riemer, Nick. 2016. "Academics, the Humanities and the Enclosure of Knowledge: The Worm in the Fruit." *The Australian Universities' Review* 58 (2):33–41.

Ringer, Fritz K. 1990. *The Decline of the German Mandarins: The German Academic Community, 1890–1933*. Wesleyan University Press.

Ritchie, James M. 1988. "The Nazi Book-Burning." *The Modern Language Review* 83 (3):627–43.

Roberts, Neil. 2019. *Freedom as Marronage*. University of Chicago Press.

Roberts, Stephen H. 2019. *The History of French Colonial Policy, 1870–1925*. Routledge.

Robins, Steven. 2014a. "Poo Wars as Matter Out of Place:'Toilets for Africa' in Cape Town" *Anthropology Today* 30 (1):1–3.

Robins, Steven. 2014b. "The 2011 Toilet Wars in South Africa: Justice and Transition between the Exceptional and the Everyday after Apartheid." *Transition and Justice: Negotiating the Terms of New Beginnings in Africa*, edited by Gerhard Anders and Olaf Zenker, 85–111. Wiley

Rodney, Walter. 1969. *The Groundings with My Brothers*. Bogle-L'Ouverture Publications.

Rodney, Walter. 1972. *How Europe Underdeveloped Africa*. Tanzania Publishing House.

Rodríguez-Ruiz, Óscar. 2009. "The Citation Indexes and the Quantification of Knowledge." *Journal of Educational Administration* 47 (2):250–66.

Roman, Meredith L. 2020. "'Armed and Dangerous': The Criminalization of Angela Davis and the Cold War Myth of America's Innocence." *Women, Gender, and Families of Color* 8 (1):87–111.

Rosenblatt, Rand K. 1967. "The Revolution at the LSE." *The Harvard Crimson*, March 23. https://www.thecrimson.com/article/1967/3/23/the-revolution-at-the-lse-plast/.

Rosenthal, Lawrence. 2021. "Does the First Amendment Protect Academic Freedom?" *Journal of College and University Law* 46 (2):223–57.

Rosman, Katherine. 2024. "On Columbia's Campus, a ProtestEncampment Grows and Tensions Flare." *The New York Times*. https://www.nytimes.com/2024/04/22/us/columbia-protests-encampment.html.

Ross, Andrew. 2009. "The Rise of the Global University." In *Towards a Global Autonomous University*, edited by Edu-Factory Collective, 18–32. Autonomedia.

Ross, Hannah. 2020. *Revolutions: How Women Changed the World on Two Wheels*. Penguin.

Ross, Janell. 2015. "How Black Lives Matter Moved from a Hashtag to a Real Political Force." *The Washington Post*. August 19, 2015. https://www.washingtonpost.com/news/the-fix/wp/2015/08/19/how-black-lives-matter-moved-from-a-hashtag-to-a-real-political-force/

Rothblatt, Sheldon, and Björn Wittrock. 1993. "Introduction: Universities and 'Higher Education'." In *The European and American University Since 1800: Historical and Sociological Essays*, edited by Sheldon Rothblatt and Björn Wittrock, 1–15. Cambridge University Press.

Rubinstein, David. 1977. "Cycling in the 1890s." *Victorian Studies* 21 (1):47–71.

Rufo, Christopher F. 2020a. "Cult Programming in Seattle." *City Journal*, July 8.

Rufo, Christopher F. 2020b. "'White Fragility' Comes to Washington." *City Journal*, July 18.

Ruiz, Carlos. 2012. "New Social Conflicts under Bachelet." *Latin American Perspectives* 39 (4):71–84.

Ryke, Benoît Beyer de. 2002. "Le moyen âge et ses dissidents religieux: Cathares et béguines, xie–xive siècles." In *Sectes et hérésies de l'antiquité à nos jours*, edited

by Anne Morelli and Alain Dierkens, 73–92. Institut d'Étude des Religions et de la Laïcité Université libre de Bruxelles.
Sagar, Paul. 2011. "On Riots and Kettles, Protests and Violence." In *Fight Back! A Reader on the Winter of Protest*, edited by Dan Hancox, 79–82. openDemocracy.
Saïd, Edward W. 1994. *Culture and Imperialim*. Vintage Books.
Said, Edward Wadie. 1992. *The Question of Palestine*. Vintage Books.
Salamanca Charria, B. E. 2016. "Early Modern Controversies of Mobility within the Spanish Empire: Francisco de Vitoria and the Peaceful Right to Travel." *Tropos* 14–21.
Sartre, Jean-Paul. 1949. "La République du silence." In *Situations III (Lendemains de Guerre)*, edited by Jean-Paul Sartre, 11–14. Gallimard.
Sartre, Jean-Paul. 1985. *Réflexions sur la question juive (1946)*. Gallimard, collection «Folio».
Sartre, Jean-Paul. 1988. *"What Is Literature?" and Other Essays*. Harvard University Press.
Sartre, Jean-Paul. 1996. "What I Learned about the Black Problem." In *Existence in Black: An Anthology of Black Existential Philosophy*, edited by Lewis R. Gordon, 81–91. Routledge.
Saruya, Hiroe. 2012. "Protests and Democracy in Japan: The Development of Movement Fields and the 1960 Anpo Protests." Ph.D., Sociology, University of Michigan.
Saul, Stephanie. 2024. "Columbia's President May Face a CensureResolution." *The New York Times*, April 22.
Sawey, Elisabeth, and Kelsie Schrader. 2015. "Protesters Use Recruiting Day to Voice Concerns about Racism at MU." *Columbia Missourian*. November 7.
Schirokauer, Conrad. 1993. "Chu Hsi' Sense of History." In *Ordering the World: Approaches to State and Society in Sung Dynasty China*, edited by Robert P. Hymes and Conrad Schirokauer, 193–220. University of California Press.
Schirokauer, Conrad. 2019. "Education in Premodern China and Japan." In *The [Oxford] Handbook of the History of Education*, edited by John L. Rury and Eileen H. Tamura, 114–31. Oxford University Press.
Schmahmann, Brenda. 2016. "The Fall of Rhodes: The Removal of a Sculpture from the University of Cape Town." *Public Art Dialogue* 6 (1):90–115.
Schrecker, Ellen W. 1986. *No Ivory Tower: McCarthyism and the Universities*. Oxford University Press.
Schroeder, Nicholas A. 2017. "Avoiding Deliberation: Why the 'Safe Space' Campus Cannot Comport with Deliberative Democracy." *Brigham Young University Education and Law Journal* 2017 (2): 325–58.
Schulthess, D. 1980. "'N. Grimaldi': L'expérience de la pensée dans la philosophie de Descartes." *Revue de Théologie Et de Philosophie* 112:211.
Schwab, Klaus and Thierry Malleret. 2020. "*COVID-19: The Great Reset*." World Economic Forum.
Schwartz, Sarah. 2023. "Map: Where Critical Race Theory Is Under Attack." *Education Week*.
Schwartz, Stuart B. 1970. "The 'Mocambo': Slave Resistance in Colonial Bahia." *Journal of Social History* 3 (4):313–33.
Schwember, Hermann, and Jerome Bear. 1981. "Chile: Free Market, Unfree Thought." *Index on Censorship* 10 (5):16–18.

Scott, James C. 1998. *Seeing Like a State: How Certain Schemes to Improve the Human Condition Have Failed*. Yale University Press.

Scott, James C. 1977a. "Protest and Profanation: Agrarian Revolt and the Little Tradition, Part I." *Theory and Society* 4 (1):1–38.

Seth, Sanjay. 2007. *Subject Lessons: The Western Education of Colonial India*. Duke University Press.

Sever, Demet. 2018. "University Students' Resistance Behaviors: Sample of Anadolu University." *Turkish Online Journal of Qualitative Inquiry* 9 (2):125–46.

Seyama, Sadi Mokhaneli. 2020. "'Hiding within the Glass Cage': Performance Management as Surveillance—A Case of Academic Spaces as Resistance Spaces." *Education as Change* 24 (1):1–19.

Shaw, Christine. 2016. "Concepts of Libertà in Renaissance Genoa." In *Communes and Despots in Medieval and Renaissance Italy*, edited by John E. Law and Bernadette Paton, 197–210. Routledge.

Sheptycki, James W. E. 1998. "The Global Cops Cometh: Reflections on Transnationalization, Knowledge Work and Policing Subculture." *British Journal of Sociology* 49 (4): 57–74.

Shimer, David, and Victor Wang. "Students Submit New Demands to Salovey." *Yale Daily News*, November 13, 2015. https://yaledailynews.com/blog/2015/11/13/students-submit-new-demands-to-salovey/.

Shimbori, Michiya. 1964. "Zengakuren: A Japanese Case Study of a Student Political Movement." *Sociology of Education* 34 (3):229–53.

Shinn, Christine H. 1980. "The Beginnings of the University Grants Committee." *History of Education* 9 (3):233–43.

Silverblatt, Irene. 2007. "Modern Inquisitions." In *Imperial Formations*, edited by Ann Laura Stoler, Carole McGranahan and Peter C. Perdue, 3–44. School for Advances Research Press.

Simon, John J. 2000. "*Sweezy v. New Hampshire*: The Radicalism of Principle." *Monthly Review* 51 (11):35–41.

Singaravélou, Pierre. 2009. "Le moment «impérial» de l'histoire des sciences sociales (1880–1910)." *Mil neuf cent. Revue d'histoire intellectuelle* 27(1):87–102.

Singer, Jonathan. 1999. "Striking in Unexpected Places." *Workplace: A Journal for Academic Labor* (No. 3): 40–46.

Small, Richard. 1969. "Introduction." In *The Groundings with my Brothers*, edited by Walter Rodney, 7–11. Bogle-L'Ouverture Publications.

Smith, Anne Kennedy. 2022. "'No Women at Cambridge': The 1897 Protests." *Anne Kennedy Smith*, 26 February.

Smith, Charlie, and Eda Ulus. 2020. "Who Cares for Academics? We Need to Talk about Emotional Well-Being including What We Avoid and Intellectualise through Macro-Discourses." *Organization* 27 (6):840–57.

Smith, Henry DeWitt. 1970. "The Origins of Student Radicalism in Japan." *Journal of Contemporary History* 5 (1):87–103.

Smith, Henry DeWitt. 1972. *Japan's First Student Radicals*. Harvard University Press.

Soffer, Reba N. 1987. "The Modern University and National Values, 1850–1930." *Historical Research* 60 (142):166–87.

Solomon, Clare, and Tania Palmieri. 2011. *Springtime: The New Student Rebellions*. Verso Books.

Somma, Nicolás. 2012. “The Chilean Student Movement of 2011–2012: Challenging the Marketization of Education.” *Interface: A Journal for and about Social Movements* 4 (2):296–309.

Sorkin, Andrew Ross, Ravi Mattu, Bernhard Warner, Sarah Kessler, Michael J. de la Merced, Lauren Hirsch, and Ephrat Livni. 2024. “Donors Stay Largely Silent Amid New Wave ofCampus Protests.” *New York Times*, April 23. https://www.nytimes.com/2024/04/23/business/dealbook/donors-protests-columbia-kraft.html.

Spalding, Hobart A. 1972. “Education in Argentina, 1890–1914: The Limits of Oligarchical Reform.” *The Journal of Interdisciplinary History* 3 (1):31–61.

Sridhar, V. 2004. “For Struggles, Global and National: Samir Amin, Interviewed by V. Sridhar.” In *The World Social Forum: Challenging Empires*, edited by Jai Sen, Anita Anand, Arturo Escobar and Peter Waterman, 5–11. The Viveka Foundation.

Stanley-Backer, Isaac. 2015a. “Hundreds March at Yale in Solidarity with Minority Students.” *The Washington Post*, November 9.

Stanley-Backer, Isaac. 2015b. “Minority Students at Yale Give List of Demands to University President.” *The Washington Post*, November 13.

Steadman, J. M. 1977. “The Asiatick Society of Bengal.” *Eighteenth-Century Studies* 10 (4):464–83.

Steinhoff, Patricia G. 2013. “Memories of New Left Protest.” *Contemporary Japan* 25 (2):127–65.

Steinmetz, George. 2017. “Sociology and Colonialism in the British and French Empires, 1945–1965.” *The Journal of Modern History* 89 (3):601–48.

Stewart-Ambo, Theresa. 2021. “The Future Is in the Past: How Land-Grab Universities Can Shape the Future of Higher Education.” *Native American and Indigenous Studies* 8 (1):162–68.

Stimie, C. M., and Caroline Geggus. 1972. *University Education in the Republic of South Africa*. Institute for Information and Special Services.

Strachey, Ray. 1928. “The Cause”: A Short History of the Women’s Movement in Great Britain. Kennikat Press.

Strika, Vincenzo, and Jabir Khalil. 1987. *The Islamic Architecture of Baghdad. The Results of a Joint Italian-Iraqi Survey*. Annali. Istituto Orientale di Napoli.

Stromquist, Nelly P., and Anita Sanyal. 2013. “Student Resistance to Neoliberalism in Chile.” *International Studies in Sociology of Education* 23 (2):152–78.

Students for a Democratic Society. 2015. “The Port Huron Statement.” In *The Port Huron Statement: Sources and Legacies of the New Left’s Founding Manifesto*, edited by Richard Flacks and Nelson Lichtenstein, 239–83. University of Pennsylvania Press.

Suman, Amit Kumar. 2020. “Colonial State and Indigenous Islamic Learning: A Case Study of Calcutta Madrasa.” *Paedagogica Historica* 1–18.

Sunada, Ichiro. 1969. “The Thought and Behavior of Zengakuren: Trends in the Japanese Student Movement.” *Asian Survey* 9 (6):457–74.

Swai, Bonaventure 1980. “An Inquiry into the Idea of the African University.” *Taamuli* 10 (1):32–54.

Szadkowski, Krystian. 2019. “The Common in Higher Education: A Conceptual Approach.” *Higher Education* 78 (2):241–55.

Taillandier, Saint-René. 1861. “La libre pensée au moyen-âge: travaux récens sur Abélard.” *Revue des Deux Mondes* (1829–1971) 34 (3):624–41.

Tarazona, Álvaro Acevedo, and Andrés David Correa Lugos. 2018. "Un siglo del Manifiesto Liminar: acción política y rebeldía en Defensa de la Universidad colombiana1." *Revista Historia de la Educación Latinoamericana* 20 (30):53–66.

Taylor, Moe. 2020. "Walter Rodney, Forbes Burnham, and the Specter of Pseudo-socialism." *Canadian Journal of Latin American and Caribbean Studies/Revue canadienne des études latino-américaines et caraïbes* 45 (2):193–211.

Taylor, Tristan S. 2016. "Social Status, Legal Status, and Legal Privilege." In *The Oxford Handbook of Roman Law and Society*, edited by Clifford Ando Paul J. du Plessis, Kaius Tuori, 349–61. Oxford University Press.

Teoh, Emily, and Sarah Wynn. 2015. "UPDATE: Swastika Drawn with Human Feces Found in MU Residence Hall." Columbia Missourian, October 30. https://www.columbiamissourian.com/news/higher_education/swastika-drawn-with-human-feces-found-in-mu-residence-hall/article_4f9c57f0-7f4c-11e5-9f88-a324bf705d1d.html.

Thompson, Edward P., ed. 1982a. *Notes on Exterminism, the Last Stage of Civilization*. Verso.

Thompson, Edward P. 1982b. *Exterminism and Cold War*, edited by New Left Books. Verso.

Thompson, Edward P. 1971. "The Moral Economy of the English Crowd in the Eighteenth Century." *Past and Present* No. 50:76–136.

Thompson, Edward P. 1983. "Notes sur L'exterminisme, Stade Suprème de la Civilisation," edited by E. P. Thompson, 72–115. Presses Universitaires de France.

Thompson, Edward Palmer. 1991. "The Moral Economy Reviewed." In *Customs In Common: Studies in Traditional Popular Culture*, 259–351. The Merlin Press.

Tikhonov Sigrist, Natalia. 2009. "Les femmes et l'université en France, 1860–1914. Pour une historiographie comparée." *Histoire de l'éducation* 122 (2):53–70.

Tillman, Hoyt Cleveland. 1991. "Intellectuals and Officials in Action: Academies and Granaries in Sung China." *Asia Major* 4 (2):1–14.

Tillman, Hoyt Cleveland. 2020. "Some Reflections on Confucian Academies in China." In *Confucian Academies in East Asia*, edited by Vladimír Glomb, Eun-Jeung Lee, and Martin Gehlmann, 21–44. Brill.

Tomiak, Julie. 2016. "Unsettling Ottawa: Settler Colonialism, Indigenous Resistance, and the Politics of Scale." *Canadian Journal of Urban Research* 25 (1):8–21.

Touraine, Alain, and Michel Wieviorka. 2018. "Du social au culturel. Entretien avec Alain Touraine." *Socio. La nouvelle revue des sciences sociales* 10:41–53.

Tracy, Marc. 2015. "Saying He Has Cancer, Missouri Coach Is Resigning." *The New York Times*, November 13.

Tracy, Marc, and Ashley Southali. 2015. "Black Football Players Lend Heft to Protests at Missouri." *The New York Times*, November 8. https://www.nytimes.com/2015/11/09/us/missouri-football-players-boycott-in-protest-of-university-president.html.

Trott, Ben. 2014. "Research and the Riots: Politics and England's 2011 Urban Uprisings." *Reviews and Critical Commentary: A Forum for Research and Commentary on Europe*.

Tsurumi, Kazuko. 1970. "Some Comments on the Japanese Student Movement in the Sixties." *Journal of Contemporary History* 5 (1):104–12.

Tsuzuki, Chushichi. 1970. "Anarchism in Japan." *Government and Opposition* 5 (4):501–22.
Tu, Wei-Ming. 1998. "Confucius and Confucianism." In *Confucianism and the Family*, edited by Walter H. Slote and George A. DeVos, 3–36. SUNY Press
Tullberg, Rita McWilliams. 1975. *Women at Cambridge*. Victor Gollancz.
Tuttle, William M, ed. 1973. *WEB Du Bois*. Prentice Hall/Spectrum Book.
Uchitelle, Louis. 2004. "Paul Sweezy, 93, Marxist Publisher and Economist, Dies." *The New York Times*, 2 March. https://www.nytimes.com/2004/03/02/business/paul-sweezy-93-marxist-publisher-and-economist-dies.html.
Université Tangeante/Tangential University. n.d. "Manifeste de l'Université Tangeante." http://utangente.free.fr/man.html.
Usami, Sho. 1968. "Zengakuren." *Japan Quarterly* 15 (2):233–44.
Vallières, Pierre. 1971. *White Niggers of America*. McLelland & Stewart.
van Aken, Mark J. 1971. "University Reform before Córdoba." *The Hispanic American Historical Review* 51 (3):447–62.
van der Pijl, Kees. 1984. *The Making of a Transnational Ruling Class*. Verso.
van der Pijl, Kees. 2006. "A Lockean Europe?" *New Left Review* 37:9–37.
Van Leeuwen, Richard. 1999. *Waqfs and Urban Structures: The Case of Ottoman Damascus*. Brill.
Vaneigem, Raoul. 1967. *Traité de savoir-vivre à l'usage des jeunes générations*. Gallimard.
Vaneigem, Raoul. 2012. *Revolution of Everyday Life*. Pm Press.
Veblen, Thorstein. 2015 (1918). *The Higher Learning in America: The Annotated Edition: A Memorandum on the Conduct of Universities by Business Men*. John Hopkins University Press.
Vereen, Linwood G., Lisa A. Wines, Taminko Lemberger-Truelove, Michael D. Hannon, Natasha Howard, and Isaac Burt. 2017. "Black Existentialism: Extending the Discourse on Meaning and Existence." *The Journal of Humanistic Counseling* 56 (1):72–84.
Verger, Jacques. 1991. "La mobilité étudiante au Moyen Âge." *Histoire de l'éducation* 50:65–90.
Verger, Jacques. 1999. *Culture, enseignement et société en Occident aux XIIe et XIIIe siècles*. PU Rennes.
Vicinus, Martha. 1985. *Independent Women: Work and Community for Single Women, 1850–1920*. University of Chicago Press.
Viénet, René. 1968. *Enragés et situationnistes dans le mouvement des occupations*. Gallimard.
Villalobos-Ruminott, Sergio. 2012. "The Chilean Winter." *Radical Philosophy* 171:11.
Vogler, Justin. 2007. "The Rise of the Penguins." *NACLA Report on the Americas* 40 (1):51–53.
Von Bülow, Marisa, and Germán Bidegain Ponte. 2015. "It Takes Two to Tango: Students, Political Parties, and Protest in Chile (2005–2013)." In *Handbook of Social Movements across Latin America*, edited by Paul Almeida and Allen Cordero Ulate, 179–94. Springer
Von Grunebaum, Gustav Edmund. 1970. *Classical Islam*. Transaction Publishers.
von Humboldt, W. 1970. "On the Spirit and Organizational Frame-work of Intellectual Institutions in Berlin. University Reform in Germany." *Minerva* 8:240–97.

von Humboldt, Wilhelm. 1976. "University Reform in Germany: Reports and Documents." *Minerva* 8:242–50.

Waddell, Helen. 1927. *The Wndering Scholars: Fontana Library: Theology and Philosophy*. Collins.

Wallace-Wells, Benjamin. 2021. "How a Conservative Activist Invented the Conflict over Critical Race Theory." *The New Yorker*, June 18.

Wallerstein, Immanuel. 1973. Review of The Spiral of Conflict: Berkeley, 1964., Max Heirich. *American Journal of Sociology* 78 (6):1573–75.

Wallerstein, Immanuel. 1996. *Open de Social Sciences :Report of the Gulbenkian Commission on the Restructuring of the Social Sciences*. Stanford University Press.

Wallerstein, Layla, and Yasu Shinozaki. 2024. "Encampment, Teach-Ins, Fundraisers Held to Support Palestine." *The Oberlin Review*, May 3.

Walter, Richard J. 1968. *Student Politics in Argentina: The University Reform And Its Effects, 1918–1964*. Basic Books.

Walter, Richard J. 1969. "The Intellectual Background of the 1918 University Reform in Argentina." *The Hispanic American Historical Review* 49 (2):233–53.

Walton, Linda. 1993. "Charitable Estates as an Aspect of Statecraft in Southern Sung China." In *Ordering the World: Approaches to State and Society in Sung Dynasty China*, edited by Robert P. Hymes and Conrad Schirokauer, 255–79. University of California Press.

Walton, Linda A. 1999a. "3. The Academy Movement: Economic and Sacred Geography." In *Academies and Society in Southern Sung China*, 87–118. University of Hawaii Press.

Walton, Linda A. 1999b. *Academies and Society in Southern Sung China*. University of Hawai'i Press.

Wang, Monica, and Victor Wang. 2015. "Students Confront Christakis about Halloween Email." *Yale News*, Novenber 5.

Warren, Jean-Philippe. 2008. "L'Opération McGill français: une page méconnue de l'histoire de la gauche nationaliste." *Bulletin d'histoire politique* 16 (2):97–115.

Warren, Jean-Philippe. 2009. "McGill brûle-t-elle?." In: *État du Québec*, edited by Miriam Fahmy, 502–4.

Watts, J., and N. Robertson. 2011. "Burnout in University Teaching Staff: A Systematic Literature Review." *Educational Research* 53 (1):33–50.

Watts, John. 2015. "The Commons in Medieval England." *La légitimité implicite*, edited by Jean-Philippe Genet,207–22. Éditions de la Sorbonne, Publications de l'École française de Rome

Weatherford, Jack. 2005. *Genghis Khan and the Making of the Modern World*. Broadway Books.

Weber, Max. 2019. *Economy and Society: A New Translation*. Translated by Keith Tribe. Harvard University Press.

Wei, Ian P. 2012. *Intellectual Culture in Medieval Paris: Theologians and the University, c. 1100–1330*. Cambridge University Press.

Weijers, Olga. 1987. *Terminologie des universités au XIII e siècle*. Edizioni dell'Ateneo.

Weijers, Olga. 1999. "De la joute dialectique à la dispute scolastique." *Comptes rendus des séances de l'Académie des Inscriptions et Belles-Lettres* 143 (2):509–18.

Weijers, Olga. 2015. *A Scholar's Paradise. Teaching and Debating in Medieval Paris*.Brepols.
Weiss, Thomas G., and Leon Gordenker, eds. 1996. *NGOs, the UN, and Global Governance*. Lynne Rienner.
Weisz, George. 1983. *The Emergence of Modern Universities in France, 1863–1914*. Princeton University Press.
Welch, Edwin. 1973. *The Peripatetic University: Cambridge local lectures 1873–1973*. Cambridge University Press.
West, M. O. 2005. "Walter Rodney and Black Power: Jamaican Intelligence and US Diplomacy." *African Journal of Criminology and Justice Studies* 1 (2):1–50.
West, Michael O. 2021. "On Fire: The Crisis at Sir George Williams University (Montreal) and the Worldwide Revolution of 1968." In *The Fire That Time*, edited by Ronald Cummings and Nalini Mohabir, 101–42. Black Rose Books.
White, Ian. 2003. "Exhibitions: Reviews-Hey Production!" *Art Monthly* (No. 226):24.
Whyte, William Hadden. 2015. *Redbrick: A Social and Architectural History of Britain's Civic Universities*. Oxford University Press.
Wilcox, Clifford. 1993. "World War I and the Attack on Professors of German at the University of Michigan." *History of Education Quarterly* 33 (1):59–84.
Williams, Dorothy. 1997. *The Road to Now: A History of Blacks in Montreal*. Vehicule Press.
Williams, Oscar R. 2006. Review of Gregory Mixon, *The Atlanta Riot: Race, Class, and Violence in a New South City*; David Fort Godshalk, *Veiled Visions: The 1906 Atlanta Race Riot and the Reshaping of American Race Relations*. *The Journal of African American History* 91 (4):478–80.
Wilson, Kathleen. 2009. "The Performance of Freedom: Maroons and the Colonial Order in Eighteenth-Century Jamaica and the Atlantic Sound." *The William and Mary Quarterly* 66 (1):45–86.
Wilson, Richard. 2001. *The Politics of Truth and Reconciliation in South Africa: Legitimizing the Post-Apartheid State*. Cambridge University Press.
Wind, Maya. 2024. *Towers of Ivory and Steel: How Israeli Universities Deny Palestinian Freedom*. Verso Books.
Winn, Joss. 2015. "Writing about Academic Labour." *Workplace: A Journal for Academic Labor* (25): 1–15.
Wintour, Patrick, and Nicholas Watt. 2010. "Prince Charles and Camilla Caught up in London Violence after Student Fees Vote." *The Guardian*, Dec 10.
Wise, Alana. 2020. "Trump Announced 'Patriotic Education' Commission, A Largely Political Move." *NPR*, September 17.
Wittenborn, Allen. 1991. "Introduction." In *Further Reflections on Things at Hand: A Reader*, edited by Chu Hsi, 1–43. University Press of America.
Wittrock, Björn. 1993. "The Modern University: The Three Transformations." In *The European and American University since 1800: Historical and Sociological Essays*, edited by Sheldon Rothblatt and Wittrock Björn, 303–63. Cambridge University Press.
Wolf, Eric R. 1982. *Europe and the People Without History*. University of California Press.
Wolf, Eric R. 2023. *L'Europe et l'Histoire des Sans-Histoires*. Translated by André C. Drainville and Martin Hébert. Écosociété.

Worthen, Helena, and Joe Berry. 1999. *Contingent Faculty in Public Higher Education in Pennsylvania, Spring 1999: Focus on the Community Colleges*. Keystone Research Center.

Wright, David Curtis. 2022. "The Mongol Conquest of the Song Empire, 1234–1279." In *The Mongol World*, edited by Timothy May and Michgael Hope, 118–36. Routledge.

Wright, Duane. 2023. "*Stamping Out the Sparks: Union Repression of Rank-and-File Activism*." Ph.D. diss., UC Davis.

Wright II, Earl. 2002. "The Atlanta Sociological Laboratory 1896–1924: A Historical Account of the First American School of Sociology." *Western Journal of Black Studies* 26 (3):165–74.

WuHantian, and Qiang Zha. 2018. "Chinese Higher Education, History of." In *Encyclopedia of Educational Philosophy and Theory*, edited by Michael A. Peters, 598–615. Springer.

Yancy, Dorothy Cowser. 1978. "William Edward Burghardt Du Bois' Atlanta Years: The Human Side–A Study Based Upon Oral Sources." *The Journal of Negro History* 63 (1):59–67.

Yancy, George. 2018. "The Ugly Truth of Being a Black Professor in America." *Chronicle of Higher Education* 64 (32).

Yastrebtseva, Anastasia. 2015. The Doctrine of Public Education of Condorcet in Light of the Discussion on Women'S Rights and Slavery at the Beginning of the Third Republic. In *Higher School of Economics Research Paper* No. WP BRP. Higher School of Economics. National Research University.

Younis, Musab. 2011. "British Tuition Fee Protest, November 9, 2010, London." *Interface: A Journal for and about Social Movements* 3 (1):172–81.

Zack, Naomi. 2014. *Philosophy of Science and Race*. Routledge.

Zack, Naomi. 2015. *White Privilege and Black Rights: The Injustice of US Police Racial Profiling and Homicide*. Rowman & Littlefield.

Zaman, Muhammad Qasim. 1999. "Religious Education and the Rhetoric of Reform: The Madrasa in British India and Pakistan." *Comparative Studies in Society and History* 41 (2):294–323.

Zeena, Feldman, and Sandoval Marisol. 2018. Metric Power and the Academic Self: Neoliberalism, Knowledge and Resistance in the British University." *Triplec: Communication,Capitalism and Critique* 16 (1): 214–33.

Zheng, Yuan. 1994. "Local Government Schools in Sung China: A Reassessment." *History of Education Quarterly* 34 (2):193–213.

Zimmerman, A. P. 1945. "The Land Policy of Argentina, with Particular Reference to the Conquest of the Southern Pampas." *Hispanic American Historical Review* 25 (1):3–26.

Žižek, Slavoj. 2011. "Shoplifters of the World Unite." *London Review of Books* 33 (No. 16. https://www.lrb.co.uk/the-paper/v33/n16/slavoj-zizek/shoplifters-of-the-world-unite

Zuberi, Tukufu. 2004. "W. E. B. Du Bois's Sociology: The Philadelphia Negro and Social Science." *The Annals of the American Academy of Political and Social Science* 595 (1):146–56.

INDEX